WARSHIP 1990

HMCS Fraser, *taken from the bridge deck of* MV Myrmidon *off Iceland, during Operation 'Ocean Safari', September 1985. The fine underwater lines and turtleback forecastle make these some of the finest rough weather warships of any NATO fleet. The conception, development and much-extended careers of these highly successful Canadian escorts are described in detail below (see page 175).* (Lyncan)

WARSHIP 1990

Edited by Robert Gardiner

Naval Institute Press

TITLE PAGE
The Japanese heavy repair ship Akashi *leaving Sasebo for sea trials, July 1939.* (Hans Lengerer)

© Conway Maritime Press Ltd 1990

First published in Great Britain by
Conway Maritime Press Ltd,
24 Bride Lane, Fleet Street,
London EC4Y 8DR

Published and distributed in the United States of America and Canada by the Naval Institute Press, Annapolis, Maryland 21402.

Library of Congress Catalog Card No. 90–62895

ISBN 1–55750–903–4

This edition is authorized for sale only in the United States of America, its territories and possessions, and in Canada.
Printed and bound in Great Britain by
Clays Ltd, St Ives plc

CONTENTS

Editorial	7
FEATURE ARTICLES	
Chapman's Frigates *by Dan G Harris*	9
Ramming *by David K Brown and Philip Pugh*	18
Sankeikan: Japan's Coast Defence Ships of the Matsushima Class *by Jiro Itani, Hans Lengerer and Tomoko Rehm-Takahara*	35
The Battleship USS Oregon *by William C Emerson*	56
Russian 'Lake' Type Submarines and the Baltic War 1914–1916 *by Dr Gene C Stevenson*	76
Engadine at Jutland *by R D Layman*	93
The Weird Sisters *by Keith McBride*	102
The Imperial Japanese Navy Repair Ship Akashi *by Jiro Itani and Hans Lengerer*	118
The Yorktown Class *by Robert F Sumrall*	132
Aircraft to Malta *by Roger Nailer*	151
The Midget Submarine Attack on the Tirpitz *by John Marriott*	166
Twilight of the St Laurents *by Thomas G Lynch*	175
REVIEW SECTION	
Warship Notes	
Danish Tumleren Torpedo Boats *by Tom Wismann*	198
Yangtsze River Gunboats – Photo Feature	202
The Mysterious Fate of the Poltava *by René Greger*	206
British Destroyer Requirements *by John English*	208
Naval Books of the Year	213
The Naval Year in Review *by Ian Sturton*	222
Index	253

EDITORIAL

Encouraged by the favourable response of the readership to the first *Warship* annual, we have made no radical changes to the balance and approach of this, the second. Of the new features, the Naval Year in Review was particularly popular, and although there was no time to modify this year's review, we plan to expand our coverage of the contemporary scene in future volumes.

Otherwise, the orientation of the annual remains firmly historical. One of the reasons that *Warship* has been reluctant to publish on modern subjects is the inaccessibility of primary sources that makes any form of original comment difficult or impossible. In Britain research is still hampered by the automatic closure of documents for thirty years, but with no guarantee that they will be released when they cross that threshold. Indeed, there have been rumours that the very effort to clear certain papers has actually provoked their destruction (they were not supposed to have been kept, but had slipped from official gaze until the inquiry brought them into the limelight once more). The USA is better placed with a Freedom of Information Act, but even there the powers-that-be have numerous subtle restraints on researchers working on defence topics. If the current global warming in the political sphere begins to reduce paranoia about the security value of decades-old data, then a whole new period opens up to the warship historian – hopefully to augment the overworked area of the Second World War.

For the first postwar generation of warships at least, this is already happening, and in this context we are pleased to have Thomas Lynch's feature on the *St Laurent* class destroyer escorts. Not only are these ships among the most successful of NATO's escorts, but the vicissitudes of their long service in effect tells the story of Canadian naval policy over the past thirty years. This gives the article a valuable extra dimension, while still concentrating on the design rationale of the class. We look forward to more original work on the ships of this era.

Over the years, it has also been suggested that more operational matter should be included. Since *Warship* is essentially devoted to ship history rather than naval history, we have tended to limit such material to actions that point up the strengths or weaknesses of a design. In this issue, for example, Keith McBride describes the little-discussed third Battle of Heligoland as the only test for the bizarre 'Large Light Cruisers' of the *Courageous* class. Similarly, Dick Layman explains *Engadine*'s role at Jutland in terms of the contemporary limitations of naval flying, so often misunderstood by modern commentators. However, more purely operational, we also have a chronicle of fighter reinforcement sorties to Malta, usefully summarised by Roger Nailer, and a new look at the midget submarine attack on the *Tirpitz*.

One particularly obscure area of naval operations illuminated in this issue is the performance of Russian submarines in the Baltic during the First World War. Previous accounts from Soviet sources have lacked both detail and historical objectivity, so Dr Gene C Stevenson's article is especially welcome in its reassessment of the Czarist navy's underwater contribution in the early years of the war. Using some recently discovered personal memorabilia, he has been able to explain for the first time the circumstances of a previously mysterious attack on the *U–9*.

The influence of tactics on design is often overlooked by warship enthusiasts, although most will be aware of why so many nineteenth century ships carried ram bows. Although the subject of much controversy at the time, no real analysis of its effectiveness as a weapon was attempted, but using modern techniques, David Brown and Phillip Pugh have scrutinised its dismal record, and produced some fascinating conclusions – particularly as to its chances of success in battle.

The mainstay of *Warship* is still the in-depth profile of individual warships or classes, and this volume includes some fine examples, ranging from major successes like the US *Yorktown* class carriers, to the peculiarly inadequate *Matsushima* type Japanese coast defence ships. An unusual, but technically interesting, subject is the heavy repair ship *Akashi*, which throws light on how the Japanese tackled the design of an entirely novel ship type.

In the Review section, one of the highlights is the collection of photographs of Yangtsze gunboats. The flow of unpublished good quality and/or historically valuable photographs has seemed to dry up of late, so these excellent and unusual photos are very welcome. Elsewhere, for lovers of the esoteric, there are some gems in Warship Notes, and the Year in Review builds on last year's success; the Books section is somewhat shorter, however, since the last twelve-month has not been a vintage year for naval publishing.

In general, the switch to an annual format has been relatively easy, and we hope readers share our conviction that the overall standard of material has improved. In only one respect do we regret the passing of the quarterly format – as some reviewers have pointed out, we no longer have a forum for an exchange of views and information. This is reflected in the reduced correspondence we receive, and makes it more difficult to assess readers' likes and dislikes. While we do not publish letters, we still want to hear from readers, and are actively in search of short pieces for Warship Notes. We do not run a club, but readers can have a real say in the contents of the annual.

Robert Gardiner

CHAPMAN'S FRIGATES

In the years 1780 to 1789 Sweden reconstructed its fleet, under the guidance of the famous naval architect F H Chapman. This ambitious programme included a series of ten 40-gun frigates of the *Bellona* class. Contrary to popular belief, it was these ships and not the US *Constitution* type which were the first frigates to be designed for 24pdr guns. Dan G Harris, the author of a recent biography of Chapman, describes these highly successful ships.

In 1771, Gustaf III ascended the throne of Sweden and, a year later, brought about sweeping changes to internal affairs and external relations. He was determined to end Danish and Russian interference in Swedish domestic politics, whereas Denmark and Russia intended to keep Sweden weak by preventing any changes to her constitution, hoping for internal chaos to be a reason for partition. Gustaf III arranged a convention with Louis XV of France to advance funds to overwhelm any opposition to his constitutional changes and to pay for the rebuilding of Sweden's land and sea forces. France saw a strong Sweden as part of a barrier against Russian intrusion in Europe.

In 1764 F H Chapman left Finland where he had held the appointment of shipwright to Sweden's Inshore Fleet, a specialist force that fought among the numerous island archipelagoes in close cooperation with the army. At Stockholm he found the opportunity to apply his knowledge of mathematics, physics, and practical experience acquired in Britain and France, when he became a member of an Establishment Commission which submitted its report in 1768. Two members of the commission were of the old school of shipbuilders and one, Gilbert Sheldon, was to be a constant opponent to Chapman's proposed changes in ship design. The commission's chairman, Colonel Ehrenbill, pointed out in his report that 'Swedish ships' lower battery decks are so close to the water that no one dares to open the gunports,' and continued, 'Shipbuilding has to become a science based on mathematics. No longer is it possible to demand that the Navy's personnel shall be shipbuilders, nor shipbuilders vice versa.' The Admiralty recommended Chapman be kept fully engaged in the Crown's service to design and build new ships for the High Seas Fleet.

King Gustaf realised that a powerful high seas fleet was essential to protect the Inshore Fleet's operations by preventing enemy vessels from entering the Skerries, to stop the Russian fleet from leaving the Gulf of Finland, and to check Denmark. The king set up a new Establishment Commission in the spring of 1780, to determine the types of vessels for the new fleet. Chapman and his friend, Admiral Henrik af Trolle, were members of the Commission which comprised the king's brother, Duke Carl, two civilian counsellors and three admirals, who favoured the old school of shipbuilders. In addition, the commission was to make comparisons between Chapman's drawings and those of Gilbert Sheldon. Unlike his predecessors' empirical methods, Chapman's warship designs originated from mathematical calculations of the weights of guns, stores, size of complement and the main areas of operation, namely the Baltic and the North Sea.

On the third day of hearings, Chapman and his ally af Trolle made a pre-emptive strike by producing a plan drawn up by Chapman for a fleet of twenty-one 60-gun ships of the line, fifteen heavy frigates, and six light frigates. The heavy frigates were to carry forty guns (18pdrs, although evidence suggests that Chapman always intended them to carry 24pdrs). All three classes of ships were to be stiff and their lower gun decks to be at least 6ft above the waterline. The Trolle–Chapman plan included cost estimates and proposed the new fleet be ready for action in seven years.

The construction

King Gustaf approved the Trolle–Chapman plan in June 1780, promoted Trolle to the rank of General-Admiral, and placed Chapman at Trolle's service. The king divided the responsibilities for the new fleet's construction: Chapman was to be responsible for the design and construction of the new ships' hulls; Admiral Tersmeden for the rigging. The division of responsibilities and personality differences between Chapman and Tersmeden caused conflicts that eventually ended after two years with Chapman becoming solely responsible for the construction of the new fleet.

Chapman had estimated that one year from the date of

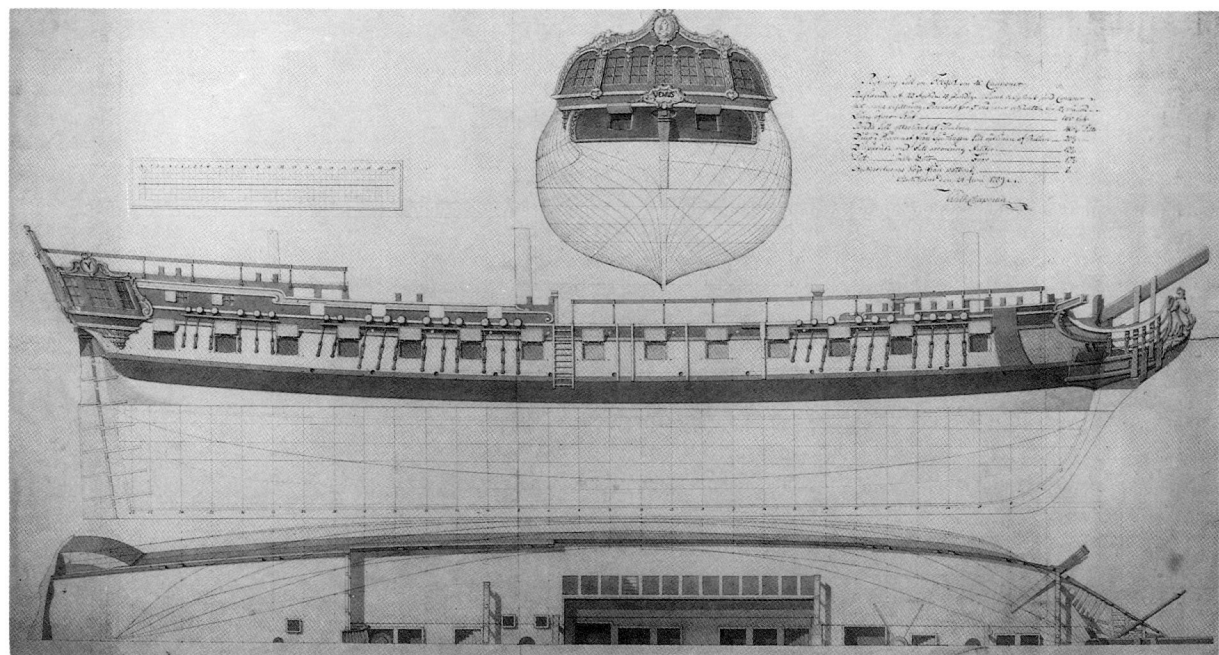

Bellona *class frigate. Coloured drawing of frigate* Venus *by Chapman's brother Wilhelm, dated 24 June 1789, showing the appearance of the class as built.* (Rigsarkivet Denmark)

the king's approval would be needed to purchase timber and to season it to prevent rot. He was to reorganise the Karlskrona dockyard, introduce new equipment and the use of prefabrication methods of construction to meet the king's stipulated deadlines.

A Royal Decree of 20 September 1783 ordered the main armament of the *Bellona* class to be increased to 24pdrs. Chapman's memorandum to the Board of Admiralty of 23 December 1784 states 'Bellona has got her new armament of 24pdr guns – the frigates need 286 guns.' All ten frigates had replaced the 18pdr guns with 24pdrs by 1800. The Swedish Navy had adopted the British style of rigging and sails. Chapman's original sail plans for the frigates show the carrying of square sails on the bowsprit but a sail plan for the frigate *Galathea* dated 1813 shows no sprit sails.

In 1793, The British Admiralty authorised the construction of the nine frigates of the *Artois* class to meet the pressing needs of the war with revolutionary France. Comparison of the draughts of the British and Swedish frigates shows the latter had greater sheer which would give better sea-keeping qualities.

Commercial yards were to build seven *Artois* class ships; the Chatham Naval Dockyard was to build two. The Karlskrona Royal Dockyard built all ten Chapman frigates. The British and Swedish dockyards used different materials for the construction. The British stipulated elm for the keel, oak for the frames, knees and most of the planking, but in practice the contract shipyards may have used elm for the underwater planking, and the gun decks. British frigates often had pine decks where the loads were light. Chapman had his frigates only partially built of oak, for economic reasons. He used pine for the outside planking from the keel to the wales, had knees made from root pine where no curved oak was available, and in addition he ordered that planking not be given the usual fine finish. Chapman reduced the decorative carvings on the sterns, reasoning that the ships were built to be shot at so why waste good money on expensive decorations? Nevertheless, Törnström the dockyard sculptor carved figureheads for all ten ships.

The British *Artois* class had their underwater hulls coppered soon after launch. Because of the urgent need to complete the new Swedish fleet, most of the frigates were sheathed in the old style with layers of tar and cowhair covered with planking (Chapman rejected a proposal to use iron sheathing). Later, Swedish frigates sent to the Mediterranean on convoy duty, were given copper sheathing, and Sjöbohm, a shipwright employed by Chapman, kept a journal that records that a 40-gun frigate required 8600sq ft of copper plates. Each plate was about 5ft long and 1½ft broad. Sjöbohm notes that a *Bellona* class frigate required '1075 copper plates and at least 120,000 nails'. Each plate required three rows of nails made ⅝ths of copper and ⅛th of tin, coated with pitch; the shipwright added that nails of copper and zinc could not be driven into oak. Apparently the shipyard had considered sheathing with zinc plates 6ft 2¾in long and 1ft 7¾in wide, but of this I have found no record.

Sjöbohm's journal states that *Bellona* class frigates carried about 124 tons of ballast, consisting of iron weights 3ft 6in long and about 3in in height. Sjöbohm notes Chapman opposed the use of old guns as ballast because of the difficulties of moving them at sea. According to Fincham, the amounts of ballast carried by similar British and French frigates were about 107 and 147 tons respectively.

The British shipyards completed an *Artois* class frigate from keel-laying to launch in about eleven months. Using prefabrication methods, Chapman was able to reduce the time to build simultaneously a *Bellona* class frigate and a

CHAPMAN'S FRIGATES

Table 1. BELLONA CLASS

The *Bellona* class frigates had the following dimensions and armament:

Dimensions		Mast heights[1]	
Length overall	156ft	Foremast	86ft
Beam	40ft	Main	92ft
Thickness of wales	7in	Mizzen	79ft
Keel width		Bowsprit 64ft (46ft outboard of the hull)	
forward	1ft 4in		
midships	1ft 5in	*Armament*	
aft	1ft 3½in		
Draught (full load)	17½ft	Twenty-six 18pdr guns	
Tonnage	1088 45/94	Fourteen 6pdr guns	
Height of gun deck above water	7ft		
Complement	350		

Table 2. ARTOIS CLASS

The dimensions and armament of the British *Artois* class of 38-gun frigates built in 1794 were as follows:

Dimensions		Mast heights	
Length overall	146ft	Fore	82ft
Beam	39ft	Main	92ft
Draught	13¾ft	Mizzen	79ft
Tonnage	999	*Armament*	
Height of gun deck above water	3.62ft	Twenty-eight 18pdr guns	
Complement	282	Eleven 9pdr guns	

ship of the line from 145 days to 45. Sjöbohm's journal records that the yard delayed the launch of *Venus* in 1783 by three weeks, because King Gustaf wanted to be present. Consequently her time on the ways was 110 days. However, affairs of state detained Gustaf in Stockholm, so when news of this arrived, the launch took place the same morning and the stempost and frames for the *Diana* were raised that same afternoon.

The names of the ten Swedish frigates were *Bellona*, *Camilla*, *Diana*, *Euredice*, *Fröja*, *Galathea*, *Minerva*, *Thetis*, *Venus*, and *Zemire*. Only ten out of the original plan for fifteen were built owing to the shortage of funds (the king had diverted part of the French subsidies for the armed forces to his other interests such as the theatre). Sjöbohm's journal states that at the end of October 1785 after *Zemire*'s launch, all work on the slipways ceased, although the work force had laid the keel and raised the stem- and sternposts for the eleventh frigate. By February 1787, the dockyard management had reduced the number of carpenters working to complete the frigates from 40 to 20. In addition, Chapman now Admiral Superintendent, held a conference in his office to discuss the proposed reduction in costs and wages for the year. The workforce had to agree to the superintendent's terms, namely skilled workers and apprentices were to earn ⅚ths of their normal rates of pay over a 9-month period.

Manning

Including Finland, Sweden in the 1780s had a population of little more than two million, so manning the ten new 60-gun ships and the ten frigates (with complements of 570 and 380 respectively) was a considerable burden on top of the requirements of the existing fleet. Unfortunately, Gustav III's interest in the fleet did not extend to an understanding of the need for competent officers, well-trained NCOs, and sufficient men.

Pay for officers was inadequate, and appointments were 'sold' by outgoing post-holders as a crude form of pension. Training was almost non-existent, although the neutrality patrols that began in 1779 provided some seatime. Tactical experience, however, could only come from those enlisting in French or British service, the former being more popular. Social position was still a key factor in career success, so the best qualified officers were not always the first choice.

The navy obtained most of its seamen from a conscription system begun in the mid-seventeenth century. The Crown set aside income from certain land holdings, for the upkeep of men who could be called upon to serve in

Bellona class frigate, original sheer draught. (Sjöhistoriska Muséet Stockholm)

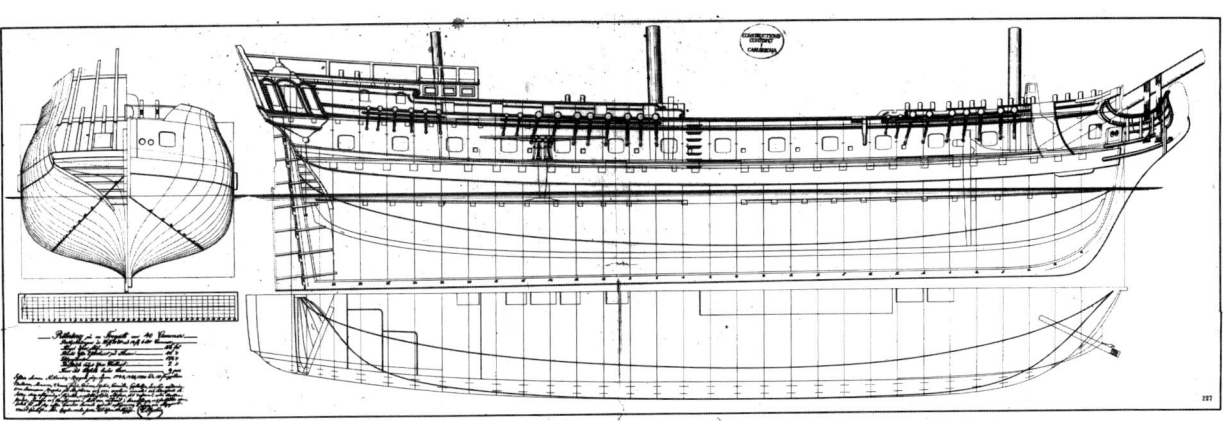

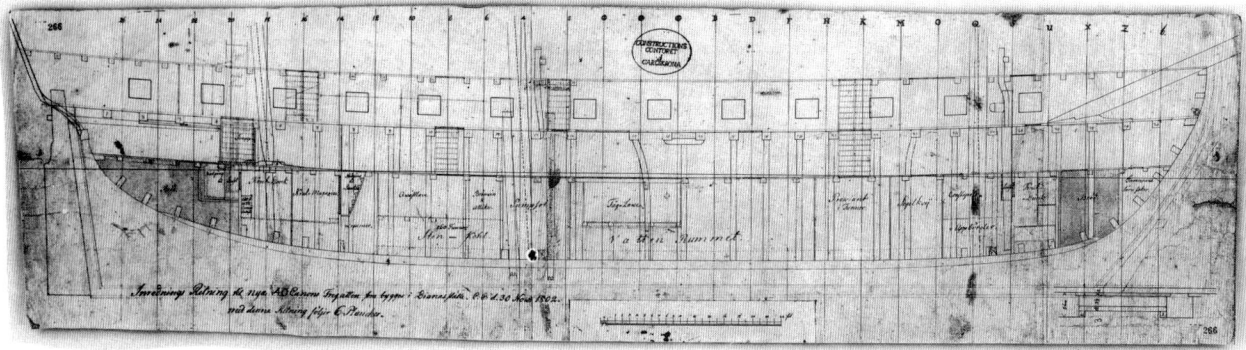

Bellona *class frigate, profile of orlop and hold spaces, dated 30 November 1802.* (Krigsarkivet Stockholm)

the navy. Certain cities were to provide one seaman for every ten of their citizens, and designated built-up areas within 10km (6 miles) of the sea were to provide up to 265 seamen for the fleet. Royal decree could increase the number. The method was similar to the British quota acts of 1795. Another system to retain men for the fleet was the military tenure establishment; it arranged for seamen to be lodged with peasant farmers in return for homestead rights, reduction in taxes, and a small payment for each seaman's food, but inspections of some homesteads revealed peasants kept the unfortunate seamen on starvation rations.

In 1780, the fleet's personnel comprised 227 commissioned officers and 11,288 other ranks. The navy was able to enrol volunteers, recruit 800 seamen from the merchant marine, and get 400 gunners. In addition, Sweden persuaded officers and men from foreign navies, including the British, to enter Swedish service. Although the number of the navy's personnel had reached 17,000 by 1790, it still lacked experienced commissioned officers, non-commissioned officers, and ratings. The Danish Ambassador wrote, 'the Swedish navy's ratings are mostly farm labourers dipped a couple of times in salt water.'

After Gustav III introduced military titles, commanders of frigates held either the rank of lieutenant-colonel or major; his officers were one captain, one lieutenant, two sub-lieutenants, and possibly two army officers. The frigates embarked a sailing master responsible for navigation and three pupils, two gunners, six armourers, six chief petty officers and three army non-commissioned officers. The ratings would include 100 soldiers and 20–35 boys. The regulations required the seamen and soldiers to be berthed separately. The frigates usually carried one barber–surgeon: the Swedish authorities encouraged several in the British Navy to join the Swedish by offering better service conditions.

In contrast, the British Navy had no problems in enrolling and training officers. The bounty system, volunteers, and the press gang provided the men. Because of Britain's many overseas interests, and the wars of the eighteenth and early nineteenth centuries, the Royal Navy's vessels were frequently at sea. As a result its efficiency was higher than in other navies. In 1809, the experienced and well trained British crews were to prove their superiority during the joint British–Swedish naval operations in the Baltic.

Service history

How did the Chapman frigates perform in comparison with, say, the British *Artois* class? Comparison is difficult because the British frigates were continuously at sea, throughout most of their service lives. One survived in British and Dutch service for 45 years: four others survived 'the raging of the sea and the violence of the enemy' and were afloat for up to 19 years. The six Chapman frigates remaining at the end of the wars of 1788–90 and 1809 had an average life of 42 years. Most of the Swedish frigates were commissioned for short periods owing too the annual icing-up of the Baltic, and the state's economic and manning problems. During the 1788–90 war with Russia, the freezing of the Baltic limited the fleet's activities to periods of seven to eight months. The frigates' longest commissions were the neutrality patrols in the North Sea, escorting merchant vessels to the Mediterranean, and during the hostilities with the Bey of Tripoli.

On completion, three frigates, *Bellona*, *Diana* and *Venus*, were stationed at Göteborg on Sweden's west coast. In 1786, *Diana* sailed for Britain with the British Minister Wroughton, nine Öland horses for the Duke of Parma, and gifts for the Sultan of Morocco. The gifts were tribute to prevent the sultan's privateers from capturing Swedish merchant vessels. *Diana*'s commander, Cristiernin, reported: 'She surpasses most frigates in Europe – in my 23 years experience at sea I have never sailed a stronger ship and she has such qualities that she surpasses most frigates in Europe.' *Diana*'s log maintains she reached a speed of 13–14kts, which would put her on a par with the very best French and British designs.

In the 1788–90 war, the west coast frigates captured a Russian 22-gun frigate, the *Kilduin*, but a Russian force attacked *Venus* in the neutral Oslofjord and dismasted and captured her. At the Battle of Hogland the frigates *Fröja* and *Minerva* were in the van and *Thetis* in the rear. In 1789 *Euredice*, *Fröja*, *Minerva* and *Zemire* were in the drawn action off Öland; *Camilla* and *Fröja* took part in the unsuccessful attack on Reval in 1790. In the same year *Zemire* was lost at the Viborg break-out, and *Minerva* blew up (cause unknown) in Carlskrona.

After the 1788–90 war most of the Swedish fleet was laid up and the crews released. Owing to the shortage of

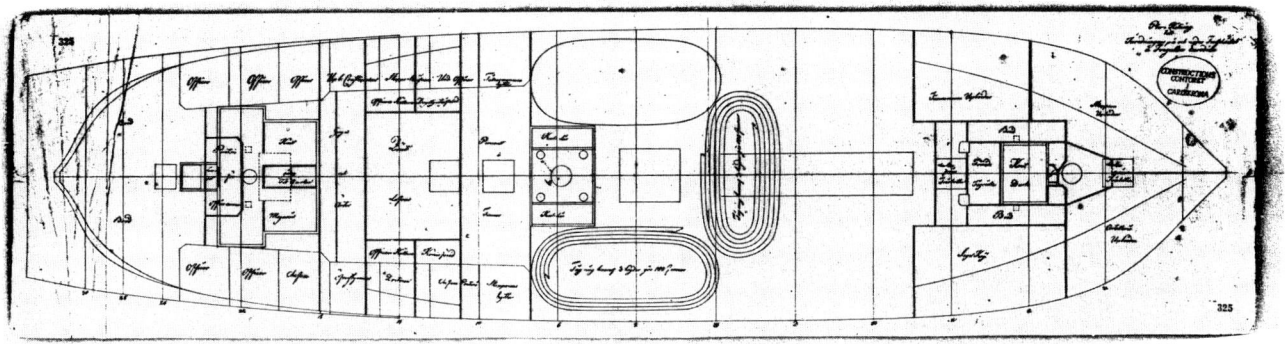

▼ Bellona *class frigate, upper and gun decks.*
(Krigsarkivet Stockholm)

▲ Bellona *class frigate, plan of orlop and hold.*
(Krigsarkivet Stockholm)

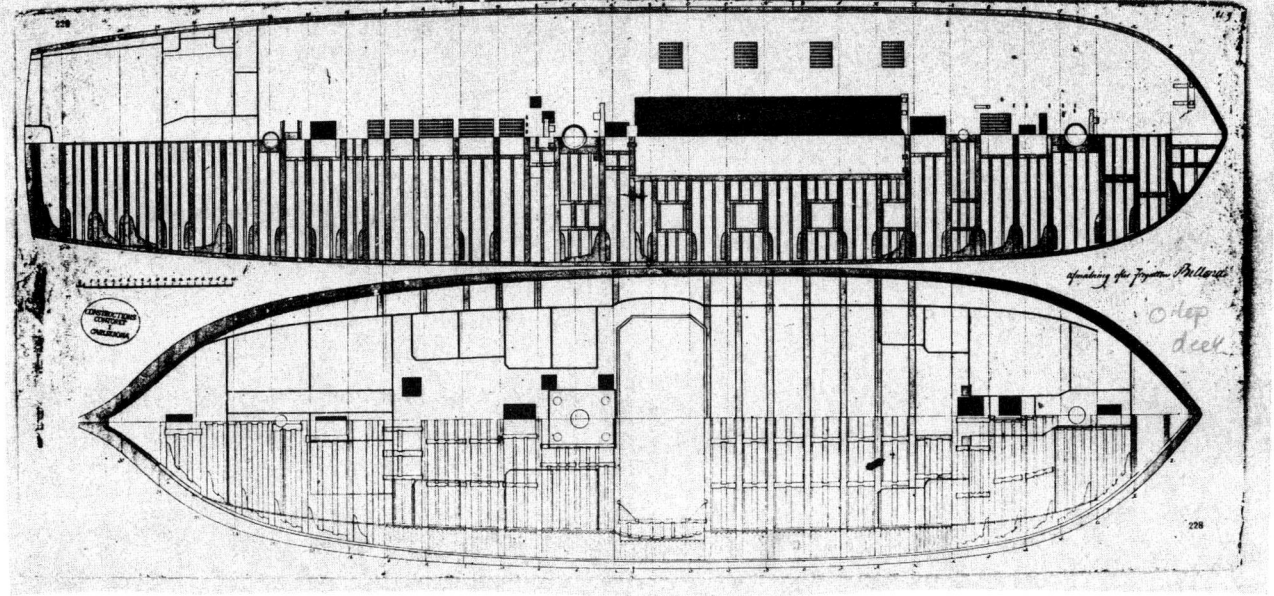

funds, many of the discharged were paid with the stores collected for the war. Nonetheless, the Crown was to commission some Chapman frigates for the North Sea neutrality patrols and to escort convoys of merchant vessels bound for the Mediterranean.

In the late seventeenth century Sweden established a commission to organise escorts for merchant vessels sailing to the Mediterranean. The commission was headed by an admiral and included members of the Merchants' Association. The owners of the vessels sailing in convoy were to pay most of the costs of the naval escort, assessed at 1 per cent of the value of cargo carried; vessels in ballast paid ⅛ riksdaler of their registered tonnage.

In 1801, Jussuf Bey of Tripoli abrogated the 1721 and 1798 treaties with Sweden. Under these treaties Sweden paid Tripoli annual sums in return for protection from the bey's piratical activities. Denmark, the Netherlands, and the United States of America had similar agreements. To bring the bey to reason, and to recover seized Swedish merchant vessels, the Crown ordered Admiral R Cederström to commission the frigates *Camilla*, *Fröja*, *Sprengporten*, and the brig *Husar*, take on stores and ammunition for six months (30 rounds per gun) and to join the frigate *Thetis* in the Mediterranean. The Crown's instructions ordered the squadron to sail to Malaga, Spain, where the admiral was to arrange for escorts to Swedish convoys in the Mediterranean. The admiral was to find out if America was still at war with Tripoli and, if so, he was to make plans with the American 'Commodore Deal' (actually Captain Dale) to damage Tripoli in any way possible. The Swedish squadron's ships were to escort American and Swedish merchant vessels from French, Spanish and Italian ports to Sicily. Cederström's squadron was to seize any Tripolitan ships found at sea and to take them either to French or Spanish ports. Cederström was to inform all Mediterranean ports of Sweden's blockade of Tripoli but was, if possible, to negotiate with Tripoli for the release of captured Swedish merchant vessels and their crews. The admiral was to obtain compensation for seized cargoes, offer a settlement of the bey's claims for tribute, and to enforce Swedish demands should the bey refuse to co-operate. The squadron was to avoid involvements or any conflicts between the fleets of the major powers.

Camilla and *Fröja* were coppered and left Karlskrona with the brig *Husar* at the end of October 1801. The force ran into heavy weather in the Kattegatt, and *Husar* disappeared; no member of her 110-man crew survived. The

A design model of a Bellona *class frigate: the rounded gunports were squared off during later refits, and in the 1800s the frigates carried three boats.* (Sjöhistoriska Muséet Stockholm)

frigates lost topmasts and spars necessitating repairs at Göteborg, where the barber–surgeons decided to go ashore, but in their place Professor Hartman and one assistant joined the force. The chosen route was to sail to the north of the Shetland Islands, thence west of Ireland, south to Spain to avoid any contacts with either the British or French fleets.

At Malaga, Cederström sent the frigate *Thetis* with presents to Tangier, arranged for *Camilla* to escort Swedish and American vessels from French and Spanish ports to Sicily, then in *Fröja* accompanied by *Sprengporten*, sailed to Toulon to meet the American commanders.

Captain D McNeil of the USS *Boston*, in a despatch to the US Counsul at Tunis, reported: 'A Swedish squadron of four frigates under Vice-Admiral Soderstrom has arrived to cruise off Tripoli – We are to cruise together off Tripoli in concert and blockade the port.' Captain Dale, commanding the American force of four frigates, met Admiral Cederström with the Swedish force at Toulon on 2 February 1802. Dale wrote to Cederström outlining the armament of the American frigates *Boston, Essex, Philadelphia,* and *President*; in addition he stated that three or four gunboats carrying 18pdr or 24pdr guns ought to be available to prevent small craft from entering or leaving Tripoli. Dale believed that the frigates should not attack the town of Tripoli, 'two bomb vessels are ideal for this purpose – it is no use to make an attack unless one is well prepared.'

The Swedish squadron was to capture several small merchant ships, but could make no impact on Tripolitan intransigence. The blockade continued, but in July three Danish frigates arrived, ignored the American–Swedish blockade and entered Tripoli. The Danish government had agreed to the bey's demands for a lump sum payment of 30,000 pesos and annual tribute of 5000 pesos in return for which Danish merchant vessels would be free from capture by the bey's privateers. Shortly thereafter, three Dutch ships of the line and two frigates arrived commanded by Admiral de Winthers. This force also ignored the American and Swedish blockade. Its arrival enabled a brig from Smyrna loaded with gunpowder and wine to enter the harbour. The Dutch Admiral agreed to pay 80,000 pesos in a lump sum, 5000 pesos annual tribute, 35,000 in the form of watches and jewels, 84 tons of gunpowder and two anchor cables. In addition there was a fine of 20,000 pesos for every month's delay in delivery. The Dutch and Danish failure to comply with the American–Swedish blockade and the appeasement of Jussuf Bey was an example of the lack of unity among the European nations, which helps to explain the long survival of the

Bellona *class frigate: framing model on the stocks. Note the portrait of Chapman in the background.* (Naval Museum Karlskrona)

Barbary pirates. Cederström came to the conclusion that his four frigates lacked sufficient force to compel Tripoli to surrender the captured Swedish merchant vessels and to release the 140 men held prisoner.

In late August a new French Consul–General arrived in Tripoli and was warmly greeted by the bey. The French gifts included a 12-gun polacka. A few days later under the flag of truce Cederström left his flagship *Fröja* and went ashore to request the new French Consul–General to offer Jussuf Bey 100,000 pesos for immediate peace and an annual tribute of 5000 pesos. Tripoli's ruler refused the offer. Negotiations ended when the Swedish offer was increased to 150,000 pesos and an annual tribute of 8000 pesos, both to be paid within six months. Jussuf would release all prisoners as soon as the King of Sweden confirmed the treaty, and the amounts had been paid. The king confirmed the treaty on 18 November 1802. The American President Madison, on receiving the news of the Swedish agreement, commented 'Sweden has made dishonourable peace with Tripoli.' The Americans were to lose the frigate *Philadelphia* in their first attempt to assault Tripoli. Only in 1815, when they sent a more powerful force under Commodore Decatur, were the Americans able to subdue Tripoli.

Cederström in *Fröja*, accompanied by *Camilla*, *Thetis* and *Jarramas*, sailed for Toulon for repairs, where *Fröja* and *Camilla* entered the drydocks to replace defective coppering. Early in March 1803 *Fröja* left Toulon with 150,000 pesos for the Bey of Tripoli – the ransom for the release of 158 merchant seamen and all of a captured Swedish prize crew, except one who had decided to embrace Islam and change his name to Ahmed Wilson. *Camilla* arrived a few days later with the annual tribute, and Jussuf Bey presented Admiral Cederström with a curved Turkish sword. Cederström refused the bey's last

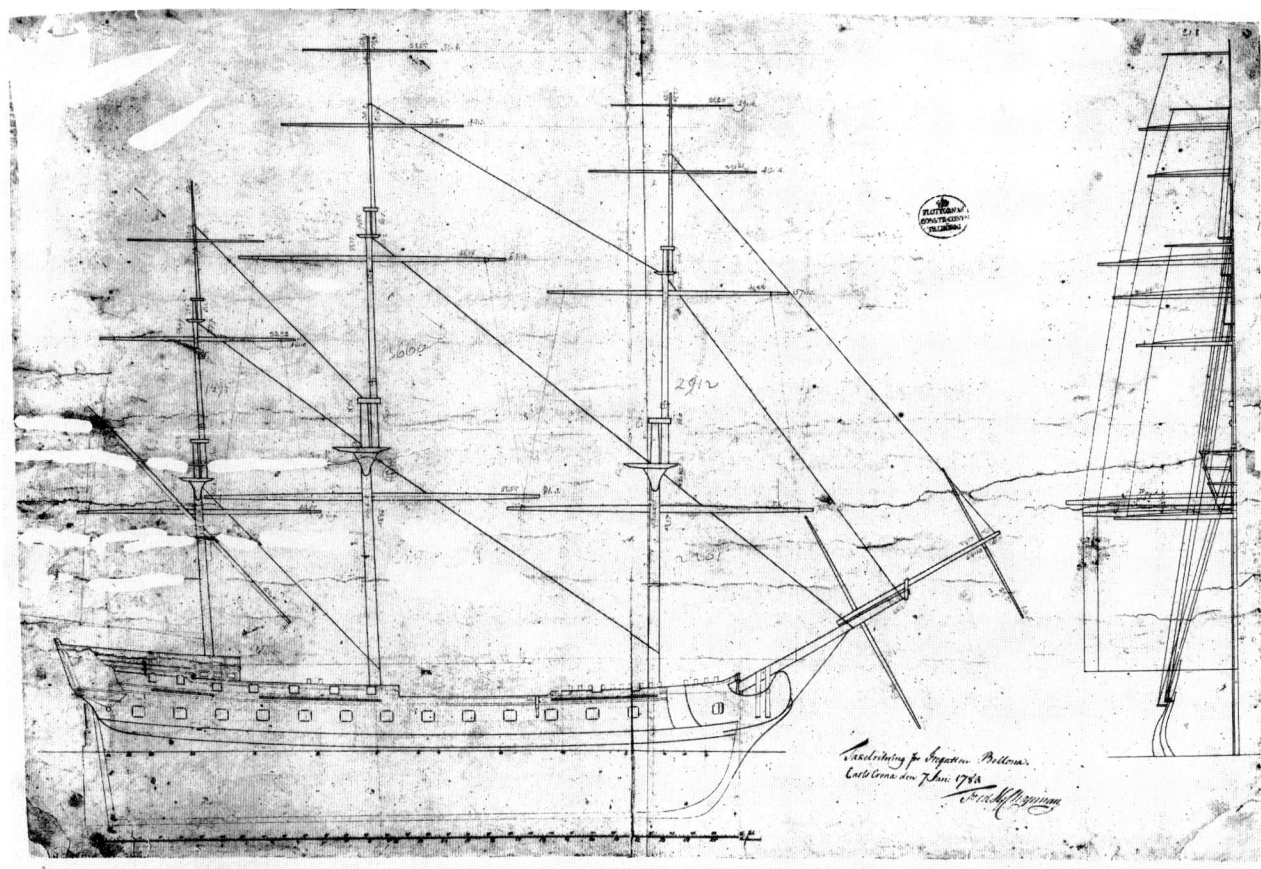

Bellona *class frigate: original sail plan dated 7 January 1783, signed by Frederik H Chapman, showing spritsail yards on bowsprit.* (Sjöhistoriska Muséet Stockholm)

request for several hundred pounds of gunpowder. On 28 March, the three frigates left for Sweden carrying the released merchant seamen, the defective copper and some paintings and sculptures for Gustav IV loaded at Leghorn.

In the Russian–Swedish War of 1808–1809 the frigate *Bellona* was part of a large force which relieved the island of Gotland occupied by a combined French and Russian force commanded by Admiral Bodisco. *Camilla* and *Euredice* joined a British force under Admiral Samuel Hood in the chase of the Russian fleet to Baltischport, the destruction of the Russian 74-gun *Ysevoloch*, and the port's blockade. In the chase, the Swedish ships could not keep up with the British ships and their well-trained crews. The Swedish High Seas Fleet, plagued with sickness, had no major role in the rest of the war, the outcome of which was decided by the defeat of the Swedish army in 1809. In that year *Bellona* went aground off Oregrund and became a wreck; *Camilla* was to take the deposed King Gustav IV, his queen and family to exile on the continent.

In 1814 Denmark ceded Norway to Sweden by the Treaty of Kiel. To enforce the treaty terms, Sweden invaded Norway and the frigates *Euredice* and *Galathea* were part of the force for the reduction of the Valorna defences. In 1815, *Galathea*, fitted with copper sheathing, sailed to the Mediterranean on a diplomatic mission to Tangier. *Camilla* had a long refit in 1824 and the records state the dockyard used the new Seppings filling method. *Camilla* sailed with the corvette *Jarramas* to Tangier with the final payment of tribute in 1828. After the French invasion of Algiers in 1829, payments to the Barbary pirate chiefs ended. Officers, cadets and seamen under training manned the frigates *Euredice*, *Fröja* and *Galathea* for short commissions in the years 1815–1830.

The fates of the Chapman series built frigates were as follows:

Bellona	wrecked off Oregrund 1809
Camilla	discarded 1842
Diana	discarded 1802
Euredice	discarded 1858
Fröja	discarded 1834
Galathea	discarded 1854
Minerva	internal explosion 1789
Thetis	discarded 1818
Venus	captured by Russians 1789 (in Neapolitan service 1840)
Zemire	sunk Viborg Bay 1789

Were the *Bellona* class frigates the most successful ships Chapman built for the High Seas Fleet? The frigates were the only units of the navy to be in commission for periods of over six months before, during and after the two Russian wars. The long commissions were for the neutrality patrols in the North Sea, convoy escort duty and diplomatic missions into the Mediterranean area. One of these was to arrest Gustaf IV's enemy, Armfelt, who had taken refuge in Naples, although the authorities refused to hand

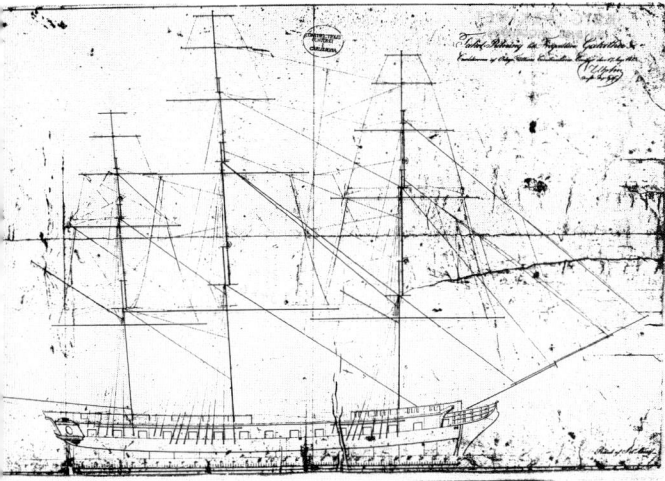

Bellona *class frigate: revised sail plan dated 1813. By this date, modifications include the removal of the poop, the addition of a main deck gunport forward, and the building up of the forecastle and quarterdeck bulwarks, making the ships very similar in appearance to the frigates of other navies at this period.* (Krigsarkivet Stockholm)

Extract from Fröja's *log for December 1801 showing sketches of Shetland Islands made by officer of the watch.* (Krigsarkivet Stockholm)

him over. The long service lives were the results of short commissions, owing to the Baltic's four- or five-month freeze-up, the few Swedish overseas interests, and the absence of teredo worms in the Baltic. In contrast, the British *Artois* class frigates had longer commissions: for example, the third commission of HMS *Diana* lasted for six years; moreover the British frigates were continuously at sea in wartime conditions from 1794 to 1814. Direct comparison between the British and the Swedish frigates is therefore difficult. The British ships were built for worldwide service, the Swedish only for the Baltic and North Sea areas, but both met successfully their navy's needs.

Sources and Bibliography
Admiraletets Kollegiets Historia, Vol 2 (Malmo 1977).
E Borg, *Svenska konsuler och Slavar* (Kristianstad 1987).
C Gyllengranat, *Sveriges Sjökrig* (Karlskrona 1840).
D Harris, *F H Chapman: The First Naval Architect and his Work* (London 1989).
E Hägg, *Under Tre Tungard Flagga* (Stockholm 1941).
J Fincham, *Naval Architecture* (London 1851).
J Harland, *Seamanship in the Age of Sail* (London 1984).
J Kreuger, *Svenges Forhållande till barbarisk Staterna* (Stockholm 1856).
Svenska Flottans Historia, Vol 2 (Malmo 1943).
G Unger, *Svenska Sjökrigs' Historia* (Stockholm 1923).
US Naval Documents: US Wars with Barbary Powers, Vol II (Washington 1940).

Unpublished Sources
Bellona 1792 Inventory (Marin Museum DV a39).
Chapman cost calculations (Sjöhistoriska muséet Inv 515).
Fröja's Journal 1801–1802 (Kungliga Krigsarkivet).
Konvoj Kommissariatet (Riks arkivet).
Rulla 1825 (Kungliga Krigsarkivet).
Sjöbohms Jounaler (Uppsala Universitets bibliotek).
Sjö expeditioner Eskader Chefers Handlinger 1801–1803 (Kungliga Krigsarkivet).

I am grateful for the assistance of Mrs Åsa Arnö of Svenska Sjöhistoriska Muséet, Stockholm; Mrs Ylva Lindström of the Naval Museum, Karlskrona; Dr E Norberg of the Royal War Archives, Stockholm; and to Captain Michel Gevrey, French Navy, for the calculation of the height of the British *Artois* class frigates' midship gunports.

RAMMING

Although it experienced a brief period of popularity in the late nineteenth century, the ram as a weapon was never the subject of serious analysis. If it had been, as David K Brown and Philip Pugh argue in this article, its shortcomings would have been evident.

Between the galley of classical times and Lissa in 1866, the first great battle between squadrons of armoured ships, there was very little interest in the use of the ram. The configuration of the sailing ship with its projecting bowsprit and headsails did not encourage ramming and its wind propulsion did not give it the tactical manoeuvrability necessary. The Battle of Lissa, in which one ironclad was sunk and others damaged (mainly slightly), led to an enthusiasm for ramming which was almost certainly unjustified. Naval officers, amongst whom Admiral Sartorius was most prominent in Britain, wrote on ramming tactics whilst warship designs commonly featured rams and a few ships were built with ramming as their primary, or even sole role.

The ram in war

The controlled mobility of the steam ship was soon seen as providing the means for the re-introduction of ramming as a tactic whilst the apparent invulnerability of *Gloire* and *Warrior* to gunfire seemed to make such methods almost essential. Baxter[1] lists a considerable number of early proposals for steam rams from all the major naval powers. Most such proposals were premature; until sails could be dispensed with or, at least, reduced to the scale at which a bowsprit was not needed, ramming was likely to be ineffective. The bowsprit and its supports absorbed most of the shock with little damage to the victim: *eg* the collision of *Warrior* and *Royal Oak* in August 1869.[2]

On the other hand, the cannon, firing solid shot, was ineffective for sinking ships and the Crimean War was to show that early shells were only a slightly greater threat to a ship with a crew trained in fire-fighting.[3] To sink a ship it is necessary to cause a massive explosion (magazine), an uncontrollable fire or to let in water.

A clear indication of the ram's potential came on 8 March 1862 when the Confederate armoured ship *Virginia* (ex-*Merrimack*) rammed and sank the sailing sloop *Cumberland* which was at anchor off Newport News. The unarmoured steam frigate *Congress* was despatched by gunfire. On the following day, during her celebrated duel with *Monitor*, the *Virginia* did manage to ram her opponent but *Monitor* was protected from damage by her projecting armour, though *Virginia* damaged her own bow, causing a leak.

There were many other incidents involving attempts to ram during the American Civil War; indeed they comprise the majority of cases of ramming in anger.[4] These incidents took place mainly in estuaries during the Union Blockade of the Confederacy and during the campaigns on the great rivers in support of the armies.[5] In these confined waters, the ram was a moderately effective weapon, particularly since even improvised armour, such as railway lines, was impervious to most guns in use. Ramming also suited the conditions of this war, for which neither side was materially prepared, since all that was required was a stout hull, a stout heart and powerful engines which could work well for a short trip.

Though European admiralties were much impressed by the duel between *Monitor* and *Virginia*, they were less impressed by the activities of rams. Their attention was concentrated on fleet actions on the high seas between squadrons which were the ultimate products of advanced armaments industries and controlled by long service, professional officers. For them the Battle of Lissa was more significant in that the Austrian Rear-Admiral Tegetthoff, recognising the inferior gun power of his squadron, planned to use ramming as his primary tactic against the Italian fleet.

The Austrian armoured ships attacked in line abreast 'at full speed' – probably about 10kts – against the disorganised van of the Italian line but the thick cloud of smoke from the first broadsides so obscured their view that the Austrian ships passed through without hitting anything. They turned and made a second attack during which *Erzherzog Ferdinand Max* struck the *Re D'Italia* a glancing blow. There followed a confused melee, shrouded in thick smoke; *Palestro* was set on fire by gunfire, rammed by *Ferdinand Max* and eventually sank. *Re D'Italia* lost her steering and stopped to avoid hitting an Austrian ship ahead of her. While stationary, she was rammed in the engine room by the *Ferdinand Max*.

The displacement of the *Ferdinand Max* was 3588 tons

Friedrich de Grosse *on slip showing her ram.*

and her speed, not recorded, was probably well under 10kts as a result of her various manoeuvres. It is said that her ram penetrated 6½ft into the *Re D'Italia*, rolling her over 25 degrees to starboard and left a hole measuring 300sq ft (another account says 12ft wide, which is reasonably consistent). The *Re D'Italia* sank very quickly; three minutes is quoted.[6] *Kaiser*, an unarmoured, wooden, steam battleship made several attempts to ram the *Re Di Portogallo*, finally succeeding. She knocked some 50ft of armour plating off the Italian ship at the cost of her bowsprit and foremast. *Ancona* attempted to ram *Ferdinand Max* and *Affondatore* tried to hit the *Kaiser* but both failed to make contact.

In the actions at Hampton Roads and at Lissa it is apparent that ships sunk by the ram were stationary at the time. It is also clear that damage to the ramming ship, *Virginia* and *Kaiser*, could be serious. These impressions are strengthened by a more careful study of Appendix 1.

Iron Duke *which rammed and sank the* Vanguard *in 1875.* (CPL)

In 1894 Laird Clowes[7] reviewed the outcome of seventy-four encounters (Appendix 1). He pointed out, correctly, that ramming had few successes when the ships were in open water and both were under control; but he then fell into the same trap as many have done, before and since, in attempting to draw conclusions from the results of battle. Working in terms of percentages and subdividing the data into numerous categories, he failed to appreciate that the apparent differences which seemed so impressive were, in fact, due to the outcome of a very few actions. These results are just as likely to be the result of chance as to have been due to general principles concerning the use of the ram.

A re-examination of Clowes' data using modern statistical methods shows (Table 1) that there was a real difference in character between actions at sea with both vessels under command on the one hand and all other incidents on the other. No clear distinction can be drawn between other categories of action; the sole point of importance is whether the vessel being rammed was free to manoeuvre or not. Any restrictions on the victim's ability to manoeuvre – at sea but out of control, restricted by narrow waters or at anchor – would be a disadvantage.

It must be supposed that the rammer would only attack when he thought the conditions were in his favour and that restrictions on the freedom of manoeuvre of the victim meant that the attacker could choose the geometry of the action. If the vessel under attack was free to move and turn it might be able to minimise the damage, avoid the blow altogether or even convert the engagement into a successful counterattack. Table 2 shows that without freedom of manoeuvre, the victim was much more likely to receive much more damage than the rammer. The table gives the best estimates of the probability of damage to both ships using Clowes' main categories.

There is a clear contrast between the indecisiveness and lack of advantage of ramming when the rammed ship was free to manoeuvre and its effectiveness when the movement of the victim was restricted. That contrast was enhanced by a correlation between the occurrence, but not the severity, of damage to rammed and rammer which was present in the first case but not in the latter. As Table 3 shows, ramming was only a useful means of attack when the target ship was unable to manoeuvre freely.

Even a prolonged engagement at sea was unlikely to bring a decisive result since analysis of Clowes' data fails to show any significant increase in susceptibility to damage as a result of an earlier ramming unless that had caused loss of control.

While Clowes' analysis may be criticised, contemporary discussion neither noted his over-reliance on too few incidents to support some detailed conclusions nor did it accept his overall, and clearly correct, conclusion that ramming was ineffective when both ships were under control in the open sea. Many officers believed that opportunities to ram would arise in the confusion of fleet actions at short range. This belief was rooted in a totally incorrect interpretation of Lissa where the only ship sunk was stopped when hit and ships under way were either missed or struck trivial, glancing blows. The doubts which were expressed on Clowes' views were based on a gross over-

Table 1.

Prior state of victim	No of incidents	Nil	Effect on victim Slight	Serious	Disabled
Under steam with sea-room	32	26	5	1	–
Under steam in narrow waters	32	9	9	3	2
Unmanageable	4	1	–	1	–
At anchor	6	–	4	–	–
Effect on the rammer	74	56	13	3	1

Table 2.

	RAMMED VESSEL (Percentage)			
	Free to manoeuvre		Restricted in manoeuvre	
	Final state of rammer	Final state of rammed	Final state of rammer	Final state of rammed
Undamaged	79	79	73	23
Damaged	16	16	19	29
Seriously damaged	3	3	5	12
Disabled	2	2	0	5
Sunk	0	0	3	31
	100	100	100	100

Table 3.

	RAMMED VESSEL (Percentage)	
OUTCOME OF ATTACK	Free to manoeuvre	Restricted in manoeuvre
Rammer more damaged	7	10
No damage to either vessel	73	21
Equal damage to both vessels	13	7
Rammed more damaged	7	62
	100	100

estimate of the effectiveness of the newly introduced automobile torpedo. Above all, any doubts on how rams were to be used were outweighed by an awesome regard for the damage which a successful attack could achieve.

The ram in accidents

Fear of the ram was enhanced by a considerable number of accidental collisions leading to the loss of several modern warships and damage to others. These incidents may also have given a false impression of the ease with which the ram might be used in action. If rammings occurred when both vessels were trying to avoid collision, it must have seemed obvious that successful ramming would be frequent when at least one ship was trying to hit.

This was a misreading of the situation. Ships collided accidentally when they were manoeuvring in close company because one or both were difficult to control, avoiding-action was delayed through poor visibility or, most frequently, because the wrong action was taken. In battle, incompetence, poor handling, low visibility and the evasive actions of the enemy made deliberate ramming more difficult in exactly the opposite way to which they made accidents more likely.

Accidents were more akin to war, when the victim was not able to manoeuvre freely, than to encounters at sea with the ship under full command. This analogy is supported by consideration of some British collisions (Table 4, probably incomplete). The proportion of accidentally rammed vessels that sank was significantly higher than the corresponding figure for open sea wartime actions and much closer to the figures for events with the victim restricted in manoeuvre. (Some of this effect was because water-tight doors, etc, were more likely to be open in a peacetime event.)

Many of the British collisions listed were quite minor and the frequency is probably not all that different from modern times when there were about 115 collisions involving British warships between 1945 and 1984 leading to the loss of a submarine and a minesweeper.[8]

Inquiries into the more serious of these incidents, including some foreign collisions (see Table 5) give some idea of the damage which would be caused to both ships in the event of a successful attempt to ram. The reasons for

Table 4. SOME BRITISH COLLISIONS

Minotaur/Bellerophon	1868
Warrior/Royal Oak	August 1869
Northumberland/Hercules	25 December 1872
Bellerophon/Flamsteed (Liner)	October 1872
Vanguard/Iron Duke	1 September 1875
Achilles/Alexandra	October 1879
Valiant/Defence	20 July 1884
Devastation/Ajax	1887
Temeraire/Orion	1888
Victoria/Camperdown	22 June 1893
Neptune/Victory and *Hero*	23 October 1903

Table 5. SOME FOREIGN COLLISIONS

Kreml sank *Oleg*	Russian	1869
Adm Spiridoff hit *Adm Lazereff*	Russian	1871
Numancia sank *Fernando el Catolica*	Spanish	1873
Jeanne D'Arc sank *Forfait*	French	1875
Thetis hit *Reine Blanche*	French	1875
König Wilhelm sank *Grosser Kurfurst*	German	1878

these collisions were, and remain, subjects of controversy, outside the scope of this article. However, the bare facts of a selection of such collisions is presented here, followed by a more detailed description of the damage.

Vanguard and Iron Duke[9]

A squadron under Vice-Admiral Sir W Tarleton left Dublin Bay on 1 September 1875 and ran into dense fog soon after midday. *Vanguard* reduced speed from 7kts to about 5kts and while manoeuvring to avoid a sailing ship was rammed by her next astern, *Iron Duke*. The collision was at 45 degrees and *Vanguard* was hit on the bulkhead between the engine and boiler rooms, flooding some 52 per cent of the length of the ship. The rising water put out the boiler fires within a few minutes which meant that the steam pumps could not be used. The rate at which she was sinking was measured at some 8 inches in 15 minutes which means that about 800–900 tons of water an hour was entering. The hand pumps had a capacity of some 30 tons per hour, minute compared with the rate at which water was flooding in but, even so, the *Vanguard*'s officers were later reprimanded for being slow in getting these pumps to work.

Iron Duke's ram struck below the *Vanguard*'s armour belt which bore the impact of the upper part of *Iron Duke*'s stem, bringing her to rest. The hole in the outer bottom was 9ft high and 3ft wide. The point of the ram did not penetrate the inner bottom but the armour was pushed in some 12 inches by the stem which cut the skin behind and tore the shelf piece forming the top of the double bottom. The evidence revealed a number of minor but important problems. Water-tight doors took a long while to close and two ventilation openings which could not be closed had been cut in the bulkhead between the engine and boiler rooms. It would also seem desirable to have a longitudinal water-tight bulkhead behind the armour to stop leaks, however caused. One may also deduce that there were a number of small leaks through distorted structure.

Grosser Kurfurst and König Wilhelm[9]

On 31 May 1878, off Folkestone, the Prussian turret ship *Grosser Kurfurst* (similar to *Monarch*), steaming at 9–10kts, turned across the bows of the *König Wilhelm* due to incorrect operation of the helm. Though the latter ship put her engines full astern it was impossible to avoid a collision. The ships hit at an angle of between 45 and 90 degrees. It is clear that much of the after end of the *Grosser Kurfurst* was ripped open and she sank in seven minutes with the loss of 284 lives. *König Wilhelm* received damage to her bows, the ram was twisted through 45 degrees, which caused considerable flooding though she was able to steam slowly to Portsmouth for temporary repairs.

Victoria and Camperdown[10]

The Mediterranean Fleet was preparing to anchor at Tripoli (Lebanon) on 22 June 1893 when Admiral Tryon

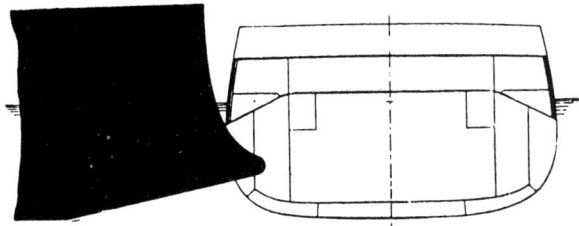

▲ *A projecting ram penetrating deep into the victim's hull below the deck.*

▼ König Wilhelm, *seriously damaged when she rammed and sank* Grosser Kurfurst. (CPL)

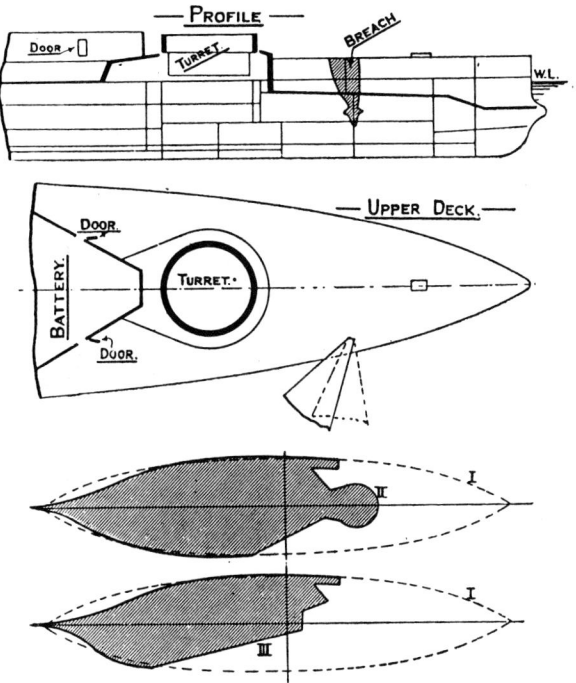

▲ *Stages in the sinking of* Victoria, *the plan view shows: I The intact waterplane II Forecastle immersed, turret still dry III Turret and battery flooding*

▶ Victoria *from the bow immediately before water entered the battery causing the final plunge.*

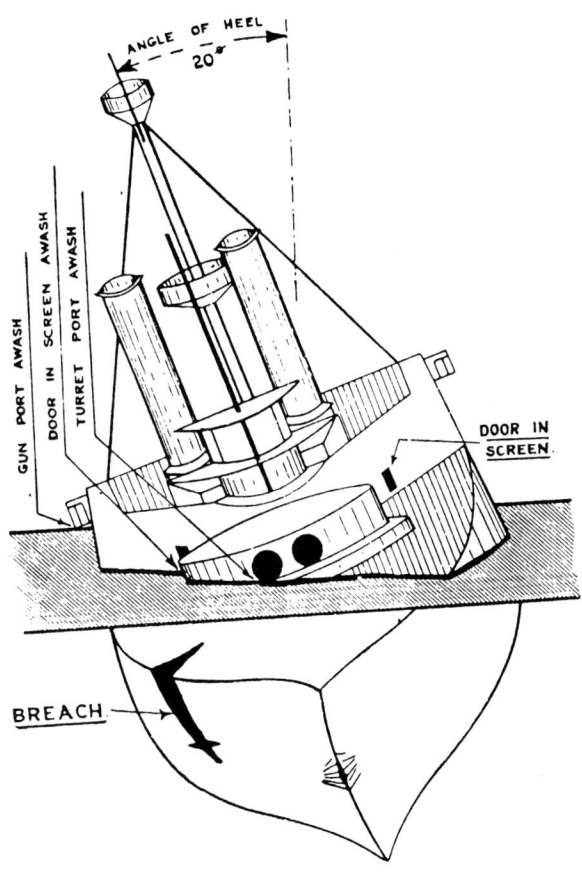

ordered the two lines of battleships to turn towards each other. Inevitably, the two leading ships collided, *Camperdown* striking *Victoria* about 65ft abaft the bow at an angle of 80 degrees (abaft the beam), slewing her bodily some 70ft to port which absorbed some of the impact. Both ships were under full helm on impact and continued to turn through a further 20 degrees while locked together. *Camperdown* was held by the protective deck of *Victoria* which prevented the two ships from moving relative to each other longitudinally.

The *Victoria*'s upper deck was damaged for about 8–11ft from the side but the actual penetration of the stem was less; marks on *Camperdown* show that her stem penetrated 5–6ft. The ram, of course, went deeper with a penetration of about 9ft at about 12ft below water. The hole in the side of *Victoria* was about 28ft deep with an area of 100–110sq ft. The hole was just forward of a main bulkhead which was damaged as the two ships slewed after the collision. Even so, had *Victoria* been prepared for battle she should have survived. However, it was a hot day and all doors, scuttles and ventilation openings were wide open. With a crew prepared for the drill, these openings could be closed in three minutes but the order to close came only one minute before impact and the crew was not ready. The damage was quite local and only in one case was there any difficulty in closing a door.

Victoria had a low freeboard forward (10ft) and flooding brought the deck under in about four minutes; two minutes later men working on the fore deck had to leave.[11] In about nine minutes from impact the water was half way up the turret and started pouring into the gunports. Water was also entering the 6in battery through the open door at the fore end. There was a sudden lurch and she capsized quite quickly to starboard. The drawings show how the waterplane area diminished rapidly as the turret and battery flooded. This is further demonstrated by the figures below.

Condition	Metacentric Height (ft)
Undamaged	5.05
Forecastle underwater, turret and battery dry	0.8
As above: turret and battery flooded	–1.8

With water-tight openings closed, she was still safe in calm water but the loss of waterplane area as turret and battery flooded meant a sudden reduction of 2.6ft in metacentric height which caused the sudden capsize. The illustrations of the model made for the inquiry show the situation as she made her final lurch.

Camperdown's bow was torn by *Victoria*'s protective deck as she slewed, tearing the skin. Water spread through open doors and was only stopped when the carpenter built a wooden coffer dam across the main deck. At that time it was said[12] that her metacentric height was almost zero. In both ships every bulkhead and every deck had drain holes which were fitted with valves but these were difficult to reach after flooding and some were jammed with dirt.

▲ *The last moments of the* Victoria. *(CPL)*

▶ Camperdown *was damaged in her fatal collision with* Victoria. *(CPL)*

▼ *Three views of the official model with water just about to enter the battery through ports and doors.*

Protection against ramming

The obvious lesson from these accidents was that when manoeuvring close to other ships or the shore, water-tight doors and hatches should be closed. Naval constructors realised that Murphy's law applies; and that if it was possible to leave a door or hatch open it would be so. In following classes the number of doors, valves, etc, in bulkheads was gradually reduced until *Dreadnought* had almost unpierced bulkheads[13] as even the best of automatic closing doors, valves, etc, fail to work after damage. It is a lesson which still applies today; the loss of the ferry *European Gateway* was largely due to water-tight doors left open while leaving harbour in busy shipping lanes.

A collision, accidental or deliberate, is almost certain to flood one main compartment with a fairly high probability of two compartments being flooded (25 per cent in modern passenger ships, rather greater in warships as there are more numerous bulkheads, closer together). There is little chance of flooding more than two compartments (*pace* the *Titanic* and, possibly, *Grosser Kurfurst*). The penetration into the hull is also likely to be fairly limited in a warship. This extent of damage is much less than that caused even by a First World War torpedo so that any ship designed to resist torpedo damage with subdivision which will preserve buoyancy with three, four or more compartments flooded should be safe from collision.

The shape and structure of the ram

The profile of the bow was a matter of considerable debate. There were those who believed that the bow should project above water, so that the ramming ship would over-ride its victim, forcing it down. This tended to be an American view, based on experience with very low freeboard ships in the Mississippi campaign. Today, an overhanging bow is rightly seen as a means of minimising collision damage.

A more substantial body of opinion supported a vertical bow, such as that in *Achilles*, claiming that such a shape would damage structure over a bigger area than that caused by the more usual spur. In most cases the ramming ship would be brought to rest, as in *Vanguard*, when its stem came up against the armour and its thick timber backing. The impulsive blow delivered by *Camperdown* was about 17,000 to 18,000ft–tons, much the same as that from a shell from a 12in 45-ton gun. A spur, projecting below and beyond the stem would pierce both inner and outer bottoms and any wing bulkheads fitted. If the impact was aft, the spur would wreck propellers, shafts and rudders. Unfortunately, the modern bulbous bow, projecting ahead of the ship is a very effective spur and was a contributory factor in the loss of *European Gateway*.

The early rams were iron forgings but from the *Royal Sovereign* onwards, cast steel was used. Ships sheathed with copper presented special difficulty since an iron ram

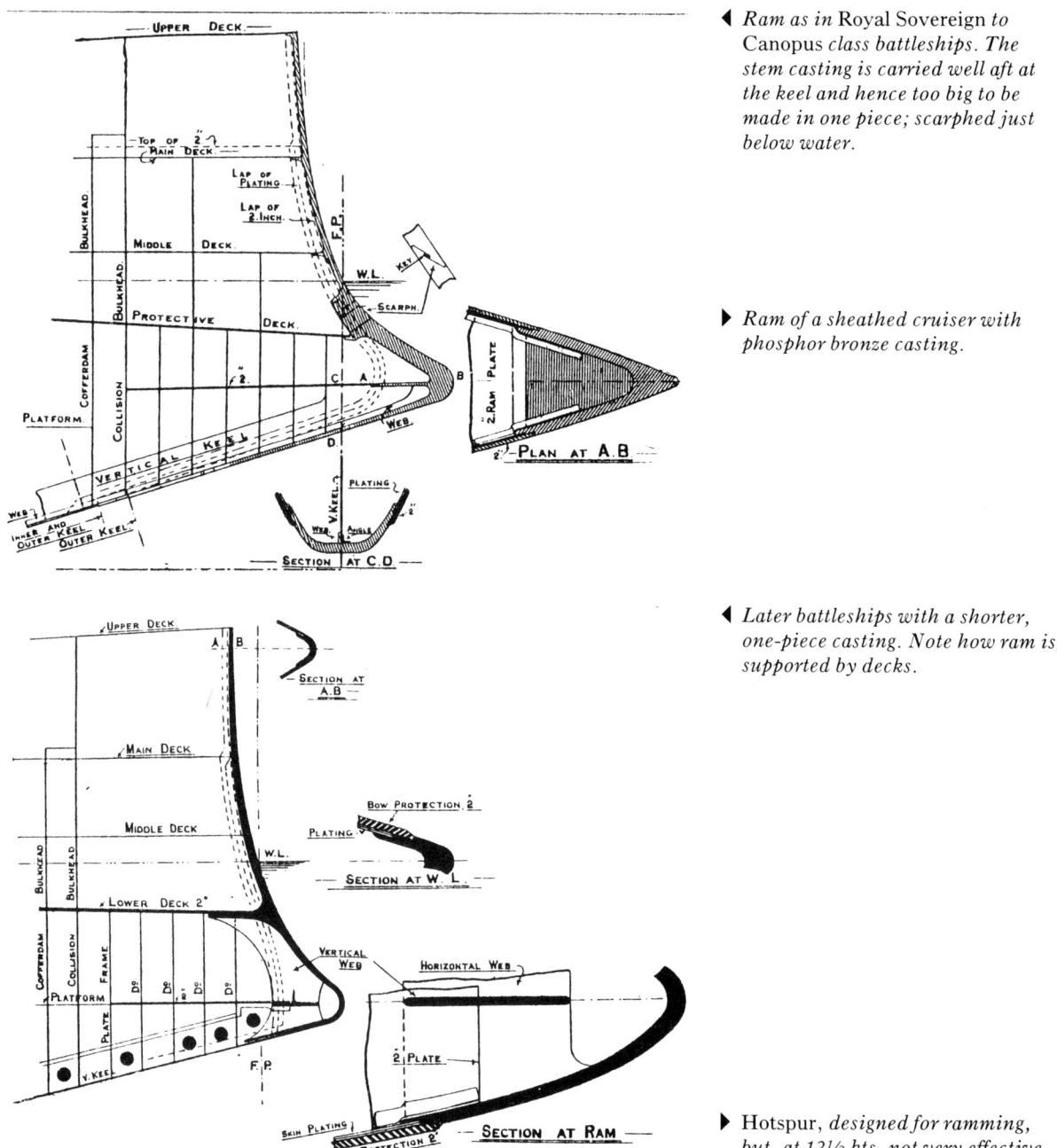

◀ Ram as in Royal Sovereign to Canopus *class battleships. The stem casting is carried well aft at the keel and hence too big to be made in one piece; scarphed just below water.*

▶ *Ram of a sheathed cruiser with phosphor bronze casting.*

◀ *Later battleships with a shorter, one-piece casting. Note how ram is supported by decks.*

▶ Hotspur, *designed for ramming, but, at 12½ kts, not very effective.* (CPL)

would form an electric battery when in contact with copper in salt water. Phosphor bronze was used in these ships but since it is a much weaker material than steel, a more massive casting was needed.

The accompanying drawing shows how the ram was integrated with the main structure of the ship to give it strength in all directions. The vertical and flat keel were run up and scarphed into the bottom of the ram casting while the top was supported by the protective deck. A platform, 2in thick, was connected to a thick horizontal web in the casting to take any sideways wrenching force such as that which damaged *Camperdown*. This thick platform was stopped one frame space forward of the collision bulkhead so that the bulkhead would not be distorted by direct impact. Even so, leaks in the main collision bulkhead were probable after ramming, so a light coffer dam bulkhead was fitted just abaft the main bulkhead to contain leaks.

Froude's model tests on *Polyphemus* showed that the ram functioned as a bulbous bow, increasing the top speed slightly. For this reason, supported by the aesthetic standards of the day, the ram shape was retained long after ramming tactics were abandoned, though made of light structure. Perhaps the most bizarre fitting was *Shannon*'s detachable ram which would only be fitted in war.

RAMMING

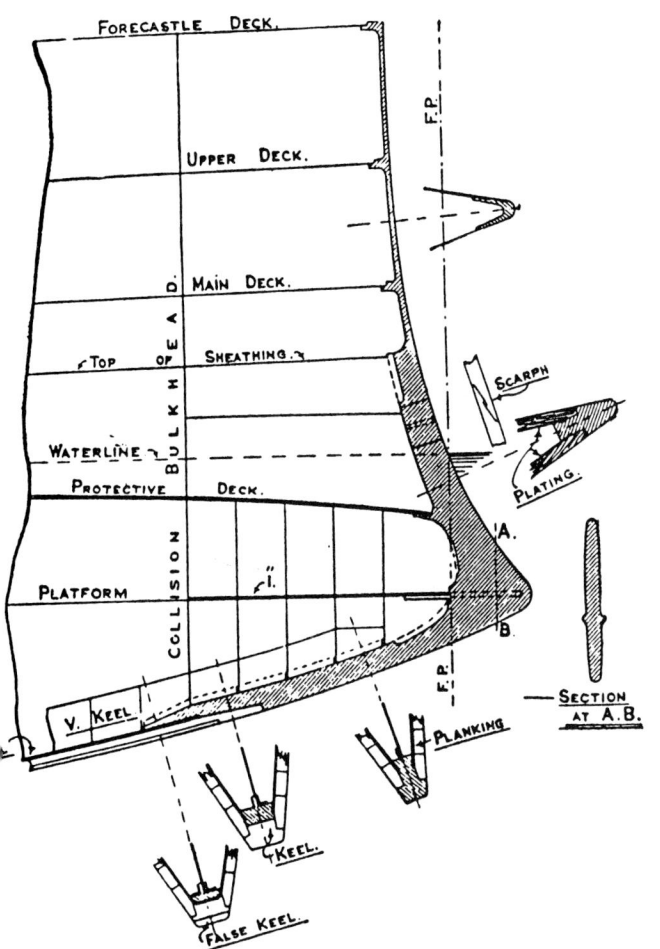

Ships designed as rams

Probably the first steam ship designed with the ram as its primary weapon was the French *Taureau*, designed by Dupuy de Lôme, and laid down in 1863. She was intended for coastal work and was a bad sea boat, though very manoeuvrable (tactical diameter 230yds). She and the four larger derivatives of the *Cerbere* class (laid down in 1865) had wooden hulls making it all too likely that they would have suffered heavily themselves in a collision.[15]

All early British armoured ships from *Warrior* onwards had bows strengthened for ramming. *Hotspur* (laid down in 1868) was the first ship designed as a ram for the Royal Navy and though very manoeuvrable was, at 12½kts, rather slow for the role. Like the French ships, her gun was mounted on a turntable inside a fixed, armoured box and, in her case, an unarmoured forecastle prevented ahead fire. A somewhat similar ship, *Rupert*, completed in 1874, had two 10in guns in a turret and was a knot faster.

The 'Ram' was viewed with considerable awe and many warships were described as rams even though their main weapon was the gun. There remains a mystery over the *Polyphemus*, laid down in 1878, and usually called a ram. From a study of contemporary documents in the Ship's Cover, Lyon[16] has shown that she was designed as an armoured torpedo vessel and that the ram was added as an afterthought. On the other hand, the Chief Constructor, Barnaby, is quite specific in his writings that the ram came first and that it was the torpedo tubes that were the afterthought. Barnaby's book was written many years later and it may merely be a case of failing memory. A full study of this fascinating ship is long overdue.

Thinking on the ram was much influenced by compari-

son of the kinetic energy of a typical shell with that of a ship at full speed. Since the latter was far greater, such comparisons seemed to show that the ram was the predominant weapon, a view endorsed by the RN Committee on Designs whose report in 1871 was influenced by the evidence of Edward Reed. As a result, some officers, notably Cdr G H Noel, were led to advocate radical changes from the traditional line of battle. Groups of three ships in triangular formation were thought better suited to ramming tactics. On the other hand, Admiral Aube and his French 'Jeune Ecole' were less concerned with details of the approach, seeking only a confused melee during which they hoped for fatal collisions occurring at random and, by 'happy chance', giving victory to the large number of small ships which they planned.

All this pseudo-thinking neglected the difficulty of hitting a manoeuvrable victim (Appendix 4). Early in the debate (1868) Admiral Warden, commanding the Channel Fleet, said that a ship 'cannot even be struck to any purpose so long as she has room and is properly handled'. The leading proponent of ramming was Sir George R Sartorious, who became Admiral of the Fleet in 1869. While an outspoken supporter of ramming he appears never to have explained how this was to be accomplished in a fleet action on the open sea.

USS *Katahdin*, of 1891, was a ram, pure and simple, with no torpedoes and only very light guns.[17] By the time she entered service, longer range guns had made the approach to close quarters more dangerous whilst protection against torpedoes had further reduced the chances of success.

Ramming of submarines

In both World Wars there were considerable numbers of submarines sunk as a result of ramming by surface ships. In the First World War, detection and location of submerged submarines was almost impossible and ramming could be a quick and effective response to a periscope sighting or to a boat detected in the act of diving. Appendix 2 shows that 19 of the 178 submarines sunk were destroyed by ramming.

It is notable that four of these sinking were due to P-boats which were built with a steel forging in the forefoot to act as a ram. If nothing else, this may have concentrated the minds of their captains on ramming. They had other useful design features; their low freeboard and small superstructure made it hard to see them and even harder to judge their course. The P-boats (Table 6) were fairly fast (20–22kts), and had good turning qualities for the day, due to a balanced rudder of 43sq ft and a long cut up.

For much of the First World War, merchant ships sailed independently and were unarmed. To conserve torpedoes, U-boats usually used their guns to sink them and the only, rather ineffective, counter available to the merchant ship was to attempt to ram the surfaced submarine. It was a tactic taken very seriously by the Germans. In June 1916 the railway steamer *Brussels* was captured by German destroyers and her master, Captain Fryatt, was tried, condemned and shot on 27 July 1916 as a combatant out of uniform following his attempt to use *Brussels* to ram *U-33* on 28 March 1915.

Table 6. *P-BOAT TURNING CHARACTERISTICS*

Tactical diameter, ft		840
Advance, ft		1160
	Min	Sec
Time to put helm over	0	7
Time to put helm hardover to hardover	0	11
Time to turn through 16 points	1	7.5
Time to turn through 32 points	2	5

In the Second World War the position was somewhat different and a considerable number of the U-boats sunk by ramming had already been damaged by depth charges and were unable to dive. The shells fired by the guns of escort vessels were relatively ineffective against surfaced submarines since the curvature of the small area of pressure hull exposed ensured a very oblique impact on the thick, tough steel. Successful ramming was not easy as the U-boats' turning circle was less than that of most escorts and several accounts mention the use of screws used in opposition to reduce the turning circle (Table 7).

A study in May 1943 showed that of 27 'incidents' in which submarines were rammed, 24 led to the submarine sinking. In roughly half the cases, depth charge damage was severe and might have caused the boat to sink anyway. In several incidents there was more than one impact and in some there were several attempts in which contact was not made. Study of accounts of the Battle of the Atlantic suggest that there was a considerable number of unsuccessful attempts to ram. However, if contact was made the chances of a sinking were high.

C-in-C, Western Approaches, asked what was the minimum speed of impact to ensure sinking, replied that 14kts seemed insufficient and that 20kts was better. The Director of Naval Construction (DNC) advised that the highest possible speed should always be used; damage to the bow was inevitable but worth incurring for the certainty of a kill.

Damage to the ramming ship was usually considerable and, on average, 7–8 weeks' repair was needed. It is not possible to be precise over the time for repair as once a ship was in hand other, much needed, work was done at the same time. In one case a destroyer was disabled by damage to both shafts, which later led to her sinking by torpedo, and another destroyer had one of her two shafts bent. It does not seem that this time out of action was an excessive price to pay for the sinking of a submarine but a better gun/projectile (*eg* 'Shark') would have done the job more cheaply and efficiently. (For that matter, in modern terms, how does one sink a disabled 'Typhoon' on the surface?) However, it seems that from mid-1943 onwards, ramming was discouraged if not forbidden and shallow-set depth charges were the approved means of attacking surfaced submarines.

Analysis using hindsight confirms that official views were right; DNC's advice was entirely valid. There was a great variation in repair times following individual incidents but repairs after ramming a previously damaged U-boat averaged 5.5 weeks while an intact one cost 8.4

Table 7. Turning Circles Of Ships Which Rammed Submarines

	Tactical diameter (yds)	at speed (kts)
Sharpshooter	300	15
'V & W' class destroyers	370	10
	405	15
	600	35
Hesperus	400	14
	480	25
	650	35
Assiniboine	430	14
	650	35
'Flower' class corvettes	170	12
Ithuriel	400	10
	410	20
	470	25
	600	30

Damage to destroyer Oribi *after ramming* U 531 *at 22kts on 6 May 1943.*

weeks. British operational research in 1942 showed that a typical escort vessel saved two or three merchant ships from sinking each year. The figures then work out at a penalty for repairs after ramming equivalent to the loss of 0.4 merchant ships. At about the same time, the gain from sinking a U-boat was calculated as equal to saving 14 merchant ships so the trade off from ramming was very advantageous. In the difficult first nine months of 1942 ramming accounted for some 20 per cent of all U-boat sinkings.

On the other hand, damage to escort vessels was to be avoided if the same result could be achieved by other means. The use of depth charges became possible towards the end of 1942 with the introduction of fuses which could be set as shallow as 15ft and with Torpex filling which increased the lethal radius to about 20ft. It was the fact that lethal radius exceeded the shallow depth setting which made possible the use of depth charges against surfaced submarines.

Conclusions on ramming

When *Warrior* and *Gloire* entered service they had armour belts which could not be penetrated by any gun afloat at fighting ranges. It was natural and correct to seek alternative means of sinking these 'invulnerable' warships. Even much later, the big armour-piercing projectiles frequently did not carry an explosive filling and the damage caused by the few such shots which hit and then penetrated the belt would be unlikely to sink a battleship.

During the late nineteenth century, the chance of hitting a moving target from a ship which was itself moving was remote indeed at ranges over a mile. If the opponent tried to ram, it would take about five minutes to cover a mile during which time the victim's guns could get off about three rounds (assuming 'one up the spout'). It seems most unlikely that enough hits could be scored from three broadsides to disable, let alone sink, the ramming ship.

On the other hand, if the victim were free to manoeuvre, it would not calmly await its fate. If it just ran away the difference in speeds would govern the length of the chase. Even if the rammer was only, say, 10 per cent faster, the time available for gunnery would increase to about 50 minutes during which time the guns capable of end-on fire should score some hits on an enemy approaching on a constant bearing at ranges over which trajectories were flat and hence accuracy of range-finding was not important.

It is likely that a slower victim would turn so as to minimise the angle of impact and if it could turn more quickly it could convert defence into attack. The time required to force a favourable position for attack depended on rate of turn. Some typical values are given in Table 8.

These indicate a minimum time of about a minute to turn through 90 degrees relative to the victim's course but even were the victim 10 per cent inferior in turn rate it could extend that time to 10 minutes. Since it is difficult to notice a change of heading of less than 10 degrees, this time would be further extended by the time required to react. Throughout this period the ships would be close together with their paths crossing and re-crossing like those of aircraft in a dogfight. There would be ample opportunity for gunfire at close range and the possibility

Table 8. Typical Turning Characteristics

Ship	Time to turn 360°	Diameter (yds)
	Min Sec	
Bellerophon	4.10	559
Pallas	4.24	573
Ocean	4.57	480
Lord Clyde	5.19	502
Hector	5.36	
Archilles	7.15	916
Warrior		1000

Launch of a predreadnought showing her ram. (CPL)

of glancing contacts but a decisive blow with the ram was most unlikely. The possibility of evasion and counter-attack are considered in Appendix 4.

It is now easy to see why decisive results were so difficult to achieve from ramming while there was sea room and both vessels were under command. The mystery is why faith in the ram persisted for so long when its weakness as a weapon might so easily be exposed by simple arguments such as those above or, perhaps more in line with nineteenth century thought, demonstrated by a few trials using steam launches.

It was often argued that ramming was an effective means of sinking a ship disabled by gunfire. This, too, is not a very convincing argument as the rammer would be exposed to the risk of severe damage (*eg Camperdown*). If the enemy was disabled, a slower but safer way of sinking her would be to lie off her stern and fire raking salvoes into her. However, even in 1894, when Clowes presented his paper to the United Services Institute which clearly showed the difficulty of ramming tactics, there was still considerable, though not universal, support for this weapon from naval officers during the discussion.

It is suggested that the one era when ramming might have been successful was around 1840 when powerful paddle ships such as *Gorgon* were entering service. Against a becalmed sailing ship the chance of ramming by a manoeuvrable paddle steamer would have been good. There was enough experience with iron stiffening to support the ram itself. Why were the early iron frigates not configured as rams?

References

[1] J P Baxter, *The Introduction of the Ironclad Warship* (Harvard 1937; reprinted 1968).
[2] J Wells, *The immortal Warrior* (Emsworth 1987).
[3] D K Brown, 'The Royal Navy in the Crimean War', *Marine & Technique au XIXe siècle* (Paris 1987).
[4] Sir William Clowes, 'The ram in action and in accident', *RUSI Journal*, No 193 (March 1894).
[5] D K Brown, 'Warships on the Mississippi', *Marine Propulsion* (May 1983).
[6] H W Wilson, *Ironclads in Action* (London 1897).
[7] As 4.
[8] G A Ransome, 'RN Accidents and losses since 1945', *Warship Supplement 91–93* (Kendal 1987–88).
[9] K C Barnaby, *Some Ship Disasters and their Causes* (London 1968).
[10] Report by Assistant Controller and Director of Naval Construction based on minutes of Proceedings of the Court Martial appointed to inquire into the loss of HMS *Victoria*.
[11] W H White, *Manual of Naval Architecture* (London 1900).
[12] O Parkes, *British Battleships* (London 1956).
[13] J H Narbeth, 'Three steps in Naval Construction', *Trans INA* (London 1922).
[14] E J Reed, *Our Ironclad Ships* (London 1869).
[15] Conway's *All the World's Fighting Ships 1860–1905* (London 1979).
[16] D Lyon, *Steam, Steel and Torpedoes* (London 1980).
[17] 'The US armoured ram *Katahdin*'. Note in *Warship International*, 3/1974, p315.

Appendix 1. *Particulars Of Attempts To Ram In Action 1861–79*

Item	Date	Nature of Area	Rammer	Rammed	Final condition of rammer	Position of rammed	Final condition of rammed
1	11.10.61	N	Manassass	Richmond	S Da	A	Da
2	10.2.62	N	Commodore Perry	Sea Bird	U	A	S
3	8.3.62	S	Virginia	Cumberland	Da	A	S
4	9.3.62	S	Monitor	Virginia	U	S	U
5	9.3.62	S	Virginia	Monitor	Da	S	U
6	24.4.62	N	Manassass	Pensacola	U	S	U
7	24.4.62	N	Manassass	Mississippi	U	S	S Da
8	24.4.62	N	Manassass	Brooklyn	U	S	S Da
9	24.4.62	N	Governor Moore	Varuna	U	S	S Da
10	24.4.62	N	Stonewall Jackson	Varuna	U	S	S
11	10.5.62	N	General Bragg	Cincinnati	U	S	S Da
12	10.5.62	N	General Price	Cincinnati	U	S	S
13	10.5.62	N	General van Dorn	Mound City	U	S	Di
14	6.6.62	N	Queen of the West	Lovell	U	S	S
15	6.6.62	N	Beauregard	Queen of the West	U	S	Di
16	6.6.62	N	Beauregard	Monarch	U	S	U
17	6.6.62	N	Price	Monarch	U	S	U
18	6.6.62	N	Monarch	Beauregard	U	S	S
19	18.7.62	N	Arkansas	Carondelet	U	S	U
20	22.7.62	N	Essex	Arkansas	U	A	Da
21	22.7.62	N	Queen of the West	Arkansas	Da	A	Da
22	1.1.63	N	Harriet Lane	Bayou City	Da	S	Da
23	1.1.63	N	Neptune	Harriet Lane	S	S	Da
24	1.1.63	N	Bayou City	Harriet Lane	Da	S	Da
25	31.1.63	S	Keystone State	Palmetto State	Da	S	U
26	14.2.63	N	Queen of the West	Indianola	U	S	Da
27	24.2.63	N	Webb	Indianola	Da	S	U
28	24.2.63	N	Webb	Indianola	U	S	Da
29	24.2.63	N	Queen of the West	Indianola	U	S	U
30	24.2.63	N	Queen of the West	Indianola	U	S	U
31	24.2.63	N	Queen of the West	Indianola	U	S	Da
32	24.2.63	N	Webb	Indianola	U	S	S
33	7.10.63	N	Wachusett	Florida	U	A	Da
34	9.11.63	S	Niphon	Ella and Anne	Da	S	Da
35	18.4.64	N	Albemarle	Miami	U	S	Da
36	18.4.64	N	Albemarle	Southfield	U	S	S
37	18.4.64	N	Albemarle	Miami	U	S	U
38	5.5.64	N	Sassacus	Albemarle	S Da	S	Da
39	5.5.64	N	Albemarle	Matabesett	U	S	U
40	5.8.64	S	Tennessee	Hartford	U	S	U
41	5.8.64	S	Monongahela	Tennessee	U	S	U
42	5.8.64	S	Ossipee	Tennessee	U	S	U
43	5.8.64	S	Monongahela	Tennessee	Da	S	Da
44	5.8.64	S	Lackawanna	Tennessee	Da	S	Da
45	5.8.64	S	Hartford	Tennessee	U	S	U
46	11.6.64	N	Amazonas	Jeguy	U	S	S
47	11.6.64	N	Amazonas	Salto	Da	S	S
48	11.6.64	N	Amazonas	Marquez de Olinda	Da	S	S
49	20.7.66	S	Erz Ferdinand Max	Re d'Italia	U	S	U
50	20.7.66	S	Erz Ferdinand Max	Palestro	U	S	Da
51	20.7.66	S	Erz Ferdinand Max	Re d'Italia	U	Un	S
52	20.7.66	S	Ancona	Erz Ferdinand Max	U	S	U
53	20.7.66	S	Kaiser	Re di Portogallo	S Da	S	S Da
54	20.7.66	S	Affondatore	Kaiser	U	S	U
55	20.7.66	S	Re di Portogallo	Schwartzenberg	U	S	U
56	20.7.66	S	Mario Pia	?	U	S	U

Item	Date	Nature of Area	Rammer	Rammed	Final condition of rammer	Position of rammed	Final condition of rammed
57	19.8.67	S	*Izzedin*	*Arcadion*	U	Un	S Da
58	9.11.69	S	*Bouvet*	*Meteor*	U	S	Da
59	29.5.77	S	*Huascar*	*Shah*	U	S	U
60	21.5.79	S	*Huascar*	*Esmeralda*	U	S	U
61	21.5.79	S	*Huascar*	*Esmeralda*	U	S	U
62	21.5.79	S	*Huascar*	*Esmeralda*	Da	Un	S
63	21.5.79	S	*Independencia*	*Covadonga*	U	S	U
64	21.5.79	S	*Independencia*	*Covadonga*	U	S	U
65	21.5.79	S	*Independencia*	*Covadonga*	RA	S	U
66	10.7.79	S	*Huascar*	*Magellanes*	U	S	U
67	10.7.79	S	*Huascar*	*Magellanes*	U	S	U
68	10.7.79	S	*Huascar*	*Magellanes*	U	S	U
69	10.7.79	S	*Huascar*	*Magellanes*	U	S	U
70	8.10.79	S	*Huascar*	*Cochrane*	U	S	U
71	8.10.79	S	*Cochrane*	*Huascar*	U	S	U
72	8.10.79	S	*Cochrane*	*Huascar*	U	S	U
73	8.10.79	S	*Huascar*	*Blanco Encalada*	U	S	U
74	8.10.79	S	*Cochrane*	*Huascar*	U	Un	U

Notes

Nature of Area: S = Sea-room, N = restricted waters.
Condition of rammer: Da = Damaged, S = Sank, RA = Missed and ran ashore.
Position of rammed: S = Under steam, A = At anchor, Un = Unmanageable.
Condition of rammed: U = Uninjured, S Da = Serious damage, Di = Disabled, S = Sunk.

Appendix 2. RAMMING OF U-BOATS IN FIRST WORLD WAR

U-Boat	Date	Area etc	By
U-15	9.8.14	N Sea	*Birmingham*
U-18	23.11.14	Pentland	Trawler 96
U-12	10.3.15	E Coast	*Ariel*
U-29	18.3.15	Irish Sea	*Dreadnought*
UC-46	8.2.17	Channel	*Liberty*
UC-26	14.5.17	Channel	*Milne*
UB-36	21.5.17	Channel	
U-44	12.8.17	Channel	*Oracle*
U-49	11.9.17	NW Spain	*ss British Transport*
UC-33	26.9.17	S Ireland	*P-61*
UC-47	18.11.17	E Coast	*P-57*
UB-18	9.12.17	W Channel	
U-87	25.12.17	W Channel	*P-56*
U-95	7.1.18	W Channel	
U-84	26.1.18	W France	*P-62*
U-89	12.2.18	N Channel	*Roxborough*
UB-78	9.5.18	W Channel	Transport *Queen Alexandra*
U-103	12.5.18	W Channel	*ss Olympic*
UC-75	31.5.18	E Coast	*Fairy*

A total of 19 rammed out of 178 U-boats lost from all causes.

Appendix 3. Ramming Of U-boats In Second World War

Rammer	Victim	Date	Speed (kts)	Angle (°)	Repairs weeks
Sunk by ram alone					
1 Hermione	Tembien	8.8.41			2
2 Sharpshooter	U-655	24.3.42	13	80	10
3 Wolverine	Dagabur	12.8.42	26	90	13
4 Viscount	U-619	15.10.42	26	60	13
Rammed, then depth charged					
5 Hesperus	U-93	15.1.42	25	glancing	8
Depth charged then rammed, ram major cause of sinking					
6 Walker	U-100	17.3.41			
Vanoc				90	10
7 Stork	U-574	19.12.41	15	20	4
8 Assiniboine	U-21	6.8.42			16
9 Oakville	U-94	28.8.42			10
10 Hesperus	U-357	26.12.42		90	11
Vanessa			10	glancing	1
11 Ville de Quebec	U-224	13.1.43			
12 Harvester	U-444	11.3.43	27	90	Later sunk
Aconite					
13 Aconite	U-432	11.3.43			4
Depth charge major cause of sinking					
14 Chambly	U-501	10.9.41	14	45	11
Moose Jaw			5		2
15 Westcott	U-581	2.2.42	25	glancing	8
16 Dianthus	U-379	8.8.42	14	60	3
17 Fame	U-353	16.10.42	14	glancing	4
18 Lulworth	Calvi	14.7.42	16	glancing	9
19 Ithuriel	Cobalto	12.8.42	12	60	7
Pathfinder					2
20 Crocus	XXXXX	16	70		1
21 Enchantress	Corallo	13.12.42	15	120	
22 Cadmus	XXXXX	4.12.42	12		2
23 USS Campbell	U-606	27.2.43			
24 Hotspur	Lafole	20.10.40			12
25 Antelope	U-31	2.11.40			3
26 Assiniboine	XXXXX	2.3.43	15		8
27 Oribi	U-531	6.5.43	22	90	

XXXXX = Not sunk

Notes to Appendix 3

1. Hit ahead of the conning tower (CT). Two small compartments flooded in *Hermione*.
3. Hit abreast aft end of CT.
4. Hit 20ft abaft CT; 4 compartments flooded in *Viscount*.
6. Hit just forward of CT; hull and CT smashed in.
7. Hit just forward of CT; 11-mile chase, *Stork* turned two complete circles before hitting.
8. Three or four unsuccessful attempts; first hit using engines to reduce turning circle just abaft CT, second ram well aft.
10. *Hesperus* used screws to turn, hit at full speed, U-boat broke in two.
11. Hit between CT and forward gun.
12. *Harvester* ran over U-boat, which jammed under propeller shafts for 10 minutes. Not certain that *Aconite* rammed this boat.
13. Ramming an accident; tried to board. U-boat sank at once.
14. U-boat turned across *Moose Jaw*'s bow.
15. At least one unsuccessful attempt. Considerable damage.
16. Four ramming contacts; last seems accidental. Four lower compartments flooded.
17. Holed in engine room and aft magazine, shaft bent.
18. Two unsuccessful attempts; hit starboard quarter.
19. Hit half way between CT and stern.
20. Two hits one between CT and stern; the other well aft. Submarine did not sink.
21. Hit between CT and stern; marks on hull seemed to show that *Enchantress* passed through submarine pressure hull but not sunk. Considerable damage.
22. Struck abreast CT; ship lifted and came down heavily on U-boat. Not sunk.
24. Considerable damage.
27. Considerable damage.

Appendix 4. THE KINEMATICS OF RAMMING

If the target ship is immobile then the attacker can execute the ideal ramming attack by approaching on the target's beam and with the target on the attacker's bow. The impact is then square on to the target's side but on the attacker's stem and in the direction of its length. Thereby, maximum injury is done to the target with only superficial hurt to the attacker.

However, if the target has way on then that much improves its situation, even if it does no more than steam slowly on a steady course. The attacker can still approach on the target's beam, but it must also match the target's forward speed (see accompanying figure). Thereby:
 i) the shock of impact is reduced, so diminishing damage to the target;
 ii) the impact is at an angle to the length of the attacker, so increasing the damage to it;
 iii) the target now has to be held at a constant angle off the bow of the attacker, so that judging the correct course is more difficult.

With an increase in the target's speed there appears a sector about its stern from within which the target is sensibly immune to ramming. An attacker located within that zone cannot commence any attack resulting in more than a glancing blow to the target. Rather, the attacker has first to use its superior speed to draw ahead out of that sector. This immune zone grows with further increase in target speed. When both ships are of equal speed the immune zone extends from beam to beam about the target's stern.

Ramming a target of superior speed is possible only if the attacker finds itself on the target's forward quarter. Even then, the impact becomes more glancing as its force increases, so that decisive blows are improbable. The difficulties of the attacker are further exacerbated by the target making a turn. For the former to remain a threat to the latter it must be capable of much more than just conforming to the target's change in course. The target can turn so as to sweep its immune zone towards the attacker – which must then use some of its speed to keep clear of that zone. Alternatively, the target can turn so as to put the attacker on its bow. Either way, there is a contest not only between the turn rates of attacker and target but also between the attacker's forward speed and the target's turn rate.

The greater the distance between the contending ships the greater the forward advance of the attacker necessary to counter a given turn by the target (in terms of keeping out of the latter's immune zone or off its bow). Thus, the contest between attacker's speed and the target's turn rate is more weighted against the former the earlier the moment in an attack at which the target begins its turn.

For a target having superior speed it is sufficient to force the attacker into its immune zone and then escape in a stern chase. Other targets (and those more aggressively disposed) would prefer to present their bows to the attacker – so promoting an even exchange of damage in the ensuing impact. A daring target could deliberately leave its turn until almost too late. Any hesitation by the attacker would then leave it on the target's bow but with the

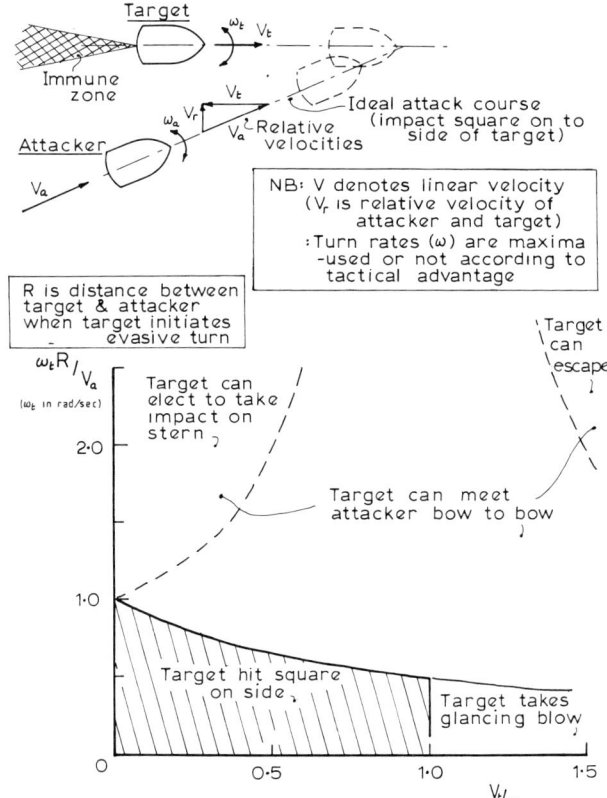

Ramming : attack and defence

target towards its forward quarter: *ie* the rôles of attacker and target would be reversed.

Such manoeuvres are susceptible to mathematical analysis (of the polygons of relative velocities) with the results shown on the accompanying graph. This graph enables the result of a ramming contest between any two vessels to be predicted, given their performances and the range at which the target initiates its evasion or counterattack. For understanding the ineffectiveness of the ram as a weapon, it is sufficient to consider the case of vessels whose performances are not greatly dissimilar. Then, the target can delay its evasive turn until the attacker has approached to within little more than half its tactical radius (*ie* a hundred yards or so) and still ensure much the same (modest) damage to the attacker as to itself.

It was no accident that the ram was a disappointment in comparison to the expectations of its nineteenth century advocates. If the target is under way, free to manoeuvre and handled competently, then basic kinematics make ramming inherently incapable of decisive results. The target has to be stationary, already damaged, not under command or caught by surprise at very close range for ramming to be an effective tactic.

SANKEIKAN: JAPAN'S COAST DEFENCE SHIPS OF THE MATSUSHIMA CLASS

As a crisis measure in the years before the outbreak of war with China, the Imperial Japanese Navy built three unusual vessels which, operating as a squadron, were intended to counter the two German-built battleships in the Chinese fleet. Named after Japan's most beautiful landscapes, they were known as *Sankeikan*. The well-known team of Jiro Itani, Hans Lengerer and Tomoko Rehm-Takahara describes these curious hybrids.

The hull structure was that of a contemporary protected cruiser, but with slightly inferior speed; they had practically no armour at all, while the main gun, one 32cm (12.6in) Canet gun of 38 calibres, was the armament of a battleship; all of which made them hybrid ships. The design was the work of the French naval architect Louis Emile Bertin and two of them were built in France, while the *Hashidate* was constructed at Yokosuka Navy Arsenal using drawings supplied by the French yard. Therefore the *Sankeikan* were different from earlier Japanese ships in that they had the French style hull form – enormous tumblehome, with secondary and lighter guns on the broadsides, large square shaped scuttles and near the waterline there were booms for torpedo net protection gear. The use of torpedo nets for ships of little more than 4000 tons in displacement was exceptional (when the French Navy had not even adopted the gear), but it might have been considered necessary because they were effectively the capital ships of the Imperial Japanese Navy (IJN) at that time.

There was one tripod mast with two superimposed fighting tops and one big cowelled funnel forward of this mast.

Their dignified appearance gave the impression of reliability but in fact these ships were troubled continuously with their boilers and the big gun was little more than a decoration. Even though the IJN had been warned not to build such ships, the naval authorities ignored the criticism. To understand the reason why they proceeded with such unbalanced ships, it is necessary to look to Japan's recent history.

Chinese armoured ships

The first decades of the new government after the Meiji Restoration can be characterised with regard to foreign policy by continuous tension between Japan and China brought about by Japanese territorial claims to Formosa (Taiwan), the Ryukyu archipelago (Tokara, Amami, Oki-

nawa Guntō), and Korea. There were skilful diplomatic manoeuvres on the Japanese side, local clashes, meetings of missions, and agreements and treaties were concluded but basically the tensions remained.

On 15 April 1875 Navy Minister Sumiyoshi Kawamura obtained permission to order the armoured frigate *Fusō* and the armoured corvettes *Kongo* and *Hiei*. All three ships were ordered by the Japanese Embassy in London from British shipyards on 2 May of the same year. Designed by the famous British naval architect Sir Edward Reed, these ships arrived at Japan during 1878 and became the most powerful ships of the IJN. The Chinese Navy recognised this development as dangerous for its supremacy at sea and after the Japanese Expedition to Formosa by which China was diplomatically outmanoeuvred and the Korean Incident peacefully settled (the Kanghwa Treaty of 27 February 1876) China began the expansion of her fleet. The order for two battleships was declined by the British government because of an ongoing border conflict between China and Russia, but it was accepted by the German Vulkan shipyard at Stettin in 1879. Four years later the Chinese Navy possessed the biggest, most heavily armed and best protected battleships in the Orient.

The IJN had no ships which could oppose them. The armoured frigate (casemate ship) *Fusō* displaced only 3718 tons and the shells of her four 24cm (9.4in) Krupp guns could not pierce the armour belt – 356mm to 250mm thick – of the Chinese central citadel ships, whose displacement at 7335 tons was about twice that of *Fusō*. The most important elements of a warship are represented by the offensive and defensive aspects of guns and armour, and

The Chinese battleship Chen Yuen *took part in the Battle of the Yalu with her sister* Tei Yuen. *Later captured at Wei-Hai-Wei, she became the Japanese 2nd class battleship* Chin Yuen. *(All photographs by courtesy of Hans Lengerer)*

Japan had no ship strong in these two decisive factors. Therefore countermeasures had to be taken.

The IJN's answer: The first period of the Naval Extension Programme

One year before the arrival of the Chinese ships and immediately after further trouble in Korea in July 1882, the Navy Minister Kawamura requested the urgent expansion of the IJN in view of the rapid technical and material progress that was being made in the navies of Western countries at that time in general, and the building of the Chinese battleships in particular, which had no comparable rival in the Far East and would become the biggest menace for the IJN. Notwithstanding these facts, the Cabinet rejected the Fifth Naval Extension Programme; but after the Imperial Rescript for military expansion had been issued on 25 December 1882, the sum of 26,640,000 Yen was granted for an 8-year building programme as an emergency measure following Kawamura's proposal of 24 February 1883 which revised his former proposal of 15 November 1882. Because of rapid technical progress it became necessary to introduce certain alterations into the scheme of the 8-year warship

The Chin Yuen *in Japanese service.*

construction programme, which became the Sixth Naval Extension Programme (92 ships, including 8 armoured ships; 75,514,242 Yen, not granted; in the same year this was reduced to 54 ships, including 2 first class (total 12,000 tons) and 4 second class coast defence ships (totalling 16,000 tons). In a Cabinet meeting early in 1886 the naval budget for warship construction (*Gunkan Seizō Hi*) was fixed at 9,903,491 Yen 20 Sen for 1883 to 1885. After deduction from the total amount granted in 1883 there remained 16,736,508 Yen 80 Sen. In order to execute the aforesaid naval expansion scheme (at least partly) it was necessary to provide 17 million Yen by means of naval loans and use them primarily for warship construction in the years after 1886. On 12 June 1886 this was sanctioned by the Emperor and between July 1886 and April 1889, 17,244,100 Yen were subscribed. While the aforementioned 9,903,491 Yen had been declared as the Warship Construction Budget, 16,967,003 Yen 67 Sen 4 Rin of the loan were first called Expenditures for other Usage (*Bettō Hi*) but became Special Expenses (*Tokubetsu Hi*) from 1887. These specific sums were allocated to the building of ships which were to be capable at least of destroying the enemy capital ships, but preferably of recovering the Japanese supremacy at sea.

Emile Bertin's design

For building these ships the eminent French naval architect Emile Bertin was engaged, after contacts were made during a tour of Europe and the USA by Deputy Minister of the Navy, Vice-Admiral Sukenori Kabayama. When the Japanese consul-general Hachizuka informed the French Navy Ministry of his government's desire to invite Bertin to Japan for three years, his duties were declared to be (1) adviser for the Navy Ministry (2) supervisor of the Navy Arsenals (placement and construction), and (3) direct employee of the Navy Construction Department; but IJN's primary expectation was that Bertin would build ships to counter the Chinese battleships.

On 2 February 1886 Bertin arrived at Yokosuka[1] (with his wife and three children) and remained in Japan until February 1890, because his contract was ultimately extended for one more year. He worked without French assistants and instead cooperated with Japanese engineers, most of whom had been educated in France.

Following his detailed investigations and drawing upon his long experience, he decided to build ships which were smaller in tonnage but superior to their Chinese opponents with regard to the calibre of the main gun and speed. In this he was responding to a very limited budget and the concept of a 'defensive navy' because Japan's financial situation did not allow the construction of armoured ships (the ship in the modified Sixth Naval Extension Programme was deleted). Therefore the building of three so-called *Kaibōjunyōkan* (coast defence cruisers) was proposed as an emergency measure. In fact these three ships were steel-hulled second class cruisers, of only 4278 tons displacement, which allowed the building of three ships instead of the two first class *Kaibōkan* (coast defence ship) of the same total tonnage in the aforementioned building programme.

WARSHIP 1990

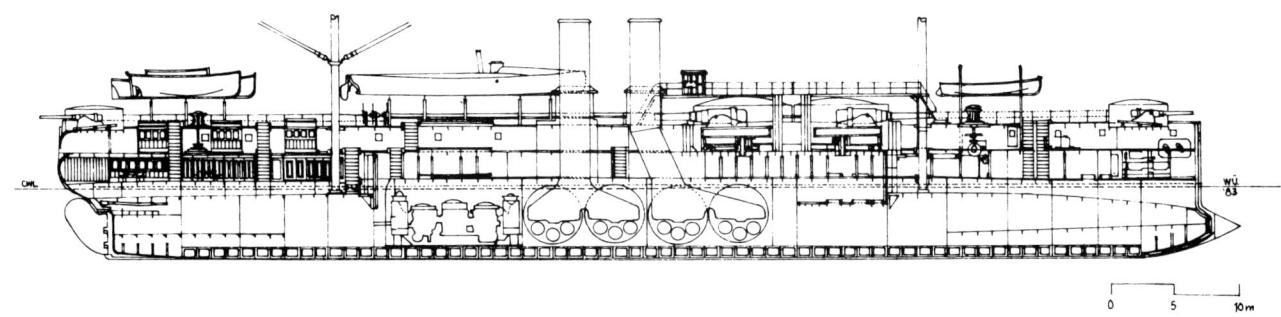

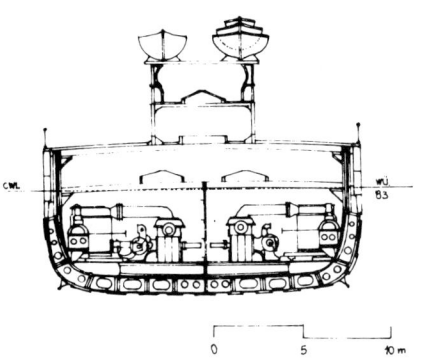

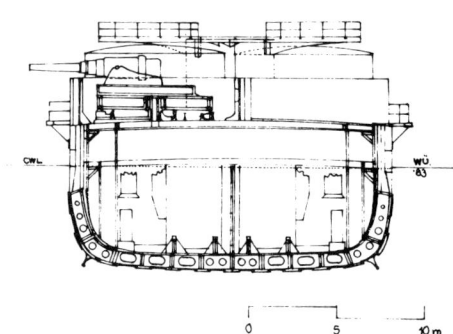

Chen Yuen: *drawings showing main features* – en echelon *main armament, auxiliary sailing rig, and torpedo-boats carried amidships*. (All drawings by Michael Wünschmann)

Matsushima, *sheer elevation, showing differences from sister ships*.

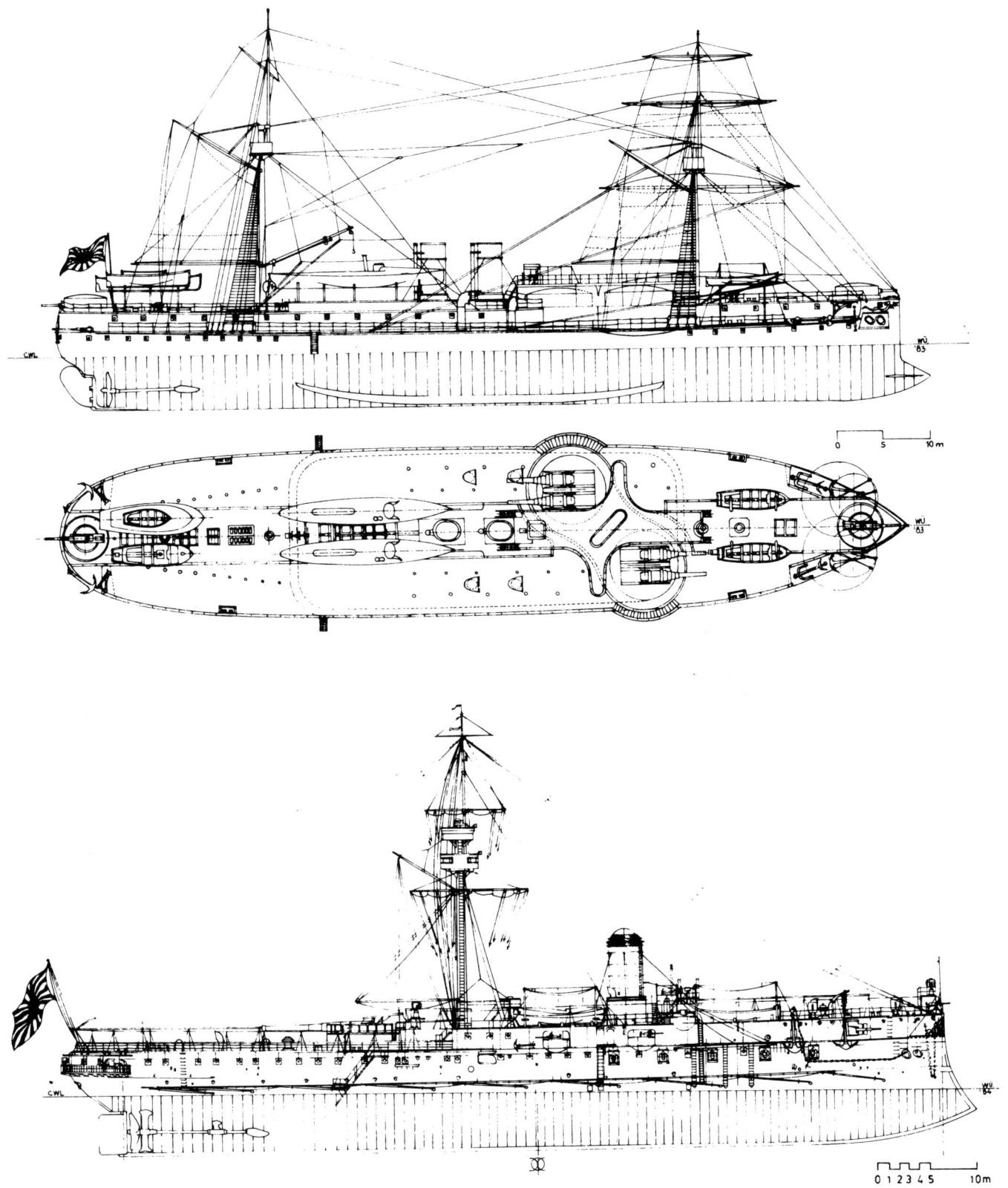

Table 1. PARTICULARS

	Itsukushima	Matsushima	Hashidate
Laid down	7.1.1888	17.2.1888	6.8.1888
Launched	18.7.1889	22.1.1890	24.3.1891
Completed	3.9.1891	5.4.1892	26.6.1894
Builder	Forges et Chantiers de la Mediterranée		Yokosuka Navy Yard
Classified as 2nd class cruiser	21.3.1898	21.3.1898	21.3.1898
Classified as 2nd class coast defence ship	28.8.1912	[sunk 30.4.1908]	28.8.1912
Removed from the list	12.3.1926	31.7.1908	25.12.1925
Length between perpendiculars (m)		90.68	
Length overall (m)		99.00	
Beam (m)		15.39	
Depth (m)		10.67	
Draught, mean (m)		6.04	
Draught, maximum (m)		6.74	
Trial displacement (as designed)		4278	
32cm I 38cal Canet gun (60 rounds)	1	1	1
12cm I 40cal Armstrong QF gun (100)	11	12	11
47mm I Hotchkiss QF gun (400)	5	6	6
37mm V Hotchkiss QF gun (1,500)	12	11	12
35.6cm Krupp TT		4	
Type 88 (Schwartzkopf) torpedoes		20 (five for each TT)	
Searchlights		4	
Armour			
Protective deck		40mm Harvey steel, slopes 30mm	
Conning Tower		100mm	
Coal (tons)		670	
Complement		360	

The beginning of the 'Big ship – big gun' principle in the IJN

These three ships were to fight in one formation (see later) in a gunnery duel against the enemy battleships. They were built with the specific intention of forcing a decisive fleet battle, because no other guns available on Japanese warships could pierce the armour protection of the Chinese ships. Because the main armament of these ships was the 30.5cm (12in) Krupp gun, Bertin proposed to use the 32cm Canet gun whose calibre was above the battleship standard of the time. The *Matsushima* class ships were no match for the Chinese capital ships in protection, so he attempted to mount a superior gun to out-shoot the enemy. (In this respect the comparison can be made with the situation before the Pacific War when the numerically inferior IJN wanted to out-gun the USN battleships with the huge main armament of the *Yamato* class.) The longer barrel length (initially the barrel was to be 42 calibres length, with a muzzle velocity of more than 700m per sec) would provide the velocity to pierce the thickest armour, while the mechanised training and elevation/depression machinery (by hydraulic pressure) was to guarantee fast firing speed. This was later called a 'mechanised gun' (*Kidō-Hō*) by the IJN and was the first gun of its type in Japan. However, contrary to all expectations, the hydraulic machinery, thought to be of so much advantage, continuously caused break-downs and in the decisive moment at the Battle of the Yalu, a splinter put the hydraulic system and thus the gun out of action aboard *Matsushima*.

Captain John Ingles, who came to Japan in 1887[2] as adviser to the Navy Ministry and assistant for the development of the Higher Technical Education system, argued against these ships and their large calibre gun and warned that the development of guns and ships was proceeding so rapidly that the IJN should not choose any class of warships upon which to place complete reliance. On the other hand, he recommended the protected cruisers *Naniwa* and *Takachiho*, just delivered by British shipyards at that time, as the best fighting ships from the viewpoint of both offensive and defensive characteristics and proposed to build at least ten more ships of this class.[3] But the IJN's principal concern was to have a gun whose shell was able to pierce the armour of any existing Chinese ship or any foreign warship likely to show her flag in the Orient.

Technical description of the Sankeikan

The decision was taken to build two ships in France and one ship at the Yokosuka Navy Arsenal (to be supervised by Bertin). The IJN ordered *Itsukushima* and *Matsushima* from Forges et Chantiers de la Mediterranée, at La

Seyne, and they were laid down on 7 January and 17 February 1888 respectively, while the construction of *Hashidate* began on 6 August of the same year.

Because of limited space this description concentrates on the main gun and propulsion plant, but before dealing with these items some general remarks may be of interest. The bow was fitted with a ram – nearly unavoidable on this type of ship since the Battle of Lissa. The protective deck by which these ships were classified consisted of Harvey steel plates of 20mm thickness rivetted over a double plating of steel, each layer 10mm in thickness, so that the total thickness became 40mm. The various openings in the protective deck, especially the boiler and engine room hatches, were protected by 50mm thick armour glacis and protective framing filled with cellulose.

The cellular belt, a longitudinal caisson from end to end and divided into numerous compartments filled with cellulose, was associated with this deck as was the coal protection. The space between the protective deck and the upper deck, about 4m in height, was subdivided by longitudinal and transverse bulkheads into a large number of water-tight compartments. This was the typical French indirect protective system in contrast to the British direct protection system, but as far as the resistance to penetration is concerned, it might be pierced by shells of 12cm (4.7in) or more in calibre, *ie* it was not very effective.

The midship section of *Hashidate* clearly shows the typically French tumblehome intended to reduce rolling. This particular hull form had some advantages (saving of weight in the upper part of the hull, easy rolling in high seas, higher speed in the same sea states), but its biggest disadvantage was the big angle of heel when the helm was put over – in fact the training of the main gun to port or starboard caused heeling of several degrees in the *Sankeikan*.

The tall tripod mast (or more correctly, a large diameter pole mast with two stays) was made of steel plates and was utilised to ventilate the interior of the ship, thus

◀ *A rare view of the* Chin Yuen *shortly after capture. The turret hoods have been removed and the white circles indicate battle damage.*

▼ Matsushima *about 1897–99. Her mast is still unaltered.*

giving an example of Bertin's concern for ventilation, the theme of his first prize-winning study. Of the two fighting tops, the lower one was used for at least four Hotchkiss revolving guns while the upper one was reserved for riflemen.

The full width bridge was placed before the funnel and each wing carried one searchlight; one more was mounted immediately aft, the fourth being located on the after superstructure.[4] The interior of the ship was entirely lit by electric light.

The main armament

After Bertin proposed a superior gun, on 27 April 1886 Navy Minister Tsugumichi Saigo ordered the Chairman of the Weapons Committee, Noriyoshi Akamatsu, to investigate which kind of gun should equip the new ships. Akamatsu was instructed that the gun would be ordered from abroad and was supplied with the necessary specifications and drawings for study by the committee members. On 25 May they decided in favour of the 42-calibre 32cm (12.6in) gun with breech screw, of more than 700m per sec muzzle velocity, with an elevation of up to 30 degrees, free loading system (3 degrees to 30 degrees) mounted in the gun carriage on the training platform with the ammunition tube hoist in the centre to be able to load the next shell immediately after firing. The mounting was to be of the barbette type with hood, the latter being 100mm in thickness. The gun should fire an AP shell weighing about 540kg by using about 170kg brown powder with the lower burning speed. The other specifications amounted to twenty-two items, concerning materials, structure, production methods, hydraulic system, prices, etc.

The Navy Construction Department (at that time *Kansenkyoku*) then approached Bertin about the design. Early in August of the following year everything was ready and the Deputy Minister of the Navy ordered the Chairman of the Weapons Committee to discuss the design quickly and secretly. In the second conference on 30 August 1887

The 32cm/38cal gun of Matsushima. *Note barrel support.*

Table 2. *MAIN ARMAMENT (FINAL DESIGN)*

Calibre	320mm
Length of the barrel	38 calibres (rifling 12.16m); total length from breech to muzzle 12.778m = 40cal; 42cal[1]
No of grooves; depth	90; 1.6mm
Breech type	Breech screw
Weight of gun barrel	65.7 tons
Elevation angle	+ 10°; 30°[1]
Depression angle	− 4°
Training angle	285°
AP shell, weight	450kg; about 540kg[1] (explosive 10.17kg)
length	112cm (3.5cal)
Common shell, weight	350kg
Propellant, type	Brown powder with lower burning speed
weight	High, 280kg; 170kg[1] Common 220 kg Reduced 160kg
Fuse	No 1 type Higo instant fuse
Muzzle velocity, AP shell	650m/s; more than 700m/s[1]; 700m/s[2]
common shell	610m/s
Muzzle energy	9690 metre-tons; 11,250 metre-tons[2]
Penetration	
at muzzle	1111mm wrought iron
at 8000m	334mm wrought iron
Effective range	8000m
Maximum range	12,000m
Type of turret	Barbette gun with hood
Thickness of shield	110mm; 160mm[1]
Thickness of shelter	40mm; 100mm[1]
Thickness of barbette	305mm
Thickness of central tube	260mm
Diameter of the barbette	7.77m
Diameter of the training platform	5.79m

Notes
[1] Decision of Weapons Conference, 27 April 1886.
[2] As altered in August 1887.

discussion ranged from the reason why the length of the barrel was shortened,[5] to the use of the barbette gun with hood,[6] the designs supplied by Krupp and Armstrong,[7] the method of test firing, the life of the gun barrel, amount of powder, prices, materials etc, and afterwards the General Staff, Navy Department and Navy Construction Department expressed their opinions and the necessary decisions were made. The final dimensions of the gun are given in Table 2.

The order to the French shipyard included the complete armament of *Hashidate*. The weight of the ordnance amounted to about 460 tons (including ammunition). At that time tacticians favoured bow fire and ram. Therefore the main gun of *Itsukushima* and *Hashidate* was mounted

Matsushima *at La Seyne around July 1892*.

on the forecastle while *Matsushima*'s gun was placed aft. Even though they were not real turret ships but were more precisely barbette ships, with hoods, they suffered all the disadvantages of turret ships of that period, like the British *Sans Pareil* and *Victoria*.

Without any doubt they were over-armed; the huge main gun barrel was 12.78m long and weighed 65.7 tons. Put another way, they were typical examples of an inadequate compromise between contradictory requirements. The barbette and the gun had to be placed as low as possible because of the disproportionate effect of the heavy weight upon stability,[8] resulting in a low freeboard and firing position, which in turn caused problems for the handling of the gun and had a detrimental influence upon seaworthiness. When this arrangement was questioned, the position of the main gun in the later *Matsushima* was shifted aft and the secondary battery brought forward to improve seaworthiness.

The barbette consisted of 305mm thick Creusot armour plates. The central tube, connected to the barbette by the training platform, was protected between the protective and upper decks with 260mm thick steel plates. Even though this ammunition hoist contributed to the protection of the barbette the gun could be put out of action relatively easily by a shell bursting underneath it. The barbette hood at the after end of the mounting was formed by 40mm thick steel plates and fitted with a weather-proof port in the front.

The gun was constructed by Schneider & Co, Chalon-sur-Saone, and built according to the general principles of the Canet system. It was of course made throughout of steel and was built up in jackets, with the inner tube (imported from Britain) extending the whole length. It was surrounded by five outer tubes (made in France) and at the aft two-thirds up to ten layers of metal wire were tightly wound. No trunnion ring was shrunk on but it was held within the cradle of the carriage by means of a grooved jacket.

The breech mechanism consisted of the cylindrical breech screw with four plain and four threaded parts, the supporting slide which carried the breech screw, and the firing device. The breech screw was worked mechanically by means of a crank and a set of toothed wheels to be successively turned in its seating, withdrawn by the opposite turning of the gear and turned on its support round the vertical hinge bolt to the right. In order to open the breech only one handle had to be operated while in earlier times three cranks had been necessary.

The obturator was of the de Bange type (plastic) and

Matsushima *entering Kobe in September 1894 after the Battle of the Yalu. The large black hole forward indicates where the 30.5cm shell exploded.*

Matsushima *at Sasebo in April 1905. She had suffered ice damage to the bow and had been repaired at Sasebo (the white areas reveal the repairs)*

was situated between the fore end of the screw block and the movable head. The firing device was mainly a bolt in the rear end of the breech screw and acted by percussion. In order to prevent premature fire it masked the vent as long as the breech was not completely closed, preventing the introduction of the percussion tube, and preventing the striker from acting.

The gun carriage consisted of three main parts, namely the two bearing blocks, one slide and the cradle. The two bearing blocks were fixed symmetrically to the training platform supported by the central tube and a comparatively thin bulkhead surrounding the tube, with the interpolation of a sole plate. The slide consisted of two heavy I-beams stayed together by transverse beams, screws and rivets. The upper surface formed the slide paths for the cradle. At the front end were the trunnions and the rear end was provided with blocks in which the piston rods of the recoil cylinders were fixed. The cradle was semi-cylindrical in shape and rested on the slide paths of the slide. Two recoil and two compensating cylinders were cast integrally with in. The recoil cylinders were of the Schneider–Canet system, *ie* the piston was drilled horizontally so that a central counter rod, connected to the bottom screw of the cylinder, could slide in it. These cylinders communicated to each other by a pipe coming from a valve box fitted at the rear of the intermediate compensating cylinders. A slide valve regulated the distribution of liquid in the various cylinders and by this arrangement full control was provided in the running out and hauling in operation of the gun.

Itsukushima *at La Seyne in 1891 towards the end of fitting-out.*

Itsukushima *as completed.*

Table 3. MACHINERY

	As completed (three ships)	After reboilering Itsukushima/ Matsushima	Hashidate
Type of engine	Horizontal, direct-acting triple expansion, three cylinders		
Diameter of cylinders	HP 390.5mm, MP 593.7mm LP 1439.9mm		
Length of stroke	1000mm		
Number of revolutions (designed)	108		
Piston speed	216m/min		
Hp, designed	5326 (5400)		
on trials	5830 (*Itsukushima*)		
Total weight of engines with water	277.7 tons		
Propellers	2		
Diameter and pitch of propellers	4.40m × 5.10m		
Steam pressure	12kg/cm^2	17kg/cm^2	12kg/cm^2
Mean pressure in LP cylinder	3.45kg/cm^2		
Type of boilers	Low cylindrical	Belleville with economisers	Miyabara
Number of boilers	6	8	8
Heating surface	1418.7m^2	1241.2m^2*	1336.7m^2
Grate surface	36m^2 (*Itsu*), 36.18m^2 (*Matsu*), 31m^2 (*Hashi*)	40.75m^2/ 39.82m^2	38.14^2
Total weight of boilers	214.65 tons (*Hashidate*) 226.3 tons	149.6 tons	139 tons
Total weight of water in the boilers (normal)	91.53 tons	11.81 tons	33.07 tons
Total weight of machinery	583.88 tons	439.11 tons	449.77 tons

* 409.2m^2 of which related to the economisers.

Owing to the heavy weights that had to be moved, hydraulic pressure was necessary for handling the gun. All movements (such as traverse and elevation, running out and hauling in, hoisting of shells and powder bags, and loading) were executed by hydraulic pressure and the gun was dependent on muscle-power only for the opening and closing of the breech screw.

Power was supplied by hydraulic pumps, the water for which was furnished by a three-cylinder steam pump at 95kg/cm^2 pressure out of a 2400-litre water tank behind the turret. In an emergency the steam pump could be replaced by a hand pump needing twenty men for operation. The water was led to a central distribution box located upon the training platform by a feed pipe and then delivered to the various controlling devices which consisted of single and double slide valves in order to guarantee the most possible uniform distribution of water. Surplus water was discharged in an upper tank and brought back to the lower tank by another pipe.

The levers and handwheels for handling the gun were all within reach of the trainer standing on the platform under the hood. To move the gun vertically jacks were placed at each side of the slide and by moving the handwheel in the desired direction (for elevation or depression) the slide made the corresponding movement. The central tube was supported by a pivot and fitted below the protective deck with a circular rack for training the gun (this tube was connected to the training platform). On each side of the tube, and in the same plane with this toothed ring, there were two hydraulic jacks provided with two small hydraulic cylinders. The ends of a pitched chain, which passed round the head pulleys of two plunger pistons, were fixed to the lugs of the small cylinders, maintaining the chain taut. For training, the handwheel that governed the mechanism was turned to the direction towards which the gun was to be moved.

Main engines

The main engines belonged to the horizontal triple expansion three-cylinder type, one in each of the fore and aft engine rooms, each driving a separate propeller shaft. The engines, which were direct-acting, could be worked either in double or triple expansion, the former being used for speeds above 10kts. In this condition the steam was sent directly to the high- and medium-pressure cylinders at the same time and the exhaust was passed to the low-pressure cylinder. The average pressure of the cylinders was thus raised to increase the horsepower and hence the speed. When working with double expansion the output was 3410hp with natural ventilation and 5400hp (designed) with forced draught. On the forced ventilation full power trials *Matsushima* obtained 16.778kts with 105rpm and

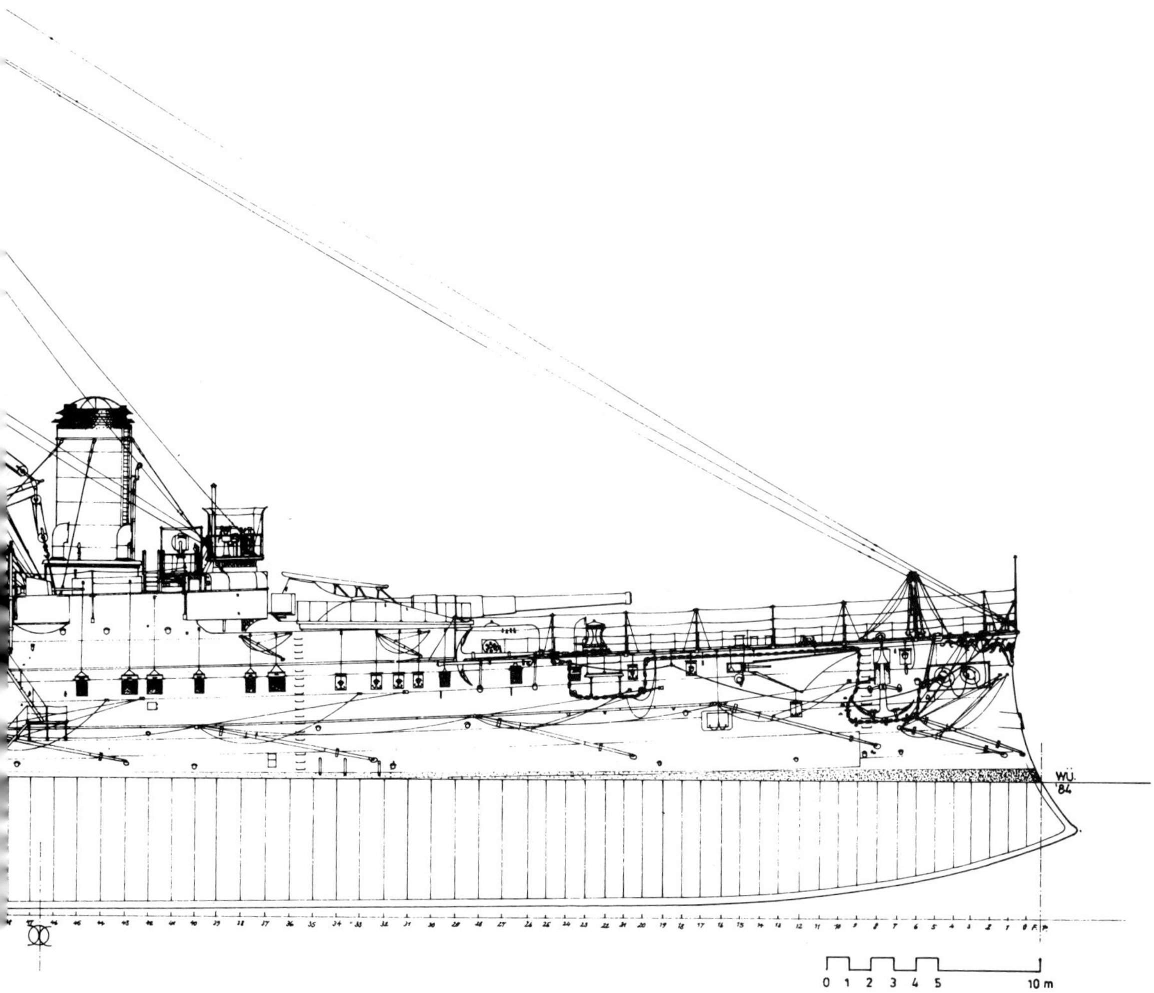

MATSUSHIMA CLASS

Hashidate *sheer elevation*.

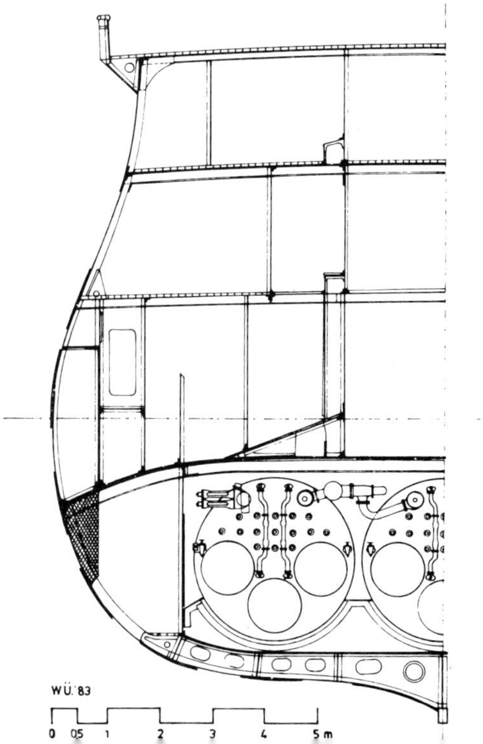

Hashidate, *midship section. The tumbletone is evident, as in the cross-hatched 'tranche cellulaire'.*

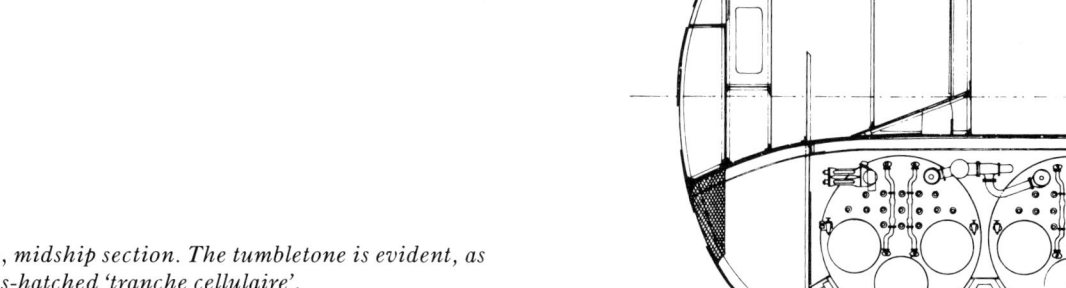

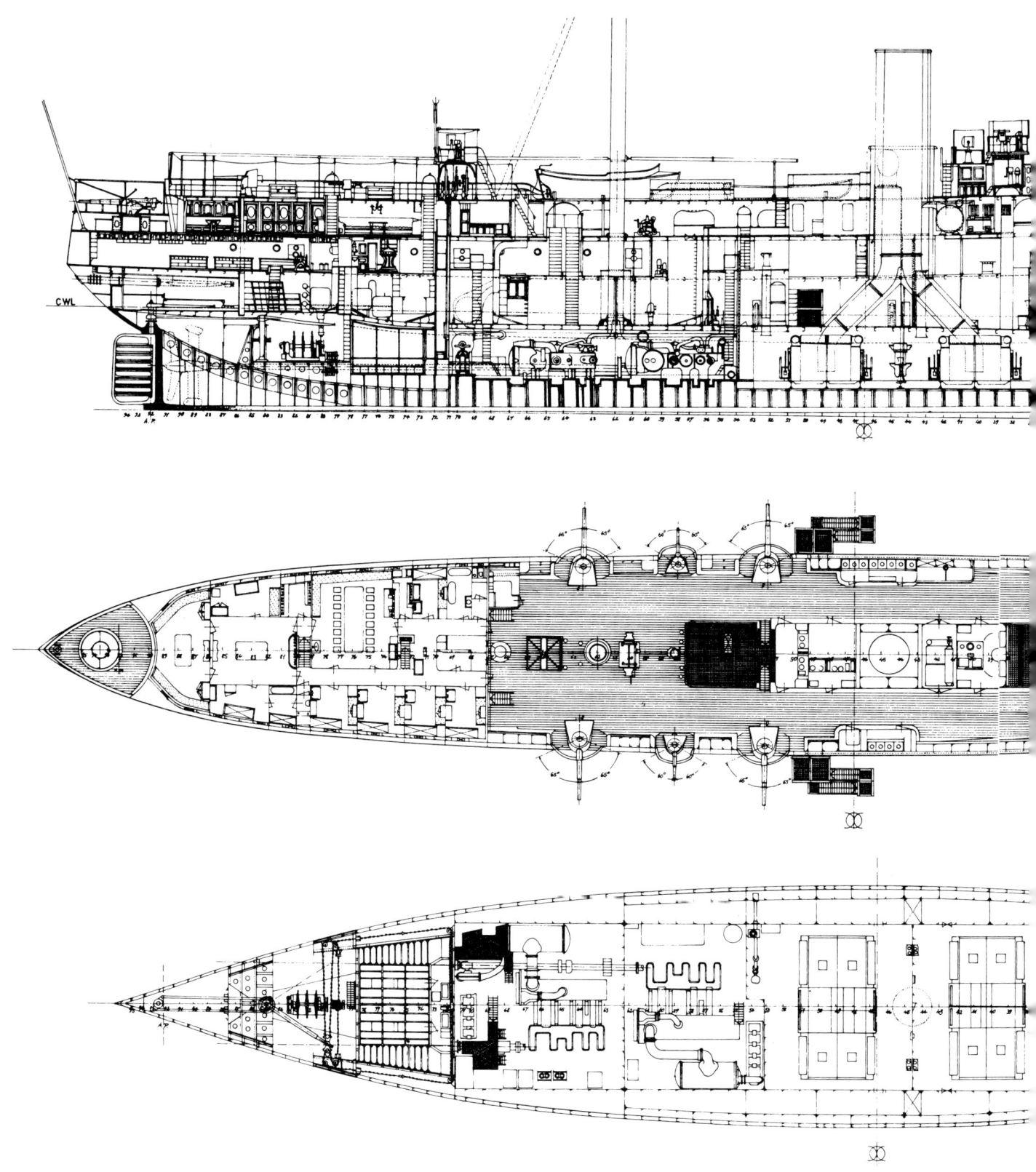

MATSUSHIMA CLASS

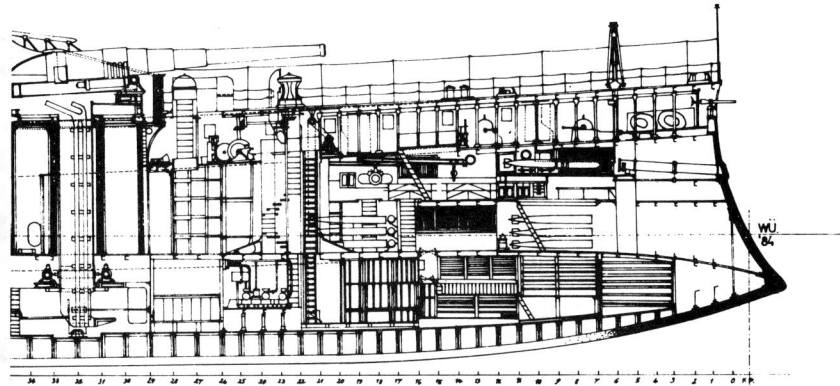

Hashidate, *internal profile. Note torpedo tube and handling arrangements forward.*

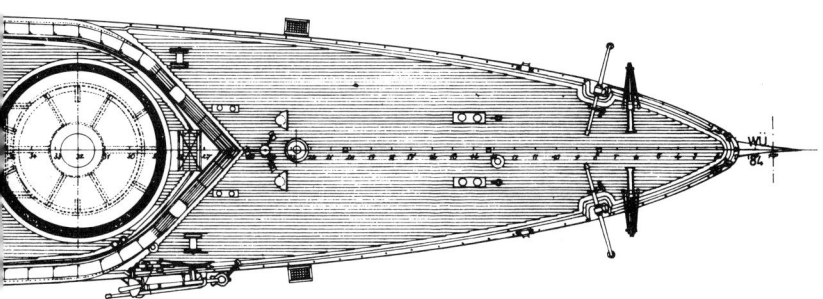

Hashidate, *forecastle deck level: 12cm and 57mm QF guns are mounted amidships.*

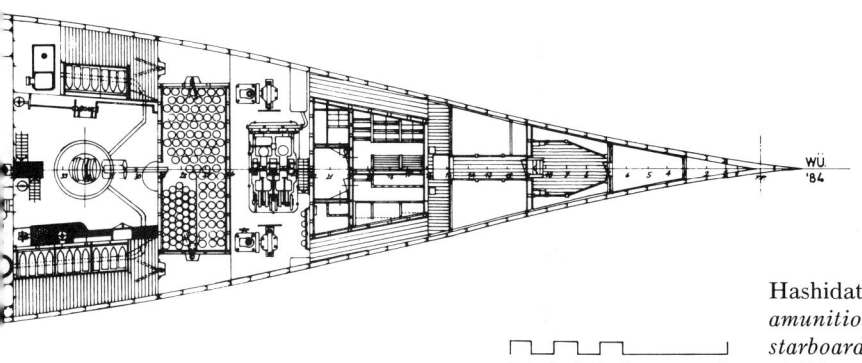

Hashidate, *lower deck. Note magazine forward of the amunition hoist and the shell rooms to port and starboard. The tiller and steering mechanism is also visible.*

Itsukushima *in the middle of 1892, with white hull and black funnel and mast.*

6519ihp, *Itsukushima* achieved 16.54kts on her trials in September 1890.

There was a condenser for each engine (6 tons/24 hours) and two auxiliary condensers were also fitted. These ships were equipped with a small workshop for repairs, the first time that this kind of facility had been provided on board.

Auxiliary machinery

The air pump was the double expansion type and the centrifugal water feed pumps and bilge pumps were driven off its crankshaft. There were four ventilating engines besides a number of other auxiliaries of which only the flywheel steam hydraulic pressure pump warrants a mention.

Boilers

The steam for the engines was provided by six low-pressure cylindrical boilers with the working pressure of 12kg/cm^2 (170.678psi). The boiler tubes were made of steel. Each boiler had three Fox corrugated furnaces, used for the first time in the IJN (the flues of *Hashidate* being the first domestically produced ones). As already stated, these ships were particularly troubled by boiler leakages and corrosion.

Itsukushima, the first completed, was delivered on 3 September 1891 and left Toulon on 12 November. On her way to Japan the boiler tubes suffered frequent leakage and the problem increased steadily. When the ship arrived at Colombo (Ceylon) on 5 January 1892, she was unable to steam further. It became necessary to send the engineers and workmen from France in order to repair the leakage of the tube plates. By adopting a new tube fitting she was able to leave Colombo on 18 April of the same year and arrived at Shinagawa on 21 May.

The breakdowns continued and the investigation concluded that the tubes were expanded very often during construction and therefore the holes of the tube plates became elliptical instead of round. This trouble was rectified by using a ferrule and completely circular holes in the tube plates.

As mentioned, *Matsushima*'s trial was successful regarding power and speed, but the boiler problems continued and she was given the same repair and improvement as *Itsukushima*. *Matsushima* was delivered on 5 April 1892, left on 23 July and arrived at Sasebo on 19 October. Benefitting from *Itsukushima*'s experience, her delivery crew made special efforts, for example when the fire was doused every part of the boiler was sealed by clay or canvas in order to prevent the intrusion of cold air.

The trial of *Hashidate* revealed no difficulties at cruising speed but at the high speed trials she had continuous problems and finally the Fox corrugated flues collapsed. Her building work had been hastened from the end of 1893 and was carried out as top priority in 1894. After changing the furnaces from Fox to Purves type she was delivered on 25 June 1894, just one month before the outbreak of the Sino-Japanese War. Because of her repaired boilers, *Matsushima* could manage full power and so she became the flagship of the Combined Fleet even though she had the rearward–firing main armament.[9]

After the war, the disorders of the boilers continued. As stated before, *Hashidate* had problems at higher speed and had to curtail her trials. No 5 boiler flue was expanded and other boilers also had some deformations. She participated in the war without using No 5 boiler and after the war the flue was renewed and could be used at the reduced pressure of 8.44kg/cm^2. Because of the condi-

From top to bottom: Itsukushima *off Kobe about 1897–98.*

Itsukushima *entering the Uraga yard's drydock about 1902. Note changes to the bridge and mast.*

Itsukushima *at Yokosuka naval base about 1908.*

tion of the boilers in general, it was decided (30 October 1896) to replace them at the next opportunity.

Itsukushima was given increased diameter boiler tubes (increased by 3mm) in September 1885 and ferrules to prevent leakage. However, during the fleet actions in February 1896 the problem arose again and later during manoeuvres, so on 27 May 1897 it was decided to use the boilers at the reduced pressure of $7kg/cm^2$. After a further outbreak of the trouble on 10 February 1900, a decision was taken to replace them completely. At that time it was reported that the boilers were fit for about one year at $8.29kg/cm^2$ pressure and 12.5kts maximum speed.

After investigations of many similar disorders[10] the following were found to be the main causes:
(1) Existence of scale
(2) Local superheating of the flue or contraction of the fire box tube plate
(3) Uncontrolled or unskilled firing (stoking) methods.

In 1901, *Itsukushima* and *Matsushima* were fitted with Belleville water-tube boilers and *Hashidate* with Miyabara boilers (invented by Vice-Admiral (Ing) Jiro Miyabara) in the following year. The post-refit trials of *Hashidate* on 20 October 1902 produces the following:

	ihp	rpm	Speed (kts)	Ventilation pressure	Combustion degree (kg)
Natural draught	3040.7	89.9	14.5	6.8	
Forced draught	4572.6	104.8	15.97	25.6	9.12

Note: Water evaporated from and at 220°F per one pound of coal was 11.9 in case of forced draught.

Prior to this (October 1901 to November 1902) a Miyabara boiler like *Hashidate*'s, a Niclausse boiler similar to *Yaeyama*'s and a Belleville boiler of the *Itsukushima* type, were tested on land by Yokosuka Navy Yard.[11] The results favoured the Miyabara boiler and proved also its superiority with regard to production and repair costs. After sea trials in *Hashidate* and other ships the Miyabara boiler was formally adopted by the IJN and used for a period of about thirteen years as a coal- and then mixed-burning boiler first without and later with superheated steam.

The Sino-Japanese War

The Battle of the Yellow Sea (known in Europe as the Battle of the Yalu) on 17 September 1895 ended with a Japanese victory which achieved control of the sea even though the Chinese battleships survived and retreated into harbour. Because of the later inactivity of the Chinese fleet the war was actually decided by this battle. At first it was believed in Japan that the gigantic guns of the *Sankeikan* had played the decisive role in the battle but detailed information was not released. Eventually it became widely known that the gun was too big for the ship and the resulting tendency to heel made it difficult to obtain the correct elevation and training angles. Furthermore the handling of the gun was difficult and time-consuming (in their later role as training ships, the cadets used to say 'By the time one shot is fired, the day is over'). To make

Itsukushima, about 1897–98. The tripod mast has already been modified.

▶ *Shipping* Hashidate's *main gun, 9 January 1893. Because Yokosuka did not have a powerful enough crane, the ship was sailed to Kure to use the specially constructed 100-ton crane seen here.*

matters worse, the recoil mechanism was inadequate and always gave trouble each time the gun was fired.

The captain of *Itsukushima* reported that the main gun fired five times, four rounds at *Tei Yuen* and one at *Chen Yuen*. The Japanese believed that one hit was made on the superstructure aft of the second funnel of *Chen Yuen* but in fact no Chinese ship was hit by any of the 13 rounds the three ships fired during the battle. The captain's record of firing is no more than a list of failures:

First shell – Recoil mechanism malfunction
Second shell – Malfunction in two places
Third shell – No problems
Fourth shell – Malfunction (uncertain if recoil or breech mechanism)
Fifth shell – Malfunction of the spring
Sixth shell – Never fired.

From the report of the captain of *Matsushima* the time interval between the firing is recorded as follows

First shot	12.58	Shell passed over *Tei Yuen*
Second shot	14.26	Shell hit on fore part of *Chen Yeun* [mistaken].
Third shot[12]	15.26	Shell dropped aft of *Tei Yuen* and *Chen Yuen*.

Just after the third or fourth round the ship was hit by

▼ Hashidate's *main 32cm gun. Details of the barbette, hood and barrel support are visible.*

Hashidate *off Kobe, 9 November 1898, during the Emperor's visit to the 'Standing Fleet' (later the Combined Fleet)*

two 30.5cm shells from *Chen Yuen* which put the main gun out of action from shock damage.

The total number of shells fired by each gun was *Itsukushima* 5, *Matsushima* and *Hashidate* 4 each. The engagement lasted for almost four hours (from 12.52 to 16.45) which means that almost an hour elapsed between rounds.[13]

Damage to Matsushima

Late in the battle (at 15.26)[14] *Matsushima* was hit by two 30.5cm (12in) shells from *Chen Yuen*. Both shells hit the port side at the height of the lower deck. One shell pierced the hull and dropped into the sea but the other hit the shield of No 4 12cm gun and exploded. Unfortunately this was a position where the 12cm QF guns were grouped and many ready-use rounds were stored alongside the guns. They, too, detonated and broke up the upper deck on both sides and caused a major fire.

Out of a crew of about 400 (including flagship personnel), 28 died instantly and 68 were injured. Most guns were destroyed and only six 12cm QF guns remained operable. The breech lever of the main gun was deformed and the ship lost most of its fighting power. *Matsushima* could not function as a flagship and after the battle the flag was shifted to *Hashidate* at 20.00.[15] Despite the serious losses and damage, the Japanese were lucky. If the hit had pierced the hull at or very near to the waterline, it might have caused enough flooding to sink the ship; and if these shells had hit at the beginning of the damage to the flagship might have had serious consequences. The damage to the *Sankeikan* in the Battle of the Yalu was as follows:

	Hits suffered	Dead	Wounded	Total
Matsushima	13	35	78	113
Hashidate	11	3	10	13
Itsukushima	8	13	18	31

Later careers

On 21 March 1898 the *Sankeikan* were classified as second class cruisers. *Matsushima* was involved in the North China Incident in 1900–1901 (as was *Itsukushima* in 1900), and was converted to Belleville water-tube boilers after returning to Sasebo in February 1901. Her sisters became the 4th Training Group for cadets and their boilers were also changed in 1901 and 1902 respectively. All three ships were used for navigation training of cadets.

After reboilering, the following figures were reported after a 6-month training cruise:

	Itsukushima	Matsushima	Hashidate
Type of boiler	Belleville	Belleville	Miyabara
Total coal used (tons)	2791	3310	3452
Boiler water bought (tons)	2630	2516	2065
Average ihp during the cruise	511	591	640
Coal, per ihp (tons)	5462	5572	5394
Cost of coal, water, oil etc, per ihp (Yen)	67.342	68.628	56.988

Hashidate *in November 1908*.

During the Russo-Japanese War, the ships participated in operations off Port Arthur, the Battle of the Yellow Sea (10 August 1904), Tsushima (27/28 May 1905), the Sakhalin operations, and so on, but mainly in escort and supporting roles. After the war the *Sankeikan* again became training ships. Commanded by Rear-Admiral Shigetaro Yoshimatsu, the three ships left Yokosuka on 25 January 1908 and arrived at Bako on 27 April, via Hongkong, Saigon, Penang, Ceylon, Batavia and Manila. Three days after their arrival, at dawn on 30 April, the magazine of *Matsushima* exploded at 04.08 or 04.09. The ship listed to starboard and sank by the stern, resting on the bottom at an angle of 16 degrees to starboard. *Matsushima* was removed from the list on 31 July and was later dismantled where she lay.

Personnel losses were high and out of 172 cadets of the 35th class aboard the three ships, 32 died. Most of the cadets who survived escaped from the previously mentioned French-type big square scuttles. The Investigation Committee concluded that the cause of the sinking was undoubtedly the explosion of the powder magazine.[16] It contained brown powder only and therefore the accident was not recognised as the spontaneous explosion of the propellant but was put down to an unintentional or intentional act by one or more members of the crew. The battleship *Mikasa* had also been sunk by a magazine explosion (11 September 1905). The circumstances of the sinkings were very similar and the Investigation Committee recognised a number of identical factors in both cases.

Itsukushima and *Hashidate* were classified as second class coast defence vessels on 28 August 1912. *Itsukushima* was removed from the active list on 1 April 1919, and became the submarine tender (*Sensuiteibōsen*, then on 1 July 1920 *Sensuibotei*) *Itsukushima Maru* and was used as a floating school until the foundation of the Submarine School from 20 September 1920 to 31 July 1924. On 12 March 1926 she was stricken and scrapped at Kure. *Hashidate* was removed from the list on 1 April 1920 and classified as a miscellaneous vessel (*Zatsuekisen*). She became the training hulk for the Yokosuka Naval Barracks until she was deleted on 25 December 1925 to be sold on 1 May of the following year and scrapped thereafter at Yokosuka.

Notes

[1] At that time Bertin was already famous in his profession. In 1864 he had won a prize for a paper on ship ventilation – especially important for French ships in China. In 1872 his study of the 'tranche cellulaire' formed the basis for the cellular belt. He also studied the rolling of ships and developed a special shape of section, with extreme tumblehome, that was widely used in the French Navy and also in the *Sankeikan* even though it was not successful.

[2] Navy Minister Tsugumichi Saigo, the successor of Kawamura since December 1885, had visited England in September 1886 and requested an adviser.

[3] The building costs for *Naniwa* and *Takachiho* amounted to 2,062,819 Yen 88 Sen 5 Rin and 1,939,111 Yen 41 Sen 3 Rin respectively, so when compared with the building costs of the *Sankeikan* the difference was not great enough to allow the implementation of Ingles' proposal. On the other hand, the Battle of the Yalu proved that the armour of the Chinese ships could not be pierced by the guns of this class.

Hashidate *as a second class coast defence ship, 1916.*

4. *Kaigun Kikan Shi* (History of Naval Equipment) identifies the type of these searchlights as 'Gramme' but this is the literal transcription of the Kanji ideographs. The authors do not know if this is right and ask any reader who knows about this subject to share his knowledge with them by writing to Hans Lengerer, c/o the Conway office.
5. In general this would mean a reduction of muzzle velocity but the weight of the shell was reduced (from 540 to 450kg) and the weight of the propellant was increased (from 170 to 280kg) and therefore it did not mean an intolerable reduction of the power.
6. An important problem was the position of the trunnion greatly forward of the centre of the training axis, by which the heeling moment became larger. Because of the gunners requirement for steadiness, the ship was given a long roll period, for which the GM was kept low, and this is thought to be one reason for the big heel when the gun was trained on the broadside.
7. At first all guns were to be ordered from Canet but later the 12cm guns were changed to Armstrong QF guns.
8. As already stated the initial barrel length was 42 calibres. The reason why it was shortened to 38cal was that the huge moment of the gun at the time of training caused the ship to heel, reducing effective elevation.
9. There are a number of other theories why *Matsushima*'s gun was placed aft other than the previously mentioned improvements to seaworthiness and the handling of the gun. One theory, accepted by Japanese and European writers like F T Jane is that these ships might form a triangle to be able to fire at least two main guns in case of chasing and fire one gun in case of being chased, thus having no dead angle. There are interesting differences in the opinions of Prof Takahashi (*Sekai no Kansen* 6/64) and Prof Aoki (same magazine 3/63) but it is impossible to discuss them here because of limited space.
10. For example in *Takasago, Miyako, Izumi, Suma, Fuso, Yashima, Fuji, Tokiwa, Akitsushima* and *Yoshino*.
11. The tests are described in *Kaigun Kikan Shi* Vol 2 (there were also dissenting voices).
12. Several records agree that *Matsushima* fired four shells. Therefore it is believed that No 2 round was actually No 3 and so on.
13. In contrast to the *Sankeikan*'s 13 rounds, the 30.5cm (12in) main guns of *Tei Yuen* and *Chen Yuen* fired 120 and 77 rounds respectively.
14. There are differences according to the sources ranging from 15.00 to 15.50. This is the time used by Prof Takahashi.
15. *Matsushima* returned to Japan and was repaired at Kure Navy Yard. She returned to the Combined Fleet in November.
16. At 04.01 the officer on duty when making his rounds smelt smoke behind the barbette of the main gun and found the smoke coming from the hoist. At about 04.05 he ordered feed water into the magazine but before this could be executed the magazine blew up.

THE BATTLESHIP USS OREGON

William C Emerson describes the design, construction and career of the *Oregon*, one of three ships which made up America's first predreadnought battleship class.

Following the American Civil War (1861–1865) settlement of the West became the prominent objective on the American agenda. As a consequence, a steep decline took place in naval forces. The fleet was left to deteriorate; by 1880 only a few dozen obsolete monitors and unarmoured craft were seaworthy. Among the most powerful elements in the remaining fleet were five unarmoured steam frigates built before the war. This antiquated naval arsenal would undoubtedly have been sunk by one contemporary European battleship.

In the early 1880s there were growing concerns over battleship acquisitions in Latin America, notably by Brazil and Chile, and disputes with Canada and Spain. In 1883 a concerned Congress finally halted the naval decline. A steady stream of Congressional Authorizations led to the construction of thirty-two capital ships – and the 'New Navy' was born. The first battleships of this revivification were the *Texas* and *Maine*. Even before their completion these ships were regarded as inferior in design, and they were designated 'second class battleships'. Thus the three ships of the *Indiana* class were the initial first class battleships of the United States Navy, the first to be comparable to contemporary European battleships. The *Oregon* was the third ship of this class.

Description

On 30 June 1890, Congress authorized the building of three heavily armoured and formidably armed battleships of the first class, known as the *Indiana* class. Primarily intended for coastal defence, they nevertheless possessed sufficient seaworthiness for extended cruises in case of offensive operations. Limited coal capacity was the main concession made to assure a wary Congress that these vessels were intended for defensive roles. The second class battleships *Maine* and *Texas* had their main armament offset from the centreline of the ship, or *en echelon*. This arrangement had been popular in earlier iron warships such as Brazil's *Riachuelo* and Great Britain's *Colossus* class. The *Indiana*s had turrets mounted on the centreline – an arrangement which proved to be superior to that used on earlier ships. No turreted ships were ever again built with the *en echelon* arrangement.

The general plans and specifications for the *Oregon* and her sisters were furnished by the Navy Department. Detailed drawings from these general designs were prepared by contractors and submitted for approval as the work progressed. This process allowed for only minor design differences between the three vessels of this class, the *Indiana, Massachusetts,* and *Oregon*.

The *Oregon* was a twin-screw battleship of 10,250 tons with a draught of 24ft. She was contracted for on 19 November 1890, and was completed three years later. The contract price for machinery and hull, exclusive of armour, was $3,180,000. Before work was commenced, however, it was decided to increase the length for the ship from 344ft to 348ft at an additional cost of $42,810. She was built at the Union Iron Works of San Francisco, California – in the slip next to the now famous cruiser, USS *Olympia*. Total cost of the vessel was $6,575,000. In 1990 dollars, this would be the equivalent of $105,200,000, a very modest price for a 'modern' first class warship.

The first keel plate was laid on 19 November 1891; the first frame was raised 19 December 1891; the first rivet was driven 14 January 1892; and the launch took place on 26 October 1893. On 14 May 1896, the *Oregon* was given her official speed trial in Santa Barbara Channel. Her average speed for the four hour run was 16.8kts, thus beating the contract speed of 15kts and earning her builders a $175,000 bonus.

Below decks, the *Oregon*'s arrangement was similar to most ships of the day. The lowest deck area aboard was the hold, which was taken up with trimming tanks, chain lockers, 5in and 8in shell rooms and magazines, 5pdr and 1pdr ammunition rooms, boilers, engines, coal bunkers,

The USS Oregon *about 1898. She is shown in the peacetime colour scheme of white and buff in this photo taken before her funnels were raised, providing her with greater draught for her boilers.* (US National Archives)

The Oregon *aground at the entrance to the Port Orchard Drydock, in Washington State in May 1897.* (US Naval Historical Center)

and hydraulic pumps for the 13in turrets. Above this, forward and aft, were the platform decks containing warheads for torpedoes, handling rooms and other stores. Above these decks and the hold was the orlop deck, with reserve coal bunkers, main ammunition passing rooms, ammunition passages and the 8in turret machinery. Above the orlop deck was the berth deck, which contained the living quarters for the officers and crew, held coal bunkers, a refrigerating plant, auxiliary boilers, workshops and torpedo rooms. Above this were the main and upper decks.

Oregon. TECHNICAL SPECIFICATION

Construction Data

Builder	Union Iron Works, San Francisco, California
Authorized	30 June 1890
Contract Signed	19 November 1890
Laid Down	19 November 1891
Launched	26 October 1893
Commissioned	15 July 1896
Construction costs	$6,575,033

Design Particulars

Displacement	11,719 tons
Length overall, inc rudder	351ft 2in
Design speed	15kts
Trial speed	16.8kts
Length load waterline	348ft 1¼in
Max breadth	69ft 3in
Mean draught	26ft 9in
Max draught aft at lowest point of keel, ship ready for sea with bunkers full	27ft 1in
Coal capacity	400 tons (normal)
	1594 tons (bunker capacity)
Coal endurance	5500nm at 10kts
Armament	
	4–13in/35cal Mk I
	8–8in/35cal
	4–6in/35cal RF
	20–6pdr
	6–1pdr Hotchkiss RF
	3–18in Whitehead torpedo tubes
	4 short Colt machine-guns
Armour	
Side belt	18in–8in
Armoured deck	3¼in
13in turrets	15in
13in barbettes	17in
8in turrets	6in
8in barbettes	8in–6in
8in turret tube	3in
6in guns	5in
6pdr guns	2in
1pdr guns	2in
Conning tower	10in
Armoured tube	7in
Machinery	
Boilers	4 double-ended
Engines	2 vertical triple expansion reciprocating
Indicated hp	13,500
Max indicated hp	17,313
Propellers	2
Diameter of propellers	15ft
Complement	34 officers
	416 men

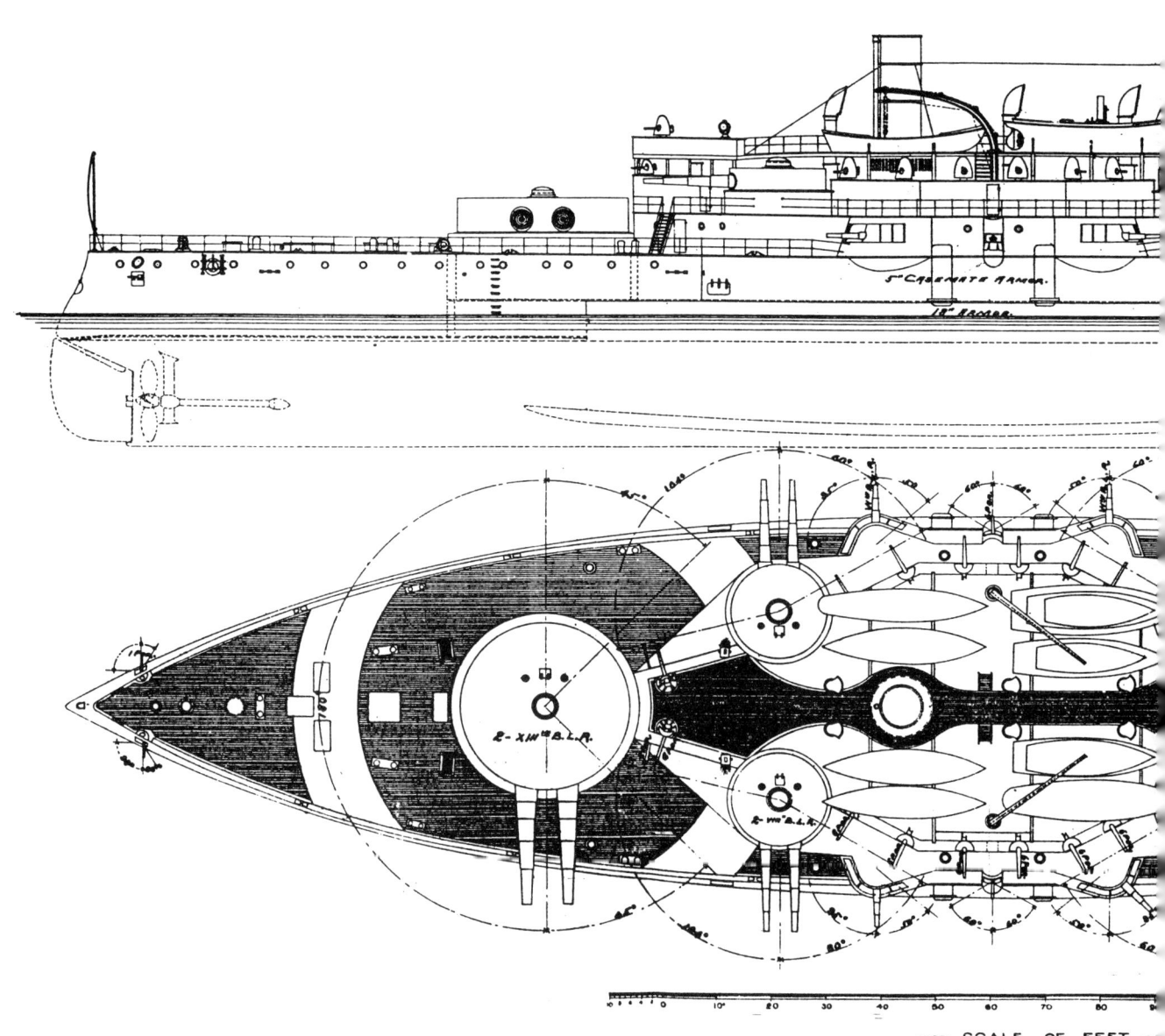

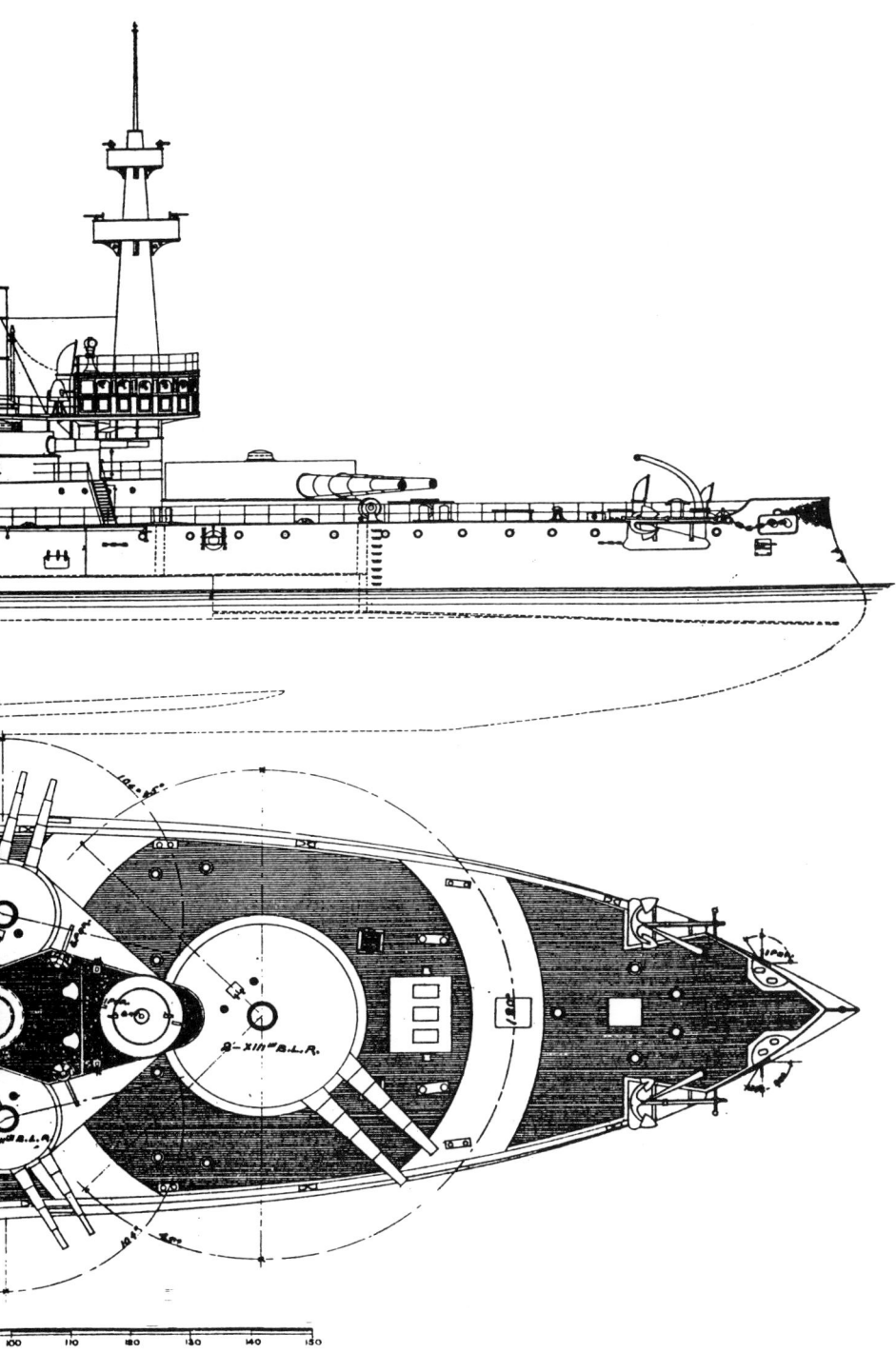

Outboard profile and plan view of Oregon *from a 1893 publication. Clearly evident is her low freeboard, which hampered operation of her forward turret in a sea. As built, the* Oregon *did not have the blast shields on the deck as shown, although both of her sister ships did.* (Society of Naval Architects and Marine Engineers)

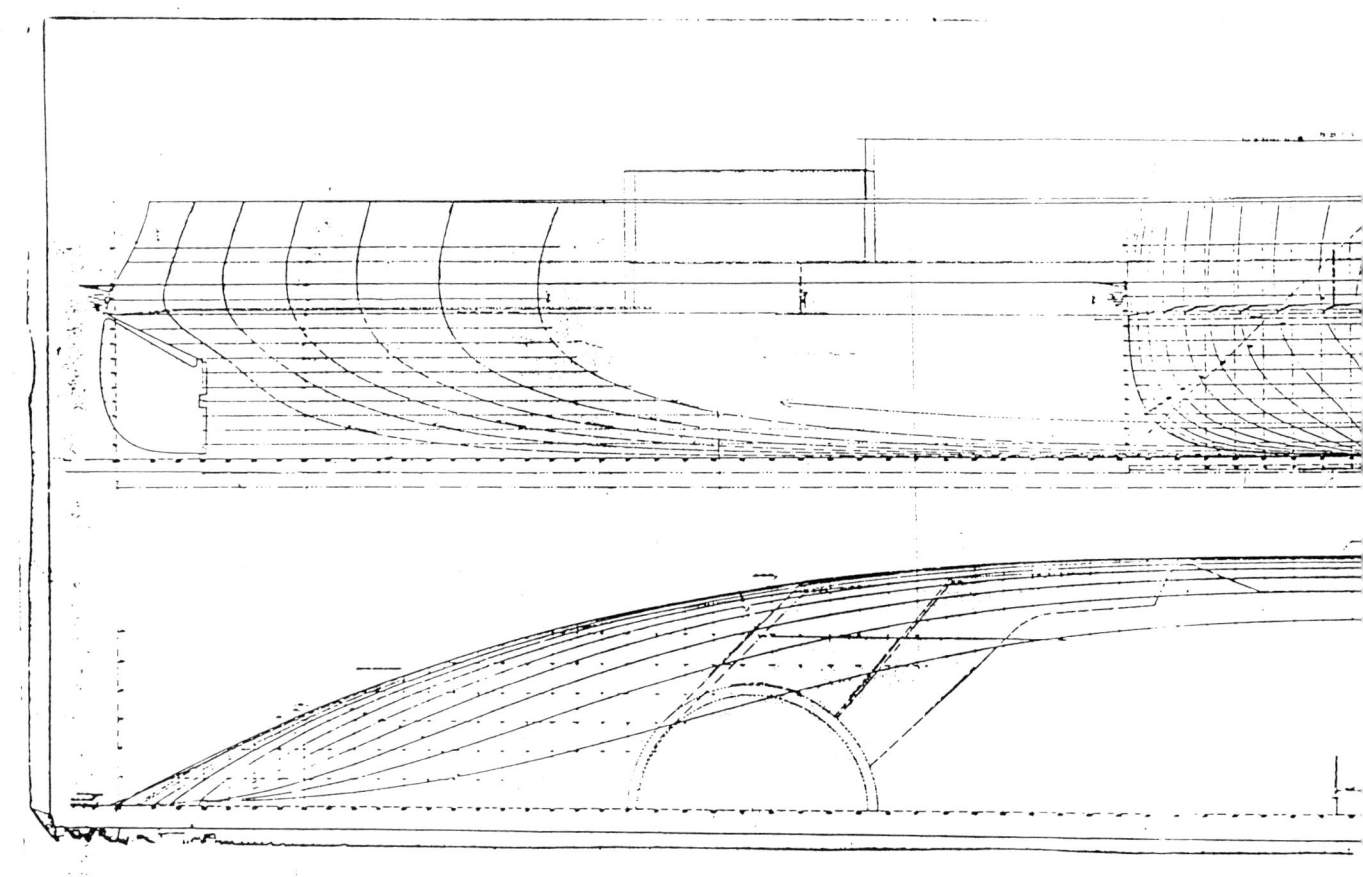

Original Navy half-breadth, body and sheer plan of 'Armoured Coast-line Battleship No 3' (US National Archives)

Bridge and stowage of boats plan for 'Armoured Coast-line Battleships Nos 1, 2 and 3'. The turrets as drawn were intended to have sloping sides, but were cylindrical as built. (US National Archives)

NO. 1.
U. S. ARMORED COAST-LINE
BATTLE-SHIPS NOS. 1, 2, AND 3.
BUREAU OF CONSTRUCTION AND REPAIR

NO. 4.
0 10 20 30 40 50 60 70 80 90 100
SCALE IN FEET
U. S. ARMORED COAST-LINE
BATTLE-SHIPS NOS. 1, 2, AND 3.

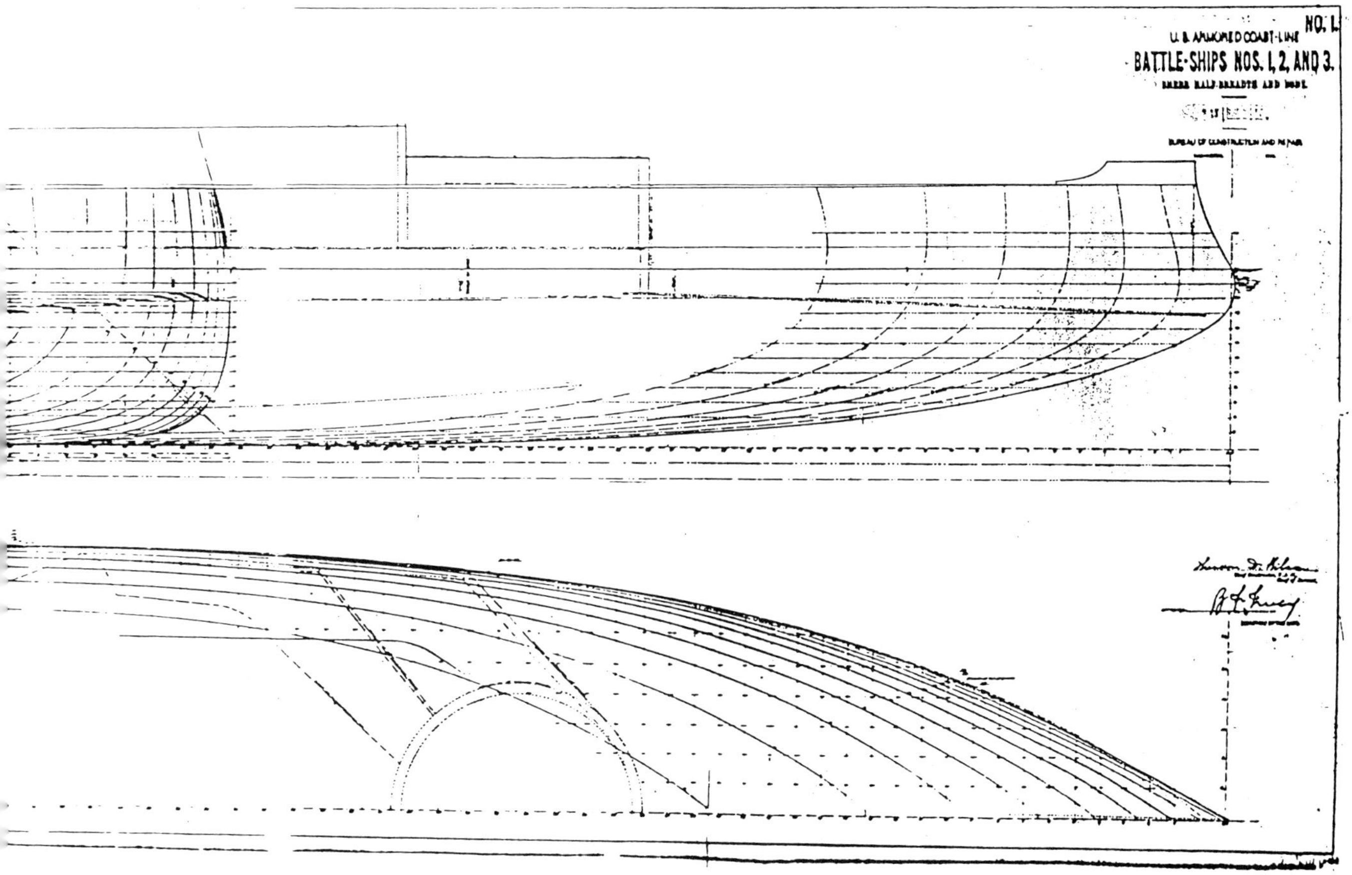

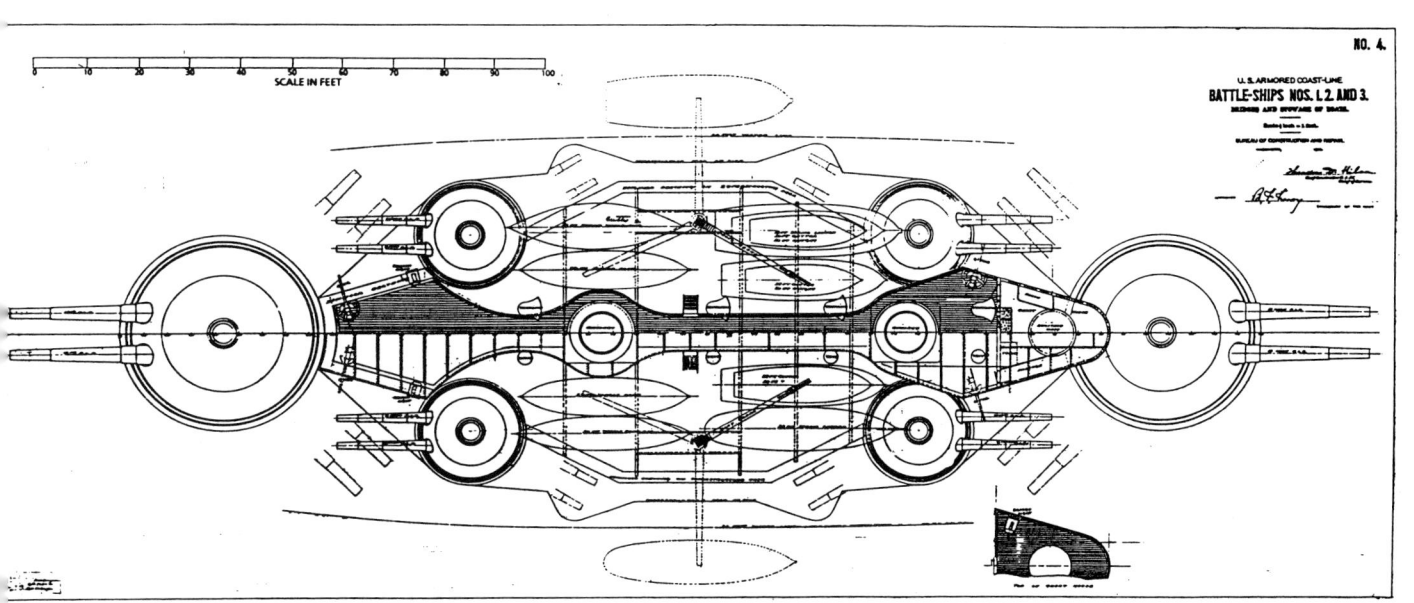

Visitors tour the Oregon *in the summer of 1898 following the successful conclusion of the Spanish war. Details of the mahogany charthouse and a 13in gun are visible.* (US Naval Historical Center)

The Oregon *returning from Cuba in 1898. She is painted in wartime grey, and shows signs of the wear and tear of many months of operational duty.* (US National Archives)

Hull

Mild steel of American manufacture was used in the construction of the hull. Frames were placed at 4ft centres amidships, and at 3ft 6in centres forward and abaft this. A double bottom extended for 196ft amidships and the hull was divided into a total of 249 water-tight compartments.

Built within the hull were twenty-eight coal bunkers with a capacity of 1594 tons of coal. Eight of these were located on the berth deck, four on the orlop deck, and sixteen located in the hold. Chutes and trunks for filling the bunkers were fitted between decks. Four chutes, for disposal of ash, were fitted to the outside of the vessel amidships. Their upper ends extended above the main deck and terminated in suitable hoppers built into the inside of the vessel. These chutes are readily visible amidships in most photos. Trolleyways lead from a number of ash hoists to the chutes.

Armament

Designed to carry the heaviest armament possible for their size, the *Oregon* and her sisters mounted four 13in/35cal guns in two heavily armoured turrets. While early designs for these and the 8in turrets featured sloped sides, the final design was the more familiar and more easily constructed cylindrical turrets. In order to minimize the size of the turret openings, the 13in guns were positioned as far forward as possible, which necessitated that the turrets be

The Oregon *receiving a fresh coat of underwater hull paint, in a New York Navy Yard drydock, around September, 1898. Notice the lack of safety precautions for the workmen.* (US Naval Historical Center)

unbalanced, with more weight forward of the axis than abaft. This proved a major design flaw – the ships listed badly when the main batteries were trained on the broadside, and during one stormy night both turrets on the *Indiana* broke loose and began swinging wildly about – several hundred sailors were required to tie the guns down.

In addition to the four 13in guns, the main battery consisted of eight 8in/35cal guns in four turrets mounted on the superstructure deck, and four 6in/35cal guns, mounted two on each side within the superstructure on the main deck. The secondary battery consisted of twenty 6pdr and six 1pdr Hotchkiss rapid-fire guns, and four light machine-guns in the military tops. Throw weight from the main and secondary batteries totalled 5664lbs.

Armour

The science of face hardening for armour was relatively new at the time that the *Oregon* was being built. In 1890 trials using a high temperature carbon-induced hardening process known as Harveyizing had demonstrated impressive improvements in protection from shell penetration, and most of the armour used for America's first battleship class was treated with this process.

Weight constraints have always limited the amount of a

ship that could be armoured. For the *Oregon* and her sister ships, the central portion of the ship was heavily armoured, while much of the superstructure and ends received little or no protection. The theory, then as now, was to defend the vital central portion of a ship, include the turrets, ammunition storage and handling areas, machinery and boilers, but leave most of the superstructure and the ends relatively unarmoured, since these areas could sustain severe damage without mortally wounding the ship. The protection consisted of side armour, casemate armour, conning tower armour, and turret and barbette armour.

Side armour extended for 149ft along the waterline of the *Oregon*, or about one-third of her length, and was nickel steel hardened with the Harvey process. It was 18in thick at the top and tapered to 12in below the waterline, and finally to a thickness of 8in at its lowest point. Amidships it extended vertically a distance of 3ft above and 4ft 6in below the normal load line and tapered slightly at the ends. From the ends of the side armour a diagonal armour plate, 14in thick, connected to the barbettes of the 13in guns, thus sealing off the machinery spaces from shots fired from ahead or astern. The casemate armour was also of nickel steel, and was 4in thick backed by 2½in steel plates. It extended vertically from the top edge of the side armour to the main deck, horizontally across the deck, and connected at the ends to the 13in gun barbettes. Conning tower armour was nickel steel 10in thick. The 13in gun turrets were armoured with 15in of Harveyized

The boilers of sister ship Massachusetts *being stoked. During her speed trial the* Oregon *consumed nearly 19 tons of coal per hour* (Library of Congress)

As a means of improving the draught of the boilers, the funnels were raised following the war. This photo of the Oregon *shows the ship about 1899. Note the simplicity of the bow decoration, which contrasted dramatically from many of the elaborately decorated US warships of the era.* (US Naval Historical Center)

Oregon. CONTRACT TRIALS
(FULL POWER, FORCED DRAUGHT)

Date of trial	14 May 1896	Vacuum in condensers, in inches of mercury	24.7	25.3
Duration of trial	4 hours			
Place of trial	Santa Barbara Channel			
Condition of sea and weather	Smooth, light breeze	Revolutions of main engines per minute	128.3	128.2
Draught, mean, on trial	24ft			
Displacement	10,250 tons			
Immersed midship section	1534sq ft	Mean engine pressures (psi)		
Type of engines	Vertical triple expansion	High-pressure cylinder	59.6	60.8
Cylinder, diameters		Intermediate-pressure	31.6	32.6
High pressure	34½ins	Low-pressure	18.7	21.2
Intermediate pressure	48ins	Equivalent on low-pressure	44.2	47.4
Low pressure	75ins			
		Indicated horsepower		
Stroke of pistons	42ins	High pressure	1486.2	1512.6
Number and type of boilers	4 double-ended	Intermediate pressure	1536.1	1586.8
		Low pressure	2233.5	2537.2
Length of boilers	18ft	Aggregate each main engine	5253.7	5636.6
Diameter of boilers	15ft	Aggregate both main engines		10,890.3
Number of furnaces (each boiler)	8	Air-pump engines	8.8	7.7
		Circulating pump engines	51.5	34.5
Grate surface (each boiler)	136sq ft	Feed pumps		44.4
Heating surface (each boiler)	4208sq ft	Other Auxiliaries		73.9
		Aggregate of all machinery		11,111.1
Screw propellers		Speed in knots		16.791
Diameter	15ft	Slip of propeller (mean)		14.3 per cent
Pitch, mean	16ft			
Pitch, adjustable	Between 15.5ft and 16.5ft	Coal		
Area developed	111sq ft (both screws)	Kind and quality used	Welsh; Harris Navigation in 96lb bags	
Number of blades	3			
		Total burned per hour	23,593.5lbs	
Steam pressure (psi)	Starboard	Port	Per hour, per ihp	2.1lbs
At engines, per guage	156.5	155.9		
In first receiver, absolute	82.1	82.2		
In second receiver, absolute	35.3	36.1		

nickel steel, and the barbettes 17in. The 8in gun turrets and barbettes had 6in of similar armour.

The displacement assigned to armament and its protection (guns and mounts, ammunition, armour used to protect guns and shields, etc.) was a very substantial 25.3 per cent. This compared with only 7.7 per cent for the *Olympia*, a typical protected cruiser of the day.

Machinery

The *Oregon* was powered by two triple expansion engines, state of the art powerplants in the 1890s, and much more efficient than earlier single and double expansion engines. In each engine there were three cylinders: a high-pressure, an intermediate-pressure, and one that worked at low pressure. The steam first entered the high-pressure cylinder and the expanding steam forced the cylinder to move. The steam was then vented to the intermediate cylinder, and then to the low-pressure cylinder. In order to extract the energy from the expanded steam, these cylinders had to be of increasingly larger diameter from the high-pressure to the low-pressure cylinder.

The engines were direct acting (connected directly to the propellers), and were placed side by side in separate water-tight compartments with access to each other by water-tight doors. The propellers were three-bladed, 15ft in diameter, and were adjustable, having axially expanding pitch. The hubs were spherical and terminated in a conical tail piece. The blades were bent backwards 6in at the tips, and were made of manganese bronze.

There were four double-ended steel boilers of the horizontal fire-tube type, placed fore and aft in four water-tight compartments with a midship passageway extending throughout the boiler space. Each boiler had eight corrugated furnaces and four combustion chambers. Each boiler was 15ft in diameter and 18ft long and produced steam at an operating pressure of 160psi.

Because the *Oregon* was a small city unto itself, there was a vast amount of auxiliary machinery aboard. This included auxiliary boilers (to power the other equipment), air and water pumps, bilge pumps, ash hoists, distilling plants, steam windlasses, steam winches, boat cranes, turret engines, an electric powerplant and refrigeration

Stern view of the Oregon *in battle grey. Her low freeboard is apparent in this photo. Her tubby shape, while uninteresting, allowed her to carry heavy armour and guns.* (US Naval Historical Center)

plants. In fact, in addition to the two main engines, there were 62 steam-driven machines aboard.

Boats

There were twelve boats carried aboard the *Oregon*; while at sea all were stowed on skids over the superstructure deck.

One 33ft steam launch	(located on forward starboard skids)
One 32ft sailing launch	(on aft starboard skids)
One 30ft steam cutter	(on aft port skids)
Two 29ft whale boats	(on aft starboard and forward port skids)
Two 28ft cutters	(on forward port and starboard skids)
One 26ft cutter	(nested in 32ft sailing launch)
One 24ft cutter	(nested in 32ft sailing launch)
Two 20ft dinghys	(nested in the 28ft cutters)
One 8ft balsa	(misc locations)

USS OREGON

Colour scheme

The peacetime colour scheme for all US capital ships of this era was basically the same – white lowers with buff uppers. In addition to the hull, the *Oregon* in 1896 had white turrets (both 8in and 13in), superstructure (below charthouse level), shields for the 6pdr guns, and boats. The military mast, funnels, boat cranes and rear platform were buff. Red lead was used on the underwater hull. The *Oregon*'s charthouse and boat trim were mahogany and the main and superstructure decks were planked with teak and were unpainted.

The wartime colour scheme was grey. In this scheme the hull, superstructure, charthouse, and stacks were all a uniform mid-grey colour with only the decks left unpainted.

▲ *The* Oregon *in 1897 in the Port Orchard Drydock, in Washington State. Despite the use of red lead to repel the growth of marine organisms, the damage of some three years in the water is readily apparent.* (US Naval Historical Center)

▼ *A view of the* Oregon's *forward turret and bridge area in 1898, from a stereo card photo published in that year. The victorious navy ships were favorite subjects of commercial photographers, many of whom produced cards for the popular stereoscopes of the day.* (US Naval Historical Center)

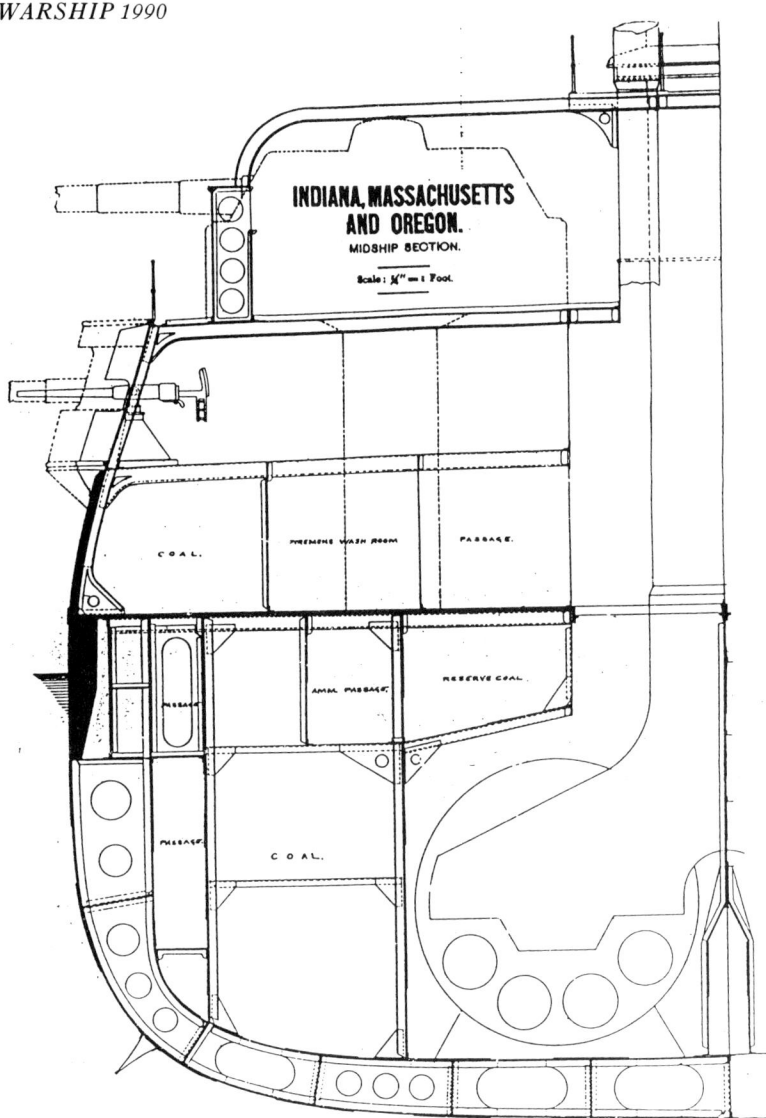

Midship section plan of the three battleships. Visible is the arrangement of the side armour and the thinner horizontal armour over the engines and ammunition storage areas. (Society of Naval Architects and Marine Engineers)

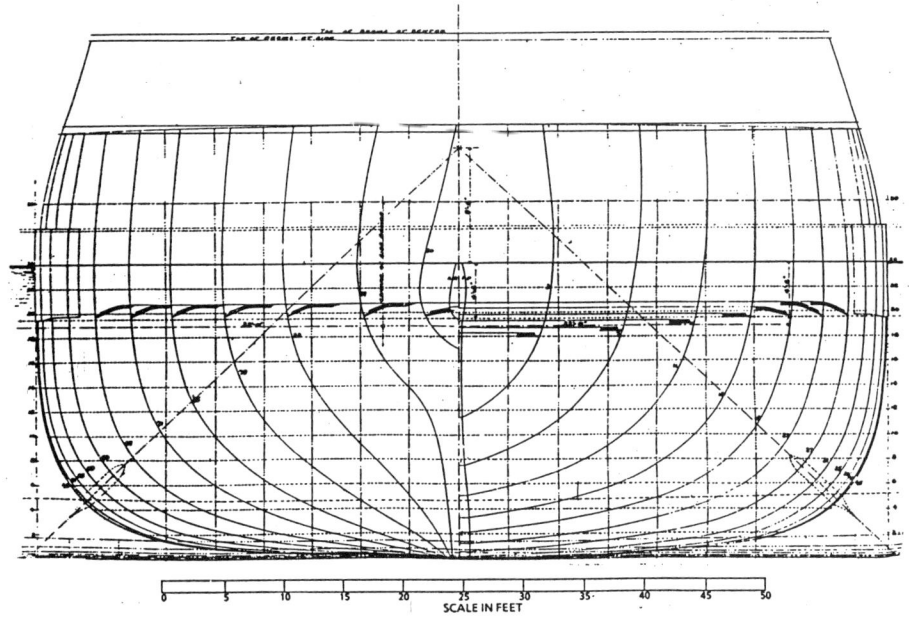

Lines of the Oregon *taken from the original construction plans. While this plan shows the side armour extending beyond the surface, as constructed the armour was flush with the ship's side.* (US National Archives)

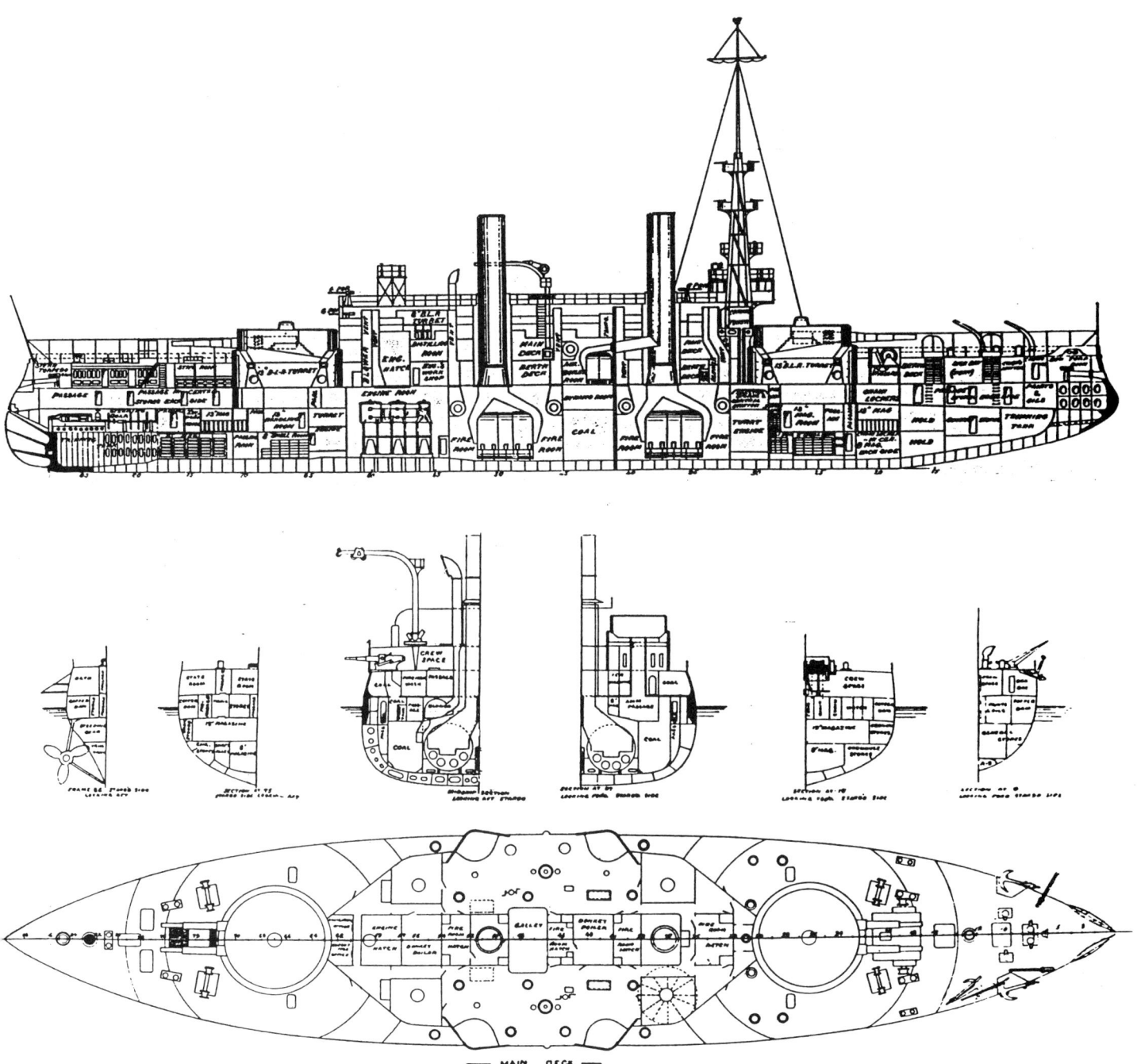

Inboard profile of sister ship Indiana. *The allocation of space devoted to machinery is readily apparent.* (American Society of Naval Engineers)

Layout of the main deck and cross-section views of the Oregon. (American Society of Naval Engineers)

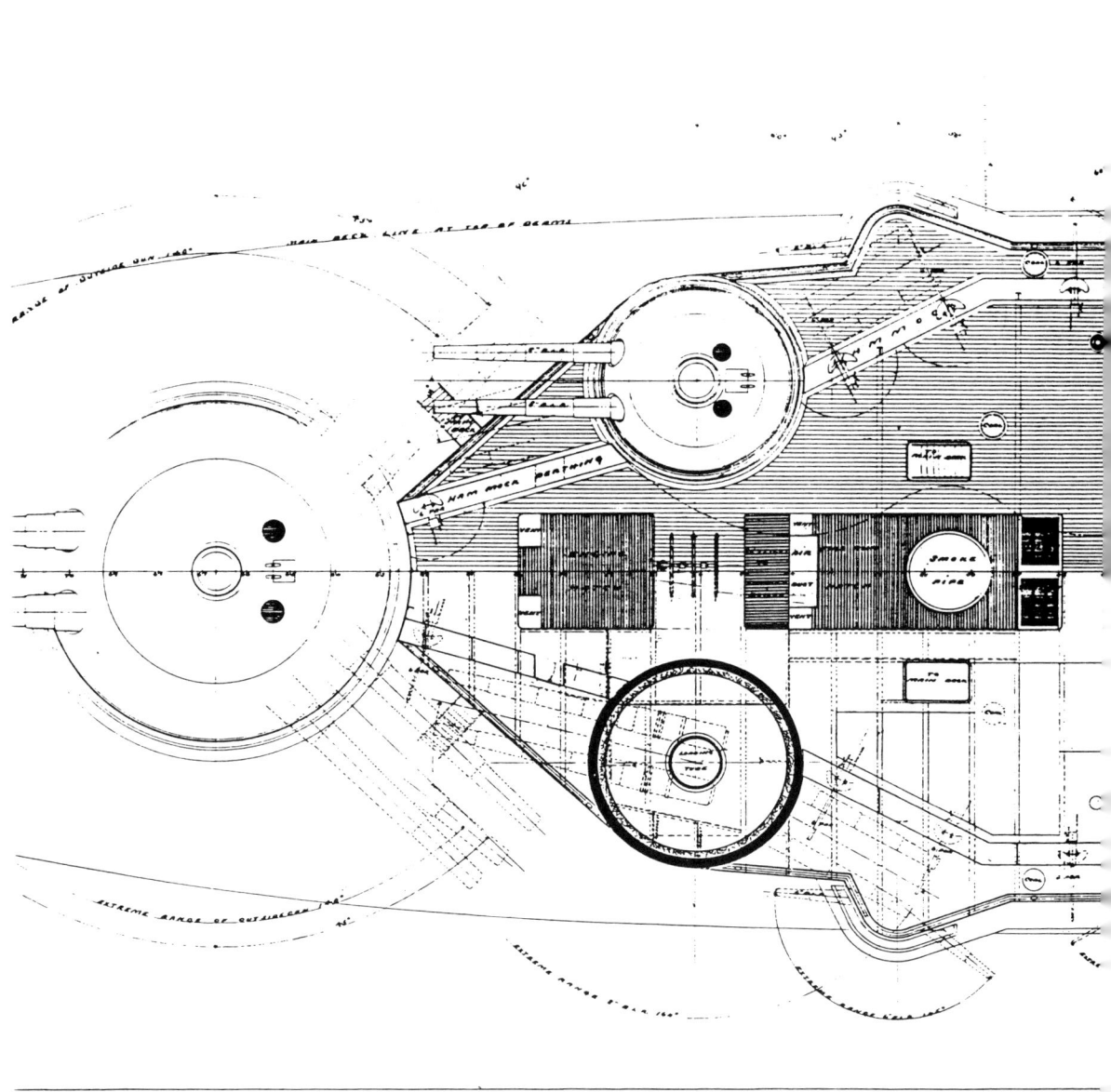

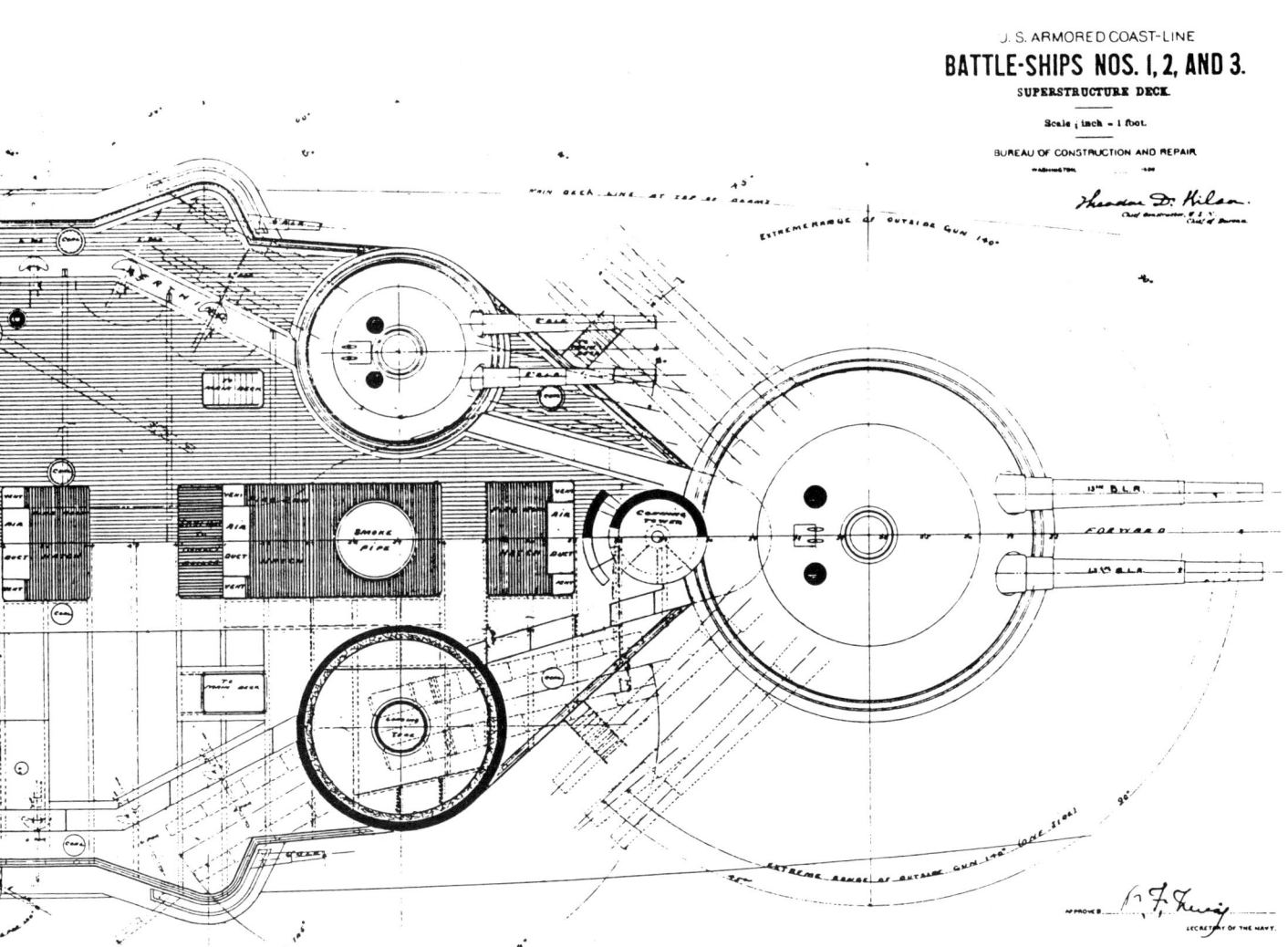

Superstructure deck plan. Except for the sloping sided turrets, the Oregon *was built as shown.* (US National Archives)

An angular, rather than curved, after bridge was one of the few characteristics that differentiated the Oregon *from her sister ships.* (US Library of Congress)

Career

The *Oregon* and both her sisters took part in the Spanish–American War. They represented most of a meagre fleet of five battleships that participated in the war. The Union Iron Works where the *Oregon* was built was in San Francisco and upon being commissioned in July 1896, she served on the Pacific Station. In mid-March 1898, it became clear that war with Spain was imminent and the *Oregon* was ordered to the East Coast. The voyage from San Francisco, in the days before the Panama Canal, was a harrowing trip of more than 14,000 miles. While passing through the Straits of Magellan a fierce gale enveloped her and she nearly foundered on the rocky coastline. After receiving news that war was declared the *Oregon* took steps to avoid Spanish ships rumoured to be hunting her. Still, after battling strong head winds and stopping several times to re-coal, the *Oregon* reached Florida just 66 days after leaving San Francisco, a remarkable achievement in the days of reciprocating engines of questionable reliability.

The *Oregon* then joined Admiral Sampson's fleet off the southern coast of Cuba in time to participate in the destruction of Admiral Cervera's fleet on 3 July 1898. Six enemy ships were destroyed that day, the two most powerful at the hands of the *Oregon* and her crew. Fol-

▲ *One of the 62 auxiliary steam engines aboard powered this generator, which in turn powered the searchlights, refrigeration plant and other electrical equipment.* (Library of Congress)

▼ *The* Oregon *arriving back in the US following the Spanish-American War. Note the after torpedo tube port at the waterline at the very stern.* (US National Archives)

lowing her return from the war, the *Oregon* was given a gala reception in New York Harbor.

In 1900, while sailing off the coast of China, she struck an unchartered rock and nearly sank. Except for this incident, the years following the Spanish–American War were relatively uneventful. During the remainder of her career she was repeatedly overhauled, decommissioned and commissioned and, though she took part in the First World War, her role was minor.

In 1924, as part of the Washington Naval Treaty, she was rendered incapable of warfare and in 1925 placed on loan to the state of Oregon, restored, and moored at Portland as a floating monument and museum. Following the attack on Pearl Harbor the scrap value of the *Oregon* was considered so high that she was sold. Scrapping was halted at the request of the navy and eventually the remaining hulk was used for ammunition storage for the re-conquest of Guam in the Pacific. Following the war the old hulk remained at Guam, and during a typhoon in November 1948, broke loose from her moorings and drifted 500 miles out to sea before search planes located her and she was towed back. Eventually she was towed to Japan and broken up.

Conclusion

Congressional restrictions on the design of the *Oregon* and her sister ships limited their size and freeboard, and required them to carry the heaviest armament possible. All this reduced her effectiveness and, at best, she was only a qualified success. Still, she fought well at Santiago Bay and the lessons learned in the design, building and use of her and her sister ships provided valuable information needed for later, more effective, battleship designs.

With a steam launch alongside, the newly refurbished Oregon, *with raised funnels, sits proudly afloat in a postwar colour scheme.* (US Naval Historical Center)

By the turn of the century, the Oregon *and her sisters were obsolete and only limited refitting was undertaken. In this photo, the* Oregon *is shown about 1910 after the addition of a cage mainmast.* (US National Archives)

Sources
1. *Conway's All the Worlds Fighting Ships 1860–1905*, Conway Maritime Press.
2. *American Battleships 1886–1923: Predreadnought Design and Construction*, by John C Reilly, Jr, and Robert L Scheina, US Naval Institute Press.
3. *American Steel Navy*, by John D Alden, US Naval Institute Press.
4. *Dictionary of American Naval Fighting Ships*, Naval History Division, Navy Department.
5. *Journal*, the American Society of Naval Engineers, August 1896.
6. Library of Congress, Washington, DC 20540 (for ship photos).
7. National Archives, Cartographic & Architectural Branch, Washington, DC 20408 (record group 19 for all ship plans).
8. Naval Historical Center, Washington Navy Yard, Washington, DC 20374 (for ship photos).
9. Still Pictures Branch (NNSP), National Archives, Washington, DC 20408 (for ship photos).
10. *Transactions*, the Society of Naval Architects and Marine Engineers (1893 edition).

RUSSIAN 'LAKE' TYPE SUBMARINES AND THE BALTIC WAR 1914–1916

Russian submarine operations in the Baltic are little known in English, and confused by unreliable and partial Soviet sources. Using some recently discovered personal memorabilia, Dr Gene C Stevenson presents the first accurate outline of the construction and wartime activities of the early Czarist *Kaiman* class submarines.

At the outbreak of war in August 1914, half of the eight operational Russian submarines commissioned in the Imperial Baltic Fleet were the four 409-ton *Kaiman* class of the 'Lake' type, built in St Petersburg and commissioned in 1911: *Alligator, Drakon, Kaiman* and *Krokodil*. Although these boats were already obsolete and outclassed by contemporary British and German submarines, they doggedly attacked various German warships and seized a few German prizes during the first two years of war in the Baltic.

Some personal effects which formerly belonged to Lieutenant (*Kapitanleitenant*) Ivan V Messer, commanding officer of *Kaiman*, have recently come to light in Germany.[1] Included among his possessions were a small group of photographs of the *Kaiman*, its commander and crew, and a hitherto unpublished handwritten report drafted by Messer himself. The document recounts a little-known torpedo engagement between the *Kaiman* and the celebrated German U-boat *U-9* at Utö island in the Baltic in the summer of 1915. This is one of only a few attacks on an enemy submarine by a Russian submarine in the First World War. Lieutenant Messer was in command of several Russian submarines from 1909 to 1917. He is credited with a total of 10,756 tons of German shipping during the First World War: four merchant ships (9629GRT) were sunk by *Volk* in 1916 and one steamer (1127GRT) was captured by *Kaiman* in 1915. Messer's manuscript and photographs provide a reliable firsthand account and very rare glimpse of one of the first Russian submarines in combat, and of the most successful Russian submarine commander in the First World War.

Russia's submarine-building programme

During the Russo-Japanese War, the Russian Imperial Fleet (*Rossikiy Imperatorskiy Flot*) lost 28 major surface warships: 14 sea-going and 3 coast defence battleships, and 5 armoured and 6 protected cruisers. After this disastrous war with Japan, an ambitious shipbuilding programme for the reconstruction and modernisation of the Russian Navy began under the supervision of the energetic commander of the Baltic Fleet (*Baltiksiy Flot*), Admiral Nikolai von Essen. The goal was to rebuild the Baltic Fleet which would reach 60 per cent of the strength of the German High Seas Fleet. Czar Nicholas II was particularly interested in building up a submarine force in the Baltic to defend the Gulf of Finland and the capital at St Petersburg. Considerable reliance was placed on foreign shipbuilders and subcontractors to build ships and to provide machinery needed for new construction, including submarines, in Baltic shipyards. Parts and equipment for

'LAKE' TYPE SUBMARINES

The silver Submarine Badge for officers of the Imperial Russian Navy was instituted on 26 January 1909. A 'Lake' type Kaiman class submarine (before the modifications of 1911) is depicted. This specimen belonged to Kapitanleitenant (Lieutenant) Ivan V Messer (Stevenson Collection).

ships were ordered from Germany and England. Complete submarines were built for Russia in shipyards in Germany, Italy and North America.

Since the middle of the nineteenth century the Imperial Russian Navy had a penchant for 'underwater boats' (*podvodnii lodki*) and was one of the first of the world's navies to explore their potentialities. During the Crimean War the Russians invited Wilhelm Bauer, a German marine engineer and inventor, to St Petersburg where he completed a test boat, the *Diable Marin* in 1855. In the second half of the nineteenth century, German and Russian engineers experimented with a variety of submarine designs with varying degrees of success.[2] However, by the turn of the century, trials with the *Forelle*, a tiny 15.5-ton experimental all-electric boat built by Krupp's Germaniawerft in Kiel, Germany, proved that a practical submarine with offensive capabilities could be built. Shortly after two Russian naval officers visited Germaniawerft in

Czarist submarine Kaiman *at sea, flying the blue and white Imperial Navy ensign of St Andrew. The* Kaiman *was launched in 1907 and completed three years later, but the four submarines of this class were not commissioned until the end of 1911, after extensive modifications had been carried out. Under the command of Lieutenant I V Messer, the* Kaiman *attacked a number of German warships and merchant ships, including the famous U-boat U–9.* (Stevenson Collection).

1904 to inspect the *Forelle*, a contract was concluded with the shipyard to design and build three 205-ton boats for the Russian Navy. The design of these *Karp* class submarines, *Karp*, *Karas* and *Kambala*, formed the basis for the development of *U-1*, the Imperial German Navy's first U-boat which was constructed simultaneously at the same shipyard.

At the beginning of this century, Simon S Lake, an American submarine engineer, served as an advisor to submarine-building programmes in Germany and Russia. In 1904 he sold the *Protector*, a small submarine he had designed and built in America, to Russia where it was renamed *Osetr*.[3] Five similar 153-ton submarines were ordered from Lake on 10 May 1904 to be built in America. They were assembled and launched in Libau in 1905 but were completed too late to see service in the Russo–Japanese War. The Russian Navy signed a contract on 1 April 1905 with the Lake Torpedo Boat Company to build in Russia four large boats of a design which was developed from that of the *Protector* and having an enlarged armament and increased radius of action. It was intended for this series of submarines to operate along the coast of Japan. In addition to carrying torpedoes, each boat would be fitted with a diving airlock which would enable it to clear minefields and cut cables underwater. The contract stipulated that the 410-ton boats would have a surface speed of 15kts and cruising radius of 3500 nautical miles, an incredible range for submarines which in those days typically did not venture out beyond 500 nautical miles. Lake claimed the submarines would be able to negotiate passage from St Petersburg to the Suez Canal (and hence to the Far East) without refuelling. Armament consisted of four torpedo tubes (2 bow and 2 stern) and two 47mm deck guns. The exposed portion of the hull was protected by 4in (101mm) armour. Construction was undertaken by the Crichton Yard in St Petersburg. Since the 1890s this privately-owned shipyard and its branch in Turku, Finland, built 200- to 535-ton torpedo boats for the Russian Navy. The first of the four 'Lake' submarines, the *Kaiman*, was launched in November 1907 and gave its name to this series. The *Alligator*, *Drakon* and *Krokodil* were launched the following year. The 'Lake' submarines are also referred to as the *Alligator* class and, occasionally, the 'Crichton Boats' and the 'Reptiles'.

During the construction of the *Kaiman* class boats which dragged on for five years – numerous design and working faults became apparent. The submarines failed to perform to the designer's ambitious projections. According to an account by a contemporary Russian observer, V A Merkushov, the submarines 'were unable to submerge and invariably stood on end, first by the bow, then by the stern'.[4] The maximum surface speed was 10.5kts, which was considerably less than the projected speed of 15kts. Diving time was slow, requiring at least 10 minutes. Mr Lake and his American engineers were unable to correct the problems and insisted that the Russian Naval Ministry accept the boats in spite of their flaws. The Russians (who had already paid Lake 3,000,000 rubles and there remained the last payment in the amount of 1,000,000 rubles) refused to accept the submarines and threatened to cancel the contract. Lake then warned that he would sell the unfinished boats to the Swedish Navy.

Table. *IMPERIAL RUSSIAN KAIMAN CLASS SUBMARINES SPECIFICATION (post-1911 modifications)*

Submarines	*Alligator, Drakon, Kaiman, Krokodil*
Designer	Simon S Lake, Lake Torpedo Boat Company, USA
Builder	Crichton Yard, St Petersburg, Russia
Contract Date	1 April 1905
Launched	1907 (*Kaiman*)
	1908 (*Alligator, Drakon, Krokodil*)
Completed	1910 (modifications completed 1911)
Commissioned	1911
Displacement (tons)	
Surfaced	409
Submerged	482
Dimensions (m)	
Length	40.2 (132ft)
Beam	4.3 (14ft)
Draught	4.9 (16ft)
Propulsion	
Surfaced	Two gasoline engines; two shafts – 800bhp
Submerged	Two electric motors; two shafts – 400shp
Speed (kts)	
Surfaced	8.4
Submerged	7.5
Range (nautical miles)	
Surfaced	1050
Submerged	40
Diving Limit (m)	27.5 (90ft)
Diving Time (sec)	180 to 300
Armament	
Torpedo tubes	4 – 457mm (18in); 2 bow, 2 stern
External torpedo launchers	2 – Dzhevetsky drop-collars
Guns	1 – 47mm high velocity gun (37mm on *Drakon*),
	1 – MG
Complement	34

After considerable negotiation, the Russians decided to take over the boats without paying the final price and utilise the spared funds unpaid to Lake and his associates to modify the submarines and to correct the design defects.

Major modifications

In 1910, with Russian crews, the four unfinished submarines sailed under their own power from the naval base at Krondstadt outside St Petersburg to Björkö in eastern Finland. A series of tests and trials were conducted in Finnish waters. The Russian engineers were able to determine that the severe instability problems were caused by the boats being excessively overloaded. In fact, the displacement was exceeded by about 12 tons. Late in the

Kapitanleitenant (Lieutenant) Ivan V Messer was the most successful Russian submarine commander in the First World War. As commanding officer of Kaiman *and* Volk, *he is credited with sinking four German merchantmen and capturing one for a total of 10,756 tons* (Stevenson Collection).

autumn of the same year, while solutions to the submarines' displacement problem were being considered, the four boats were taken to the naval yard at Reval where, in the course of the winter, they were essentially rebuilt. In an unusually pragmatic and unprecedented move, the Naval Ministry authorised the individual commanders of the *Kaiman* class submarines to spend up to 1,000,000 rubles in any way they saw fit in order to make their boats operational. The conversions which were completed in 1911 included the rather drastic removal of a four-cylinder section from each of the submarine's two engines, removal of the useless 47mm conning tower gun, and the installation of a ballast-compensation system to offset the loss of fuel during operations with an equal amount of water. The torpedo armament was increased by the addition of two external, reversible Dzhevetsky drop-collar launchers mounted on the deck and able to fire in traverse.

Even after the modifications the 'Lake' submarines were not considered to be particularly successful or seaworthy. The removal of four cylinders from each of the submarine's two engines reduced the engine output from 1200bhp to 800bhp and consequently reduced the surface speed from a modest 10.5kts to a slow 8.4kts. Fitting the boats with volatile and temperamental gasoline engines was dangerous, for this entailed a high risk of explosion and suffocation. Furthermore, the submarines could not tolerate rough weather at sea. The hulls were sheathed with 15cm wooden slats which, in turn, were sheathed with galvanised iron. The decks were made up of 7.5cm thick wood. In the summer months, if the boats were not submerged at regular intervals, the wood dried out and warped. During periods of frequent and protracted submersion, the wood swelled and twisted. This frequent working of the wooden slats caused numerous leaks to develop in the superstructure. The absorption of water by the wooden construction also destroyed buoyancy. Consequently, cruising in these submarines in rough seas was very hazardous. The weak hull limited submersion to about 90ft. On the other hand, the diving time was reduced to between 3 and 5 minutes and underwater handling characteristics improved substantially. The submerged speed actually increased by more than one knot: 7.5kts instead of the projected speed of 6kts. The weight reduction and the use of bow and stern pairs of hydroplanes enabled the boats to dive on an even keel. The radius of action was still an impressive 1050 nautical miles.

Commissioned at the end of 1911, the four *Kaiman* class submarines formed the 2nd Division of the Baltic Fleet's Submarine Brigade. In spite of their shortcomings, they proved to be very active in the Baltic during the early stages of the First World War. They were superseded by the more modern *Bars* class which began to appear in 1915. All the *Kaiman* class submarines were withdrawn from active service by the end of 1916.

In accordance with the primary strategic concept in the years before the First World War, the Russians placed increased emphasis upon the defence of St Petersburg. Under the defence plan of 1910, work began on an extensive series of naval bases and artillery fortresses on both shores of the Gulf of Finland guarding access to the Russian capital. The main base for the Baltic Fleet was under construction at Reval, but as work was not completed during the war, most of the surface warships operated from the temporary main base at Helsinki. Since 1809 Finland had enjoyed an autonomous status as a Grand Duchy of Russia, but the Finns strongly resisted the harsh 'Russification' policy of Czar Nicholas II. Ever since the assassination of Governor-General Nicholay Bobrikov in 1904 and the mutiny of the army garrison at Sveaborg in July 1906, Finland was regarded by the government in St Petersburg as being politically unreliable. Consequently, it did not greatly benefit from the surge of shipbuilding and construction activity. However, besides the construction of a few torpedo boats in Turku and Helsinki, a defensive network of coastal artillery batteries were built on the islands of the Åland and Turku Archipelagoes in south-western Finland. During the First World War the *Kaiman* class submarines frequently operated from these Finnish bases.

Russian submarine warfare in the Baltic, 1914–1916

Officers and Seamen of the Submarine Brigade on board the Russian destroyer Donskoi-Kasak. Lt I V Messer is seated in the second row, second from the right. (Stevenson Collection).

The Baltic Fleet's Submarine Brigade was formed in 1910. At the outset of war in August 1914, the eight operational submarines of the Brigade were already obsolete as compared with the best submarines then produced in France, Germany and the United States. The new *Bars* class were under construction but were still many months from being ready for service; their building was delayed by the incompetence and shortages experienced in the Russian shipyards and, after the war started, by non-delivery of parts including engines from Germany. The Brigade was commanded by Rear-Admiral Levitskij and was divided into two operational divisions. The 1st Division, based at Reval, was composed of the Bubnov-designed *Akula, Minoga, Makrel* and *Okun* and supported by the tender *Khabarovsk*. The four boats of the *Kaiman* class and the tender *Yevropa* formed the 2nd Division, which was based in the Finnish archipelago off Turku. All Russian submarines were fitted with gasoline engines except *Akula* and *Minoga* which had diesels. A submarine training school had been established at the naval base at Libau in 1906 and consisted of four old and small submarines: three Holland-type boats (105 tons) of 1904 vintage and the Lake-designed *Sig* (153 tons) built in 1905. Notwithstanding the reinforcement of four more small boats which soon arrived in the Gulf of Finland after being shipped to St Petersburg by rail from Vladivostok and the Black Sea, the effectiveness of the flotilla remained unchanged since these boats were also old and inefficient.

When war broke out, the submarine support organisation was still in its infancy. The limited repair and maintenance facilities available contributed to the low operational readiness of the Russian Submarine Brigade and significantly hampered its effectiveness. The diversity of different submarine classes and types also complicated and strained the Russian shipyards' ability to keep their submarines at sea. Since good service and repair facilities were available at the large naval base at Reval, the 1st Division submarine base and the headquarters for the Submarine Brigade were established there. During the shipping seasons (generally from May to November), the *Kaiman* class boats of the 2nd Division operated out of bases in the Turku Archipelago, particularly at the small island of Utö which is situated between the important shipping lanes of the archipelago and the open waters of the Baltic. In 1915 a squadron of small, old submarines was also based at the port of Mariehamn in the Åland Islands. After the new submarines (*Bars* and 'AG' classes) came into service in 1916, they generally operated out of the Hanko–Lappohja area. The submarines were usually docked for the winter in the vicinity of shipyards, except at Hanko which was situated close to open waters.

As part of the extensive Czarist naval defence system and in accordance with the 1912 'Plan of operation of the naval forces of the Baltic Sea', the Brigade of Submarines was integrated with the coastal artillery batteries, minefields and surface warships from the Baltic Fleet to protect the 'Forward Defence Position' (Hanko–Dagö) at the entrance to the Gulf of Finland. This strategically important operational area guarded access to the Gulf and St Petersburg. Russian submarines were deployed to intercept enemy forces attempting to break through the mine–artillery barrier. In the Russian Navy the prevailing notions of the main purpose and missions of submarines perceived them as primarily static coastal defence weapons; they were expected to take up pre-arranged patrol positions and to wait for the enemy ships to approach before attacking. Consequently, realistic offensive tactics were not developed nor practised by the Submarine Brigade before the war to the extent they were, for example, in the Germany Navy.

The Russian High Command did not comprehend the concept of combined naval and military operations. The Baltic Fleet was placed under the direct orders of General von der Fleet, the Commander of the Russian Sixth

During the First World War Utö Island was fortified by the Russians in contravention of the terms of the Treaty of Paris of 1856. The Russian Imperial Navy used the island's small natural harbour as a submarine base. (Finnish Military Museum)

The German light cruiser Lübeck *(built 1904) was part of a squadron reconnoitering the waters south of the Åland Islands in December 1914 to investigate the reports of Russian submarine bases being established in the area. As the cruiser approached Utö island, her lookouts spotted the* Alligator, Drakon *and* Kaiman *proceeding out from the island toward it. Expecting torpedo attacks, the Germans quickly withdrew. (WZ-Bilddienst)*

Army, where Admiral von Essen had just about as much freedom of action as any of the army corps commanders on that front. Hence, Russian offensive actions against the Germans at sea were generally confined to minelaying operations and submarine patrols. 'The principal role of the Baltic Fleet submarines during the first year of war,' according to an American naval historian, 'was twofold: reconnaissance and early warning of enemy surface forces approaching the . . . mine–artillery barrier in the Gulf of Finland, and the screening of minelaying vessels against enemy surface attack.'[5] Minelaying forces were usually protected by a screen of three submarines.

The Russian submarine commanders, although professionally competent, were handicapped by operating in defensive roles and with only old and inefficient boats. After completing fourteen patrols by the end of 1914, they failed to score any hits against German vessels. The larger Russian submarines' nearly constant need of repair limited their operational deployment to an average of only five or six days at sea each month. The Russian naval command was compelled to admit that the Submarine Brigade could not be expected to achieve much with such obsolete units. Nonetheless, there was one incident in December 1914 when the *Kaiman* class submarines caused the Germans some anxious moments.

The Åland Archipelago lies strategically astride the approaches to the Gulf of Bothnia between Finland and Sweden. In the earlier stages of the war the Germans suspected that the Russians, contrary to the terms of the Treaty of Paris of 1856 which guaranteed the demilitarization of the Åland Islands, had begun to fortify them. The Russians considered this area vital for several reasons. As the German Navy impeded enemy merchant shipping in the central Baltic, the Russian war effort became increasingly dependent upon the trade with neutral Sweden. The numerous Finnish islands of the Åland and Turku skerries provided shelter and cover for Russian merchant vessels which could sail with minimum risk between Finnish ports and the Swedish territorial waters. The islands posed a natural barrier and the area was considered to be an important constituent part of the Imperial Russian naval defence system.[6] This region is also less affected by winter ice and is situated close to open waters even in winter.

Soon after the outbreak of war, the Germans received reports that the Russians were establishing submarine bases on some of these islands. A German reconnaissance squadron under Rear-Admiral Ehler Behrings departed from Danzig and was scouting the area between 15 and 18 December. As the light cruiser *Lübeck* was steaming south of the Ålands, near the island of Utö, the lookouts on the ship spotted *Alligator, Drakon* and *Kaiman* with their 'smoke-vomiting' gasoline engines rushing out toward the ship from the island and then diving. To the Germans, the unexpected appearance of the anachronistic submarines must have borne a resemblance to prehistoric sea creatures, but the threat of impending torpedo attacks caused the cruiser to withdraw quickly, followed by the rest of the ships in the formation. The standard operational tactic employed by Russian submarines awaiting the approach of an enemy warship was to be trimmed down (with decks awash) so as to present the smallest possible profile and to facilitate more rapid diving. The submarine would then submerge and attack with torpedoes fired in salvoes. Despite their obsolesence, each boat of the *Kaiman* class was capable of firing a salvo of four torpedoes forward as well as aft and, consequently, commanded a healthy respect.

Other than some skirmishes between German and Russian cruisers, any serious damage to ships on either side in the Baltic was nearly always accomplished by underwater weapons. The Russians undertook a number of cleverly planned minelaying operations off German ports and in the Gulf of Finland. As a result of these mines, the German armoured cruiser *Friedrich Carl* and several minesweeping and merchant vessels were sunk and the light cruisers *Augsburg* and *Gazelle* suffered heavy damage.[7] This meant that half of the German striking power in the Baltic was put out of action. However, the Russians failed to continue the mine warfare with the same momentum after the death of Admiral von Essen in the spring of 1915. The Germans, on the other hand, were more successful with U-boats which penetrated into Russian waters than with their mine warfare. In October 1914 British submarines began to enter the Baltic to cooperate with the Russians, whose fleet contained no modern submarines. Although the Germans continued to regard the Russian submarines as worthy opponents, the British boats proved to be distinctly more effective. The difference is clearly noted in a General Instruction issued to the German U-boats by Grand-Admiral Prince Heinrich of Prussia, brother of Kaiser Wilhelm II and the German Naval Commander-in-Chief in the Baltic:

> I consider the destruction of a Russian submarine will be a great success, but I regard the destruction of a British submarine as being at least as valuable as that of a Russian armoured cruiser.[8]

By the end of April the five-month long ice-pack in the Baltic had melted and the 1915 sailing season began. The Russian submarines failed to do appreciably better than the previous year: 50 torpedoes were fired in 20 separate attacks but none had found a target. In contrast, the sinking of 13 merchant vessels and 2 warships (the cruisers *Prinz Adalbert* and *Undine*) in the Baltic were credited to the British submarines. The unsatisfactory performance of the Russian Submarine Brigade was due to the shortcomings of outmoded equipment, intractable torpedo problems and failure to develop adequate offensive tactics. The first three boats of the new *Bars* class became operational and joined the flotilla too late in the year to influence the outcome of the 1915 submarine campaign; *Bars* and *Gepard* arrival in Reval from Kronstadt on 17 July and *Viepr* in mid-September.

The early Whitehead torpedoes were very expensive, extraordinarily complicated and sensitive instruments. The Russian torpedoes' depth-keeping ability was notoriously unreliable[9] – virtually identical to the torpedo problems which bedevilled the Royal Navy early in the war and, for that matter, the navies of America, Germany and Italy during the Second World War. In practice the Russian torpedoes proved to be temperamental and erratic: torpedoes often ran deeper than their preselected depth and passed underneath targets without exploding; some dived to the bottom and exploded there, sometimes quite close to the intended victims, the blast suggesting a hit; not infrequently some broke surface soon after firing and would run on the surface with a slight bow-up angle making a large plume of spray; a few would swerve to one side after leaving the tube and then either straighten out or run in circles, missing the targets; occasionally they would fail to run at all and would sink after being ejected from the tube; finally, some Russian submariners suffered the mortification of having their torpedoes strike the targets but fail to explode. Exacerbating the low reliability of the torpedo was the widespread use in the Russian Navy of the Dzhevetsky drop-collar external launchers on submarines. The constant exposure to salt water and air outside the hull unquestionably led to rapid deterioration in torpedo performance.

All torpedoes of the First World War were driven by compressed air which left a visible wake on the surface of the water. The torpedo itself would be several yards ahead of where its wake and track appeared. Lookouts were posted on ships to spot the tracks and give warning of torpedo attacks. In order to ensure a hit against a fast warship a submarine had to fire as close to the target as possible so the ship would not be able to detect and outmanoeuvre the torpedo. Firing from a substantial distance was to be avoided, especially in smooth waters. The long series of torpedo failures and mishandling which were characteristic of the Russian submarine service before the 1917 Revolution bear a marked resemblance to the meagre performance of the Soviet submarines in the Baltic during the Second World War.

The most active Russian submarine in 1915 was the *Drakon* commanded by Lieutenant N N Iljinskij and operating out of Utö. Eighteen sorties were carried out during which Iljinskij attacked three cruisers and a destroyer, expending twelve torpedoes in the process but without scoring any hits. His bad luck was generally due to the fact that he fired at too great a range and the torpedo tracks were easily seen and avoided in calm seas. This was the case off Bogskär Island west of the Gulf of Finland on 14 May when Iljinskij attacked the light cruiser *Thetis* with two torpedoes and the accompanying destroyer *G-135* with one. At the time of the attack, the *Thetis* was towing the U-boat *U-4* toward the Gulf of Finland. Three hours later *Drakon* again fired at *Thetis*. This time the torpedo came within a hair's breadth of hitting the cruiser but passed by when the ship turned sharply to port to avoid it. The destroyer attempted to ram *Drakon* and fired at its periscope. Later the same evening *U-4* tried to catch up with the Russian submarine off Utö but did not get there in time to intercept it. As a result of *Drakon*'s attacks the Germans cancelled the laying of a planned mine barrage in the area.

The lucky and ubiquitous *Thetis* was attacked again by another *Kaiman* class submarine the following month. The cruiser was screening the minelayer *Albatross* in the vicinity of Bogskär at dusk on 16 June when three torpe-

The German light cruiser Thetis *(built 1900) was operating west of the Gulf of Finland in May and June 1915 when she was the target of several separate attacks by the Russian submarines* Drakon *and* Alligator. *She managed to out-manoeuvre more than a half-dozen torpedoes fired at her. (WZ-Bilddienst)*

does were fired at it by Lieutenant R Valrond in the *Alligator*. The torpedo tracks were spotted in time by lookouts aboard the destroyer *S-142* who sounded the alarm with a steam whistle. As *Thetis* turned, all the torpedoes hissed pass both ships, leaving white bubbled streaks in the water.

Iljinskij in *Drakon* attacked another light cruiser, the *Bremen*, on 14 July off Windau. Two torpedoes were fired; one surfaced in plain view while running and the other missed. The cruiser then attempted to chase after the Russian submarine but was met by another salvo from *Drakon*. Only by quickly turning and going full astern was she just able to evade the second pair of torpedoes. Due to this near-miss, the German naval command subsequently prohibited the larger warships from hunting submarines and relegated the task to smaller and more manoeuvrable ships. In December the energetic but luckless Iljinskij took over the command of the new *Bars*.[10]

On 18 July, just four days after *Drakon*'s failed attack against *Bremen* near Windau, the German army reached and captured that key port. The Germans were soon in control of the southern shores of the Irben Straits at the entrance of the Gulf of Riga. The Russian Naval Staff responded by sending an extensive operational group – including the old battleship *Slava* and six submarines – to the Gulf to support the hard-pressed Courland Army and to prevent enemy entry into the Gulf. The protracted fight for supremacy there was to continue for more than two years. On 8 August the German Navy's first attempt to penetrate the Straits was stalled in the extended Russian minefields which were defended by the *Slava* and its supporting destroyers and gunboats. A few days later off the entrance to the Gulf, the *Alligator* attempted to attack the cruiser *Pillau* and the *Drakon* tackled the cruiser *Kolberg*. Although both assaults were futile, they did force the Germans to keep alert for torpedoes.

To reinforce the German Navy's efforts to penetrate the Gulf of Riga, a very large and powerful force of heavy ships from the High Seas Fleet was sent to the Baltic in August. A support force comprised of the battlecruisers *Seydlitz*, *Moltke* and *Von der Tann* and accompanying destroyers under the command of Vice-Admiral Hipper made a sortie up toward Utö on the 10th. During the bombardment of Utö, the *Von der Tann* exchanged fire with the local coastal batteries and the Russian cruiser *Makaroff*. From the islands behind Utö, the submarines *Kaiman* and *Krokodil* came out to attack the German ships. Since the weather was very calm, the Russian periscopes were easily spotted in the smooth seas. The Germans were not willing to risk the big ships to torpedo attacks so the battlecruisers turned and withdrew, steaming away to the south while the destroyer screen chased after the *Kaiman* and *Krokodil*, forcing them to stay submerged. In accordance with the Imperial Decree which stipulated that adequate precautions should be taken in order not to risk any losses of the big ships, Admiral Hipper suspended the battlecruisers' operation when the presence of enemy submarines was confirmed.

On 16 August the Germans began another attempt to force their way into the Gulf of Riga. This time the German warships passed through the minefields and were able to enter the Gulf. There followed considerable activity by naval units on both sides. With the Russians still in

'LAKE' TYPE SUBMARINES

The 25,000-ton Moltke *(built 1910) was one of three German battlecruisers which attacked Utö on 10 August 1915. Nine days later the* Moltke *was put out of action with a single torpedo hit by the British submarine E-1.* (WZ-Bilddienst)

On 10 August 1915 Vice-Admiral Hipper's battlecruiser squadron attempted to bombard the Russian submarine base at Utö. Participating in the attack were the Seydlitz *(left) and the* Von der Tann *(right). The* Von der Tann *was engaged in an artillery duel with the coastal batteries on the island. The presence of the Russian submarines* Kaiman *and* Krokodil *compelled the German formation to break off and withdraw.* (WZ-Bilddienst)

command of the coast and the large number of submarine warnings, the Germans decided to withdraw from the Gulf several days later. Meanwhile, on the 19th, the British submarine *E-1*, which was positioned seaward of the approaches to the Irben Straits, managed to damage the 25,000-ton battlecruiser *Moltke* with a single torpedo hit.

Kaiman and U-9

The few German U-boats operating in the Baltic in July and August had become active again at the entrance to the Gulf of Finland. Since the sinking of the Russian armoured cruiser *Pallada* by *U-26* the preceding

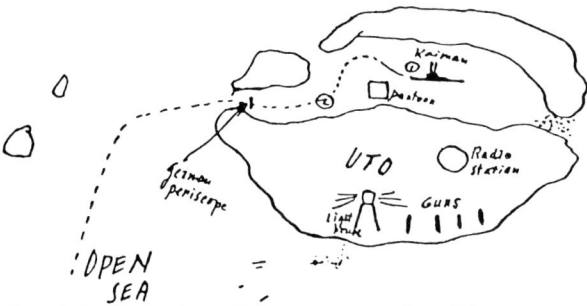

A map drawn by Ivan Messer, commander of the submarine Kaiman, *illustrating his torpedo attack on the German U-boat* U-9 *at Utö island in August 1915. Situated between the entrances to the important shipping fairways in the Åland and Turku Archipelagos and the open water of the Baltic Sea, the fortified natural harbour of Utö was used by Russia as a strategic submarine base in the First World War. (From Messer's manuscript)*

autumn,[11] no U-boat had ventured that far. Soon after her arrival at Danzig from the North Sea in July, *U-9*, the most famous U-boat of the First World War, was one of several U-boats sent to patrol the waters off the mouth of the Gulf.[12] She departed from Danzig on 17 July but did not find any suitable target and was forced to return eleven days later after all the drinking water had been consumed. The 493-ton *U-9* was an older U-boat, built in 1910 and somewhat old-fashioned with its paraffin-burning Körting engines which emitted white exhaust smoke that could clearly be seen from a great distance. The *U-9* had achieved outstanding success under the command of Otto Weddigen when on 22 September 1914, in the second month of the war, she sank three British cruisers in the North Sea within an hour. Weddigen went on to a new command, *U-29*, and was later the first German naval officer in the war to be awarded the Pour le Merite. *U-9* was accorded the distinctive honour of affixing the Iron Cross insignia to the sides of its conning tower and was dispatched to the Baltic under its new commander, Johanes Spiess, who had been Weddigen's watch officer from 1912 to 1914. *U-9* returned to the same general area on her next Baltic patrol in August. The U-boat was cruising north of Dagö Island on the morning of the 13th when Spiess sighted the British submarine *E-9* on the surface. He took his boat down and managed to manoeuvre to within 600 metres of the enemy submarine. But before the German commander was in a position to fire a torpedo, the U-boat's periscope was detected and *E-9* immediately dived out of sight. Contact between the two submarines was then lost. Four days later, while on the way back to Danzig, *U-9* made a detour to Dagö waters and at the entrance to Moon Sound (between Dagö and the Estonian coast) intercepted the *Serbino* (2205GRT). The Russian steamer was attempting to escape from Riga carrying the besieged city's possessions, including a statue of Peter the Great and church bells. It was sunk after the passengers were brought ashore.

On 25 August *U-9* attempted to enter Utö harbor to attack the Russian submarines which were based there. By this time the Germans were well aware of the Russian submarine activities around this island as was made evident by the experience of Admiral Hipper's battlecruisers two weeks earlier. After the war, Lieutenant Ivan Messer, commanding officer of the *Kaiman*, described his encounter with *U-9*:

> The place [where the incident with *U-9* occurred] was the small natural harbour of Utö which was fortified during the War. It also had a lighthouse, a radio station and a telegraph station. A narrow channel connected the anchorage to the open sea. The value of this base was its location, which was close to the open Baltic Sea.
>
> One afternoon [24 August] four Russian submarines were in Utö harbour, ready to depart for patrols in the Baltic. Our superior officer, Count K [Count Keller, Commander of the Submarine Division] received orders to transfer the submarines 20 miles to the north, further away from the Baltic, to between the numerous islands in Finnish waters. The reason for this was the expected visit to Utö waters by a German U-boat. Our intelligence was good and sometimes it gave us very reliable information. Utö had already been bombarded by the Germans who knew that this was a Russian submarine base. Count K departed from Utö with all the submarines except the *Kaiman*, in case it would be necessary to rush one submarine to sea. The difficult narrow passage between the inlet and the open sea with several underwater rocks was a natural protection against enemy submarines, so we thought. The lookout service on the island was always on duty.
>
> It was quiet the next day. About one hour before sunset, I ordered a small steam launch to inspect the channel leading to the open sea and the surrounding waters. Soon after the launch departed, I began to manoeuvre my boat out of the harbour, following the route indicated on the sketch from position No 1 [by the pontoon on the map], keeping a sharp lookout and preparing for a quick dive once we were in open waters. When my boat reached position No 2 [the anchorage end of the channel] the lookout discovered a periscope of the German U-boat straight ahead in the entrance to the bay [in the seaward entrance of the channel]. I opened fire with my small gun and ordered both bow torpedoes ready for firing. I stopped my boat in the channel, making a narrow target [profile]. The German periscope disappeared. When I saw the periscope again, it was out of the channel area and heading into the open sea. I fired both torpedoes, one after another. They passed above the U-boat, very close to its periscope. I sent a radio message about the German U-boat and one hour later a Russian destroyer arrived in the area. However, the German did not show his periscope any more that evening . . . After this episode, our submarines stopped at Utö only on occasions and then for only a short time.[13]

Lieutenant Johanes Spiess, commander of *U-9*, survived the war and he gave his own account of the near-fatal confrontation with the *Kaiman*:

The penetration of an enemy harbour is one of the rarest and most daring exploits asked of a submarine captain. But 25 August 1915, found our faithful old *U-9* dodging mines and stealing stealthily into the Russian fortified harbour of Utö. . . . We scouted around the harbour, submerged of course, and were taking a periscope look at what was to be seen when suddenly, as I studied the picture of bay and shore, I spied a Russian submarine. It was hardly distinguishable against the rocky background, but there it was, lying on the water in a small inlet. Alongside was a small steam launch, such as we had often seen on Russian warships visiting Kiel. The situation seemed clear. The Russian submarine officers were leaving their boat to spend the night on shore or onboard the submarine tender that lay a little distance away. . . . All we had to do now was to enter the channel on the side across from our Russian cousin, then turn in a quarter circle, and, with a torpedo tube pointing at him, let her rip. I steered for the entrance of the channel and ordered the bow torpedoes made ready for the shallow run.

The steam launch left the Russian submarine and started out for the tender. . . . We were entering the channel, sliding along near one rocky bank. I took a leisurely look around with the periscope to make sure that there would be no interference, no destroyers steaming suddenly into the harbour or similar unpleasantness. No sign of any danger. The water was aglow with the setting sun and the encircling shore dusky with the shadow of evening.

When I turned the 'eye' to the enemy again, whew! My hair nearly pushed my cap through the steel hull. That submarine was coming towards us!

My scheme had gone wrong. What a fool I'd been! Here they were, headed right for us, or at any rate bound for the open sea. Our one chance for a shot now was a lightning quick turn and a pot shot at her on the wing . . . Our old *U-9* always turned like a fat old lady. . . .

'Hard aport,' I called through the speaking tube. 'Port engine full speed astern. Starboard engine full ahead. Leave periscope out.'

We came around with our most powerful turning movement, while I watched the Russian as he slowly approached us. Then came a shock, a lurch, and a horrible grinding noise. In swinging around, we had hit a rocky projection on the side of the narrow channel. I stopped both engines, not knowing what was going to happen. I could hear shots popping. The Russian was firing at our periscope.

'In periscope,' I called mechanically and, I fear, rather hopelessly.

The chief engineer on his own initiative trimmed the boat down to eight metres in an effort to clear the rocks. It seemed impossible to me that the collision of our stern with the ledge had not damaged our propellers and depth rudders and put us out of commission. The voice of the helmsman in the conning tower sang out: 'She obeys the rudder!'

That one cheering announcement seemed to jerk me out of my fit of hopelessness. I ran the periscope out and cautiously started the port engine. She steered. Hurrah! We were getting clear of the rocks.

Now came the worst. I had to look through the periscope to see that we were steering away from the craggy bank. The Russian, who was watching, saw the stick, of course. It gave him his mark. I saw a track of bubbles coming at us and my blood ran cold. It seemed to lengthen out ever so slowly. I had never thought a torpedo could dillydally along

*In this view of Utö taken in 1921, the lighthouse and several gun emplacements along the crest of the hill can be seen. (*Finnish Military Museum*)*

U-9, *the most celebrated German U-boat in the First World War, barely escaped destruction at Utö in August 1915 when the two torpedoes fired by Lt Messer in the* Kaiman *narrowly missed it. U-9 had been attempting to enter the anchorage at the island to attack the squadron of Russian 'Lake' submarines based there.* (WZ-Bilddienst)

like that. But, of course, it was only my fear that made it seem so slow. I swung the boat as best I could to avoid it. Thank heaven, she missed! But would it bang into the rocks behind us? For a moment I did not realize that the Russian was lying up channel from us. But, even so, the torpedo might hit a projecting rock near us. I waited with a panicky feeling for the explosion. None came. The torpedo had slid on out into the bay.

Our periscope was down now. The whole thing must have seemed eerie and mysterious to the Russian – too mysterious, perhaps, for we saw no more of him. As for ourselves, we were glad enough to get out of the harbour before night fell.[14]

Apparently Spiess was even luckier than he imagined. According to the Russian commander, two torpedoes, not one, were fired at *U-9*. The engagement between the *Kaiman* and *U-9* has remained an obscure incident overlooked by naval historians. This is no doubt due to the fact that the identity of the Russian submarine in Spiess' account was unknown and was not revealed until the recent discovery of Messer's manuscript.

Although the encounter between the *Kaiman* and *U-9* at Utö was inconclusive, it is significant for there were very few recorded attacks between Russian and German submarines in the First World War. It should be pointed out that not a single submarine, Russian, British or German was successful in destroying another one during the entire war in the Baltic.

U-9 made its last patrol to the entrance of the Gulf of Finland in December 1915. The veteran German U-boat was retired from operational service in April the following year and transferred to a U-boat training school.

With Riga apparently safe for the time being, the four *Kaiman* class submarines were withdrawn from Utö and transferred to the port of Mariehamn in the Ålands on 1 October 1915 for repairs and servicing. At this time, a fundamental change in policy was made by the Russian Naval Staff regarding submarine warfare. Since the start of the war, German shipping in the western part of the Baltic Sea had been trading unimpeded. This was due partly to the Russians' preoccupation with the security of the Gulf of Finland and to the fact that Russian pre-war plans apparently had not considered the possibility of offensive operations against enemy maritime communications. The Baltic was the only sea route for the importation of raw materials into Germany which was not effectively closed by the Allied blockade. The German armament industry was dependent on iron ore brought by sea from Sweden; German ores contained only 25 per cent iron and were difficult to smelt compared with the 60 per cent found in Swedish ores. Following the practice started by the British submarines in the Baltic, the Russian boats were ordered to interdict German merchant shipping. The first victim of a Russian attack may have been ss *Gedania* (1477GRT) which was probably sunk by *Gepard* (*Bars* class) on 17 October near Landsort (south of Stockholm). The Russian submarines extended their area of operation into the southern part of the Gulf of Bothnia. Instead of German warships, their primary targets were now the loaded iron ore transports heading for Germany.

After its spectacular destruction of three British cruisers in the North Sea on 22 September 1914, U-9 was sent to operate in the Baltic the following summer. In this view of U-9 the outer doors of the twin stern torpedo tubes are clearly seen. (WZ-Bilddienst)

Kaiman and *Drakon* departed from Mariehamn on patrol on 20 October. *Krokodil*, *Alligator* and two other small Russian boats, *Makrel* and *Som*, departed shortly afterwards. Lieutenant Valrond, commanding officer of the *Alligator*, had their first success on the 24th, chasing two steamers near Öregundsgrepen (north-east of Uppsala); *Pietá* escaped but the *Gerda Vith* (1801GRT) was taken as a prize into a Finnish port. On the 29th the *Kaiman*, commanded by Lieutenant Messer, captured ss *Stahleck* (1127GRT) in the Åland Sea. The captured ships were incorporated into the Russian Baltic Fleet under the names *Petsjora* and *U*. At least one of these captures was probably illegal since it had been taken while in neutral Swedish waters, a fact which remained unknown until 1918 when the crews of the ships were repatriated to Germany. Although the number of vessels intercepted by the Russian and British submarines was small in relation to Germany's total Baltic shipping, the attempt at interference in the iron ore traffic forced more than a dozen loaded transports to be held up in Luleå for some time while additional escorts were being transferred from the North Sea. The *Kaiman*, *Drakon* and *Alligator* sought in vain after new targets upon the empty sea. Only a few weeks of patrols carried out in open water could be expected, after which winter would set in and the sea would freeze, ending another season's campaign. Messer recorded his impressions during this frustrating period as the Russian submarines hunted enemy merchantmen off Sweden's east coast:

> This Division of Russian submarines [which included the *Kaiman* class boats] patrolled close to the Swedish coast where there was a traffic of merchant ships, including Germans carrying coal to Sweden and iron ore back to Germany. In the cold, bad weather of October, November and December we tried to find protection from the weather in Swedish waters. Many times the Swedish patrol boats ordered us to get out of their waters. I remember that once, in very cold weather, the captain of a Swedish boat sent to the captain of a small Russian submarine a bottle of cognac to warm him up. It was accepted. This incident was later related to Czar Nicholas, who enjoyed it very much. The Czar was very fond of his fleet . . .[15]

Messer's later career

During the winter months of 1915/16 Lieutenant Messer left the *Kaiman* to take command of the newly completed *Bars* class submarine *Volk*. By the beginning of May 1916 the ice conditions in the Gulf of Finland permitted the Russian and British submarines to depart from Reval on operational patrols. The *Volk* was sent out on the 14th to attack enemy shipping along Sweden's eastern coast. The Germans had taken steps to protect the vital Swedish iron ore trade by keeping their merchant ships within Swedish territorial waters as much as possible. On the 17th when he was south-east of Hävringe in the Bay of Norrköping, Messer came across three unescorted German colliers *Hera* (2800GRT), *Kolga* (2086GRT) and *Bianca*

(1054GRT). They did not immediately obey the warning shot that was fired over them. All three vessels were torpedoed. Two of the captains were taken prisoner and most of the crew were rescued by Swedish steamers in the area. However, the *Kolga* sank so quickly she took the captain and five men down with her. These sinkings (5940GRT) were successes which were not to be exceeded by any Russian submarine commander until the sinking in the Baltic of the German liners *Wilhem Gustloff* (25,484GRT) on 31 January 1945 and *General Steuben* (14,660GRT) ten days later with the combined losses of many thousands of lives by Captain Third Rank Aleksandr Marinesko in the Soviet submarine *S-13*. Messer's last success occurred on 8 July when the *Volk* was operating off Örnsköldsvik in the southern part of the Gulf of Bothnia and intercepted ss *Dorita* (3689GRT). The steamer was sunk by gunfire after being hit with several shells.

The last German steamship sunk in the year occurred the following week when *Viepr* torpedoed ss *Syria* (3597GRT). There was a burst of outrage in Sweden after the *Krokodil* seized the steamer *Desterro* in the fog on 18 August. The German ship was lying at anchor near land in neutral Swedish waters at the time of its capture. After considerable diplomatic pressure from the Swedes, the Russian government eventually acquiesced and released the ship. The final recorded attack by a *Kaiman* class boat took place six days later when the steamer *Schwaben* barely avoided a torpedo fired at it by the *Kaiman*. Again the Swedes claimed that the incident occurred within their territorial waters.

In November 1916 submarine campaigning in the Baltic came to an end. Although the results of the year's operations by the Russian and British submarines were meagre – five steamers sunk – they are all credited to the Russians (four for *Volk*; one for *Viepr*). The British boats fared poorly. *E-18*'s torpedo-hit which blew the bow off the German destroyer *V-100* on 26 May was the sole British success for the season.

By the close of the year, the Baltic Fleet's Submarine Brigade had received a large number of reinforcements in the form of five 'AG' class submarines and the new *Bars* class boats completed in the Baltic shipyards. The old *Kaiman* class submarines were deleted from the naval list on 15 November and their experienced commanders and crews were transferred to the newly commissioned boats. The boats were hulked at Reval where *Krokodil* served as a charging plant. The submarines had been dismantled, discarded and were frozen in the ice-sheets of Reval harbour when they were abandoned by the retreating Russians before the Germans seized the port in February 1918.

In 1916, when the four pre-war Kaiman *class submarines were being phased out of service by the more modern 644-ton* Bars *series, Messer was transferred from the* Kaiman *to the new* Volk. *This photograph, taken in 1916 probably at Reval, shows the bridge of the* Volk *with the submarine's officers.*
(Stevenson Collection).

The Volk *and eight other former Czarist* Bars *class boats were taken over by the Soviet after the October 1917 Revolution and served in the Red Banner Baltic Fleet. Seen here is a sister-ship, the* Tur *(renamed* Tovarishch*), under the Soviet ensign. (WZ-Bilddienst)*

Conclusion

Offensive operations conducted by the Russian Baltic Fleet in 1914 and 1915 were accomplished by the use of mines and submarines. The Russian submarine commanders were active and capable but before the arrival of newly-built submarines in 1915–16, they were hampered by the inadequate performance of their obsolete boats and were plagued with persistent torpedo failures. Hence the operations by the four *Kaiman* class boats which were designed in 1905 had only limited effect on Russia's war effort and never seriously menaced the German Navy's domination of the Baltic. The Russian submarine commanders of these boats compiled no records of tonnage sunk. Obvious tactical success was confined to the seizure of some merchantmen, but the fact remains that the presence of the *Kaiman* class in the Baltic presented a threat to the Germans out of all proportion to their actual effectiveness. As a result of their attacks and the sense of alarm created by their existence at sea, they compelled the Germans to disrupt major offensive naval operations, to interrupt and delay their essential merchant shipping and to use heavier escort forces than would otherwise have been the case, thus diverting German warships from tactical operations against the beleagured Russian naval and land units. The German Navy repeatedly demonstrated cautious respect for these four Czarist submarines. As pointed out by American naval historian B M Kassel, the effectiveness of the *Kaiman* class boats against the enemy resulted from the human character rather than weapon technology:

> Everything being equal, the fighting qualities of the [*Kaiman* class] boats appear to have been determined by the aggressiveness of the commanding officers, and in view of the historical data, the courage and ability of the men who manned these boats was of the highest order.[16]

In light of the activities by the submarines of the *Kaiman* class as related in this study, a reassessment of their proper strategic role in harrassing the German naval effort and influencing the course of the warfare in the Baltic may be in order.

In the vast drama of the First World War and the upheaval of the 1917 Russian Revolution, the exploits of these four submarines quickly faded away to oblivion. Nonetheless, their legacy was to manifest itself during the interwar years with the reconstruction and emergence of the new German U-boat service. In September 1926, nineteen years after the launching of the *Kaiman*, contracts were signed between the Finnish branch of the shipyard which built the boats – now renamed Crichton-Vulcan Oy[17] – and the Finnish Ministry of Defence to build three 493-ton *Vetehinen* class submarines to a German design for the Finnish Navy. Financed and directed by the German shipbuilding industry and the German Navy, a secret Dutch U-boat construction office 'IvS' collaborated clandestinely with the Finnish shipyard in Turku to construct and test the prototype of the German Navy's Type VIIA series, and later, Type IIA series U-boats which were completed between 1930 and 1933.[18] These Finnish submarines were prototypes of the new generation of German U-boats that was destined to wreak havoc on the seas in the Second World War.

Sources and footnotes

The conspicuous achievements by the British and German submarines in the Baltic during the First World War are noted and described in a number of published accounts. However, the operations of the Russian submarines attacking German naval vessels and commerce have received little attention in the past. Most of what has been written, especially in English, about the Russian submarines – whose performances were much more modest and overshadowed by those of the British and Germans – has been only cursory, incomplete and frequently inaccurate. The paucity of information is also due, in part, to the shroud of secrecy which surrounded the Czarist Navy. In spite of a large number of works in the Soviet Union dealing with the history of naval warfare, descriptions of submarine development and usage by Soviet historians are notoriously unreliable and lack objectivity. The most readily available and perhaps the most authentic material on the wartime operations of the Imperial Russian submarines can be found in a book published in Finland in 1983 which recounts the submarine war in the Baltic during both World Wars. The principal published sources are listed below.

For review of British submarine operations in the Baltic see K Edwards, *We Dive At Dawn* (Chicago 1941), pp183–235; and M Wilson, *Baltic Assignment: British Submarines in Russia 1914–1919* (London 1985). For German U-boat operations see B Herzog, *Die deutschen U-boote 1906–45* (Munich 1959). For discussions of Soviet naval literary sources see K Kijanen, *Sukellushalytys: Suomalaiset Sukellusveneet Sodan ja Rauhan Toimissa [Under the Seas: Finnish Submarines in War and Peace]* (Lahti 1977), p168; and J Meister, *Soviet Warships of the Second World War* (New York 1977), pp1–3. On wartime Russian operations see Per-Olof Ekman, Swedish language edition: *Havsvargar: Ubåtar och Ubåtskrig i Östersjön [Sea Wolves: Submarines and Submarine War in the Baltic]* (Jakobstad 1983); Finnish language edition: *Sukellusvenesotaa Itämerellä [Submarine War in the Baltic]* (Helsinki 1986).

1. I V Messer, autograph manuscript signed, in English, 2-page quarto, Cleveland, Ohio, 10 December 1936. Illustrated with several figures and a sketch map.
2. For a review of early submarine development in Russia see B M Kassell, 'Russia's Submarine Development (1850–1918)', *Journal of American Society of Naval Engineers* Vol 63, No 4 (November 1951), pp831–50.
3. The *Protector (Osetr)* was launched at Bridgeport, Connecticut, on 1 November 1902. Like its predecessor, the *Argonaut*, the 136-ton *Protector* was equipped with retractable wheels for running along sea bottoms and an airlock which permitted divers to leave and re-enter the craft underwater.
4. V A Merkushov, 'Brief Outline of the Development of the Russian Submarine Fleet, 1901–1917', unpublished manuscript, translated from Russian and quoted in B M Kassell, *op cit*, p840.
5. J Breemer, *Soviet Submarines: Design, Development and Tactics* (Coulsdon 1989), p31.
6. Tomas Ries, a researcher specialising in Nordic security, describes how the geographic features of the archipelagoes off Finland's south-western coast complement naval defence in the region: '. . . Finland's entire coastline . . . is protected by a coastal archipelago. . . . This island belt is particularly thick in the south-west. This limits shipping to a few navigable channels which are easily blocked, and makes navigation in these waters difficult in peacetime, and, combined with passive and active defences integrated in the archipelago, provides a formidable obstacle in wartime. The islands and underwater reefs consist of granite which permits the construction of very resistant artillery fortifications. . . . All Finland's territorial waters are shallow and particularly suited for minelaying with no areas where mines cannot be laid.' T Ries, *Cold Will: The Defence of Finland* (London 1988), pp336–7.
7. For a review of Russian minelaying operations in the Baltic see F Ruge, 'Die Minenwaffe in ihrer Entiwicklung und Anwendung' ['Mines – Their Development and Application'], *Nauticus – 1938, Jahrbuch für Deutschlands Seeinteressen* (Berlin 1938), pp139–157.
8. K Edwards, *op cit*, p185.
9. Several explanations have been offered to explain this phenomenon: the warheads being heavier than the peacetime practice heads; the colder waters of the Baltic Sea affecting the delicate hydrostatic device which regulated depth control; and suspectibility to the changes in the ambient air pressure that built up inside a submarine submerged during a prolonged dive.
10. Lieutenant Iljinskij and twenty-three men perished when the *Bars* was depth-charged and sunk by German escorts in the Bay of Hävringe on 28 May 1917.
11. The *U-26* commanded by Egewolf von Berchheim was the most successful German U-boat in the Baltic. It was the only U-boat to torpedo and sink large warships (over 1000 tons) in the Baltic: the *Pallada* (7770 tons) was lost with all hands south of Russarö (at the entrance to the Gulf of Finland) on 11 October 1914 and the Russian minelayer *Jenisei* (3000 tons) was sunk west of Paldiski, not far from Odensholm, on 4 June 1915 with a heavy loss of lives.
12. In September and October 1914 three of Germany's newest diesel-equipped U-boats, *U-23*, *U-25* and *U-27*, were sent to the Baltic from the North Sea. The *U-9* together with two companion boats, *U-10* and *U-17*, were sent to the Baltic in the following summer as replacements to relieve the three U-boats which had been operating there for nearly a year. *U-23* and *U-25* were withdrawn and redeployed back in the North Sea where the U-boat war was now requiring all the best boats available. *U-26* disappeared west of Dagö Island on 30 August, probably the victim of a mine.
13. I V Messer, *loc cit*.
14. L Thomas, *Raiders of the Deep* (New York 1928), pp40–3. Messer wrote his report in 1936 after he read this account by Spiess in Lowell Thomas's book which recounted '. . . an exact description of the episode where the Russian submarine *Kaiman* was the supposed target for the German submarine *U-9*. This happened in August of 1915 when I was captain of the *Kaiman*.' I V Messer, *loc cit*.
15. I V Messer, *loc cit*.
16. B M Kassell, *op cit*, p847.
17. In the summer of 1924 two shipyards in Turku, Crichton & Co and Oy Vulcan, merged to form AB Crichton-Vulcan Oy. Oy Vulcan had been strongly connected with the Dutch firm 'Ingenieurskantoor voor Scheepsbouw' or 'IvS' which was secretly established and directed by the German shipbuilding industry in The Hague in 1922 to circumvent the stipulations in the Treaty of Versailles which prohibited Germany from building or designing submarines.
18. Crichton-Vulcan Oy completed and launched the *Vetehinen*, *Vesihiisi* and *Iku-Turso* (prototypes for *U-27*) in 1930 and 1931. The 250-ton CV707/*Vesikko* (prototype for *U-1*) was launched in 1933. The first German U-boat, *U-1*, was not fitted out at Kiel until June 1935.

Acknowledgements

Grateful acknowledgement is made to the publisher for permission to reprint excerpts from the chapter 'Raiding Russian Ports', from *Raiders of the Deep* by Lowell Thomas, copyright © 1928 by Doubleday, a division of Bantam, Doubleday, Dell Publishing Group, Inc.

Photographs are reproduced by courtesy of the Finnish Military Museum (FMM), Helsinki; and WZ-Bilddienst (WZ-B), Wilhelmshaven, West Germany. The photographs from the author's collection are unpublished private photographs which were formerly the personal possessions of I V Messer.

The author wishes to express his appreciation to Markku Melko, Director of the Finnish Military Museum, Helsinki, and to Patty Maddocks, Director of Library and Photographic Services, United States Naval Institute, Annapolis, for their kind cooperation and assistance.

ENGADINE AT JUTLAND

Rarely does an account of the Battle of Jutland fail to mention that the scouting flight from the seaplane carrier *Engadine* marked the first employment of a shipboard aircraft in a naval battle; seldom is it noted that this was also the *last* such event to occur during a major fleet action.[1] It therefore constitutes a unique, if brief, chapter in aeronaval history. In this article, R D Layman describes in more detail than it has previously been accorded a story that also encompasses an episode of seamanship and life-saving in the finest tradition of the Royal Navy.

Aeronautics, in the form of the rigid airship, was the single most important factor in determining where and when Jutland would be fought. The rigid airship, with range and endurance far greater than any contemporary aeroplane, plus ability to loft the bulky long-range wireless apparatus of the period, made it in theory an excellent maritime scouting craft, and the virtual monopoly of the type enjoyed by Germany gave, again in theory, the High Seas Fleet a considerable advantage in aerial reconnaissance over Britain's Grand Fleet as they confronted each other across the North Sea.[2]

The German navy possessed only one rigid when war began, but they were soon constructed in number to compensate for the High Seas Fleet's deficiency in scouting cruisers. From early 1915 on, every move of that fleet was predicated upon the availability of airships for scouting – an availability that was totally dependent on weather.

Airships were accorded a prominent role in an operation conceived in early May 1916 by Vice-Admiral Reinhard Scheer, commander of the High Seas Fleet since the previous January. Like previous plans, it was to be an attempt to bring an isolated portion of Britain's Grand Fleet into action against a superior force. In this case, a bombardment of Sunderland on the British east coast by the battlecruisers of Vice-Admiral Franz Hipper's Scouting Group I was intended to lure Vice-Admiral Sir David Beatty's Battlecruiser Fleet out of the Firth of Forth, whereupon, after an ambush by submarines, it would be engaged by the German main body before Vice-Admiral Sir John Jellicoe's Battle Fleet sailing from Scapa Flow could intervene.

To ensure that he would not be surprised and cut off from his bases by Jellicoe, Scheer planned to rely heavily on airship scouting to the north and west. This was an innovation, for whereas previously the airships had functioned as a slightly advanced tactical screen, they were now loosed for long-range strategic reconnaissance.

Scheer's operation, scheduled for 17 May, was delayed until the 23rd and then the 29th by the need to repair mine damage to the battlecruiser *Seydlitz* and correct problems with the condensers of Battle Squadron III. Meanwhile, the submarines, which were essential to the plan, had left to take station off British bases. By the 29th time was running short for the operation as conceived, since the submarines would reach the limit of their endurance on 1 June.

But now the weather turned against Scheer. Strong winds from the east and north kept the airships grounded, for they could make only slow or uncertain progress, or none at all, under these conditions. Cross-winds even kept some of them immobilized in their giant hangars.

The adverse winds continued when the German fleet sailed for the alternative operation devised by Scheer should the airships be unable to cooperate. This was an advance northward off the Danish coast to snap up British cruisers and/or merchantmen in the Skagerrak and adjacent waters. A movement in this direction, Scheer wrote later, 'offered a certain cover against surprise. An extensive aerial reconnaissance was an imperative necessity for an advance on Sunderland [but] on the course now to be adopted . . . aerial reconnaissance was desirable, though not absolutely necessary.'[3] Consequently, as the leading historian of the German rigid airship has noted, that craft's 'inability to cover the High Seas Fleet in the western part of the North Sea determined in a negative way the place as well as the time of the Battle of Jutland.'[4]

Airships finally did get aloft on the afternoon of Jutland, but far too late to have any influence on the action. British expectation of their earlier arrival, however, was one prime reason for *Engadine*'s presence at Jutland.

HMS Engadine

Engadine and a sister, *Riviera*, were completed in 1911 by William Denny & Brothers at Dumbarton as cross-Channel packets for the South-Eastern & Chatham Railway Company. *Engadine* displaced 2550 tons under naval standards (1676grt), measured 316ft overall and was powered by three sets of Parsons direct-drive turbines and six coal-fired boilers that produced 13,800shp and drove her triple screws to 22kts.

Both vessels were hired (and eventually purchased) by the Admiralty on 11 August 1914 for conversion to seaplane carriers. This work, performed speedily but crudely at Chatham Dockyard, installed canvas seaplane shelters and handling booms fore and aft, and mounted two or three low-angle 12pdr guns. One seaplane could be carried forward and two aft. *Engadine* ran sea trials in her new guise on 1 September.

It had been intended to send *Engadine* and *Riviera* to Scapa Flow but instead they went to the Harwich Force and, joined by a similarly converted packet, *Empress*, they made a number of unsuccessful attempts to attack airship bases on the German mainland. These operations pointed up inadequacies in their crude aircraft arrangements, and in early February 1915 *Engadine* and *Riviera* were remodelled by the Cunard Steamship Company at Liverpool in work that replaced the canvas shelters with large permanent aft hangars, improved aircraft handling arrangements, increased seaplane capacity to four, and added a pair of AA guns.

Engadine returned for another stint at Harwich but after a few months was dispatched to Rosyth on the Firth of Forth as an aviation vessel for Beatty. For nearly a year she took part in North Sea sweeps and continued attempts to attack the German coast. Her most important contribution, however, was a series of experiments proving the feasibility of high-speed towing of kite balloons. Between times, *Engadine* swung at a mooring far up the Forth, nearly at Bo'ness, making it a long haul for boats taking liberty parties to South Queensferry, the terminus for transit to Edinburgh.

Engadine, *date unknown. A Short 184 like the one flown at Jutland can be seen aft of the permanent hangar, which was added during her 1915 refit. Apart from the light funnel tops, this was the ship's appearance during the battle.* (Author's collection)

Engadine's commanding officer was Lieutenant Charles G Robinson, RN, with Lieutenant Handcock, RNR, her former peacetime captain, as his second. For tactical purposes, the carrier was attached to Rear-Admiral Trevylyan D W Napier's 3rd Light Cruiser Squadron, whose four vessels – *Falmouth* (flag), *Birkenhead*, *Yarmouth* and *Gloucester* – were a heterogeneous collection of three different classes. *Engadine*'s standard aerial complement, which she carried at Jutland, consisted of two Short Admiralty Type 184 seaplanes and two Sopwith Baby seaplanes. Both types were twin-float, single-engine biplanes. The two-seat Short, whose wings folded for shipboard accommodation, had been designed as a torpedo carrier but ultimately proved too underpowered for that role and instead was widely employed as a reconnaissance-bomber. Those used for scouting were equipped with wireless. The smaller, single-seat, fixed-wing Sopwiths were assigned an anti-airship role, although their weapons – a single Lewis machine gun and/or explosive darts – were inadequate for that task, and their floats had a distressing tendency to break up in even moderately rough water.

On Tuesday 30 May, the day that the Grand Fleet would receive a series of Admiralty messages indicating activity by the High Seas Fleet, *Engadine*'s hands were called at 04.45 and soon spent two hours coaling ship, loading more than 350 tons. Admiral Napier came aboard at 11.30 and may have stayed for noon dinner. At 17.45 the carrier received Beatty's signal for all ships to raise steam for 22kts. Shortly after 20.00, following Beatty's receipt of Jellicoe's instruction for rendezvous with the Battle Fleet, she steamed out of the Forth, passing May Island at 23.40. Among her complement was a 20-year-old Royal Naval Air Service flight lieutenant, Graham

Donald, who precisely 52 years later would write a vivid account of a portion of the next day's activity.

Before the flight

As the Battlecruiser Fleet steamed towards the scheduled rendezvous with Jellicoe during the early afternoon of 31 May, *Engadine* was in her assigned station in the cruiser scouting line, roughly 2½ miles to port of *Falmouth* and an equal distance to starboard of *Inconstant* and *Cordelia* of the 1st Light Cruiser Squadron. Soon after Beatty shifted the axis of his advance to the right, she forged about 4 miles ahead of the cruisers, making her the foremost vessel of the force.

This movement, as well as *Engadine*'s position in the scouting line in the first place, has been criticised on the basis that had she been stationed to the rear of the battlecrusiers she would have less exposed to possible enemy action, while her aircraft, because of their speed, could have easily scouted ahead. This view fails to consider or to realise that a 1916 seaplane carrier required up to half an hour to ready an aircraft for flight and then had to stop to hoist it onto the water. Moreover, takeoff would be impossible in the roiled sea created by the wakes of the battlecruisers and their attendant vessels; the carrier would have to wait until the turbulence abated or haul off to seek a quieter stretch. The delay these factors imposed could place the carrier stationed astern of an advancing fleet well behind it by the time the aircraft got aloft, possibly even out of visual contact. Since even at her 22kts *Engadine* was the slowest of Beatty's ships, catching up would at best involve a long stern chase; it might even be impossible because of further delay during aircraft recovery, for which the ship had again to stop and for which again smooth water was *sine qua non*. Given these considerations, *Engadine*'s advanced position, where she could launch aircraft in unruffled waters and then fall in with the advancing fleet, was eminently logical.

It was from this position that *Engadine* may have been one of the first British ships to spot the enemy. According to Frost, at 14.20 the carrier 'sighted two enemy cruisers bearing east . . . but made no report.'[5] If so, the vessels were almost certainly the large destroyers *B109* and *B110* that *Galatea* of the 1st Light Cruiser Squadron had sighted two minutes earlier in the first contact of the battle and had also misidentified as cruisers. *Engadine*'s log, however, makes no mention of sighting enemy vessels until 14.55. This is only the first of many discrepancies between times entered in the log and those in published sources, which themselves are often conflicting.

Short 184 No 8359, the aircraft flown at Jutland, lying astern of Engadine *in May 1916. Rutland (extreme left, wearing flying cap) had just given a demonstration flight to a French official who is alighting along the starboard float. No 8359 was built by Westland Aviation Works, Yeovil, Somerset. Its original 225hp Sunbeam Mohawk engine was later replaced by a 240hp Sunbeam Gurkha. The seaplane was exhibited at the Imperial War Museum until damaged by German bombing in the Second World War. Further damage inflicted accidentally during its removal from the Museum resulted in a decision that restoration would be prohibitively expensive. (Fleet Air Arm Museum)*

Just before the first contact with the German ships, Beatty had changed course to north for the rendezvous with Jellicoe. This left *Engadine* as the fleet's rearmost ship, unknowingly the nearest to the advancing German main body, which was as yet undetected. This was of no immediate consequence to aerial operations, for they would not be required during the period before the rendezvous. Her position, however, worried Napier, who at 14.31 ordered her to close the battlecruisers. Whatever his motivation for this order, it was unfortunate, for Beatty, after cruiser skirmishing had broken out to the north-east, had signalled the fleet to prepare for a radical change of course to the south-south-east – a manoeuvre intended to cut off what then appeared to be the German main force (but which was actually only an outer screen) from its line of retreat. This change was executed one minute after Napier's order to *Engadine* and had she not obeyed his order she would have regained her assigned station. After issuing that order, Napier had marched off to the sound of the guns in the north-east and thereafter the carrier became the least of his concerns.

Engadine obediently turned north and then north-west, increasing speed from 18 to 22kts. At their combined speeds of 44kts the carrier and the battlecruisers gained sight of each other within a quarter of an hour, and Beatty ordered *Engadine* by visual signal to make an aerial search to the north-north-east 9°. This was the wrong course in which to seek the enemy main body, and Frost berates Beatty for sending an aircraft 'in the wrong direction'. But a search in that direction certainly must have seemed reasonable at the time; it was in that direction that contact had been made with the enemy, and it was not until well after 15.00 that Hipper's squadron was spotted to the south-east.

At the same time as his signal to *Engadine*, Beatty ordered the light cruiser *Champion*, flagship of the 13th Flotilla, to send two destroyers to screen the carrier from submarines while she was stopped to hoist out aircraft. *Moresby* and *Onslow* were dispatched, but as we shall see arrived too late.

Upon receipt of Beatty's order, *Engadine* passed between the two battlecruiser squadrons, which were steaming in parallel, then turned sharply under the stern of *Indefatigable*, second ship of the 2nd Battlecruiser Squadron, and steered north-east to seek calmer water.

The timing of Beatty's signal to *Engadine* is disputed. Beatty himself wrote that it was made at 14.45, and most accounts have accepted this. The official British air history, however, gives it as 14.40 and states that *Engadine*'s seaplane was airborne within 28 minutes of its receipt. The carrier's log does not record the signal but rather tends to support the earlier time, for it states that the ship's engines were stopped at 15.05 and the aircraft took off two minutes later – exactly 27 minutes after 14.40. The air historian considers this a praiseworthy achievement, for 'To get a machine on the water when the ship was rolling in a swell was no easy matter' and even in harbour it had never been accomplished in less than 20 minutes.[6]

The air history's account refutes Frost's contention that *Engadine* needlessly delayed the aerial search by steaming north-west between the battlecruiser squadrons, instead of north, to clear them. It is obvious that the time required

Flight Lieutenant Frederick J Rutland, pilot of the seaplane flown at Jutland. (Fleet Airm Arm Museum)

to get a seaplane aloft would have been the same no matter what course was taken.

The flight

As noted above, the seaplane, Short 184 No 8359, took off at 15.07. It was piloted by Flight Lieutenant Frederick J Rutland, and thus inevitably became known as 'Rutland of Jutland,' a sobriquet that overshadowed his later and far more important and influential work as a pioneer of deck flying. The observer, who manned the wireless set, was Assistant Paymaster G S Trewin. Rutland later described him as 'one of the most courageous men I have ever met' because 'he was obviously scared stiff whenever he was in the air and yet he always stuck to it and did his job well under any conditions.'

Conditions for aerial observation were far from favourable that afternoon. A low cloud ceiling restricted the Short's altitude to under 1000ft, and visibility from aloft varied down to 4 miles – in a paradox of North Sea weather not infrequently encountered, visibility was much clearer on the surface.

Less than 20 minutes' flight time brought the seaplane within sight of vessels that Trewin correctly identified as German after Rutland descended for a closer look. At

ENGADINE AT JUTLAND

this directive, which greatly chagrined Rutland, remains inexplicable.

Engadine's log reports that the seaplane rejoined the ship at 15.47 and was hoisted aboard at 16.04. Meanwhile, according to the log, *Moresby* and *Onslow* had reached the carrier at 15.34, nearly half an hour too late to screen her while the aircraft was launched but at least able to stand guard during its recovery. Frost is justified in his criticism that, if escorts were deemed necessary for *Engadine*, arrangements for them should have been made much earlier. Unmentioned by Frost, but even more puzzling, is the failure to provide her with escorts while she was steaming in the fleet's van, where she would have been even more vulnerable to submarine attack. Fortunately, although it could not have been known at the time, there were no U-boats anywhere in the vicinity.

Although *Engadine* had launched and recovered her aircraft quite successfully, the 40-minute flight was a failure as a reconnaissance mission. This was not the fault of Rutland, who had handled the seaplane expertly in poor visibility and under enemy fire, or of Trewin, whose reports were accurate and timely, but because *Engadine* was unable to relay the aerial observations. Efforts to pass Trewin's reports by searchlight to *Lion* and to *Barham*, flagship of the 5th Battle Squadron of four battleships supporting the battlecruisers, were unavailing. Apparently no attempt was made to send them by wireless – perhaps, as Frost speculates, because no frequency was allotted to *Engadine* (which if true was a lamentable lack of foresight). Or perhaps a wireless message was sent but was lost in the welter of signals pouring into *Lion* at the time. The problem may have been compounded by the notorious incompetence of Beatty's flag lieutenant, Lieutenant-Commander Ralph Seymour. Jellicoe, in his history of his command of the Grand Fleet, stated that an aerial report of four German cruisers *was* received by *Lion* at 15.30, but there seems no doubt that he was mistaken.[7]

Trewin's report of the cruisers' radical change of course could have been a valuable piece of information; fortunately, its failure to get to *Lion* was redeemed by a similar report from *Galatea* received a minute or so before Trewin's message.

Succour of Warrior

Engadine's position after recovering the seaplane was to the north of the 5th Battle Squadron as it began turning to follow Beatty into the first big-gun action of the battle, the so-called 'Run to the South'. The carrier followed suit and, accompanied by the two destroyers, trailed the capital ships about 4 miles astern, a position from which her crew 'had a "grand-stand" view of the afternoon's activities,'[8] including the devastating explosions that destroyed *Indefatigable* and *Queen Mary*.

Sometime during the furious half an hour after 16.00, *Moresby* and *Onslow* were detached[9] and *Engadine* steamed on alone. In the absence of orders she made no further attempts to launch aircraft; this would have been impossible anyhow, for as both Robinson and Rutland stated later, she was sailing through the turbulence of

Assistant Paymaster G S Trewin, the observer/wireless operator during the Jutland flight. (Fleet Air Arm Museum)

15.30 he signalled *Engadine*: 'Three enemy cruisers and five destroyers, distance from me 10 miles bearing 90 degrees, steering course NW.'

The cruisers were in fact *Frankfurt*, *Pillau* and *Elbing* of Scouting Group II which, accompanied by fifteen destroyers, formed Hipper's advanced screen. These three had closed up after contact had been made with British cruisers; a fourth unit, *Wiesbaden*, had not yet been able to join them. The ships opened fire at the Short, which was unscathed, at the same time reversing course nearly 180 degrees to the south-east, a movement Trewin reported at 15.33. A few minutes later he wirelessed: 'Three enemy cruisers and ten destroyers steering south.' He was preparing a message that he could now see a fourth cruiser – undoubtedly *Wiesbaden* catching up – when the Short's fuel line ruptured and Rutland was forced to alight on the sea.

Rutland was able to repair the line and Trewin signalled that the plane was ready to take off, but the reply was an order to close *Engadine* on the surface. The reason for

The officers – and mascot – of Engadine *in October 1916.*
(J M Brice/G S Leslie collection)

water churned up by the criss-crossing wakes of scores of ships.

Soon after 17.00 *Engadine* reversed course 180 degrees to follow the fleet in the 'Run to the North,' steering first north-north-west and then north-north-east. Around 18.00, shortly before Jellicoe's and Scheer's main bodies clashed for the first time, she was to the rear and port of the 5th Battle Squadron, roughly parallel and to port of the 2nd Light Cruiser Squadron. At this point she sails off the battle charts of Jutland.

She was soon, however, a spectator to the destruction by German gunfire of the armoured cruiser *Defence* of the 1st Cruiser Squadron and the crippling of her near-sister, *Warrior*. The latter, severely damaged by an estimated fifteen hits from 11in or 12in and six 5.9in shells, veered out of action at 18.30 and ten minutes later fell in with *Engadine*, according to the carrier's log (all times given hereafter are from the log).

With engines still running in her abandoned and partly flooded engine rooms and her rudder jammed hard over, the cruiser was turning in tight circles, making it impossible for *Engadine* to close her for some time. *Warrior* finally came to a halt when her steam ran out, and at 19.45 *Engadine* prepared to take her in tow, lowering her starboard motorboat to bring a line back since the carrier possessed no line strong enough for the task.

'After a certain amount of difficulty,' Donald wrote more than half a century later,

as her decks were a shambles – one or two fires tween decks – no steam for capstans etc and many casualties to be located – we managed to lead over a reasonably heavy wire cable. . . . This cable was of course much too heavy for our light passenger-ship bollards – but we lashed the b[lood]y thing on to every bollard or projection we could find.

The line was secured at 20.45, but the first attempt to tow the cruiser at slow ahead stopped *Engadine* dead in the water 'with a shower of sparks shooting up from the aftermost bollards.' The fault was *Warrior*'s jammed rudder, which was causing her to veer to starboard. Robinson signalled a query asking if the rudder could be hand-trained amidships. 'This they did – quite rapidly – and at the next effort the little *Engadine* got the *Warrior* well and truly under way.' By 21.30 the carrier was creeping along at 8kts, while her engines were making revolutions for 19, with course shaped for Cromarty Firth.

The morning of 1 June found *Warrior* in desperate straits, her quarterdeck awash, obviously near the point of sinking. Robinson and the cruiser's commanding officer, Captain Vincent B Molteno, agreed that she be abandoned after her crew was transferred to *Engadine*. At

07.20 *Engadine* slipped the tow – the 3½in wire hawser sweeping overside with it a box of 12pdr shells and assorted pieces of deck gear – and at 08.00 came alongside *Warrior*. 'The manoeuvre was tricky,' Donald wrote. 'Rather a nasty little slop of sea was now running.' (*Engadine*'s log gives the condition at the time as sea state 4.) The excellent seamanship of Robinson and Handcock was helped in the accomplishment by the fact that *Engadine* retained her peacetime fenders, although these wooden structures began to break up as the ships ground together. At one point, one of *Warrior*'s casemated guns, which were now dipping under water, punched through *Engadine*'s stokehold below the waterline, but 'a cheery stoker jammed his cap in the hole [and] the rest of the lads soon had it securely packed and wedged.'

Then came a dramatic moment.

> Just as we were about ready for 'Boarders' – the *Warrior* gave a nasty little shudder which meant the end was near, and (for a brief moment) there was *almost* a flicker of panic on some of the faces of the lads waiting to leap over to us – and the *Warrior*'s bugler sounded the 'Still!' Every man-jack sprang to attention and stood stock-still. (At the moment I knew exactly what Rudyard Kipling meant when he wrote – 'To stand and be still – to the Birkenhead drill. . . .'[10]

Donald was the recipient of the first of *Warrior*'s company off the cruiser – a teenage ship's boy 'not quite able to make the jump . . . two big seamen picked him up and heaved him through the air to me. I was able to catch him – but landed fairly flat on my back in the process.'

'After that,' Donald continues, 'it was a slightly hectic process of shepherding the Warriors as rapidly as possible to our starboard side so that the weight of 600–700 bod[ie]s all on our port side would not capsize the ship.' Approximately 675 officers and men made the transfer to *Engadine*, including about 30 seriously wounded who were handed over on stretchers, up to six at a time. Another moment of drama came when the last of these fell from his stretcher into the water between the ships. Robinson forbade anyone to attempt a rescue under these dangerous conditions, but Rutland seized a rope two seamen were trying to lower to the victim, dropped over the side, swam to the man and secured him to the line. Both were hauled aboard safely.[11]

The transfer of the cruiser's company took less than an hour, and by 09.00 *Engadine* was pulling away as *Warrior* 'disappeared astern of us – her funnels hanging over the side – her 9.2in guns pointing skywards – and her White Ensign gallantly fluttering in the morning sun.' The position was 57°18′N/3°54′E.[12]

In a change of destination apparently due to the fact that *Warrior* was no longer in tow, *Engadine* headed for the Firth of Forth 'with the entire North Sea all to ourselves.' Speed was kept at 11–12kts in deference to the wounded aboard. Two of these died during the day and were buried at sea at 17.15. At 23.36 *Engadine* passed May Island and headed up the Forth.

The next day Beatty honoured her with 'the finest gesture ever made by a fighting Admiral to a Little Ship' by assigning her to the berth near the Forth Bridge that had been occupied by the sunken *Queen Mary*; there the carrier lay in line with *Lion, Tiger* and *Princess Royal*.

Conclusions

'The seaplane had added nothing of importance to Beatty's information'[13] is a typical assessment of *Engadine*'s work at Jutland, and its truth must be admitted. The failure has often been criticised in histories of the battle, sometimes in condescending or even scornful terms. Much of this adverse comment, however, stems from ignorance of the state of the art of shipboard aviation, and its perceived and possible roles, in 1916, as well as lack of knowledge of the fundamental limitations of aircraft of the period.

Such ignorance is the reason why, as noted earlier, Frost's belief that *Engadine*'s captain delayed the seaplane flight was unfounded. Also unfounded is Marder's criticism that the carrier had not 'fulfilled her reconnaissance role'[14] because she launched only one of her four aircraft. Marder apparently did not apprehend that reconnaissance was only one of two roles assigned to *Engadine*; the other was defence against airships – which is why she carried the Sopwith Babies, machines useless for reconnaissance because they lacked wireless. Only two aircraft were capable of scouting, and while both could have been launched in response to Beatty's order, common sense dictated that one be kept in reserve for whatever forthcoming missions might be required.

Some writers have condemned the British policy, incorporated in Jellicoe's battle orders, of restricting shipboard flight operations until contact was made with the enemy. There were several good reasons for this doctrine. Until the advent of the flight-deck carrier, an aircraft operating beyond range of land had perforce to be a seaplane unless every flight were to be a one-shot sacrifice mission. And the seaplane was totally dependent on sea conditions – by their nature unpredictable – for take-off and recovery. A 1916 admiral simply could not be certain that he could order aerial reconnaissance whenever he desired, and if his aircraft did get aloft he could never be sure they would be able to return.

Nor could he be certain that any information they obtained would be reliable. Aerial navigation at sea was very much in its infancy; the instruments permitting accurate position-finding did not yet exist, and there was no guarantee that an aerial observer who spotted an enemy ship or fleet could report its location correctly. Even the German airships, whose navigational facilities were relatively much roomier and more stable than those in a seaplane cockpit, consistently mistook their own positions and those of ships sighted.

Still another handicap was the fact that the seaplanes lacked the radius and endurance for sustained long-range reconnaissance. But above all, aeroplanes were undependable because of mechanical unreliability. The fuel line breakage of *Engadine*'s Short is an example.

The reasons for the Grand Fleet's seaplane doctrine were well summarised by Beatty's authorised biographer:

Engadine *later in the war, with dazzle camouflage.* (CPL)

> ... the range of her [*Engadine*'s] seaplanes was very limited, and once they had flown off the water it was problematical if they would ever return. It was not possible to maintain an air reconnaissance patrol for any length of time, so [for these reasons] it was the usual practice to conserve the seaplanes until there was some indication that the enemy was in the immediate vicinity.[15]

There was greater hope for the utility of aerial reconnaissance 'in the immediate vicinity', because the airmen could take, and maintain for a reasonable distance, bearings from friendly ships and so be able to relate them to enemy vessels.

As we have seen, the proximate cause of the failure of the Rutland–Trewin flight was a mechanical mishap, but there was a more basic underlying problem that had nothing to do with aeronautics and would have prevailed had *Engadine* sent ten seaplanes aloft: the disorganised state of Grand Fleet communications. This problem had been evident since the Heligoland Bight action of August 1914, but apparently little had been done to correct it. Every detailed account of Jutland is replete with mentions of signals, by flag, searchlight or wireless, that were misleading, incorrect, incomplete, tardy, unreceived or misread. *Engadine*'s seaplane was one more victim of this muddle.

Like so many aeronaval ventures of 1914–18, the work of *Engadine* at Jutland was more influential in demonstrating potential for the future than in immediate results. Beatty, whose air-mindedness has never been adequately stressed by his biographers, was impressed with that potential. Praising Rutland and Trewin for 'the clarity of their reports', he declared 'their achievement . . . indicates that seaplanes under such circumstances are of distinct value.'[16] He expounded on this view seven years later with the forecast that

> The intelligent use of the air for reconnaissance purposes will improve the quality of the information which the admiral now possesses derived from Light Cruisers; and it may well be that in the future the Commander-in-Chief of a fleet with his staff may be quartered on board an aircraft carrier . . .[17]

Since those words were uttered, hundreds of millions of miles have been flown in emulation of those first few logged by *Engadine*'s seaplane on 31 May 1916.

Notes

(Bibliographical citations refer to sources listed below)

[1] Until Jutland, all Royal Navy operational (as distinct from experimental) use of shipboard aircraft had been to scout or bomb land objectives or to attempt to attack airships after they had been sighted from the surface. After Jutland, it would seem that the only clash of dreadnoughts in which shipboard aircraft (except carrier aircraft) were used for observation was the Italo–British encounter of 9 July 1940, when battleships of both sides catapulted seaplanes. This skirmish, involving a total of only five capital ships, can hardly be termed a fleet action.

[2] The airships were almost universally called Zeppelins, although not all were produced by the firm founded by Count Ferdinand von Zeppelin, creator of the first successful rigid airship. They were never as useful as the Germans hoped and the British feared; their operations were greatly restricted by weather, they were prone to navigational error, and their crews often misidentified ships.

[3] Scheer, p136.

[4] Robinson, p147.

[5] Frost, p149. No source is cited for this assertion.

[6] Jones, p407.

A group of officers at Bacton in 1917, including Trewin (right centre). (J M Brice/G S Leslie collection)

7. Jellicoe, p320.
8. This and all following quotations in this section are from Graham Donald.
9. *Onslow* later took part in a gallant torpedo attack against the German battlecruisers. Her captain was Lieutenant-Commander John C Tovey, who was to command the Home Fleet in 1940–43 and end his distinguished career as Admiral of the Fleet Lord Tovey, first Baron of Langton Maltavers. One wonders if his thoughts might have returned to his duty as *Engadine*'s escort when, 25 years later almost to the day, he ordered aircraft from the carrier *Victorious* to search for *Bismarck*.
10. A mispunctuated line from the fifth stanza of *Soldier an' Sailor Too*; Kipling's reference was to the stoic bravery of the 74th Highlanders when the troopship *Birkenhead* sank in 1852.
11. The rescued man died later, but for his gallant feat Rutland was awarded the First Class (gold) Albert Medal for lifesaving at sea. He was at the time the only living recipient of this rarely bestowed decoration. For his aerial work at Jutland, Rutland received the Distinguished Flying Cross and a promotion to lieutenant-commander.
12. The position given by Jellicoe, who, fearing *Warrior* might remain afloat and fall into German hands, later dispatched two light cruiser squadrons to search for her. The search, which continued until 23 June, was unavailing. The location of *Warrior*'s watery grave remains unknown, but from her condition as described by her survivors and *Engadine*'s officers, she must have gone down fairly soon after parting company with the carrier.
13. Gibson and Harper, p115.
14. Marder, p56.
15. Chalmers, p225.
16. Quoted in Jellicoe, p469.
17. From Beatty's speech at the Lord Mayor's banquet, 9 November 1923, quoted in Chalmers, p468.

Acknowledgements
The author is grateful for the assistance of Peter F G Wright and Joseph D Fama.

Sources
Primary sources were Adm 53/40888, log of HMS *Engadine* for 30 May–1 June 1916, Public Record Office, and a letter dated 31 May 1968 addressed by Graham Donald, RN (retd), to the commanding officer of helicopter support ship RFA *Engadine*.
Secondary sources included:
Geoffrey Bennett, *Naval Battles of the First World War* (London 1983).
W S Chalmers, *The Life and Letters of David, Earl Beatty* (London 1951).
Sir Julian S Corbett, *Naval Operations*, Vol 3 (text) and Vol 3 (maps) (London 1923).
John R Cuneo, *The Air Weapon 1914–1916* (Harrisburg, 1947).
Holloway H Frost, *The Battle of Jutland* (Annapolis 1936).
Langhorne Gibson and J E T Harper, *The Riddle of Jutland* (New York 1934).
Sir Arthur Hezlet, *Aircraft and Sea Power* (New York 1970).
Viscount Jellicoe of Scapa, *The Grand Fleet 1914–1916* (New York 1919).
H A Jones, *The War in the Air*, Vol 2 (Oxford 1928).
Peter H Liddle, *The Sailor's War 1914–18* (Poole 1985).
Arthur J Marder, *From the Dreadnought to Scapa Flow*, Vol 3 (London 1966).
Douglas H Robinson, *The Zeppelin in Combat* (London 1962).
Reinhard Scheer, *Germany's High Seas Fleet in the World War* (London 1920).
Desmond Young, *Rutland of Jutland* (London 1963).

THE WEIRD SISTERS

The British 'Large Light Cruisers' or 'Light Battlecruisers' *Courageous*, *Glorious* and *Furious* have generally been regarded as among the most useless warships ever built. Churchill called them 'An Old Man's Children'; in a recent book, G M Stephen referred to them as 'Something very special in the way of madness'; and in the Fleet their nicknames were 'Outrageous', 'Curious' and 'Spurious'. It has been suggested that their parent, Lord Fisher, had finally gone completely mad. Nevertheless, they *were* built, served for many years, and two of them saw action in their original form. In this article Keith McBride seeks to find out why they were built and how they performed.

As is common with such documents in the 1914–18 period, the Ship's Cover leaves many gaps. It begins at the point in January 1915 when the design had been approved in its main outline, but I suspect that the concept goes back many years before that.

The Italians had been building battlecruisers, though not calling them such, since the 1870s, and the trend towards long-range gunfire had become widespread by the late 1890s. At the same time, though the sun did not set on the British Empire and Britannia ruled the waves, many British thinkers were worried as to how British naval supremacy was to be maintained if and when the giant powers, Russia, America – even perhaps China – started to exploit their vast potential. To Sir John Fisher, as he then was, the development by Arthur Hungerford Pollen of a system of 'Aim Correction' – in later parlance, Fire Control – seemed to offer the possibility of overwhelming an enemy from beyond the range at which he could reply effectively, or even reply at all. In Fisher's thinking, this would permit British ships to do without armour, thus keeping their size and cost within Britain's limited though considerable resources.

This lay behind Fisher's enthusiasm for the battlecruiser, which was vigorously developed during his 1904–1910 term as First Sea Lord and was as near to his ideal as he could hope to get past the Admiralty and Parliament. There were several caveats to this ideal: it depended on keeping a monopoly of the Pollen system and on no-one else developing anything like it. Also, the ships would have to be long for speed, fairly wide to accommodate heavy turrets, and hence of considerable size, while very bulky machinery would be needed. A further point was that Fisher never seemed to consider the possibility of meeting the enemy in bad weather, darkness, or where there was insufficient sea-room to outrange the enemy. Was this a reflection of many years spent in the Mediterranean or the tropics, where, at least in memory, the horizon was always clear and the sky blue?

It is often said that the point of the *Dreadnought* was her uniform eight-gun broadside, permitting controlled long-range salvoes, but it is by no means clear that this was intended, though it came out that way. Fisher thought mainly in terms of cheapness and simplicity of construction and ammunition supply. (She was a very cheap ship for her size.) He was perfectly prepared to revert to fewer guns if necessary. Moreover, the *Dreadnought*'s armour was thinner and less extensive than that of her predecessors, being sacrificed for her 21kt speed.

During the 1900s, the battlecruiser and the Pollen and other fire control systems were developed rapidly, the system being fitted in the *Orion* of the 1909/10 programme and the four *King George V*s and *Queen Mary* of the 1910/11 one. That, however, was high tide. In 1912, the partnership between the Royal Navy and Arthur Pollen collapsed amid mutual recriminations. The reasons may be read in his son's book, the main ones being:

a) Naval preference for simple equipment worked by highly trained men, rather than automatic devices which would be splendid until they went wrong.
b) A feeling that the sophistication of the Pollen system was unnecessary; fleets would approach with steps heavy, solemn and slow, turn into line ahead and blast away on parallel courses at almost constant range and deflection.

By this time Fisher had retired; he had never under-

Glorious as completed. Note the large 4in triple mountings. (IWM)

stood the minutiae of fire control developments and was happy to accept any system that would do what he wanted. His design ideas had not changed and he had vast behind-the-scenes influence. He nearly got Winston Churchill to have four *Tigers* instead of four *Queen Elizabeths* (plus the *Malaya*) in the 1912/13 programme. This may explain Churchill's interest in boosting the *Tiger*'s power from the original 76,000shp to 108,000shp. As it was, his successors ordered no battlecruisers in 1912/13, 1913/14 or 1914/15. Had war not broken out when it did, the *Tiger* might have been the last of her line.

Early First World War experience

When war did break out and for some time thereafter, the battlecruiser seemed to justify all Fisher's hopes. The British ones saved the day – partly at any rate – at Heligoland, and he sent them to sort out the situation after Coronel, which they did satisfactorily, though at great expenditure of ammunition. A portent for the future was that they were much hampered by smoke. This had been a problem since the first guns went to sea, especially after the introduction of steam. During the 1900s, Sir A K Wilson conceived of using smoke deliberately, thereby producing night and fog whenever desired.

It is well known that, on his return to the Admiralty, Fisher used the material from two of the 1914/15 'R' class battleships to produce the *Repulse* and *Renown*. In his mind, this pair were closely linked with the *Courageous* class, which followed them by a few weeks in time and had many features in common. The reason for having two different types was apparently lack of turrets and guns. Although four battleships had been ordered in 1914/15, it seems that only twelve twin 15in turrets were under construction. Six of these were seized for the *Repulses* and two for monitors, leaving only four. (The initial plan was for two turrets apiece in the *Repulses*, but this was changed within 24 hours.) At this point the plot thickens considerably.

On 25 January, Fisher sent a note, marked BURN (but not of course burnt) to Tennyson D'Eyncourt, the Director of Naval Construction (DNC), confiding that:

> I had a fierce time with the First Lord – *Very* fierce!

but we are to have two – 1 at Harland & Wolff and 1 at Elswick, if only we can make a good story for the Cabinet:
    a) They must be both ready to fight within the year.
    b) They must be said to cost quite approx in *Round* terms probably not more than a million but in view of the cost [?] it is difficult to forecast what they will cost. [This was presumably to allow for wartime cost increases.]
    c) We must state that the construction of these two ships are [*sic*] demanded by these two firms who can undertake them without interfering with current government work.

For example, riveters and such like today cannot affect current work, as these classes of workmen are only required in the initial stages and cannot be turned into joiners or (onto) submarine work. The First Lord thinks you can be any d--d thing at any moment.
    d) We must stick to it that the draught of water will not exceed 22½ft, this is vital for Baltic work. It's on the Baltic undertaking that he will carry them through in the Cabinet.
    e) Speed 32kts – don't say anything about being deep or light.
    f) Enlarge on the unprecedented combination in one hull of 4 15in guns, 22½ feet draught of water and 32kts speed with a radius of 11,000 miles and so small a personnel in lieu of the 1000 in the *Derfflinger* and the [?] 885 in the *Moltke*.

Came to see you with a very high impression of [?] mine. Please explain to 3rd Sea Lord.

D'Eyncourt included almost all Fisher's points in his minute of 28 January to his immediate superior, the Controller and Third Sea Lord, Rear-Admiral F C T Tudor. The only difference was that he gave the 'Peacetime' cost as £1,180,000, which presumably excludes the borrowed 15in and their turrets. (For comparison, the *Queen Elizabeth*s cost £3 million apiece.) Fisher saw the memorandum in draft and minuted 'Could not be better'.

Early design

At this stage, the Large Light Cruisers were already close to their final form, except that their legend displacement was first 17,400 tons, then 17,800, and their secondary armament was sixteen 4in in four triples and two singles, which leaves a couple adrift. There is one reference in May to seventeen 4in, but this may be an error. The main armament was four 15in Mk I in Mk I* mountings, with improved doors on the hoists. The 15in ammunition outfit was first planned as 80 rounds per gun, but was soon increased to 120 as in the *Repulse* – a reaction to the very heavy expenditure at the Falklands.

Dimensions were 735ft between perpendiculars, 786ft 3in overall, beam 80ft, load draught 21ft forward and 22½ft aft (21¾ft on an even keel) at 17,400 tons. Freeboard forward was 30½ft, aft 18½ft, and the axial heights of the 15in were 33ft for 'A' and 23ft for 'Y' turrets. For comparison, the 17,250-ton *Invincible* was 530ft × 78½ft × 26ft. The writer has only just noticed that no ice-breaking bow was provided, as would be expected for Baltic operations. The actual designer seems to have been Stanley Goodall, supervised by W J Berry.

Machinery

The power, to come from two sets of *Champion*-type geared turbines fed by 18 small-tube boilers, was 90,000shp (41,000 in *Invincible*), giving 32kts. This was 3 kts faster than contemporary light cruisers. Fuel supply was 750 tons legend and 3250 tons full, from which 6000

Table 1. CHARACTERISTICS

Courageous and *Glorious*

Length pp	735ft
Length oa	786ft 3in
Beam	81ft
Draught	21–22ft
Legend displacement	17,800 tons
Normal displacement	19,320 tons
Deep load displacement	22,690 tons
Freeboard (normal)	28ft fwd, 17ft aft
Armament:	4–15in
	18–4in
	2–3in AA
	2–21in TT (submerged)
	12–21in TT (above water)
Armour	
Side	2in on 1in
Decks	1in/¾in forecastle; 1 in upper; 1in/¼in main
Turrets	9in/7in/11in; 4¼in in roofs
Barbettes	7in max
CT	10in
Power	90,000shp
Speed	31¼/31¾kts
Radius of action	? at 31kts; 6000nm at 20kts; 11,000nm at 10kts
Cost	£2,000,000 including armament

Furious
As above except:

Beam	88ft
Draught (designed)	20ft 6in/21ft 6in
Legend displacement	19,100 tons
Normal displacement	19,513 tons
Deep load displacement	22,890 tons
Armament	2–18in
	11–5.5in
	2–3in
	2–3pdr
	2–21in TT (submerged)
	16–21 TT (above water)
Speed	30¼kts

THE WEIRD SISTERS

Despite Oscar Parkes' assertion that originally Courageous *had her funnel searchlights on one level, and* Glorious *on two, the original of this photo is clear enough to reveal that the ship's name on the quarter is* Courageous. *(IWM)*

miles at 20kts and 11,000 miles at economic speed – presumably 10kts – was expected, which was a bit lavish for the Baltic. Cruising turbines were planned but not actually fitted.

This 'Great Leap Forward' was made under the pressure of wartime; Sir Philip Watts had wanted to make it in the *Tiger* of 1911, but the ship and engine builders had muttered in their beards. If he had gone ahead regardless, they would no doubt have ensured that the experiment was a failure. The Germans had used small-tube boilers and un-geared turbines for years.

Protection

Armour was on a true light cruiser scale, 2in on a 1in side over 465ft length, and extending from 23ft above to 1½ft below load waterline, with 2in plating beyond that and 2 + 1in bulkheads. The only heavy armour was on the turrets, which were as in the *Repulse*; 9in fronts, 7in sides, 11in rears, presumably for balance, and 4½in high-quality roofs; and the conning tower, which was planned as 7in and 9in, but later thickened to 10in, the after one being 6in. The deck was ¾in and 1in, the uptakes ¾in.

Battle scouts and torpedo battleships

In the meantime, in neutral America, Admiral Frank Fletcher was reporting to the Secretary of the Navy on a disastrous Fleet Problem. The 'Blue' (US) Fleet had been trying to keep the two halves of the 'Red' (British) fleet apart. At that time, the USN had plenty of old but slow armoured and protected cruisers, but only three modern ones – the *Salem*s. There were doubts about the battlecruiser – too big, costly and vulnerable (one design study came out at 79,000 tons) – and the light cruiser, which was too slow in bad weather. To fill the gap USN destroyers had been built extra big and strong in the hope that they could fill the scouting role.

During the January 1915 Fleet Problem, as on previous occasions, the weather proved too tough for them, wrecked 'Blue's' carefully arranged scouting plans, and enabled the two halves of 'Red' to join up and win the game. This brought the scouting problem to a head, and Admiral Fletcher recommended a 'Heavy Scout', big enough to maintain a 5kt margin over 21kt dreadnoughts in almost any weather.

The upshot was that in April, the USN Bureau of Construction and Repair produced a fleet of 'Battle Scout' studies of ships able to do just this and to shoot their way through an enemy's scouting line. The studies were produced in sets of three, each set having a common armament, but one being completely unarmoured, one having light cruiser armour (4in side and 1½in deck), and one having battlecruiser armour (8in side and 3in deck). To ensure the necessary rough weather speed, a trial speed of 35kts was provided for.

This meant some very big ships; even those with only ten 6in came out well over 10,000 tons, despite a 2000-ton saving from designing to cruiser, rather than battleship, standards. To do the 'shooting through' most carried 12in, 14in or 16in guns. Six carried four 14in or 16in each; details are in Table 2 and it will be seen that similar problems led different design teams to very similar solutions. The 'Battle Scouts' were not intended to fight battleships, but to destroy light cruisers and torpedo craft and to fight battlecruisers on fairly even terms. No 126, the battlecruiser-armoured 14in design, was selected for development and, after many changes, became the 43,000-ton 1919 battlecruiser, which was transmuted into an aircraft carrier by the Washington Treaty, and fought at the Coral Sea under another Admiral Fletcher.

In 1912, the USN had studied a 'Torpedo Battleship', with four big guns, high speed and heavy torpedo arma-

Table 2. SIX USN 'BATTLE SCOUT' PROJECTS, APRIL 1915

Project	124	125	126	130	131	132
Normal displacement	15,500	19,500	25,000	16,500	20,500	26,800
LWL (ft)	720	760	800	720	775	800
Beam (ft)	71	77	85	73	79	88
Draught (ft)	19½	21½	24	20½	22	26
Battery	4–14in	4–14in	4–14in	4–16in	4–16in	4–16in
	7–5in	7–5in	7–5in	7–5in	7–5in	7–5in
Belt	Nil	4in	8in	Nil	4in	8in
Deck	Nil	1½in	3in	Nil	1½in	3in
Belt height	Nil	17½ft	17½ft	Nil	17½ft	17½ft
Boiler rooms	9	10	11	10	10	12
ehp (50 per cent)	68,500	76,500	86,000	73,000	77,000	92,500
Weights (tons)						
Hull, fittings	7050	8467	10,450	7169	8826	10,892
Protective deck	Nil	485	1430	Nil	493	1575
Armour	Nil	1085	2330	Nil	1087	2470
Machinery	4375	4860	5500	4670	4920	5910
Reserve feed water	913	1017	1150	974	1028	1235
Battery	1080	1080	1080	1325	1325	1325
Equipment	465	585	750	496	616	789
Outfit	511	643	825	545	676	868
Fuel Oil	1106	1278	1485	1142	1320	1532

ment. Wargaming suggested that one such ship at each end of the battle line could create havoc in the enemy's line.

Back in Whitehall, Board of Admiralty approval was given to the *Courageous* design on 29 January 1915, Winston Churchill writing to the Secretary on 3 February that 'I am notifying the Treasury separately.' Strict secrecy was enjoined on the design staff and everyone else concerned. The name ship was laid down at Walker on 28 April (No 895) and *Glorious* (No 482) at Belfast on 1 May. Fisher had hoped for three or even four ships, but had to be content for the moment with two, probably through shortage of heavy mountings.

The user angle

Dogger Bank had been fought on 23 January 1915, but does not seem to have affected the design in the least. On 28 January 1916 Admiral Beatty wrote privately to D'Eyncourt:

> Dear D'Eyncourt,
> Can you give me any information on the new cruisers of which you sent me the specifications and of which Lord Fisher showed me the model a year ago? Have they materialised along the lines originally laid down?

D'Eyncourt endorsed this: 'Ans 1st is *Repulse* launched last month to complete about July. She is practically identical with the model you saw 6 × 15in, 27,000 tons.'

When he did receive details of 'the three smaller ships' Beatty was very critical, saying that four guns were too few to permit accurate shooting, while the armour was far too thin: '*Lion* would have been lost but for her armour' [*ie* at Dogger Bank].

Secondary armament gave rise to a lot of problems and some vacillation. The decision for 4in – as in the *Repulse* – was probably due to Jellicoe, a former Director of Naval Ordnance and Controller, who considered the 1911 reversion to 6in an error, overloading the ships and unnecessary to stop destroyers. There was also a feeling that the 6in was too large to be a true hand-loader, even in big ships. (There is some social history here; the shrinking size of British recruits caused much concern and eventually led to the Welfare State. It was noticed that Japanese sailors were as big as most British, and much stronger.)

The 4.7in 50pdr had been in limbo since the middle 1890s, a 5in 60pdr had been designed but not built, leaving nothing immediately available between the 4in 31pdr and the 6in 100pdr. The triple 4in was intended to provide volume of fire; it required twenty-six men to work, against eleven for a 6in. The original disposition was apparently two triples on the centreline, one and a single on each side, plus two others as yet unlocated. At first it was intended to rely on gunlayer control, with Evershed's bearing indicators to put them on target, after which the fire gong would sound and each mount would blaze away. This would permit the use of QF or 'semi-automatic' 4in, which were far more accurate than their BL Mk VII cousins. However, during April, it was decided to fit secondary director control, which involved developing a new gun, the BL Mk IX, which was designed in a week.

There were also two 3in 20cwt AA guns with 150rpg, five Maxims with 5000 rpg and two submerged 21in tubes with a total of ten torpedoes.

THE WEIRD SISTERS

Courageous *with modified searchlight arrangements, and a flying-off platform on 'A' turret. (CPL)*

Furious *as completed. (IWM)*

Courageous *and* Glorious *at sea. (IWM)*

Furious

At the same time, the third sister, *Furious*, was ordered as Elswick's No 896. Nothing is recorded of the major decision to fit her with 18in and 5.5in guns, though this involved widening her by 7ft. The 18in was ordered by the Admiralty (*ie* Fisher) direct from Elswick, the only firm with the plant to handle such huge pieces. The Ordnance Board were simply by-passed, which was probably illegal. The gun was essentially a further development of the 13.5/15in medium velocity series, and apart from being a bit heavy (149 tons) in proportion to its 3320lb shell, was very orthodox. Muzzle velocity was 2472fps. The single mountings were so designed as to fit into normal twin 15in barbettes, though with a bit of overlap at the top and an additional 150 tons weight per mounting; 120 of the huge shells were carried per gun. Sets of spare 15in guns and mountings were made for *Furious* and two were used in the monitor *Erebus*. The first 18in passed trials in September 1916.

Furious's secondary armament was first set at eight 5.5in. This calibre came in with the ex-Greek *Chesters*, and there were 38 spare guns on hand, 22 of which were being sub-contracted by the Coventry Ordnance Works for the Greek battleship *Vassilis Giorgious* under construction in France. The gun fired an 82lb shell and required nine men. Range at 25 degrees elevation was 16,498yds against 13,840yds for the 4in. Its adoption may have reflected doubts about the 4in, or may have been to free 4in for destroyers and light cruisers. The disposition adopted was four guns sided forward of the funnel, two on the centreline abaft it, and two abreast 24ft apart, firing over the after turret. Seven 6in, weighing about the same, were also considered. (When the Germans, 'inspired' by the events of 17 November 1917, designed 'anti-*Courageous*es' they used very similar layouts, no doubt meeting similar space and weight problems.)

This was still not the end; in June, the 4in in the first pair were increased to eighteen and the third ship was given eleven 5.5in. This meant six 4in triples per ship, and in *Furious* an additional pair abreast the funnel and the foremost centreline gun replaced by a sided pair. It was noted that the 5.5in 'would be useful against other light cruisers in certain contingencies'. 5in were proposed and 5.5in used in the early *Hood* designs, some of which had a few centreline guns. All this suggests that someone had doubts about the ships' ability to deal with small, agile targets – a contingency which did arise. The 4in triples had spray shields, the 5.5in *Birmingham*-type shields, though spray shields would have saved 30 tons topweight.

Displacement and speed

The various additions, including torpedo bulkheads to protect the inner shaft machinery only, extra ammunition, overweight armament – 40 tons per 15in turret and at least 6.6 tons per triple 4in – and extra fire control, made nonsense of the never very realistic legend displacement. By 1918, it had risen to 19,320 tons and full load was 22,690. The designed 32kts was reckoned cut to 31¾ in deep water at 18,600 tons, about 31½kts at Skelmorlie (40 fathoms), 30kts at Polperro (25 fathoms) and the optimum to 31kts at deep load in deep water.

Research and development

All sorts of problems had to be solved as the designers and the builders worked; gun pumps were 'borrowed' from the *Ramillies*, the last of the 1913/14 ships, fittings were included for torpedo nets, and turret arrangements made as much like the *Repulse* as possible. After much dithering, it was decided to fit the *Courageous* as a flagship, and plans were made for carrying two Sopwith Baby seaplanes. Incidentally, *Glorious* was apparently not weighed by Harland & Wolff during construction.

In May 1915, both Fisher and Churchill fell from power, the latter making the first reference to 'Light Battle Cruisers' in commending the ships to his successor, Balfour, whose first appearance in the papers is a letter urging the Constructors to get enough leave. Wise, no doubt – at least one RCNC man worked himself to death – but hardly Churchill's or Fisher's way of making war.

In March, Fisher had lamented that

> I fear we are not going to get even two out of the four owing to the Parliamentary bugbear of delaying 4 last ships of the *Royal Sovereign* type. *It's a great pity & it will be very greatly regretted.'*
>
> The present light small cruisers get their speed knocked down from full to 15kts in heavy weather, so will be no use to accompany & scout for the BCs & if caught may fall prey to the enemy's BCs if caught by them scouting in heavy weather.

At a later date the Controller, Admiral Tudor, wrote that '. . . they were originally intended to act as light cruisers attached to the battlecruisers.' This was very close to the American 'Battle Scout' concept, though even the Controller may not have been fully aware of Fisher's ideas.

Hull

The beam of the first pair was increased by 1ft during design to allow for the extra weight, *Furious* was 7ft wider still and appreciably larger. A bulge, for hydrodynamic reasons only, was worked in below the waterline. The hull-form was excellent and was used later as the starting point for light fleet carriers and the unbuilt CVA-01. Compartmentation was considered fairly good; counter-flooding scuttles were fitted. The weak spot was regarded as the junction of the transverse and longditudinal bulkheads at station 110. A hit here would flood No 3 Boiler room and cause the first pair to heel 13½ degrees or in *Furious* 14½. Metacentric height of *Courageous* was 3.5ft at 21ft 8½in draught, 4ft light and 6ft at extreme draught of 25ft 8in. For *Furious* in her original state, the figures were: 3.17ft extreme light, 3.2ft light, 3.5ft legend and 5.3ft deep load, with ranges of 89, 80, 76 and 74 degrees. Her speed was reckoned to be ¼kt to ½kt slower than her half-sisters.

Once Fisher and Churchill had gone, construction slowed down; probably the dates were optimistic anyway, and Admiral Tudor told Elswick to shift their main effort from *Furious* to *Courageous*. The two 15in ships were completed in January 1917, and *Furious*, much altered, on 4 July 1917. The decision to convert *Furious*'s sharp end into a carrier had been taken in March. In May, Captain Miller of the *Glorious* proposed the fitting of numerous above-water tubes, as the class had the ability to get into good torpedo-firing positions, and this idea was adopted, twelve 21in tubes in pairs being added. This came very near to the American 'Torpedo Battleship' scheme of 1912.

In the meantime, trials took place and produced some problems. On the night of 8/9 January 1917, *Courageous* was working up to full speed in what was thought to be a 'State 4' sea (waves 7ft high) when her sides and deck began to buckle. Both sides were damaged from stations 50 to 54 from the upper to the forecastle deck. Water got into the torpedo flat and wings and there were also signs of strain under 'Y' turret. The ship was able to continue with gunnery and torpedo exercises, but a naval Court of Enquiry wanted to say that she was structurally weak. The Constructor member, Victor Shepheard, a very junior Assistant Constructor, refused to sign the report and insisted on a signal being sent out asking all ships in the North Sea that night what the sea state was. The consensus was 'State 7' – waves 16ft to 18ft high, a much tougher proposition. *Courageous* was strengthened as soon as possible, *Glorious* not until after 17 November; worries were expressed about the ships in winter if not strengthened. It was thought that with the bridge so far back from the bow, the Captain had not sensed the state of the sea quickly enough.

There were other minor troubles with the astern turbines and *Courageous* had an argument with a buoy. Turning circle was reported as less than 1500yds, good for such long, slim ships.

The question now was what to do with the monsters? There was nothing afloat remotely like them, the Baltic Landing was now dead, even if it had been really intended, and Jutland had led to a revulsion against lightly protected ships. (Fisher was very bitter about the misunderstanding of his ideas; he endorsed a letter from Beatty about the light protection of the battlecruisers, 'Never intended to come within range of the enemy' and prophesied 'Hang Fisher; now they will build ships armoured like Noah's Ark.')

The two 15in ships were formed into the new 1st Cruiser Squadron (the Germans had abolished the old one) and, when the Light Cruiser Force was formed, *Courageous* became its flagship, too.

The Germans, it seems, never heard of the type until they met it in person at 07.30 on 17 November; British security in the First World War was excellent.

Minelayers v minesweepers

Although the Grand Fleet had been much strengthened since Jutland, the Admiralty was not keen on a further fleet action, shifting to a policy of mining the Germans in, which was effective both against the High Seas Fleet and the much more dangerous U-boats. Mines were laid by big conventional minelayers, submarines and destroyers. A good mine, the Russian-designed H2, was available in quantity, and a struggle developed between the British layers and the German sweepers. Soon the latter were forced to work up to 100 miles seaward of Heligoland, which brought them within striking range of British surface ships. On 31 October, the latter sank ten small ships in the Kattegat.

In mid-November, the Admiralty planned Operation 'FR', a really big anti-sweeper operation, intended to annihilate a whole group of sweepers and the light cruisers and destroyers which were known to accompany them. It was based on radio intelligence. The plan was that, at a pre-arranged time, Force A (The 1st Cruiser Squadron, 1st and 6th Light Cruiser Squadrons – four ships each – and twelve destroyers) should arrive at Rendezvous X, 55°N, 5°55'E. It would be followed and supported by Force B (1st Battlecruiser Squadron – five ships – and eight destroyers led by the light cruiser *Champion*). Forces A and B would sweep on 349° true to meet with Force C (1st Battle Squadron – three 'R's, *Canada* and two *Iron Dukes* with eleven destroyers), who would reach Rendezvous Y in 56°N, 5°33'E at the same time. British information was that a German 'Probe Voyage' by minesweepers, light cruisers and destroyers would reach Rendezvous X at 06.00 and steer 349°, searching for newly-laid British mines.

If things went reasonably well, a handsome victory, to equal the Army's at Cambrai and also to avenge the Scandinavian convoy, might be expected. The three forces included contingents from the Battlecruiser and Light Cruiser Forces, and the Grand Fleet. The ships set out on the 15th, but an intercepted German weather report showed that the 16th would be too rough for sweeping, and the forces were recalled for a hasty top-up at Rosyth.

Other forces were at sea for exercises, in which submarine *K-1* was lost, and Beatty ordered all signals to be reported to him. In the late afternoon of the 16th, the ships sailed again, to be at their rendezvous by 08.00 of the 17th. The approach was made without detection during a very dark night, thereby avoiding air reconnaissance. Between 05.00 and 06.00, Forces A and B passed the South Dogger light vessel, gaining a vital fix. Only ten of Force A's destroyers were present.

Force A was commanded by Vice-Admiral T D M Napier, who had had the 3rd Light Cruiser Squadron at Jutland, Force B by Vice-Admiral Pakenham, formerly of the 2nd Battlecruiser Squadron – his old flagship *New Zealand*, keeping up nobly with the *Lions* and *Repulse*. The two Light Cruiser Squadrons in Force A were the 1st (Commodore Cowan – ex-*Princess Royal* – *Caledon* and three *Arethusas*) and 6th (Rear-Admiral E S Alexander-Sinclair – ex-1st Light Cruiser Squadron – two *Cardiffs* and two more *Caledons*).

Despite the careful planning and the overwhelming force assigned, the seeds of failure had already been planted. Information on minefields was kept on a strict 'need to know' basis and while Pakenham had full information, his subordinates had progressively less down the chain of command. Rendezvous X was almost on the line beyond which British ships could not go without special permission, and Napier had put on his chart a line beyond which he was reluctant to go and another which was an absolute limit.

The Germans had no idea what was bearing down on them, though they were ready for destroyer or light cruiser raids, but they had the battleships *Kaiserin* and *Kaiser* in support off Heligoland some 80 miles to the east-southeast, with the battlecruisers *Hindenburg* and *Moltke* backing them up; it is not clear if the British knew of this precaution.

The proof of the pudding – the Third Battle of Heligoland

It was very dark during the approach; *Glorious* noted visibility as two miles at 06.15, with the light cruisers not yet in sight and the ships making remarkably little smoke (except *Calypso*, who was told off about this). At 06.30, *Vendetta* reported to *Caledon*: 'I can hear Telefunken German Naval Code signals strength 10.' The sun rose out of a fog bank at 07.17 and visibility increased to 7½ miles, with a light wind from west or south-west. Expectations were high. Napier told Force A that enemy minesweepers might be met and were to be attacked.

Force A was making 24kts until 07.26, when it reduced to 22kts. Course was east and the two Large Light Cruisers had their four attendant destroyers round them. The 6th LCS had dropped back to their port beam – a tricky manoeuvre in the darkness – with their four 'V' class. The 1st, with two destroyers, were three miles astern instead of on the starboard beam and the five battlecruisers and their screen ten miles one point on the starboard quarter. At 07.25, *Vendetta* heard more German morse and, at 07.30, ships were sighted ahead with Force A still some ten miles short of the Rendezvous.

The enemy were much as the planners had hoped; the four light cruisers of Scouting Group II, *Königsberg* (Flag of Rear-Admiral Ludwig von Reuter, who commanded the whole force and had been Commodore of Scouting Group IV at Jutland), *Nurnburg, Pillau* and *Frankfurt*, eight destroyers, three divisions of minesweepers, eight 'sperrbrechers' (cork-filled trawlers, to clear mines the hard way) and, last but not least, two trawlers as danlayers. One of these was the *Kehdingen* (Lt zur See H von Bredow). The latter had anchored at 06.00 to mark the starting point of the probe.

At the moment of contact, some minesweepers and a

couple of destroyers were on the British port bow, six or eight 'submarines' (the sperrbrechers) and two destroyers right ahead and two or more light cruisers with destroyers fine on the starboard bow. The 'submarines' appeared to be stopped, the rest to be crossing Force A's bows on a north-north-west course. Either the Germans were behind schedule or British Intelligence had got the timing wrong; contact had been made just before the victims entered the jaws of the trap.

Courageous and *Cardiff* opened fire with their forward guns at 07.37, quickly followed by other ships, and enemy reports were sent. Speed was increased to 25kts, the 6th LCS pulling ahead rapidly. The flagship used her 15in against a light cruiser and her 4in on a minesweeper, which was soon hit. The Germans very promptly began making smoke from funnels, floats and smoke generators, and were hidden within a few minutes. A mushroom cloud from behind the screen suggested that *Courageous*'s 15in had been on target, too. The minesweepers appeared to turn away to the north-east. 'The submarines appeared

Calypso *and other light cruisers, taken from* Cardiff, *possibly on 17 November 1917.* (IWM)

to take a long time to dive.' When last seen, the light cruisers were still on their original course.

Von Reuter and his men had been completely surprised, through no fault of their own, but they reacted quickly. The light was against them and at first they could see nothing but gun-flashes and shell splashes. The *Kehdingen* was disabled at once, but by no means finished. Von Reuter kept on his course to find out what he was up against, but by 07.53 realised that he was outgunned and reversed course to east-south-east to fall back on his supports, getting his cruisers into port quarter line. At 07.52 he radioed that he was under attack by 'strong enemy forces', and the battleships set off to the rescue, followed by the battlecruisers, while seaplanes took off from their bases, despite the poor visibility. Though in a tight corner, von Reuter had hopes of turning the tables with the help of his battleships, unless 'the English' sank him first. *Vendetta* noted 'very frantic telegraphing'.

At 07.45 the 6th LCS came round to the southward, crossing *Courageous*'s bows; the latter altered to north and later to north-east to clear them. Just afterwards the Germans turned away, so that a lot of ground was lost. The *Kehdingen* was left behind, exchanging fire with the

Repulse *firing a broadside, date unknown.* (IWM)

many British ships that passed. As most of the 30 to 35 shells which hit her passed through without exploding, she took a lot of finishing off, being sunk at 08.50 by Force B's destroyers, who picked up most of her crew and were much impressed by them, except Leading Seaman V Peters, snobbishly described as 'of a lower type'. In return, von Bredow was equally impressed by the *Courageous, Glorious,* and *Repulse,* wanting to know what they were, and by the 'V' destroyers, which he took for light cruisers.

The 1st Cruiser Squadron were round on to east-south-east by 07.51 and to south-south-east by 08.10, but the range had opened to 14,000yds and only brief glimpses of the enemy were possible. Return fire was spasmodic and at this stage mostly short. The four 'V's originally with the 6th LCS made a lunge at the minesweepers but soon lost them in the smoke, and the battle turned into a chase after the four light cruisers. Commodore Cowan's 1st LCS opened fire at 07.50, coming round to south-south-east and coming under fire at 08.04. They saw nothing of the minesweepers, but engaged the light cruisers, preferably those in the rear; in practice, any that showed themselves. The three *Arethusa*s, apart from being in a poor position, had only two 6in each and those of limited range. Captain Marten of *Inconstant* remarked that he had been at Jutland in *Galatea* and had been outranged there, too. Pleas had been made long before for the class to be rearmed, and these proved only too justified. (*Royalist* to *Caledon*: 'Range too great for us (08.15). Reply: 'Am closing'.)

Commodore Cowan handed *Caledon* over to his Executive Officer, while he concentrated on fighting the squadron. *Royalist* had been out of dockyard hands for only three days and had had no time for refresher training, but everything worked. *Galatea*'s fire control circuits had been dismantled in preparation for the fitting of a director; Chief Electrical Artificer Plaskett had to rig a series of 'lash-ups' but these met the test. The lack of directors was severely felt.

The two big ships continued the chase, firing as opportunity offered. At 08.02, Pakenham, following along behind, told the 31kt *Repulse*: 'Support *Caledon* bearing 130' and she began to pull ahead. Shortly after, at 08.38, the rest of the battlecruisers, thinking that they had reached the Rendezvous and were not needed, turned back and 'stood off and on' to the northward.

Courageous and *Glorious* used both main and secondary armament without much success; the former was only able to shoot continuously from 08.02 to 08.06, and the latter, like that in the light cruisers, was mostly outranged. It was also shaken up by the 15in, causing many electrical failures. One 15in hit was made, on a gun shield in *Pillau*, but without stopping her. In *Courageous*, Midshipman Jerome was speechless with a sore throat, so had to leave his turret's crew to get on with it, which they did satisfactorily. However, at 08.33, *Glorious* suffered a premature in the lefthand gun of her 'A' turret, the gun being wrecked.

Two minutes later, the Germans began laying smoke with renewed vigour; as he was approaching his 'Line B', the penultimate safety line, Napier altered eight points to port, possibly to see round the north end of the smoke. He then resumed the chase, but another five miles had been lost. At 09.30, they reached the limit, 'Line C' and turned south, parallel to it. They had never exceeded 25kts, and their battle was over. The Germans claimed some hits on them, but these seem to have been illusory.

In the meantime, the world's biggest, longest and hardest light cruiser battle was raging; the 6th LCS had got to about 'Green 140' from the Germans, at ranges of from 10,000yds to 14,000yds. This exposed them to German torpedo fire and made their own heavy torpedo armament useless. The Germans frequently made smoke and fired torpedoes, while all ships kept up a hot fire, twisting and turning to keep guns bearing or avoid salvoes. Mines were believed to be on both sides, periscopes and torpedoes were frequently reported, and the German seaplanes had joined in. Speed was by now about 28kts, and this gave a relative wind just on the Germans' engaged bow, hiding all but the leading ship much of the time.

From about 08.45, conditions improved for a while, and several British ships were able to have a long shoot. *Ceres* claimed twelve straddles and eight hits on the German No 3, noting that her opponent began with five guns, was down to three, and finished with four. She fired 498 rounds without a single mishap, but her rangefinders got only one range, at the outset. *Calypso* was evidently engaging the same ship, and claimed a number of hits and two fires; however, the target extinguished her fires and steamed on regardless. Most of the time, *Calypso* fired salvoes in pairs with an 'Up 200' correction and then lost the target. *Caradoc*, at the rear of the squadron, fired much less; she claimed what seem to have been the same hits as *Ceres*. At 08.26 the latter had momentary engine

The light cruiser Royalist *before she was fitted with a tripod mast and spotting top.* (IWM)

trouble and asked her next astern to pass, but was able to resume her position.

Apart from the smoke, some British ships had the sun in their eyes through gaps in the overcast. Conditions were difficult and most resorted to 'laddering' – walking their salvoes across the target and trusting that their numerous straddles included some hits. The return fire was mostly slower than their own, with closely bunched salvoes and a long time of flight. All the latest fire control gadgets were used, but all too often the target could be seen only briefly.

The Germans sent many torpedoes through the British ranks, but only *Galatea* was hit, by a dud. She also tried to ram a U-boat, which may have been either a torpedo or 'an old Leon mine with a spar attached'. It was noticed that, although the wind was light and on the quarter, whenever ships turned anywhere near it, waves up to 4ft high swooshed along the forecastle. The superfiring No 2 gun in *Cardiff* and *Ceres* no doubt came in handy here. Whenever the Germans fired a torpedo, a white flare was seen from their ships, which may have been the impulse charge.

Cardiff and *Caledon*, the two flagships, came under heavy fire, though they did a lot of shooting themselves. The former was hit four or five times; once on the bridge, once or possibly twice in the torpedo dividing space under the forecastle, once in the after superstructure and once through the after funnel. Casualties amounted to seven killed and thirteen wounded. There was a lot of splinter

The light cruiser Caledon, *the flagship of the 1st Light Cruiser Squadron at Heligoland. (IWM)*

damage, one splinter entering a torpedo warhead. *Caledon* received one bad 5.9in hit on the bridge, which killed two signalmen and two of No 2 gun's crew, just aft of it, wounding seven of the other nine. Ordinary Seaman J H Carless, the rammer number, was almost disembowelled. He lifted one more shell, helped to clear away casualties, cheered on the replacement gunners, and so died, being posthumously awarded the VC.

It was noticed towards the end of the action that fire had slowed on both sides, due to the exhaustion of the guns' crews; spreads had also increased. *Caledon*'s No 1 gun had fired over 200 rounds.

At 09.42, one of *Calypso*'s signalmen was just logging in 'Your . . .' when a shell arrived. She was observed to swerve out of line. The shell burst while passing through the roof of the conning tower, killing all inside, creating havoc on the bridge, putting the rangefinder out of action and cutting the director leads. A torpedo was fired inadvertently. Casualties amounted to seven killed or mortally wounded, including Captain Edwards, and thirteen wounded, many by flying fragments of Triplex glass. The Control Top and Transmitting Station felt the hit, and challenged the bridge by voice-pipe. The badly wounded Navigator got the ship back into station, by which time the Gunnery Officer had come down from the top to take command. The ship was just recovering from this blow when four large ships were sighted ahead, two of which at once opened fire with great accuracy.

The destroyers on each side had not had much opportunity; the German ones stayed with their cruisers, firing through gaps and launching occasional torpedoes. On the British side, most wound up with the wrong set of big ships. The four 'V's with the 6th LCS found themselves at 08.20 on the port quarter of the German cruisers. *Valentine* and *Vanquisher* tried an attack, but found themselves unsupported and had to retire. The division took station on the port side of the 1st LCS; *Galatea* was a bit worried by one of them having a torpedo most of the way out of its tube and pointing at her.

Ursa, *Urchin*, *Umpire* and *Nerissa*, originally with the 1st Cruiser Squadron, and *Vendetta* and *Medway*, from the 1st LCS, formed up on the disengaged bow of the 6th LCS, firing at the Germans at extreme range. *Ursa*, commanded by Cdr J C Tovey, of Jutland and later fame, fired one torpedo in the opening minutes. The elderly *Nerissa* claimed to have attained 33.3kts in keeping with the 'Modified Rs'; she blew up a manoeuvring valve, but kept going on her evaporator. At 09.15, Alexander-Sinclair ordered the destroyers to take station astern.

All this time, *Repulse* had been coming up. She flew the flag of Rear-Admiral R F Phillimore, second-in-command of the battlecruisers, and was commanded by Captain Boyle, both aggressive characters. The latter had just come from supporting Lawrence of Arabia in the 1500-ton auxiliary *Perth*, and found the giant battlecruiser rather a change. He had told his coxswain to have refreshments ready, in case the engagement should be prolonged, and throughout the battle was aware of a huge hand, full of raisins, lurking near his left ear. Raisins and all, the ship pressed on: she had only limited information on the minefields, but replied 'yes' to an enquiry from Napier about whether she had sufficient. Between 09.02 and 09.04, she tried three salvoes from her forward turrets – *Vendetta* noted large splashes going up 'apparently from the port quarter.' However, no harm was done, and at 09.15 she resumed, this time at the enemy. Like everyone else, she found conditions difficult and had to check fire frequently, getting off eight salvoes between 09.15 and 09.37. At 09.45 she was surprised to see small-calibre splashes round her, only on reaching port and hearing the German communique did she realise that she was being bombed. At about 09.47 she got a clear view of a four-funnelled German cruiser and got off five double salvoes, of which the last scored a definite hit.

For all their efforts, the British cruisers had only made three 6in hits; there was a lot of duplication and splash confusion, and it was apparently not realised that the Germans were in a wide quarter line. There are many

Table 3. FIVE GERMAN 'SCHNELLER GROSSKAMPFSCHIFFE', MARCH 1918

	GK3021	GK3022	GK3521	GK4021	GK4521
Construction					
displacement (tons)	29,526	29,526	34,447	39,368	44,289
LWL (ft)	787.2	787.2	787.2	787.2	787.2
Beam (ft)	88.56	88.56	96.76	108.24	109.88
Draught (ft)	27.88	27.284	29.52	29.52	32.8
Battery	4–13.8in	4–13.8in	4–15in	4–16.5in	4–16.5in
	10–5.9in	10–5.9in	12–5.9in	12–5.9in	12–5.9in
Armour					
Belt (in)	6	4	11.8	11.8	13.8
Deck (in)	1.2/2.5	1.2	1.2/2.5	2	3.5
Height (ft)	15.7	25.8	7.8	11.8	15.7
Boilers (oil & coal)	16 + 16	40 + 8	?	14 + 16	16 + 16
Power	140,000	200,000	?	?	180,000

references to 'four-funnelled' German ships; all had three. None of the Germans was slowed down permanently, and it was thought that their ships, nominally 27½-knotters, were in fact ¾kt–1kt faster than the British. The British engineers were equally effective; 30,000hp *Inconstant* kept up 35,000hp for four hours and 40,000hp *Caledon*, 50,000hp for some time. The *Arethusa*s were reckoned good for 27½kts in service; *Galatea* had been 7½ months out of dock, but the trio kept up with *Caledon* at 28kts. Towards the end of the action the 1st LCS apart from the *Caledon*, was virtually out of the battle (though they would have been admirably placed to finish off any cripples). *Inconstant* received one hit, without serious effect.

By 09.00 with 80 miles to go and a closing speed of 45kts or thereabouts, the battleships should have been in sight and Admiral von Reuter was wondering where they had got to. In fact, they were coming at full speed, but in the wrong direction. The *Königsberg*'s initial contact report had given the wrong grid square, 45 miles south of the correct one. Not until a further report of 08.30 was the correct position given. The battleships hastily altered course to the north. At 09.25 they sighted the *Königsberg*. This error actually helped von Reuter's plan to trap the British, and he ordered the battleships 'Kurs NordWest', to get round the enemy's southern flank. Unfortunately, at the same time, *Kaiserin* was sending a position report, asking 'Where is the enemy?' and reporting that she was in action. This proved too much for her signal organisation, and she did not receive the vital order, altering instead to south-east and *reducing* to 15kts. Von Reuter was unable to correct the error; his flagship had been reduced to 17½kts by *Repulse*'s shell, which went through all three funnels and exploded in a bunker.

At 09.40, a radio warning was sent to Napier: 'Enemy's battleships may be in support' – it was received at 10.06. The British ships sighted what were variously reported as *Bayern*s and battlecruisers just after 09.44. The opening salvoes were very accurate; the 6th LCS at once reversed course altogether. (The much-tried *Calypso* was near-missed by two bombs from a seaplane just after turning.) The 1st LCS ran on for a few minutes and then turned, *Caledon* being hit on the quarter just afterwards. The shell tipped up a pair of torpedo tubes, but otherwise did surprisingly little damage. *Repulse* was just getting her guns onto the *Kaiserin* when Phillimore gave the order to retire. No attempt was made to cover the retreat by smoke or torpedo attack, but the action was broken off quickly. Shortly afterwards, the British ships ran into dense fog – some, no doubt, smoke from the battle – and Third Heligoland had passed into history. The British force remained at sea and repeated the sweep on the 18th, but of course found nothing.

No further attempt was made to attack the German minesweepers and their escorts in this way, and both sides were left feeling cheated of victory. The battle bears an uncanny resemblance to that off Samar twenty-seven years later.

The *Repulse* was laid up for a day with engine trouble, and the *Glorious* for five days. It is interesting that the final batches of 'C' and 'D' class light cruisers were given a trawler bow, possibly a lesson from the battle. It is noteworthy that, as actually fought, the battle resembled the 'Shooting-a-way-through-the-enemy's-screen' envisaged by the Americans; the result showed that a well-handled screen took a lot of shooting through. It was not a fair trial of the Large Light Cruisers, but it was to be the only one they got. In later life, the *Furious* showed what could be done by outranging the enemy with weapons of a different kind.

Aftermath

The Germans, as mentioned already, were quite impressed by the Large Light Cruisers; their Construction Department was heavily overworked already, designing slow, medium and high speed battleships, battlecruisers and fast 'Grosskampfschiffe' – Capital Ships. The Kaiser lnow added to their burden by ordering the design of 'Schneller Grosskampfschiffe' like those of Cousin George. The weary designers dutifully responded with GK 3021 and 3022, lightly-armoured 30,000-tonners with four 13.8in and a mixture of low and high-angle 5.9in, GK 3521, with four 15in and *Lutzow* armour, and the giant

▲ *The improved superfiring arrangement of main armament introduced in the* Ceres *class is clearly shown in this fine portrait of* Cardiff *at anchor. (IWM)*

▼ Caledon, *showing the damage caused by the 12in hit on the starboard quarter. (IWM)*

Table 4. AMMUNITION EXPENDITURE AND DAMAGE SUSTAINED, 17 NOVEMBER 1917

Ship	15in	6in	4in	Other	Torpedoes	Damage and hits
Courageous	92					Blast and concussion damage
Glorious	57		393			15in burst, 1–15in hit between them
Repulse	54		Some			1 hit on *Königsberg*
Cardiff		310		?		Received 4 or 5–5.9in hits (9 killed, 13 wounded)
Calypso		498		9	1 (accidental)	Received 1–5.9in hit (7 killed, 13 wounded)
Ceres		485				
Caradoc		300				
Caledon		609				Received 1–5.9in, 1–12in hit (5 killed, 17 wounded)
Royalist		182	60			Received 1–5.9in hit (insignificant)
Inconstant		96	102			Received 1 torpedo hit (dud)
Galatea		58	?96			
Valentine			186		1	2 torpedoes misfired
Vanquisher			162		1	
Vimiera			138			
Vehement			53			
Ursa			?		1	Charge failed; torpedo slid out anyway

Expenditure for the other five destroyers is unknown. *Umpire* and *Urchin* experienced steering failures. *Vendetta* had 2 wounded, apparently by splinters.

GK 4021 and 4521, with four 16.5in, the former having *Lutzow* armour and the latter the full battleship scale, with 13.8in sides. A design with six 13.8in was considered but not apparently worked out. All the two-turret ships were 240m long – the same as the British ships.

Of the two 30,000-ton designs, 3021 had 'armoured cruiser' armour, with 6in sides, 16 coal- and 16 oil-fired boilers and 32kts trial, 31kts in service, speed from 140,000shp. GK 3022 was much more daring, with an almost complete coat of 4in armour, making her theoretically light cruiser-proof, 40 oil- and 8 coal-fired boilers on two decks, giving 200,000shp and 34/33kts. The idea of the two-decked boilers was presumably borrowed from the Americans. These projects would have been a case of 'either/or': Germany lacked the resources to build them *and* more orthodox ships; she finally decided on a medium-speed battleship, L20e Alpha, in October 1918. The increased size due to older-type machinery is noticeable. The GK two-turret series at least proves that the Germans could be as daft as the British when the mood seized them.

After the war, as Fisher had prophesied, heavy armour became mandatory for such few battleships as were built. However, the Large Light Cruiser idea did not die entirely. The 8in cruisers spawned by the Washington Treaty were initially described as 'light' – they certainly were not armoured – and the Americans retained an interest in 'soft' but well-armed ships of the same general size. The two British 15in ships were used as turret drill ships, then laid up until converted into aircraft carriers. Both were virtually thrown away early in the Second World War, but the *Furious*, after three main and several minor transformations, was left to end the story when she launched part of the strike against the *Tirpitz* on 21 April 1944.

Sources
ADM 138/453 (Ship's Cover).
ADM 137/584–6 (Action of 17 November 1917).
ADM 137/587–9.
DEY/16–17 (D'Eyncourt Papers) & 17 ADM 137/3877.
Nordsee, Vol VII.
Oscar Parkes, *British Battleships* (London 1966).
Lord Fisher, *Memories & Records*.
Winston Churchill, *The World Crisis*.
N J M Campbell, *Battle Cruisers* (London 1978).
Newbolt, *Naval Operations*, Vol V.
A Pollen, *The Great Gunnery Scandal* (London 1980).
Conways' All the World's Fighting Ships 1906–22 (London 1985).
Lord Cork & Orrery, *Memoirs*.
Lionel Dawson, *Fighting Sailor*.
Forstmeier & Breyer, *Deutsche Grosskampfschiffe* (Munich 1970).
Norman Friedman, *US Cruisers* (Annapolis 1985).
Information from David Brown, John Campbell and Gerhard Koop, and much help from the staffs of the National Maritime Museum (Draught Room and Library), MoD Library, and Public Record Office.

THE IMPERIAL JAPANESE NAVY REPAIR SHIP AKASHI

Although far from glamorous, the repair ship is essential to the operational efficiency of any blue-water navy. Jiro Itani and Hans Lengerer look at Japan's only purpose-built example of the type, the problems of designing such a sophisticated ship without previous experience, and conclude with details of the kind of work that *Akashi* was called upon to perform during the Pacific War.

The term 'Repair Ship' is a rather literal translation of the Japanese classification *Kōsakukan*. A more correct rendering might be 'Factory Ship' because it expresses the true character of this ship type more precisely, *ie* this type of vessel contained various workshops equipped with many machine tools, and in general appearance heavy derricks and cranes were prominent. In the organisation of the ship the Repair Section was paramount and under the command of the chief of this section worked officers, engineers, special duty officers, assistant engineers, warrant and petty officers and skilled workers of all professions who were mostly drawn from the Navy Arsenals.

The function of the repair ship was to accompany the fleet and take charge of maintaining ships, engines and weapons. It was also important for making emergency and other repairs in advanced bases, supporting overseas repair yards with very restricted facilities, assisting with the salvage of sunken ships and at home it could assist the Navy Arsenals (dockyards).

Being well aware of the importance of this ship type, the Imperial Japanese Navy (IJN) used converted vessels at first, since its strategic plan was to wait for the enemy fleet to advance across the Pacific and to destroy it near the homeland. The first was *Kantō*, the ex-Russian steamer *Manchuria*. This ship had been captured in the Russo–Japanese War, converted and commissioned as a *Kōsakukan*. However, *Kantō* ran on to rocks in Wakasa Bay in 1924 and became a total loss, so the victualling ship *Mamiya* was equipped with some facilities for limited repair work. She was not convenient for this purpose,[1] so the old battleship *Asahi* was taken in hand. She had had a chequered career, having been classified as a first class coast defence ship (*Kaibōkan*) in September 1921, then as a special service training ship (*Renshū Tokumukan*) and was later converted to a submarine salvage ship (because of the sinking of the submarines *No 43* and *No 70* in 1923 and 1924). *Asahi* was hastily equipped as a repair ship in 1937,[2] and sent to Shanghai to deal with the many damaged IJN ships on the Chinese coast; she was to remain there for a long time.

As *Kantō* had become a loss and *Asahi* not only lacked sufficient capacity for the fleet repair ship but was also too slow, the requirement arose for a specially designed ship in order to fulfil a request from the fleet and to supplement the insufficient capacity of the Navy Arsenals. To this requirement the first and last *Kōsakukan* of the IJN was designed and constructed.

Four more repair ships were planned before and after the outbreak of the war in the Pacific, but abandoned before construction could begin. Therefore the IJN was very short of repair capacity in the Pacific War and had to fit and equip merchantmen as special repair ships (*Tokusetsu Kōsakukan*). Besides the eight ships in this category, two captured Chinese warships were classified as *Kōsakusen* in the miscellaneous service vessel category.[3]

AKASHI

Akashi *leaving Sasebo for initial trials, July 1939. (By courtesy of Hans Lengerer)*

Design and construction

The IJN had wanted a new type *Kōsakukan* for a long time, but mainly due to budgetary restrictions, it was postponed until 1933. In this year the Navy General Staff ordered a Navy Arsenal and *Kōsaku Gakko* (Repair School) to produce requirements for the fabrication capacity of the new *Kōsakukan*. The Washington and (First) London Disarmament Treaties and the Manchurian and (First) Shanghai Incidents contributed to international tension and the operation of more warships along the Chinese coast was foreseen. The amount of general repair work on ships of the Combined Fleet was also increased by the intensive training and numerous manoeuvres. Therefore the necessity to have a ship for repairing damage far from the homeland and to assist the Navy Yards in general repair work became more urgent.

The Navy General Staff formally requested the Navy Ministry to build the fleet *Kōsakukan* by Navy General Staff Secret Document No 176 dated 11 September 1930 and again when the proposal for the Second Navy Replenishment Programme was forwarded to the Navy Ministry by Navy General Staff Secret Document No 199 on 14 June 1933. In the appendix is the requirement for one repair ship of 10,000 tons, with a maximum speed of 18kts, radius of 8000nm at 14kts and an armament of four 12.7cm (5in) high-angle guns and more than four AA machine-guns. The Navy Minister Kiyotane Abo's estimate of costs to Prime Minister Yūkō Hamaguchi (Secretariat Secret Document No 943, 7 October 1930) was 6,900,000 Yen but even before construction was actually begun the building costs had risen dramatically to 10,000,000.

The Second Navy Replenishment Programme became law on 20 March 1934, which approved the building of one *Kōsakukan*, later called *Akashi*. The Navy Technical Department (*Kaigun Kansei Honbu*) was formally ordered to produce the design of the repair ship in close cooperation with the Navy Arsenals and the Navy Repair School on the basis of the requirements outlined in June 1933.

Since the IJN had no experience in building repair ships, the designers faced considerable difficulties, especially with regard to allocating space for every workshop and store which are the most important items in the design of this kind of ship. The only design information available in the Navy Technical Department related to the US repair ship *Medusa* and the British repair ship *Resource* and submarine tender *Medway*. Analysis of this data was the first step towards the design of the *Akashi*, which used the USS *Medusa* as its model. The internal arrangements and the positioning of machine tools in the various workshops were fully studied by making full-size wooden models at Sasebo Navy Arsenal and thus *Akashi*'s capacities were an improvement over its prototype.

Since it was considered that this ship must also have some salvage facilities, the next problem was the proportion of her facilities to be devoted to this task. Study of salvage records suggested that the minimum requirement was to be able to secure a damaged ship alongside, make it water-tight, pump out flooded compartments and finally make the necessary repair. In the case of very substantial damage *Akashi* would only give 'first aid' and anything more serious was to be done by dedicated salvage ships. It was decided to give limited salvage facilities to this ship and in service *Akashi* had many opportunities to use them.

The design was discussed and finalised in the Technical Conference of April 1936, about two years after the formal

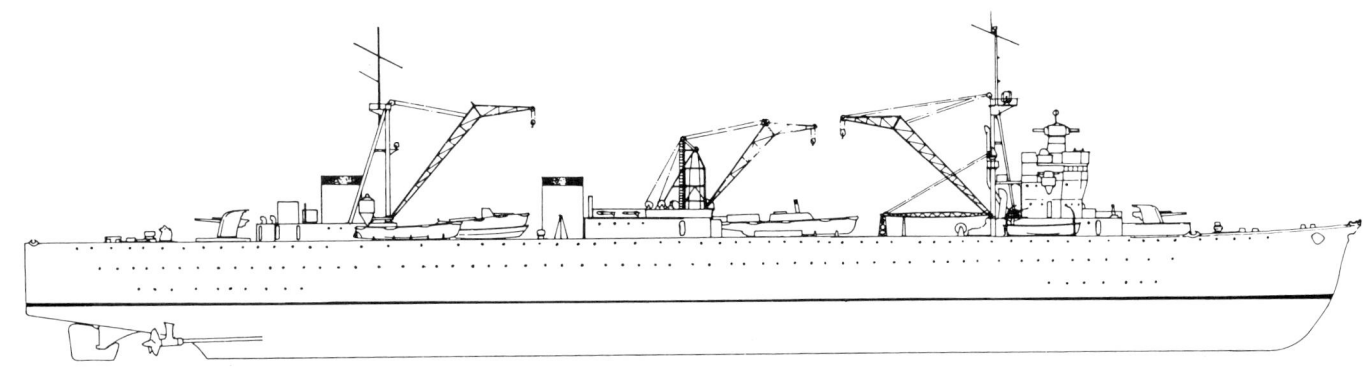

General arrangement of Akashi *as completed. (*Drawing by Takao Ishibashi*)*

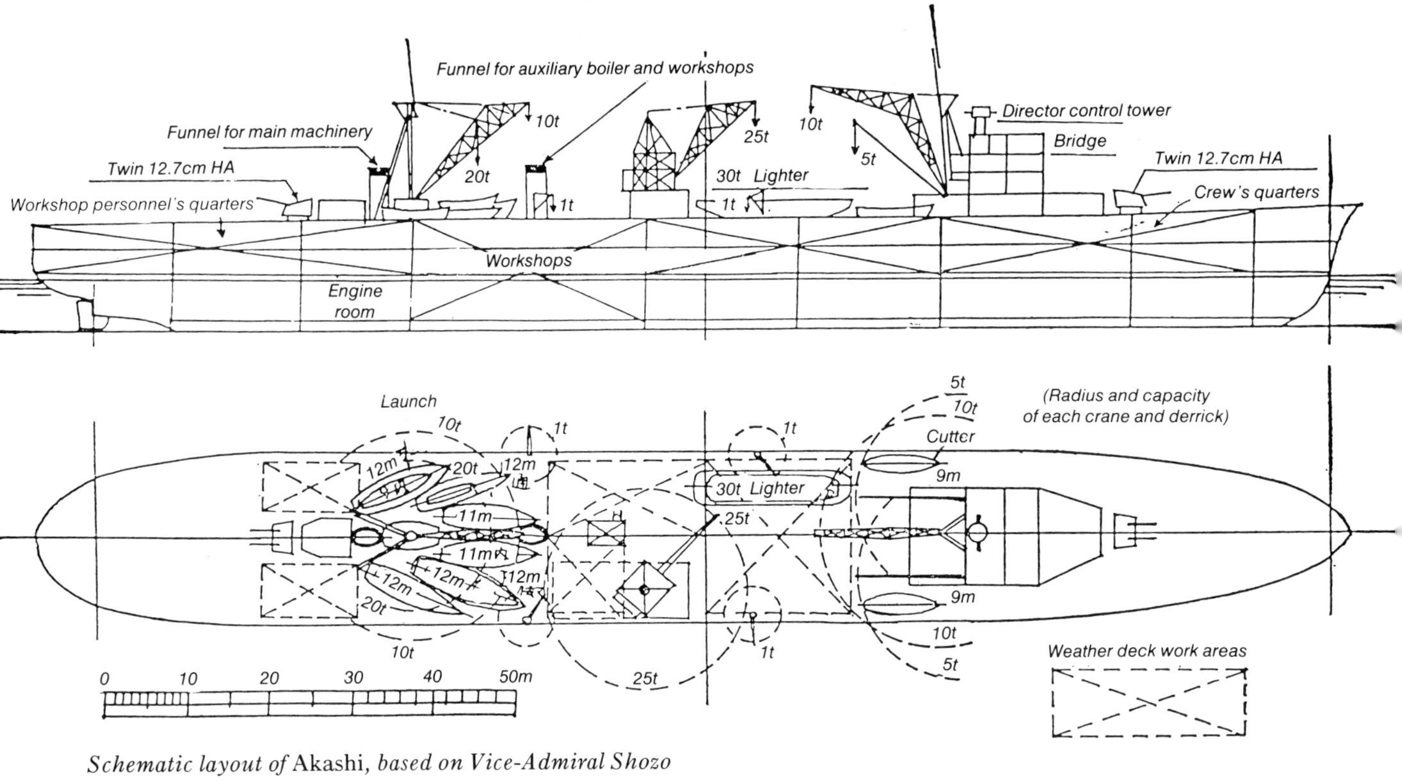

Schematic layout of Akashi*, based on Vice-Admiral Shozo Niwada's* Kenkon Hiwa.

order to proceed. It turned out to be a large vessel, like USS *Medusa*, and intended to be capable of independent action for three months without resupply of material or fuel.

The keel was laid at No 1 berth of Sasebo Navy Arsenal on 18 January 1937. When the ship was launched on 29 June 1938 and named *Akashi* she was the largest vessel ever launched from this slip and also the last of this size. Her length was 158.5m (520ft), practically the same as a *Kuma* class light cruiser of the Taishō Era (1912–1926) and it was considered that this was the absolute maximum size that could be built there. For this reason Vice-Admiral Shōzō Niwada had recommended building her in a drydock in order to avoid possible difficulties with the launch; fortunately the launching went off without incident. It was, incidentally, the last launching ceremony open to the public at this Navy Yard.

Fitting out began soon after launching and was completed within about one year when *Akashi* was officially completed and commissioned on 31 July 1939. The completed ship displaced about 500 tons less (including fabrication material) than designed and the official displacement was revised to 10,500 metric tonnes in trial condition and the stability was also improved. This was unusual in the IJN at this time where ships generally exceeded the planned displacement by 5 to 10 per cent. Also noteworthy is that *Akashi* was painted in naval grey, unlike the special service ships whose hulls were black.

Table 1. STABILITY (REPORT ON AKASHI, 1 AUGUST 1939)

Condition	Initial design			Revised design		As built	
	Light	Trial	Full	Trial	Full load	Trial	Full load
Displacement (long tons and metric tons)	8288	11,000	11,516	10,500	11,046	10,317	10,853
KG (m)	–	7.10	–	–	–	–	–
GM (m)	0.52	1.54	1.60	1.80	1.96	1.53	1.70
GZ, max (°)	–	58	–	–	–	–	–
OG (m)	3.19	0.39	−0.02	0.41	0.0	0.77	0.35
Range (°)	85	116.6	119.5	122.0	120.0	114.2	117.2
Side area $\frac{\text{above Wl}}{\text{below Wl}}$	–	1.667	–	1.77	–	–	–
Roll period (sec)	11.6						

Notes: At the time of the Technical Conference (April 1936) it was decided that
(1) trial condition should include 240 tons of fabrication material in the workshops
(2) two supplementary light load conditions were to be used: (A) and (B) with the following stability data

	Displacement	GM	OG	Range
(A)	8613	0.72	2.78	91
(B)	9259	1.06	2.00	99

Light condition (A) is the state in which the ship carries 325 tons of water, ballast; light condition (B) is (A) plus 646 tons of water ballast.

Appearance and general arrangement

Akashi's very specific duties were reflected in her unusual appearance. In order to have space for the workshops the depth of the hull was great, with high freeboard and comparatively deep draughted, surmounted by a flush upper deck, the latter also being very convenient for fabrication work. The superstructures were reduced to the minimum for the same reason and in fact she had more space than the USS *Medusa*. Most prominent were the derricks of many sizes concentrated around the midship working places and the large number of boats of various kinds around the mainmast. The bridge was the warship type with a 4.5m rangefinder on top. One 12.7cm HA gun mounting was placed in front of the bridge and one abaft the after tripod mast.

The upper deck was divided into areas for the Ship Section and the Repair Section, and internally the ship followed this distinct partition. The middle and lower decks were mostly occupied by the Repair Section (workshops and living compartments) and only the fore compartments of these decks were allotted to the ship's crew. Some small workshops were also in the hold which was mainly used for the storage of material, etc.

Structure

The structure of the *Akashi* was essentially that of an unarmoured warship even though classified as a special service ship. Great attention was paid to the simplification of the structure in order to reduce the building costs and resulted in the saving of nearly 400 tons of weight. Despite this it was something of a half measure when compared with the degree adopted during the war and the authors of *Kaigun Zosen Gijutsu Gaiyō* express their regret that the designers did not make a full study of structural simplification.

Weight breakdown

The weight distribution of this ship is given in detail in Table 4 in order to show her remarkable features. Apart from the hull, the major proportion of the weight was given over to the workshops and material store, amounting to more than 20 per cent of the total. The workshops were the *raison d'être* of this ship so this seems quite natural, but when compared with, say, the armament of a battleship (roughly 17 per cent in *Yamato* class), it becomes evident how much space and weight was allotted for industrial purposes.

The fittings were also divided into Ship Section and Repair Section. This was a fundamental way of thinking in the IJN (later repeated in survey ship *Tsukushi*) but from the viewpoint of economy and efficiency such discrimination should have been avoided. This weight group consisted of mainly steering arrangements, boat davits and winches, piping arrangements, ventilation, communications (doors, hatches, companionways), deck and outboard fittings, heating, lighting, accommodation, etc.

The weight allowed to both equipment groups was nearly 7 per cent and this was much greater than the 1.5 per cent of *Yamato* and the 2 per cent in heavy cruisers. The fixed equipment was principally anchors, anchor chains, hawsers, masts, spares, derricks, davits and this

Table 2. MANOUEVRABILITY (REPORT OF TRIALS OF AKASHI, 1 AUGUST 1939)

(1) Turning

Condition	Revised design	As built	
Displacement (metric tons)	10,500	10,304	
Speed (8/10 full)	17.9	17.5	
Rudder angle (°)	35	34.1 (starb)	34.2 (port)
Max heel (°)	4.5	3.8	3.7
D_T/L	3.5	3.1	3.3
D_A/L	3.2	3.2	3.0

(2) Speed

Condition	Initial design	Revised design	As built
Displacement	11,000	10,500	10,317
Shp	10,000	10,000	10,107
Rpm	157	157	161.4
Speed	19.00	19.20	19.38

Notes: 1. D_T/L = Tactical diameter/waterline length
2. D_A/L = Advance/waterline length
Distance/per ton of fuel at 14kts = 19.2 miles
Manoeuvrability becomes dangerous going full astern at 11kts, rudder angle 25° and pressure 105kg/cm^2.

Table 3. CHARACTERISTICS

Principal dimensions

Length, overall (m)	158.50
Length, waterline (m)	154.66 (152.00 in original design)
Length, between perpendiculars (m)	146.60
Breadth at Wl (m)	20.50
Depth (m)	14.00
Standard displacement (long tons)	9000
Standard draught (m)	6.29
Trials displacement (metric tons)	10,500 (11,000 in original design)
Trials draught (m)	6.55
Main engines	Two Yokohama MAN type 60 multiple double-acting diesels
Number of shafts	2
Rpm	157
Shp	10,000 (5000 × 2)
Boilers	Two Ro Gō Kampon shiki heavy oil burning auxiliary boilers
Fuel (full) (metric tons)	1493 (1420 in original design)
Radius (nautical miles/kts)	8000/14
Speed (kts)	19.2
Generators	Eight AC 600 KVA, 450, diesel
Armament	Four 12.7cm L/40 type 89 HA (2 × 2)
	Four 25mm L/100 type 96 AA MG (2 × 2)

Building data

Building Yard	Sasebo Navy Arsenal
Laid down	18 January 1937
Launched	29 June 1938
Completed	31 July 1939
Sunk	30 March 1944 by enemy air attack at Palau
Deleted from Navy List	10 May 1944

Table 4. *WEIGHT BREAKDOWN*

	Full load (metric tons)		
	Initial design	Percentage	As built
Hull	4550.00	39.54	4174.00
Fittings	700.00	6.07	635.00
Workshops	2320.50	20.14	2419.20
Equipment, fixed	316.70	2.75	354.50
Equipment, consumable	460.80	4.00	453.60
Guns	117.00	1.02	113.70
Torpedo	74.20	0.60	74.90
Aviation, Optics			10.80
Electrical	556.90	4.8	340.00
Wireless			4.80
Engines	1049.00	9.1	1050.00
Heavy oil	1100.00	9.6	1134.40
Light oil (gasoline)	20.00		39.50
Lubricants	65.00	1.01	77.70
Reserve water	32.00		31.00
Contingency margin	158.30	1.37	122.90
Total	11,520.50	100.00	11,036.30

ship had many heavy duty derricks and cranes. The ship's boats also belonged to this heading and *Akashi* had nearly twice as many boats as ordinary warships. Consumable equipment covered stores, comestibles, the crew, personal effects, provisions, fresh water, medical stores, etc, and she had a much larger complement for the Repair Section than was normal for a ship of this size. The equipment and fittings related to loading and unloading are a very important factor for a repair ship, but in the case of *Akashi* the size and number of derricks, the dimensions of the hatches and the number and types of the ship's boats were more than adequate, even though design weight for these items was exceeded.

The gun armament was very weak because of the particular duties of this ship, but in other areas the design included some notable features. The torpedo facilities, for example, included an air compressor (*Tokuyō asskūki*) and its generator for fuelling the top secret oxygen torpedo. The electrics ratio was 3.12 per cent in the completed ship – much less than designed, but still larger than the 1.6 per cent of the *Yamato* and the 2.5 per cent to 3 per cent in heavy cruisers. The main reason was the eight diesel generators (450v, triple-phased, 600kva) mostly used for the operation of the machine tools and electric welding.

Machinery weights were rather large compared to the output, even allowing for the two auxiliary boilers. Here the discrimination between the Ship Section and Repair Section was also evident in the use of the boilers and the funnels. The after funnel was for the main propelling machinery, but the fore one was solely for the workshops which needed the steam for several purposes other than the heating of accommodation.

This was the first design of a ship of this type undertaken by the Japanese so a large contingency reserve of tonnage was allowed, which had not been employed previously in conventional ship design, even if it was somewhat reduced during the actual construction.

Workshop facilities

The workshops inside the hull had a deck area of 2424m² and those on the upper deck 675m², making a total of 3099m² compared to the 2831m² of *Medusa*. The upper deck also made a significant contribution to the total area of 9658m² as against *Medusa*'s 8998m²; 32 per cent of the total area of the ship was allotted to the workshops and a further 2558m² was used for the storage of all kinds of material, semi-finished products, replacement parts, etc, making a total of roughly 58 per cent of the deck area for the Repair Section.

There were twenty-three large and small workshops in total. The seventeen main shops inside the ship occupied 2236m² of the deck area and they were equipped with 114 machine tools of the most modern type, including some German made (as against 109 in *Medusa*). The most important workshops were the forge and metal plate factory, machinery workshop, casting foundry, finishing and fabrication factory, welding shop, copper workshop, hardening factory, carpenter's shop, and workshops specialising in electrical equipment, weapons (gun, torpedo, optics), radio and electronics, and navigational instruments; there was also a material testing room, a drawing office, a blueprint room, and so forth.

In the forge and metal plate factory there was a 350-ton hydraulic press and punching machine, a plate-bending machine, a cutting machine, and so on. Most of the aforementioned 114 machine tools were in the machinery workshops – 62 in total, including an 8m lathe. The

Table 5. ELECTRIC DERRICKS ON THE UPPER DECK

Load capacity (tons)	Number	Location	Use
25	1	Superstructure amidships, starboard	For heavy lift
10	2	Mainmast (1)	For boats
		Foremast (1)	General
5	2	Aft of the bridge	General

Table 6. BOATS

Type	Hp	For ship	For workshop	Total	CA
11m motor boat	60	1	1	2	1
9m motor boat	30	–	1	1	1
12m motor launch	30	1	2	3	2
12m transport boat	30	–	1	1	–
12m *Temmasen* (for divers)	30	–	1	1	–
9m cutter		2	–	2	3
6m transport boat		1	–	1	–
30-ton lighter (self-propelled)		–	1	1	–
Total		5	7	12	7

Note: The boats of a heavy cruiser (CA) given for comparison.

foundry was equipped with 13 furnaces for cast steel and iron and also with a high frequency electric furnace for alloys. Overhead cranes of 5 tons and 3 tons lifting capacity and 3-ton jib cranes were used for transportation purposes in the workshops where necessary.

Compared with *Medusa*, the only inferior point was the forge and metal plate factory whose deck area was roughly 60 per cent of that in the American ship. The designers feared that *Akashi* could not provide the well-balanced fabrication capacity needed of a fleet repair ship and, in fact, there were sometimes complaints about this facility. However, the ship could produce articles of forged and cast iron as heavy as 1 ton and steel structures of about 20 tons.

These workshops employed more than 400 men under the direction of the Chief of the Repair Section. They were specialists covering all aspects of shipbuilding, marine engineering, and weapons production, and it was calculated that *Akashi* could manage about 40 per cent of the general repair work for the Combined Fleet in peacetime, estimated at about 350,000 man-days.

The material, instruments and consumable articles for fabrication, repair and salvage included, for example, 930 tons of material which was estimated to be sufficient for three months' repair without resupply, plus thirteen portable discharge pumps for salvage with a total capacity of about 3000 tons per hour. Every kind of anchor, anchor chain, steel hawser, sinkers, and buoy were also carried.

Service history

Following completion in July 1939, *Akashi* went to Kure to finish her trials and joined the Combined Fleet on 15 November, where she was responsible for most of the general repair work during 1940 and 1941. In the early months of the Pacific War, she carried out repairs at Palau (6 December – 2 January 1942), Davao (4 January – 15 February), Staring Bay (18 February – 27 March) and Ambon (28 March – 23 April), before returning to Kure for a short refit.

She was based at Truk from 4 June until February 1944, with occasional trips to Kure for replenishment or refit. *Akashi* was not damaged in the heavy air attacks by TF-58 on 17 and 18 February, but it was decided to transfer her to Palau. Ironically, there she was sunk on 30 March by the same TF, and the wreck lay abandoned until raised for scrap in 1954.

Notes to Table 7

Notes: 1. Mainly for the shipbuilding division.
2. Mainly for the weapon division.
3. Commonly used by all divisions.
No number. Mainly for the engine division.
Su type = 2 Schneider or Sperry type gyro compass [original source not clear].
An type = Armstrong type gyro compass.

Sources: 1. *Kaigun Zosen Gijutsu Gaiyo*, Vol 4, p850.
2. Vice-Admiral Shōzō Niwada, *Kenkan Hiwa*, p95.
3. Rear-Admiral Yoshiyuki Amari, *Progress of the engines of IJN after WWI*. (3 cited in 1).

Table 7. OUTLINE OF FABRICATION CAPACITY

Workshop	Location	Area (m²)	No of principal machines	Notes
(1) Internal workshops				
No 1 Machinery	Lower deck	520	42	Large machine factory, one 3-ton overhead crane
No 2 Machinery	Lowest deck	110	20	Small machine and tool factory
No 1 Fabrication	Lower deck, port	140	2	Fabrication and finishing shop equipped with pressure meters, oil pressure test pumps, shore hardness tester, 10-ton material tester, etc.
No 2 Fabrication	Middle deck	80 (excl passage)	6	
No 1 Casting	Hold	248	10	Melting and casting factory, one 5-ton overhead crane, high frequency electric furnace, etc
No 2 Casting	Lowest deck, starboard			Core factory
No 3 Casting	Lowest deck, port	100	3	Sand treatment
Forge and plate	Lower deck	305	14	One 350-ton hydraulic press, one 3-ton jib crane, etc
Tool room	Lower deck, port of No 1 Machinery Shop	35		
Welding	Middle deck, port	100	9	All kind of welding apparatus acetylene generators, etc
Copper	Middle deck, port	100	4	–
Forging	Upper deck, starboard	75	18	Air forging, each one unit of ⅙ and ⅒ tons
Wood[1]	Middle deck, starboard	170	13	
Electric[2]	Lower deck, starboard	100	8	
Wireless[2]		50		
Weapons[2]	Middle deck, port	110	8	Guns, torpedoes, optics
Navigation[2]		13		
Su type Gyro Room[2]		10		
An type Gyro Room[2]		13		
Sonar, Hydrophone[2]		15		
Steel hardening process[3] (inc material testing room)	Lowest deck	80	2	
Photo[3]		15		
Blueprint[3]	Middle deck	10	1	
Drawing[3]		25		
Total (1)		2424	160	
(2) Workshops on deck				
Steel plate[1]	Upper deck amidship within the range of the heavy crane	555		Cast iron, copper
Weapon[2]		120		Torpedo cleaning, control station for vertical rudder of submarines
Total (2)		675		
Grand Total		3099	160	

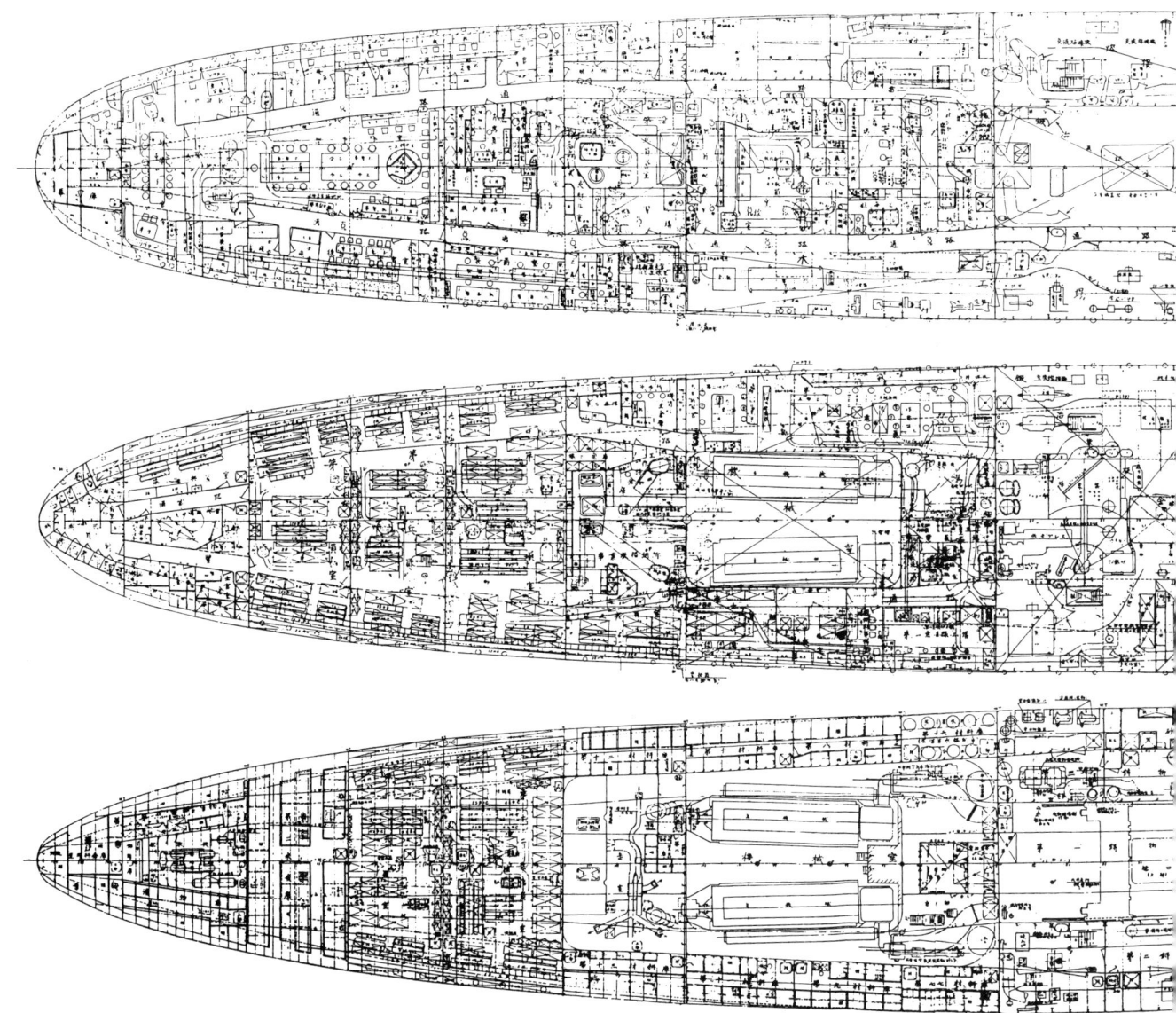

AKASHI

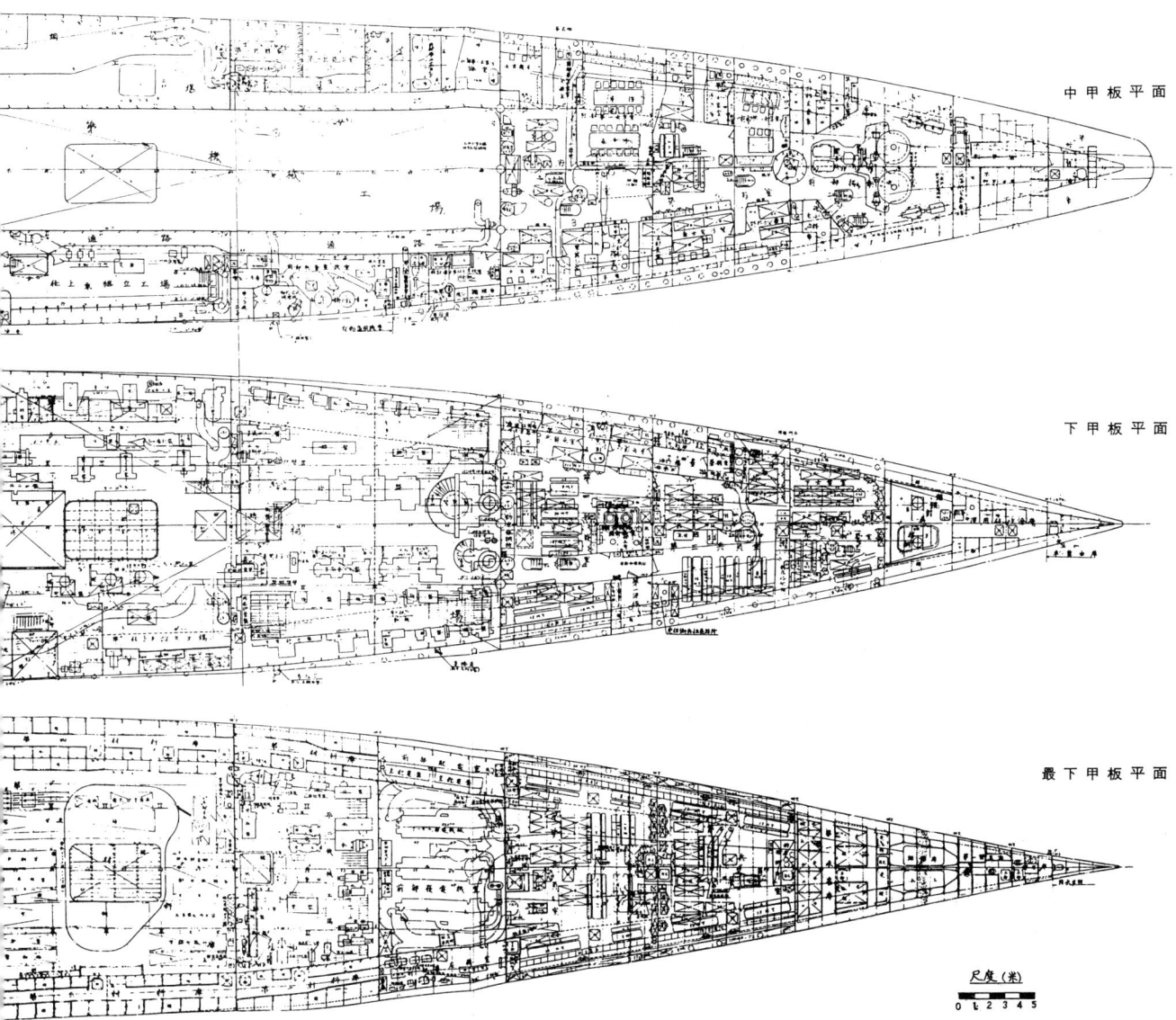

中甲板平面

下甲板平面

最下甲板平面

尺度(米)
0 1 2 3 4 5

The original general arrangement drawings of Akashi. *(By courtesy of Hans Lengerer)*

Table 8. COMPLEMENT

	Initial design	Actual
Ship's crew		
Officers and warrant officers	24	31
Petty officers and ratings	275	305
Total	299	336
Workshops		
Officers and engineers, incl chief of factory	13	13
Special duty officers, warrant officers, junior engineers	20	19
Repair and construction petty officers and workmen (each division total)	400	400
Total	433	432
Grand total	732	768

Table 9. WEIGHT BREAKDOWN FOR WORKSHOPS

	Full load (metric tons)		
	Initial design	Percentage	Actual
Total weight	2320.50	20.2	2419.20
Machines (for fabrication)			534.0
Tools			26.0
Transport system			46.0
Ventilation	643	(5.6)	17.0 } 664
Smoke ducts and funnel			8.0
Piping system and fittings			15.0
Water and oil			18.0
Material, instruments, and consumable articles for fabrication, repair and salvage	1677.5	(14.6)	1755.2
including			
Lubricants			(18)
Water			(80)
Distilled water			(10)
Light oil			(10
Heavy oil			(320)
Coal			(10)
Cokes			(5)
Charcoal			(5)

During her active career she had assisted such famous names as the battleship *Yamato* (following torpedo damage), the heavy cruiser *Mogami* and a host of destroyers and smaller craft. However, as an example in detail of the work of a wartime repair ship, the urgent repair of the light cruiser *Agano* is noteworthy. While at Rabaul on 11 November 1943, *Agano* was hit by an aerial torpedo which damaged her inner propeller shafts, but during the transfer to *Akashi*'s base at Truk, the cruiser was torpedoed again, by the submarine *Scamp*. This hit, on the No 3 boiler room, disabled *Agano* and she had to be towed to Truk.

On arrival at Truk *Agano* was on the point of sinking, with only 1m of freeboard remaining, and part of the transom, both inner shafts and the rudder blown away. A 12m × 7m hole caused by the submarine torpedo had damaged Nos 1 and 3 boiler rooms and 2 and 4 were also flooded. The most pressing task was to stop further flooding, but there was no suitable drydock at Truk so the *Akashi*'s Repair Section had to fabricate and fit a cofferdam approximately 15m long by 7m. Fitting this was tricky, but with the aid of a 25-ton floating crane, four cables were passed around *Agano* transversely and another four longitudinally. By adjusting these, the cof-

Two close-ups of Akashi's *superstructure. (By courtesy of Hans Lengerer)*

ferdam was positioned accurately and welded into place by divers.

Two 300-ton per hour pumps were set to work, but the water level did not reduce. On investigation, divers discovered many splinter holes in the bottom plating caused by near-misses during air attacks at Rabaul. Once these were stopped, the ship was pumped dry in three days. However, further splinter damage to the longitudinal bulkhead had caused the flooding of Nos 2 and 4 boiler rooms. The turbines were undamaged, so although there was no time to repair boilers 2 and 4 and no question of replacing the inner propeller shafts, the ship could be got under way by using boilers 5 and 6 and the outer shafts.

The major difficulty was the lack of a rudder, and a pair of oval jury rudders were fabricated and fitted to the damaged after end of the hull. Trials in Truk lagoon were satisfactory and so, despite the threat of further air attacks, the decision was taken to return the ship to Japan for full repairs. *Agano* sailed on 16 February 1944 escorted

The crew of Akashi *photographed at Truk, probably in October 1942. The damaged heavy cruiser* Aoba *is alongside. (By courtesy of Hans Lengerer)*

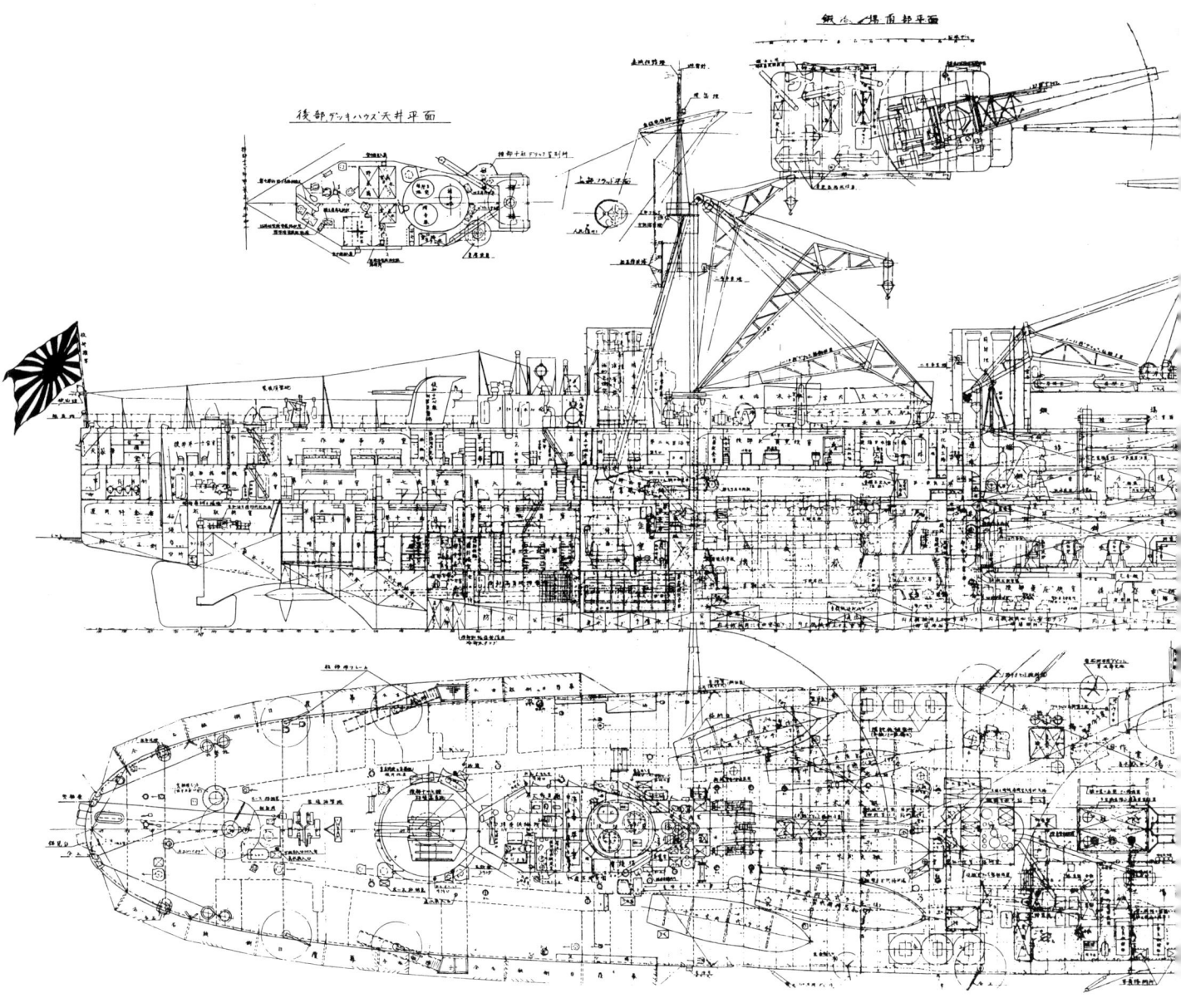

by the destroyer *Oikaze* and the sub-chaser *Ch 28*, but was promptly torpedoed by the US submarine *Skate* on the same day. Two hits reduced the cruiser to a blazing wreck, which sank early the following day. In this case *Akashi*'s good work was wasted, but the example points up the highly sophisticated and ingenious capabilities of Japan's only purpose-built repair ship.

Notes

1. Shōzō Niwada, *Kenkan Hiwa*, p93.
2. The conversion was done at the Kure Navy Arsenal and was completed on 15 August 1937.
3. *Hitonose* ex-*Ming Sen* and *Hayase* ex-*Chin Chiang*. Both belonged to No 1 Naval Repair Yard and operated as salvage and repair ships on the Yangtze river.

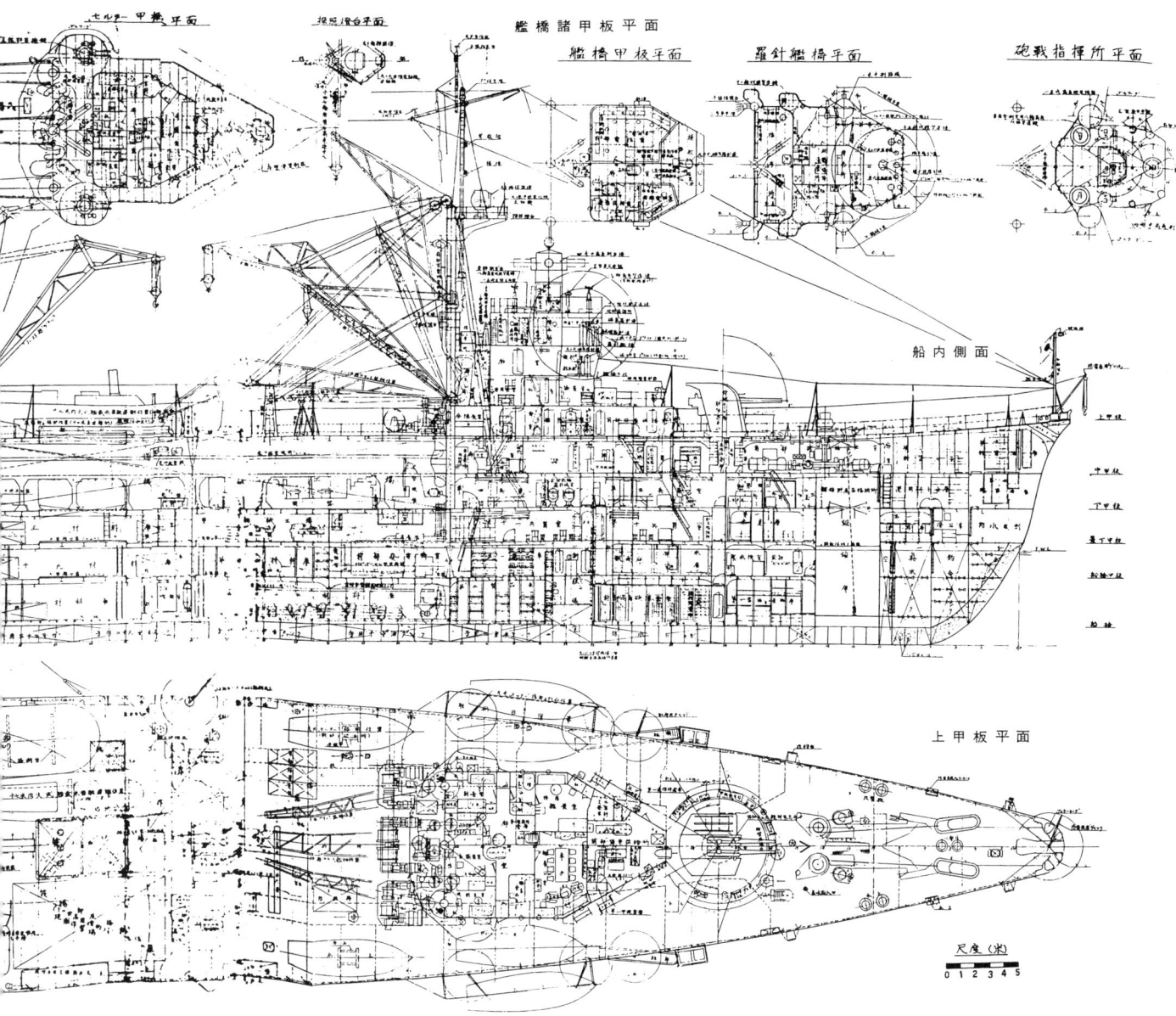

The original general arrangement drawings of Akashi. *(By courtesy of Hans Lengerer)*

Sources

Shigeru Makino, Shizuo Fukui (eds), *Kaigun Zosen Gijutsu Gaiyo* (Outline of Shipbuilding Techniques in IJN), Vol 4. (This work consists of seven handwritten volumes each of about 200 pages and was published between 1949 and 1953.)

Shizuo Fukui, *Nihon no gunkan* (The Japanese Warship), (Tokyo 1963).

Shigeru Makino, Sekina Onozuka, Takashi Yoshida, Shizuo Fukui, *Zosenkan no Kiroku* (Records of Naval Architects), published in 1966 by the Association of Naval Architects.

Shōzō Niwada, *Kenkan Hiwa* (Secret History of [Japanese] Warships).

Tabular Records of various ships (including *Agano*).

Action Records of various ships (including *Agano*).

Maru Special No 34, published by Maru Publishing Group.

Showa Zōsenshi (History of Shipbuilding in Shōwa Era), Vol 1 (up to the end of the war).

Blueprints of the general arrangement drawings of *Akashi*.

THE YORKTOWN CLASS

On 4 June 1942, in the battle for Midway Island, the US Navy aircraft carriers *Yorktown* (CV–5), *Enterprise* (CV–6) and *Hornet* (CV–8) fought together for the last time. The *Yorktown* was lost in the action and within five months the *Hornet* would be lost in the battle for the Santa Cruz Islands. Both absorbed far more battle damage than they were designed to resist. Built within restrictive treaty limitations, the three ships of the *Yorktown* class were arguably the first modern fleet carriers. In this article Robert F Sumrall argues that they were a significant and very necessary step in the evolution of the next and highly successful *Essex* (CV–9) class and even in their loss, the *Yorktown* and *Hornet* supplied important information that would influence future naval tactics and carrier design.

The beginning of the end for the *Yorktown* was just before noon on 4 June 1942 when she was hit by three bombs from aircraft of the Japanese strike force. Fires blazed above and below decks, steam was lost, the ship slowed and finally lost all way. At 14.30, the *Yorktown* was underway again when a second attack wave hit. Two torpedoes breached the carrier's port fuel tanks disabling the ship's generators and causing extensive flooding. Without power, the rudder jammed and it was impossible to restore stability by counterflooding. Within twenty minutes the *Yorktown* was listing 26 degrees. Just before 15.00, the order was given to abandon ship.

Guarded by destroyers, the crippled carrier remained afloat, but on the afternoon of 6 June, she was discovered by the Japanese submarine *I–158*. Manoeuvring through the destroyer screen, the *I–158* was able to fire a spread of four torpedoes, two of which found the carrier. By dawn on 7 June, she was listing beyond the point of recovery and at 06.00, the *Yorktown* rolled over and sank.

Nearly five months later, the *Enterprise* and *Hornet* were operating north of the Santa Cruz Islands. Both ships were at general quarters on the morning of 26 October 1942, when their radar picked up incoming enemy aircraft. The *Enterprise*, with Task Force 16, was steaming under cover of an early morning rain squall. Enemy aircraft did not find her until noon. Ten miles away, however, the *Hornet* and the other ships of Task Force 17 were under clear skies and caught the full force of the morning's assault. Within ten minutes, the carrier was hit by three bombs, two torpedoes and two dive-bombers which crashed on to the ship. The ship was aflame, but of greater seriousness, one of the torpedoes had caused the flooding of the forward engine room and the loss of all electrical power and propulsion. The *Hornet* was dead in the water with a list of 7 degrees.

Under continued enemy attacks, the *Northampton* (CA-26) tried unsuccessfully to take the *Hornet* in tow. Finally, the cruiser was driven off and the *Hornet* was hit again by a torpedo, which this time resulted in the flooding of the after engine room, destroying any possibility of restoring the ship's power. By 16.50, the *Hornet* was listing 18 degrees and the order was given to abandon ship. In the process of evacuating the crew, the *Hornet* was hit twice more by bombs, but she remained afloat. As darkness fell, the destroyers *Mustin* (DD-413) and *Anderson* (DD-411) returned to finish her off so that the *Hornet* would not fall into enemy hands. She had absorbed hits from nine torpedoes and 369 rounds of 5in ammunition when the destroyers abandoned the task in order to escape an approaching enemy force. On their arrival, Japanese destroyers fired four more torpedoes into the *Hornet*, sending her to the bottom at last at 01.35 on 27 October.

Significant in the loss of both the *Yorktown* and the *Hornet* is the fact that they survived extreme punishment to their hulls. That the damage from multiple torpedo and bomb hits and two plane crashes did not sink the *Hornet* is impressive. Like her sister ship the *Yorktown*, the *Hornet*'s resistance to damage exceeded all reasonable expectations. Had it been possible to tow the carriers out of the battle zones, it is very likely that both could have been saved. Beyond what was learned in terms of survivability of the *Yorktown*s, similar losses were prevented from occurring in the future with the addition of fleet tugs and salvage vessels as supporting units of a task force to remove badly damaged ships from the area of battle. The point here, however, is not to study tactical matters, but

The Yorktown *is shown late in the afternoon of 4 June 1942 after she was hit by three bombs and two torpedoes during the Battle of Midway. The order to abandon has been given and she is listing over 20 degrees to port. Still afloat two days later, the* Yorktown *was torpedoed twice more by the submarine I-158. She rolled over and finally sank early on the morning of 7 June.* (All photos: USN)

rather the characteristics of the design of the *Yorktown* class that contributed to their survivability and influenced future carrier construction.

The Northampton *moves into position to take the badly damaged* Hornet *in tow during the Battle of the Santa Cruz Islands on 26 October 1942. During the action, the* Hornet *was hit by four bombs, three torpedoes and two dive bombers crashing into the ship. Towing and salvage operations had to be abandoned. Two American destroyers fired 9 torpedoes and 369 rounds of 5in ammunition into her hull before leaving the battle area. Upon their arrival, Japanese destroyers hit her with four more torpedoes. Shortly after midnight, the* Hornet *finally sank.*

Design background

Naval aviation progressed very rapidly during the First World War. Most of the major naval powers converted vessels to handle aircraft. The British were the first to introduce a vessel having a 'landing deck' which could both launch and recover aircraft when the *Argus* was completed in September 1918. She was the first carrier to have a full length flight deck and a large aircraft hangar. Her design and operational experience influenced the development of the aircraft carrier as we know it today. By the end of the First World War the British had two additional aircraft carriers under construction, the *Eagle* and the *Hermes* (which was the world's first ship to be designed and built as an aircraft carrier).

The next ship to be designed and built as an aircraft carrier was the Japanese *Hosho*, which was the first purpose-built carrier to enter service being completed in December 1922, some fourteen months ahead of the British *Hermes*.

The US Navy benefited greatly from the opportunity to observe British aircraft carrier development during the Great War. In the summer of 1919, the US Navy began its

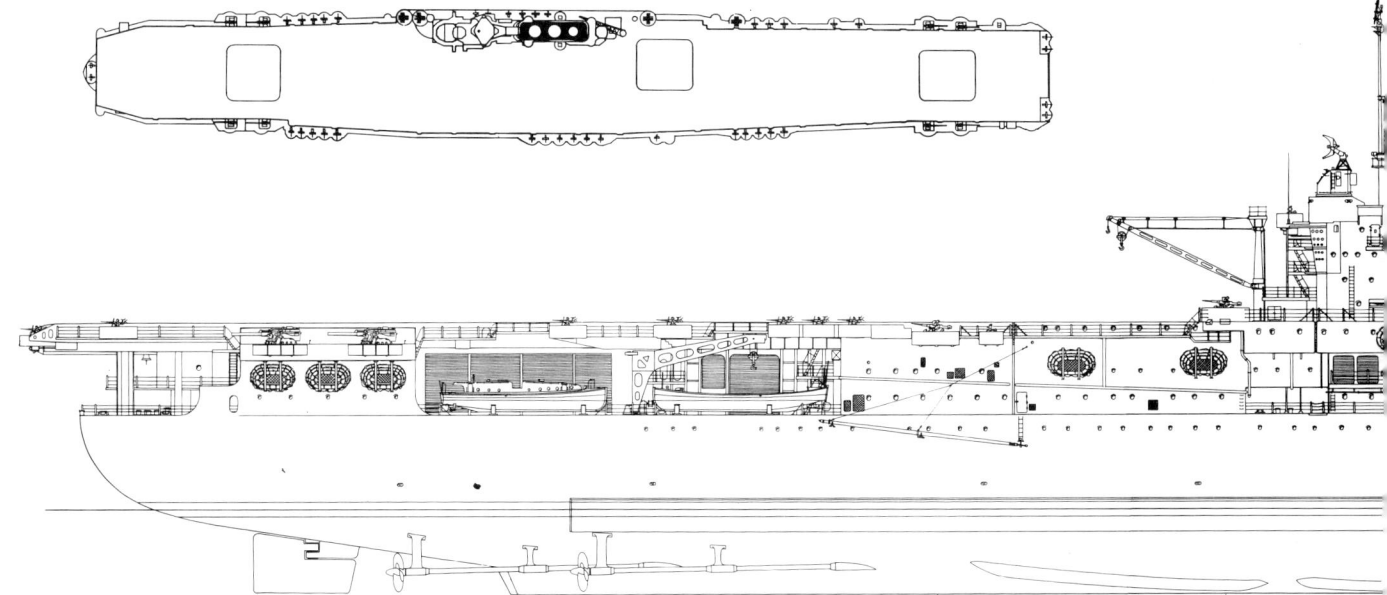

carrier programme with the conversion of the collier *Jupiter* (AC-3) to an aircraft carrier, renamed *Langley* (CV-1). Too small and slow to operate effectively as a fleet carrier, she served to train aviators in take-off and landing techniques at sea and to develop aircraft launching and recovery systems and equipment.

When the Washington Treaty was signed on 6 February 1922, the US Navy was allotted a total of 135,000 standard tons of aircraft carrier construction. Within that total, no single ship could exceed 27,000 tons with the exception that each country could convert two capital ships to aircraft carriers, not to exceed 33,000 tons each. The US Navy used 66,000 tons to convert the incomplete battle-cruisers *Lexington* (CC-1) and *Saratoga* (CC-2).

From 1922 to 1929 the BuC&R (Bureau of Construction and Repair) conducted design studies to determine how the 69,000 tons of aircraft carrier construction remaining under the Treaty could best be spent. By 1927 a five-year shipbuilding programme had been drawn up which recommended the construction of one 13,800-ton carrier a year to use the balance of the 69,000 tons allotted by the Treaty. The plan became part of the Fiscal Year 1929 appropriations (FY 1929).

There was little or no operating experience upon which the new design could be based. Most of the information and experience on launching, retrieving and handling aircraft was obtained from the *Langley*'s operations with the fleet. Not only were the *Lexington* and *Saratoga* much larger, but they did not commission until late in 1927 and contributed little in the way of operational experience for the design of the next carrier.

The BuC&R prepared design plans for the FY 1929 carrier which became the *Ranger* (CV-4). The *Ranger* was completed on 4 June 1934 at 14,500 tons and was the first US Navy carrier designed and built from the keel up as an

The Yorktown *is shown off Rockland, Maine where speed trials were conducted in December 1937. Her light anti-aircraft armament has not yet been installed. Note the clean and graceful lines of her hull. (All photos by courtesy of the author)*

THE YORKTOWN CLASS

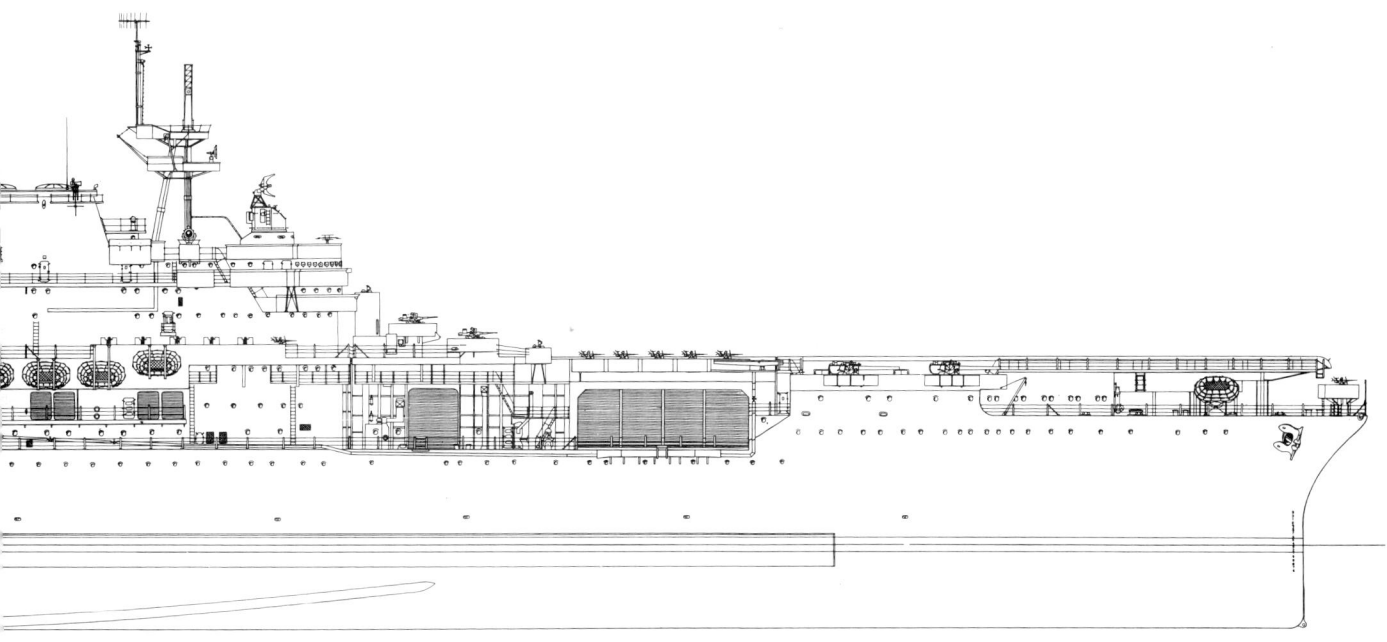

USS Hornet *as outfitted 1942. Inset: Flight deck arrangement for CV-5 class, June 1942.* (Drawings by the author)

aircraft carrier. Although designed from limited operational experience, the *Ranger* incorporated a number of features which would become standard for future US carriers, including an open hangar deck and a gallery deck around and partially under the flight deck. In subsequent years, the Navy was unable to obtain authorization for the planned sister ships of the *Ranger*. In 1933, when the Congress finally authorized construction of additional carriers, it was for larger units.

The *Yorktown*s were the first carriers designed from operational experience with the fleet. Naval operations in the late 1920s had helped to formulate tactics for future carrier operations. They were the first modern carriers to be designed by the US Navy and, even with their design deficiencies, strongly influenced the following CV-9 class. Design of the *Yorktown* class began in May 1931 and was finally completed in 1934. Two carriers were authorized to be built on 16 June 1933. Design work was sufficiently advanced to proceed to the contract stage and on 3 August 1933 contracts for the *Yorktown* (CV-5) and *Enterprise* (CV-6) were awarded to Newport News Shipbuilding which assisted in finalizing the design. A third ship, the *Hornet* (CV-8) was ordered on 30 March 1939. The design had the following basic characteristics:

Displacement	19,900 tons standard
	25,600 tons full
Dimensions	809ft 6in length overall, hull
	824ft 9in length overall, hull and flight deck
	83ft 1in beam at waterline
	28ft 0in draught
Speed	32.5kts
Shaft horsepower	120,000
Aircraft	85–100
Armament	8–5in, 4–1.1in (quad), 24–0.50cal

Characteristics were fixed to meet the requirements for aircraft carriers, as practicable, within the limitations established by the naval treaties then in effect. Because of the multiple roles envisioned for carriers, and the various threats which could be encountered, special emphasis was placed on protection and the ability to remain operational as long as possible after damage. It was recognized that a carrier of 20,000 tons could not be given the same degree of protection against the effects of gunfire, bombing, torpedoes and mining as could the much heavier battleships. It was intended to provide the best degree of protection against torpedoes as possible. Within the imposed limitations, penetration of the shallowest portions of the torpedo defence system had to be expected. This was especially evident regarding hits from the larger more powerful torpedoes carried by surface ships and submarines. Torpedoes carried by aircraft were smaller and considered less effective.

As their battle experience would prove, all three *Yorktown*s suffered severe battle damage and absorbed far more than they were designed to resist. The *Enterprise* survived the war after having been damaged several times. The carriers' performance far exceeded the expectations of their designers.

With the construction of the *Yorktown* and *Enterprise*, the US Navy had a carrier force of 120,300 tons. There remained 14,700 tons from the original Treaty limit of 135,000 tons and in March 1934, the Congress authorized the remaining tonnage to be used for the *Wasp* (CV-7).

The return to the small carrier was a statutory requirement and she became a mixture of the *Ranger* and *Yorktown* designs. The desire was to incorporate as many of the *Yorktown*'s features as possible, but due to the new carrier's limited size, it was necessary to adopt a machinery arrangement with only two shafts similar to that in the *Ranger*. Economy measures of the mid-1930s also took

The second ship of the class, the Enterprise, *is shown on 6 April 1938 returning to Newport News, Virginia after completion of her builder's trials. Note the Newport News Shipbuilding houseflag on the fore topmast.*

their toll. One of three elevators originally planned was deleted. As compensation, a small T-shaped lift was fitted forward on the port side. This introduced the deck-edge elevator to US carrier design.

The *Hornet* was authorized under the Naval Expansion Act of 17 May 1938 providing for 40,000 tons of needed new aircraft carrier construction. She was ordered on 30 March 1939 from Newport News to a slightly improved *Yorktown* design. This basic design was used for the *Hornet* because of the urgency for new carrier construction. The *Hornet* was laid down on 25 September 1939 using about half of the authorized tonnage. She was the last US Navy carrier affected by Treaty limitations.

Design features

The main offensive weapon of an aircraft carrier is its air group, therefore, the primary function of a carrier is the launching, recovery and stowage of aircraft. In order to perform these functions the general arrangement is vastly different from any other type of surface warship. Externally the differences are quite noticeable but internally they are not as apparent, nor is the interrelationship between them as obvious.

Carrier design and general arrangement are determined by the size and configuration of the flight deck which, in turn, is a function of the size of the intended air group. The *Yorktown* class was designed to operate 90 aircraft, but in actual operations, they could only fly off about 81 planes. The decrease was largely because of the growth in the size and weight of first line aircraft during the time the ships were being built. US Navy carrier tactics were to launch a full air group at one time for maximum strike efficiency. For the launching to proceed quickly, it was necessary that the air group be deck-loaded on the flight deck. The aircraft were spotted on the flight deck by weight, including ordnance loads, with the lighter planes forward. The lighter planes required a shorter run to become airborne and some could be catapulted over the bow. Operation of the elevators interfered with operations on the flight deck, therefore, only a limited number of planes could be brought up from the hangar deck after flight operations had begun. The entire design of a carrier, therefore, is intended to accommodate the operations of its air group.

The hull

Underwater, the *Yorktown*s had a moderate bulbous bow to reduce resistance at high speed, a round bilge and a cruiser stern with a single counterbalanced rudder. A fuller bilge would have provided more volume for the side protection system, but could not be accommodated on the limited displacement. Typical bilge keels were fitted and a stub skeg was located on the centreline, which gave the ship more directional stability and helped to support the stern overhang when in drydock. The four three-bladed propellers were supported by struts and an additional bearing support was provided for the long, exposed run of each shaft. Above the waterline, the stem curved forward up to the forecastle deck forming a graceful clipper bow. The shell rose almost vertically from the turn of the bilge and flared slightly before joining the main deck. The cruiser stern was curved upward and was faired into the main deck.

The main, or hangar deck, formed the top of the hull girder. The gallery and flight decks were actually part of the superstructure and did not contribute to the strength of the girder. The flight deck surface was wood laid over light steel plate which served as a fire break. A large portion of the hangar deck was open along the sides, which was the result of the requirement for aircraft to

The Hornet was ordered six years after contracts for the first two ships of the class were awarded. Although a number of improvements were incorporated in her design, the Hornet was essentially the third ship of the class. She is shown here at Norfolk, Virginia on 28 February 1942 shortly before leaving for the Pacific.

warm up their engines before being lifted to the flight deck. The hangar deck could be closed to the weather and/or blacked out for night operations by large roller curtains.

General arrangement

Within the hull proper there were four continuous decks numbered from hangar deck, or 1st deck, down. The 2nd deck was mainly used for accommodation and workshops with almost free access fore and aft. There was also accommodation on the 3rd deck shared with numerous store rooms and workshops, but fore and aft access was somewhat more restricted. Access on the 4th deck was limited to within the main water-tight transverse bulkheads. This deck was mainly devoted to weapons workshops and store rooms; it covered the machinery spaces amidships, the gasoline tanks forward, and magazines on each end of the ship. The 1st and 2nd platform decks extended forward and aft of the machinery spaces below the 4th deck. The lowest deck in the ship was the hold, which supported the foundations for the main machinery and formed the double bottom with the shell of the ship inside the side protection system.

The uptakes from the boilers penetrated the 4th deck and were trunked to starboard where they turned upward and rose through the hull to the flight deck forming the stack portion of the island structure. Forward of the stack in the island was the bridge area for conning and navigating the ship and the control of flight operations. The forward fire control director was directly above the bridge decks and a heavy tripod mast was located between the director and the stack. The island aft of the stack supported the aft fire control director and a stub pole mainmast rose from the aft end of the stack.

Aviation features

The main armament of an aircraft carrier is her aircraft. While by no means complete, this overview of air operations is intended to give the reader a basic understanding of how the aircraft were operated from the carriers. Also included are some of the vital support systems and equipment designed to move, service, launch and recover aircraft in order to achieve an efficient use of the air group.

The Air Group – Composition and Operations

The *Yorktown* class was designed to operate an 84-plane air group and a 6-plane utility unit. The standard prewar

THE YORKTOWN CLASS

▲ *The progress of construction aft is shown in this view taken on 3 January 1940. Looking forward to the machinery spaces, the additional depth of the side protection system is clearly visible. The four round objects half buried in the bottom plating nearest the viewer are the stuffing tubes for the propeller shafts.*

◀ *The* Hornet *begins to take shape in this view also taken on 3 January 1940 at Newport News Shipbuilding. Looking aft, the three bulkheads of the side protective system are in place as are several of her main transverse bulkheads. The inner bottom forward has not yet been plated.*

air group organization was one fighter (VF) squadron, one scouting-bombing (VSB) squadron, one bombing (VB) squadron and one torpedo (VT) squadron. Each squadron included 18 aircraft, plus 3 more in reserve. During the war, the number of aircraft actually carried depended on the mix of types and, later in the war, the *Enterprise* carried an air group equipped for special night operations.

Prewar US carrier doctrine required planes to be warmed-up on the hangar deck and quickly brought up to the flight deck for launching. There was an additional requirement to launch scouting-bombing types from the hangar deck prior to standard flight operations. It was also envisioned that, under certain conditions, aircraft might be required to land over the bow instead of the stern.

During standard flight operations, the carrier would turn into the wind and steam at full power for launching operations. The aircraft were launched over the bow after a deck run from about amidships or by the catapults located on the forward end of the flight deck. The effect of the ship steaming full speed into the wind increased the lift and the effective speed of the aircraft during launching.

During strike operations, the air group would be spotted on the after end of the flight deck with the lightest aircraft forward so that the heaviest aircraft would have the longest run possible and attain the maximum amount of effective speed and lift. The aircraft were armed, serviced and warmed up just prior to launching. The entire air group, or 'deck load', was launched in one operation, clearing the flight deck.

In standard recovery operations, the returning aircraft would land over the stern where they would be caught by one of the arrestor wires. They would then taxi to the forward end of the flight deck for parking. Although the forward elevator could move some of the landed planes to the hangar deck, a jam of planes could not be avoided. If one of the returning planes was damaged, or it appeared that it might miss the arrestor wires, barriers would be rigged to prevent it from crashing into the parked aircraft forward. In case the after portion of the flight deck was damaged preventing recovery, aircraft could be landed over the bow where a set of arrestor wires was also installed as a back-up.

After recovery, those aircraft needing repairs or major servicing were removed to facilities on the hangar deck. The balance of the air group, and any replacements from the hangar deck, would then be spotted on the aft end of the flight deck where they could be readied for the next strike.

Elevators

The *Yorktown* class was equipped with three in-deck aircraft elevators, two on the centreline and one slightly offset. One centreline elevator was located in the forward end of the forward hangar bay and the other was in the after end of the aft hangar bay. The third elevator was installed in the aft end of the centre hangar bay with about two-thirds of its area to starboard of the centreline. The offset allowed aircraft to be moved around the port side of the elevator at both hangar and flight deck levels while the elevator was in operation. At the flight deck level, the centre elevator came up just aft of the island. Each elevator measured 48ft by 44ft and had a 17,000lb lifting capacity. The size and capacity of the elevators reflected the expected growth in aircraft size and weight. The elevators had to lift an empty aircraft to the flight deck for loading and, in the locked-up position, bear the weight of the loaded aircraft as it rolled across during take-off. Most of the standard Second World War aircraft could be handled; however, postwar jets, and heavier attack and ASW aircraft could not be accommodated without increasing the capacity of the elevators.

Catapults

Originally, three H-2 type, flush-deck catapults were fitted. Two were located at the forward end of the flight deck and one was on the hangar deck in the forward hangar bay right aft of the forward elevator. The H-2

hydraulic catapult, developed in the early 1930s, had a 1.8 million ft–lb capacity and could launch a 7000lb aircraft at a speed of 70mph. The function of the flight deck catapults was to assist in putting the main part of the air group into the air quickly. As the ship turned into the wind at speed to launch aircraft, the combined effect of the wind and the ship's speed added to the effect of the catapult, making it possible to launch greater loads than with unassisted take-offs. The purpose of the hangar deck catapult was to allow a scout, or scouts, to be launched without disturbing the aircraft spotted on the flight deck or flight operations if in progress. In wartime operations, the hangar deck catapult was seldom used and it was removed from the *Enterprise* and *Hornet* at Pearl Harbor in June 1942 after the Battle of Midway, the *Yorktown* having gone down with hers in that action.

Arresting Gear and Barriers

When completed, the *Yorktown* class was fitted with arrestor wires forward as well as aft to satisfy the requirement for landing aircraft over the bow in the event of the after portion of the flight deck being disabled. The arresting gear was an improved version of the Mk 4 hydraulic type developed about 1930 and first installed in the *Ranger*. Arresting gear, in contrast to a catapult, is an energy-absorbing device which works on the principle of a ram, displacing fluid from a cylinder into a partially air-filled accumulator. When the landing load is released, the air compressed in the accumulator returns the arrestor wire to the battery position. As in the case of the hangar deck catapult, the forward arrestor wires were never used in actual operations and were also eventually removed from the *Enterprise*.

Wooden barricades, or landing barriers were provided which could be erected during recovery operations to

The Enterprise *is at anchor off Puerto Rico in the photo taken 23 July 1938. One of her earliest air groups is shown which included biplane as well as single-wing types. Note that both rows of her barriers are raised forward, probably as a windbreak for the flight deck judging from her flags standing nearly full. The barriers were intended to stop a plane in the event it could not hook an arrestor wire.*

catch an aircraft which failed to hook any of the arrestor wires. They were intended to prevent a damaged or mishandled plane from crashing into aircraft parked on the forward end of the flight deck during landing operations. They could also be used when recovering aircraft over the bow. By the time the war began, the old wooden walls had been replaced with wire-supported, canvas sling type barriers which were easier on both plane and pilot.

Armament

A carrier's air group, while being the main offensive weapon, was also her main defence against attack, but it was recognized that the carrier would not always be able to defend herself with only the use of her own aircraft. Therefore, guns were still considered necessary, for protection against aircraft which penetrated the Combat Air Patrol, against surface attack at night, or in bad weather when the air group was unable to operate.

Main Battery

When the *Yorktown* class was designed, the type of surface attack envisioned was a cruiser scouting force with 6in and 8in armament. The *Lexington* and *Saratoga* carried eight 8in guns in four twin turrets as allowed by the

THE YORKTOWN CLASS

Washington Treaty of 1922. Two turrets were fitted forward and two aft of the island with wide arcs of fire for each turret. In service, these batteries proved ineffective because they could not fire across the flight deck without causing blast damage. The subsequent London Treaty of 1930 further restricted the maximum gun size for carriers to 6.1in. The US Navy did not have a dual-purpose 6in gun in the early 1930s, nor was one even envisaged at that time. A mixed battery of 6.1in and 5in guns was impossible on the *Yorktown*'s 19,900-ton displacement, so the new dual-purpose 5in/38cal single mount, which had been fitted on the *Ranger*, was selected as the main battery gun.

The 5in/38cal Mk 12 gun, which first appeared on the *Farragut* (DD-348) class destroyers in 1931, was developed for long-range air defence, surface engagement and shore bombardment duties. It was developed from the 5in/25cal Mk X gun which had replaced the 3in/50cal anti-aircraft guns aboard the *Tennessee* (BB-43) and *Colorado* (BB-45) class battleships. The new, longer gun had a greater muzzle velocity, which made it more effective against surface as well as air targets.

Eight 5in guns were mounted, two at each corner of the flight deck. This arrangement necessitated a cut-out at each corner of the flight deck, but the loss of flight deck area was kept to a minimum by fitting the mounts on large sponsons flaired out from the hull and carried up to the gallery deck. The pedestal-type mount was power operated with director control for rapid pointing and training. The gun fired a semi-fixed round with a 54lb projectile and a 28lb shell case, which included a 15lb powder charge. A fuze-setter was mounted on the pedestal to the left and aft of the breech. Fuzes were cut just prior to loading. Ammunition was brought up from the magazines by dredger type chain hoists and stored in ready-service boxes on the sponsons adjacent to the mounts.

Anti-aircraft Battery

When the CV-5 class design was completed, the 5in main battery was intended to handle the long-range air defence; the intermediate and close-in ranges were to be handled by heavy and light machine guns. The heavy machine gun was a 1.1in multiple barrel mount and the light machine gun was the standard 0.50 calibre single. The effective use of aircraft during the Spanish Civil War made it apparent that heavier replacements for both of these weapons would soon be necessary. The Bureau of Ordnance selected the Swedish 40mm Bofors to replace the 1.1in and the Swiss 20mm Oerlikon for the 0.50 calibre. Negotiations began in 1939 and by the end of 1940, an all-out development and manufacturing programme was underway on the new weapons.

The *Yorktown* and *Hornet* were lost too early in the war to have the new 40mm guns installed, but the *Enterprise*, which survived the war, was extensively fitted with them. The development of the 20mm gun, which was smaller

The Landing Signal Officer (LSO) watches, right, as a Dauntless SBD-3 dive bomber returns to the Enterprise *from a raid on the Marshall Islands in early February 1942. The bomber's tail hook is down to catch one of the arrestor wires which have been rigged across the deck. A portion of the after aircraft elevator and an ordnance elevator are in the foreground.*

and considerably less complex, moved more rapidly. It was possible to fit many ships with them early in the war, including the *Yorktown* and *Hornet*. The *Enterprise* carried a large number of them later.

The 1.1in heavy machine gun was a four-barrelled, water cooled, power operated mount which could be director controlled. The first prototype was tested in 1931 but production did not begin until 1934. The gun fired a shell weighing about 1lb at a rate of 140 rounds per minute. In service, the mount experienced a number of difficulties and its tendency to jam after it was warmed up made it unpopular with the operating forces. All three of the *Yorktown*s had four quadruple 1.1in mounts. They were mounted on the starboard side with two each being fitted just forward and aft of the island.

The 40mm gun was an adaptation of the Swedish Bofors which was developed by Krupp near the end of the First World War. It could be mounted in arrangements with single, twin and quadruple barrels. Each gun was capable of firing a 2lb shell at the rate of 160 rounds per minute. The 40mm was considered one of the more potent anti-aircraft weapons of the war. At the end of 1942, the *Enterprise* replaced her 1.1in with quadruple 40mm on a one-for-one basis but by mid-1945, she carried eleven quadruple and five twin 40mm mounts.

The light machine gun was a water cooled version of the standard US Army 0.50 calibre Browning automatic which had been in service since the First World War. It was a free swinging, hand aimed gun in a special, single shipboard mounting allowing it to be pointed and trained with ease. It had a rate of fire of well over 700 rounds per minute, but the projectile weighed only 1.71oz. Although it was a well proven weapon, the small size of the round required a large number of hits to bring down a target and, on many ships, there was just not sufficient space for mounting the number of guns necessary for a satisfactory weight of fire. Still, there was no replacement until the 20mm was adopted, and the 0.50 calibre was used as an anti-aircraft weapon well into the Second World War.

For their time, the Yorktowns *provided a large and reasonably stable platform from which a variety of aircraft could be launched. The* Hornet *is shown launching US Army B-25 bombers on 18 April 1942 for the raid on Tokyo and other important Japanese cities. The striking force, lead by Lt-Col James H Doolittle, consisted of twenty-six of these large twin-engined aircraft.*

The *Yorktown* class had an allowance of twenty-five 0.50 calibre mounts, some of which were unofficially retained after the new 20mm guns were installed.

In many respects, the 20mm gun was similar to the 0.50 calibre that it replaced. Adapted from the Swiss Oerlikon, it was a free swinging mount, requiring no external power source and could be literally bolted almost anywhere. The shell weighed about ¼lb and the gun could fire at the rate of 450 rounds per minute. The gun was produced in single and twin mountings and in experimental triple and quadruple mounts also. In 1943, the twin and triple mountings were tested aboard the *Enterprise*. The twin mount was later produced in quantity, but loading the centre gun of the triple mount proved awkward and further development was discontinued. All three *Yorktown*s were initially fitted with thirty-two single 20mm guns in 1942 at Pearl Harbor. In mid-1944, the number aboard the *Enterprise* had increased to fifty singles and she finished the war with sixteen twins.

Fire control

The ability to track and hit a target quickly and consistently was a very important consideration, especially for the 5in/38cal dual-purpose main battery selected for the *Yorktown* class. Existing hand-trained directors could handle the surface fire control problem, but they were inadequate against the newer, faster aircraft being developed. This led to the development of a new family of power-operated directors: the Mks 33 and 37. It eventually became necessary to develop systems for the anti-aircraft battery also, which resulted in the Mk 14 gunsight and the Mk 44 and 51 directors.

Main Battery

When the *Yorktown* class carriers were being designed, the power-operated Mk 33 director was also under development specifically for use with the new 5in/38cal dual-purpose gun which had been selected as the main armament. The US Navy had two dual-purpose directors for control of the 5in/25cal anti-aircraft gun, the Mk 19 and Mk 28. Both were hand driven, which made target acquisition and tracking of aircraft difficult, so neither could easily be adapted for use with the new 5in gun. The *Yorktown* and *Enterprise* were, therefore, fitted with Mk 33s, but the *Hornet*, which was ordered several years later, received the newer Mk 37s, which had become the standard 5in/38cal director.

The Mk 33 was the US Navy's third generation of long-range, dual-purpose directors, which first went to sea in the *Farragut* class destroyers. It was similar to the Mk 28 in that it used the same model rangefinder, range keeper and stable element. The Mk 33's chief advantage over earlier directors was its power drive which enabled it to provide solutions for higher target speeds and angularity. The range keeper, which was actually a mechanical computer, and the stable element were incorporated into the director proper, which, in effect, limited the growth of the director. To provide solutions for faster moving aircraft, it would have to increase in size and weight. As originally completed, two Mk 33 directors were fitted to the *Yorktown* and *Enterprise*. One was mounted forward and one aft of the stack atop the highest level of the superstructure.

The first US fire control radar for dual-purpose guns was the FD or Mk 4. The set could be fitted to both the Mk 33 and Mk 37 directors. It was very successful against surface and general airborne targets, but the radiating beams produced a side effect which was duplicated in the returning signal. It was also ineffective against low-flying aircraft. The *Yorktown* was lost before the new FD could be installed, but the *Enterprise* was fitted with one set on each Mk 33 director in September 1942.

The Mk 37 director, also designed to control the 5in/38 cal gun against air or surface targets, represented a con-

During recovery operations, as soon as a plane landed it was spotted forward to clear the landing area for the next aircraft. An Avenger TBM-3 is about to touch down aft while others just recovered are being serviced forward. Note the metal tie-down strips, spaced about 4 ft apart, which could be used to secure aircraft in heavy weather.

siderable advancement in capabilities over the Mk 33. The Mk 37 system was comprised of three major units: a director with radar, a stable element, and a computer with associated instruments at the gun. In the Mk 37 the stable and computing elements were located below decks and not in the director as in the Mk 33, which allowed the system to grow considerably. The Mk 37 was a linear-rate system, which measured target position in three coordinates: range, relative bearing and elevation. The *Hornet* was completed with the Mk 37 directors in the same location as the Mk 33s in the earlier ships. The *Enterprise* was fitted with Mk 37s during her mid-1943 overhaul.

FD was radar installed on the *Hornet*'s Mk 37 directors during her post-shakedown overhaul at Norfolk in January 1942. On the *Enterprise*, the FDs from her Mk 33s were fitted to the new Mk 37 directors when they were installed during her July to October 1943 overhaul at Puget Sound. In September 1945, when repaired at Puget Sound after major battle damage, the *Enterprise* received the new Mk 12/22 fire control radar sets for her Mk 37 directors. The Mk 12 was similar in appearance and function to the FD but it reduced the side effect of the returning signal. The Mk 22, often referred to as 'orange peel', was mounted on the right side of the Mk 12. Its function was to track low-flying targets which were obscured on the Mk 12 because of signal reflection from the surface of the water.

The Enterprise *stands out of Pearl Harbor on one of her early war patrols. Note how a censor has skillfully removed her CXAM-1 radar antenna from its position in the foretop. The sponson for her hangar deck catapult can be seen projecting outboard from the side at the forward hangar bay opening. Note how the roller curtains are open enough for personnel to pass under.*

Anti-aircraft Battery

Designed and built by the Naval Gun Factory during the War Emergency period, the Mk 44 was the US Navy's first director for automatic anti-aircraft weapons. It was a simple 'dummy gun' type director which was manually trained and elevated. Intended to control the pointing and spotting of the 1.1in heavy machine gun, which originally used only ring sight and tracer control, the Mk 44 carried optics and a spotting glass but had no lead-angle computing elements. The Mk 44 director was fitted to all three *Yorktown*s in 1941. They were replaced on the *Enterprise* by the new Mk 51s in July 1943 when the ship was overhauled.

The 0.50 calibre machine guns used only ring sight and tracer control but their replacement, the 20mm gun mount, could be controlled by ring sights or the Mk 14 gunsight which was the primary element of the Mk 51 director. Tracers were also used with the 20mm as a means of correcting fire.

The first lead-angle computing mechanism, the Mk 14 gunsight, was developed for use with the 20mm gun. Lead angles were generated by two rate-of-turn gyros, one for train and one for elevation, and a simple computer moved the sight relative to the gun so the gun led the target correctly.

The Mk 51 was also a 'dummy gun' type director developed to control the 40mm gun mounts. It used the Mk 14 gunsight and was trained and elevated with a set of handlebars similar to the 20mm gun. A range estimate was manually set on the side of the director and the lead angles computed by the Mk 14 gunsight were transmitted to the power drives of the 40mm mounts.

place. The SC set was moved to the stub mainmast as a back-up. In addition, a YE antenna was mounted atop the fore topmast. The YE served as a homing beacon for returning aircraft and could identify friendly or enemy aircraft. Both the *Yorktown* and *Hornet* were lost before additional equipment could be fitted.

The *Enterprise*, however, eventually received a radar suite comparable to that of an *Essex* class carrier. By the end of 1942, she mounted the new SG surface search set on her foremast and an SC-1 antenna was bracketed outboard from her stack. During a major refit in late 1943, the CXAM-1 set was replaced by the powerful new SK radar with a range of 100nm (nautical miles). Also added during this period was the new altitude-finding SM radar and a YG antenna as an additional homing beacon. She finished the war in substantially this configuration, except for the replacement of the SC set with the SR radar for greater bearing accuracy.

Radar

There was no consideration given to the installation of radar when the *Yorktown* class was designed, since the principle itself was little known outside the laboratory. Fortunately, the *Yorktown*s had a substantial island superstructure with a heavy tripod foremast and a large stack to support the antennas which they would eventually receive. The nature of carrier operations requires a heavier concentration of radar, communications and electronics than on any other type of ship and it was remarkable how the designers accommodated all of this equipment.

Experimental work conducted by the Naval Research Laboratory in the early 1930s led to a series of radar sets that became operational just prior to the war. The earliest radars were for air and surface search and, although they did not have the precision required for gunnery fire control, could be used for relative target bearing and distance. The *Yorktown* was the first US carrier to be fitted with radar, a model CXAM in July 1940, followed by the *Enterprise* with a CXAM-1 in late 1941. The *Hornet* was originally fitted with the new SC radar at Norfolk in January 1942. The large, tripod-supported foretop was an ideal platform for these sets. The SC proved disappointing in terms of range, and the CXAM set from the battleship *California* (BB-44) was installed on the *Hornet* in its

The Enterprise *is shown in Pearl Harbor in April 1942 for resupply and repair of minor damage by a near-miss bomb explosion during action in the Marshall Islands. Note the large CXAM-1 radar antenna on her foretop and the YE aircraft homing beacon on the topmast. The exterior degaussing cables are also clearly visible just below the side of the main deck.*

The *Enterprise* was also one of the earliest ships to have Airborne Early Warning (AEW) radar capabilities. The system, referred to as Project Cadillac, used a converted torpedo bomber (TBM-3W) to carry a large radar antenna aloft. Flying at 20,000ft, the system could detect a battleship at about 200nm and low-flying aircraft at about 75nm. Signal information was relayed back to the carrier forming a data link, arguably the forerunner of the Naval Tactical Data System (NTDS).

Recognition – IFF

Recognition, or Identification Friend or Foe (IFF), is not radar but a system that is closely associated with radar to provide identification at the point of contact. A Mk III IFF system was installed aboard the *Enterprise* in October 1943. It could identify radar contacts and furnish its identity to challengers by using a number of interrogator–

responsor and transponder units. Coded signals were sent out from the interrogator–responsor units. If the signal was received by a friendly contact, it activated a transponder unit in the contact which sent out a favourable return signal. An enemy unit would be unable to respond with the proper signal or on the required frequency.

The antennas for the interrogator–responsors were mounted on the radar antenna frame which they served. Both signals were sent out and received together but were displayed separately. The transponder antennas were free-standing units mounted as high as possible, usually on yardarms, to avoid signal interference from the ship's structure.

Electronics

Electronic warfare developed almost as quickly as radar itself, because the signals sent out to detect an enemy can also inform him of your presence and the direction of your transmission. The equipment used for electronic warfare consisted of passive devices to intercept and listen to enemy transmissions, units to deceive and jam enemy transmissions and measures to negate the enemy's use of electronics.

During 1945, the *Enterprise* was equipped for signal-jamming and direct noise amplification. Rotating and stationary antennas, from the DBM and AS series, formed the passive part of the system and the active portion used the omni-directional TDY antenna. Aimed in the directions furnished by the passive antennas, the TDY generated a continuous noise which appeared as 'grass' on the enemy's display or a high powered pulse which rendered the enemy's returning signal illegible.

Protection

When the *Yorktown* class was designed, the primary threats were considered to be shellfire from surface ships, bombing from high-level or dive-bombers and torpedo attack by aircraft, surface ships and submarines. The armour and underwater protection systems were designed with these threats in mind but the size of the *Yorktown*s, as limited by the Naval Treaties then in effect, made a number of compromises inevitable.

Armour protection

Heavy armour was provided for protection against surface gunfire and aerial bombing. The carrier's speed, it was reasoned, would enable her to outrun enemy battleships, so the armour was designed to protect against shellfire from cruisers. Japan, the most probable enemy, had a number of 8in and 6in gunned cruisers which were fast enough to engage carriers. It proved impossible to provide protection against 8in fire on the allotted displacement, so the *Yorktown* class was armoured against 6in shellfire.

A 4in side belt approximately 9ft deep was installed in way of the machinery spaces, magazines and gasoline

The Enterprise *is recovering aircraft on 22 November 1943 during the Gilbert Islands operations. Her air group has a number of special 'bat teams' equipped with radar for night operations. Each three-plane, radar-equipped team was composed of one Avenger TBM-3N torpedo plane and two Hellcat F6F-3N fighters. These teams were very successful in combating night attacks against the carriers.*

THE YORKTOWN CLASS

The Enterprise *shows the effects of a near-miss bomb detonation during action in the Eastern Solomons campaign. The degaussing cables were severely damaged, there was considerable structural deformation inboard and the column of water deformed a portion of the overhanging flight deck about 8 in upward.*

stowage tanks. It extended down from the 4th deck to 6ft below the waterline, with the lower 4ft tapering to 2.5in. The side armour was covered over by 1in of armour on the 4th deck at the sides over the tanks of the side protective system and 1.5in of armour over the machinery between the tanks. The ends were closed off by 4in armour bulkheads extending from the 4th deck to the bottom of the ship. The steering machinery aft had comparable protection and lighter protection was given to the uptakes, conning tower and fire control tubes. There was also a limited amount of splinter protection for exposed personnel.

Underwater Protection

Protection against the effects of torpedoes, mining and near-miss bombing was provided by the side protective and double bottom systems. They were both multi-layered and intended to absorb the energy from underwater explosions. The double bottom extended the entire length of the ship and the side protective system covered about the same area as the armour belt – essentially, the vitals.

It was realized that within the size and displacement of the *Yorktowns*, a side protection system of adequate depth could not be provided. The intent was to provide the best degree of protection against torpedoes as possible; therefore, within these constraints, penetration of the shallowest portions of the system had to be expected.

The side protective system consisted of three tanks on the outboard side of the hull extending from the 4th deck down to the turn of the bilge. The tanks were formed by three vertical, longitudinal bulkheads. The innermost was the holding bulkhead and the inner tank was kept void while the outer tanks were liquid-loaded with fuel oil or ballast. In theory the liquid was to absorb the shock of the explosion and stop any fragments. The void was to provide for leakage from the damaged liquid layer. This arrangement was carried as far aft as possible, stepping up and in as necessary for the sharply rising bottom. Protection for the engine rooms was increased by placing an additional bulkhead inboard of the holding bulkhead in the area of the two engine rooms and the after auxiliary machinery rooms. Additionally, the *Enterprise* was blistered during a major refit in October 1943, which considerably increased the depth of her side protective system and improved stability.

Engineering

The engineering areas of the ship are those spaces that house the main and auxiliary machinery, the steering gear, the refrigeration plant, the ventilating equipment, fire-fighting stations, repair lockers, etc. These spaces consume about one-third of the total volume of the ship. This discussion cannot hope to cover all of the machinery that was aboard the *Yorktown* class and is, necessarily, limited to the main propulsion and auxiliaries used to move and service the ship.

Propulsion

The power plant produced 120,000shp (shaft horsepower) which was necessary to meet the 32.5kt speed requirement at 25,600 tons displacement. Steam for the plant was furnished by nine boilers and delivered to four sets of geared turbines. The turbines were direct-coupled to single reduction gears which drove the shafts. The propulsion machinery was arranged in five compartments below the 4th deck with all fire rooms forward and the engine rooms aft. There were nine boilers set three abreast in three rows and each separately enclosed in its own compartment. The first two rows of boilers generated saturated steam to the last row which superheated the steam delivered to the turbines. Two large machinery spaces were located directly aft of this cluster of fire rooms. Both the forward and after machinery spaces contained two sets of geared turbines coupled to their main reduction gears with the forward engines driving the outboard shafts and the after engines driving the inboard shafts.

An alternating fire room/engine room arrangement for the machinery would have been more desirable, but with the uneven number and two types of boilers, such an arrangement was impossible. The arrangement and location of the boilers was a consideration in the topside positioning of the island. The complexity of the uptake leads was thus reduced to a minimum.

The six boilers located forward were of the three-drum, single furnace 'A' type which generated saturated steam at 450psi. The saturated steam was delivered to the three after superheater boilers which raised the steam to 650 degrees F at 400psi. The superheated steam was then delivered to the two engine rooms. The boilers, manufactured by Babcock & Wilcox, were of the new welded steam drum type, which permitted a more efficient arrangement of the tube bank as compared with the older riveted drum type.

Her battle damage repaired, the Enterprise *runs trials in Puget Sound on 13 September 1945. The war with Japan ended on 15 August while repairs were still underway. She steamed west again only to help return the thousands of combat personnel stationed in the vast areas of the Pacific where she had once fought.*

Each turbine set consisted of a high-pressure and low-pressure turbine driving into a reduction gear. The high-pressure turbine was of the Curtiss impulse type, while the low-pressure turbine was of the Parsons reaction type with astern elements to reverse the rotation of the shafts for going astern. Each turbine drove its own pinion which engaged directly the larger main, or 'bull' gear accomplishing the necessary reduction in one step. The turbine sets were manufactured by the shipbuilder under licence from the Curtiss and Parsons companies. The main gears were also manufactured by the shipbuilder for the *Yorktown* and *Enterprise*. In service, however, they proved unsuccessful, primarily because of excessive airborne noise. They were later replaced with a Falk designed and built gear, so that by the time the *Hornet* was ordered, the new gear had proved to be acceptable in the first two ships and was incorporated in her design as well.

Auxiliaries

Electrical power was provided by four 1000kW turbo generators. Two each were located in spaces forward and aft of the main machinery rooms adjacent to their distribution panels. They furnished power to hundreds of electrical motors that operated the ordnance, fire control, radar and aircraft servicing equipment as well as the ship's hotel load. There were also two 250kW diesel generators to provide emergency power if any or all of the ship's service generators failed. The emergency sets had their own compartments, one forward and one aft of the main generating rooms.

The distilling plant was just aft of the aft main generating room and above the emergency generator. The large triple-effect evaporators processed sea water into boiler feed water and potable water for drinking, cooking and personal cleaning.

The steering gear was of the electro-hydraulic, twin ram type. The rams were set fore and aft, angled inboard toward the stern and directly over the rudder stock. A double-yoke tiller was fitted to the top of the rudder stock and each side of the yoke was attached to a ram through a connecting rod and pin. Steering signals from the wheel on the bridge or the secondary conning station were transmitted by an electro-hydraulic transmission system.

Overhaul and refits

The *Enterprise* was in twenty-one different engagements in the Asiatic-Pacific Theatre of operations between 7 December 1941 and 2 September 1945. She was damaged in six of those engagements by a total of six bomb hits, six near-misses from bombs, one dud bomb and two 'friendly' shell hits. Some of the damage was severe, but in all except one case she was able to remain operational. The last time she was damaged, on 14 May 1945, her forward elevator was blown completely out of the ship and she had to retire from the battle area. Even then she was able to recover most of her aircraft.

With the losses of the *Lexington, Yorktown* and *Hornet,*

Early in the morning of 14 May 1945 the Enterprise *was hit by a Kamikaze while operating off the south-east coast of Kyushu, Japan. The plane hit the flight deck just aft of the forward elevator and passed through the flight deck into the elevator pit. The resulting explosion caused structural damage in and below the elevator pit and blew the forward elevator completely out of the ship and caused the* Enterprise *to return to the States for repairs.*

the *Saratoga* and *Enterprise* were the only American carriers in the Pacific in late 1942. Although both were badly in need of overhaul, neither could be spared from combat operations. After the arrival of some of the new *Essex* and *Independence* class carriers in early 1943, *Enterprise* was released for refit.

The *Enterprise* received a complete overhaul at the Puget Sound Navy Yard from July to October 1943. Of major importance was the fitting of a blister and the reworking of the gasoline storage tanks. Blistering was considered necessary in order to increase displacement and improve stability to compensate for the considerable additions to the light anti-aircraft battery, fire control systems, radar and electronics gear and the newer, heavier aircraft she was about to receive. While the blisters were being installed, material improvements in the gasoline storage system were accomplished at the same time.

A 6ft bulge was added to each side of the ship between the forward and after armoured bulkheads covering the area protected by the armour belt. It extended from the main deck down around the turn of the bilge and was faired smoothly into the hull forward and aft. The effect was to increase the displacement by 6576 tons to 32,060 tons in the fully loaded condition. An extra benefit of the blistering was the additional depth gained by the side protection system.

The improvements made to the gasoline storage tanks required some major structural changes including modifications to the inner bottom. The old cellular-type tanks were removed and replaced with saddle-type tanks which had recently been developed as an improvement for the *Essex* class gasoline storage system. The new system consisted of a large centre tank surrounded on the sides and top with another tank fitted over like a saddle. The saddle

tank was in turn surrounded in similar fashion by a cofferdam. This provided a greater measure of protection for the volatile liquid against underwater attack, shells, bombs and splinters.

A number of other improvements were also made as a result of experience gained in combat operations. These included the revision of the entire ventilation system, improved fire-fighting facilities, reworking of the aircraft fuelling system and the installation of internal degaussing cables.

With these improvements accomplished, the *Enterprise* was brought up nearly to the standards of the *Essex* class. When the war ended, the *Enterprise* was again at Puget Sound for the repair of bomb damage delivered by a 'Kamakazi' in May 1945. After the war, efforts by the state of New York to preserve her as a war memorial never materialized. On 17 February 1947, she was laid up

This row of carriers, photographed on 16 November 1945, at the Naval Air Station, Alameda, California represents all of the major types which served in the Pacific during the Second World War. From left to right are the Saratoga, Enterprise, Hornet (II) and San Jacinto. This was the last time the Enterprise and her contemporaries, the warhorses of the Pacific, appeared together.

in reserve at the Bayonne annex of the New York Navy Yard. She was reclassified as an Anti-Submarine Warfare (ASW) support carrier (CVS) in 1949. No work was ever done towards her CVS designation and on 2 October 1956 the *Enterprise* was declared surplus and stricken from the Navy List. She was sold for scrap on 1 July 1958 and broken up at Kearney, New Jersey.

AIRCRAFT TO MALTA

The role of USS *Wasp* and Operation 'Bowery' is well known to most students of the Second World War, but this was only one of a succession of such operations carried out by the Royal Navy. Roger Nailer outlines these sorties, and reveals the considerable cost and hazard to the Navy of these missions which, in the final analysis, barely maintained the island as a viable base.

Most readers will recall 'Faith', 'Hope' and 'Charity', three Sea Gladiators which, flown by RAF bomber pilots, initially formed the sole air defence of Malta from June 1940. Quite shortly after the start of hostilities with Italy, reinforcements of Hurricanes were flown in by *Argus*, with a second batch over three months later. Tragically, two-thirds of the second flight never arrived in Malta. From April 1941 the tempo of reinforcement increased with the fleet carriers becoming involved. At this juncture the Royal Navy was obliged to use *Argus* and occasionally *Furious* as ferry carriers from Britain to Gibraltar, being thus deprived of the services of those ships (*Argus* was much needed as the sole training carrier available, while *Furious* was – and would be until 1944 – a front-line carrier). Once at Gibraltar, Force H was obliged to conduct a major operation to convey the ferried aircraft to within flying range of Malta, *ie* to within attack range from the Axis forces. During this period the deck park of non-folding aircraft precluded any reconnaissance or defence by the carriers concerned, which were only too often the only carriers present. It is remarkable that the Royal Navy managed to escape unscathed from these ventures so far as loss was concerned (apart from the sinking of *Ark Royal*), though the effect on operational efficiency and operations themselves is more difficult to assess.

It is of interest to note contemporary comment in *Periscope View* by Rear-Admiral G W G Simpson, at that time commanding the 10th Submarine Flotilla in Malta, which force was finally forced to withdraw in the face of overwhelming air attack. He is scathing regarding the failure of the politicians to deploy more, and more modern, aircraft to Malta earlier, and the local RAF commander (with practical experience of the Battle of Britain) is forced to comment that at the height of Malta's need there were three times as many fighter squadrons in Britain as there had been in October 1940. At that point not a single Spitfire had arrived in Malta. Again, it is of interest that the same source quotes the serviceable aircraft in Malta on 31 March 1942 as nine Spitfires and five Hurricanes. Deliveries via Gibraltar up to that date included 334 Hurricanes and 31 Spitfires, and indicates a dreadful rate of attrition caused by combat loss, bombing and the serious problem of shrapnel from the intense barrage fire over the airfields.

That the Royal Air Force in Malta managed to survive at all speaks volumes for the fortitude of its officers and men on the island, and for the Royal Navy in delivering such aircraft as were made available. It is somewhat less to the credit of the Air Staff and their political masters responsible (or not, as the case may be) for the directives towards the island's reinforcement. Likewise the rather bitter feelings of naval pilots who were required to defend their carriers and fleet with Mk I Hurricanes, while ferrying much later marks, a situation to be repeated in the Indian Ocean in 1942 when similar exercises were undertaken to bolster the defences of Singapore. We can at least be thankful that the Royal Navy finally acquired the control of its own supplies to a greater extent before irreparable harm was done to the Fleet Air Arm.

It is now appropriate to describe the actual operations that ensured Malta's aerial survival. Actually, there were four ways of taking aircraft to Malta: overland through Europe; by merchant ship and carrier round the Cape and up the Red Sea; by merchant ship and carrier to the west coast of Africa; and by carrier via Gibraltar.

Overland through Europe

On 4 June 1940, just prior to the outbreak of war with Italy, six Hurricanes flew from England via France and Tunis to Malta, where they were to be refuelled for further flight to Egypt. In spite of a request by the Governor that they be allowed to remain on the island the Fleet base at Alexandria was adjudged to have priority and all six were ordered to continue. One, however, had been delayed in Tunis for repairs and was allowed to stay in

Argus was the first carrier to be involved in the ferry operations, in the late summer of 1940. At this stage of the war her 'normal' aircraft were Swordfish, one of which can be seen on her deck. (FAA Museum)

Malta when the others departed.

Twelve more flew out from England on the 18th, with six allocated to Malta. Bad weather and various disasters conspired to reduce to six the number that actually arrived in Malta, and only four were permitted to remain there. By the end of June 1940 the total fighter strength in Malta was four serviceable Hurricanes plus two of the original Sea Gladiators, fast wearing out, and another 'injection' of Hurricanes became essential. The Cape route took too long, the West African route had not yet been set up, and aircraft carriers were thus the only method by which the fighters could be delivered.

Malta's potential as a base for naval and air operations was capable of realisation only if the island were properly defended by many more fighters than the five that had been retained after flying across France. The initial intention was that twelve should be carried in a merchant ship but both Admirals Cunningham and Somerville considered this to be impracticable and the latter suggested that an aircraft carrier should take them to a position south of Sardinia where they would be flown off. The men and stores could be transported in a couple of submarines. The first of the operations was code-named 'Hurry'.

Operation 'Hurry' (2 August 1940)

The pattern of the early ferry operations was simple and was established by 'Hurry': *Argus* (the Home Fleet training carrier) landed all her own aircraft and embarked 12 Mk I Hurricanes of 418 Flight RAF on 20 July at Govan in the Clyde and then, escorted by *Encounter*, *Gallant*, *Greyhound* and *Hotspur*, sailed on the 24th for Gibraltar.

Six days later she was met by Force H and escorted to a position (37°N, 07° 20′E) to the west of Sicily, well within range of Malta. Here, on 2 August, the RAF pilots made their first (and sometimes their last!) take-off from a carrier and headed for Malta. A couple of Skuas, also from *Argus*, accompanied the Hurricanes to act as guides; being two-seat machines the Skuas had the luxury of an observer who was better at over-sea navigation than the otherwise-occupied pilots of the single-seat fighters. While all this was going on, Swordfish from Force H (in the form of *Ark Royal*) were attacking the airfields at Cagliari and mining the harbour there as a diversion. All 12 Hurricanes arrived at Malta (though one crashed on landing) and formed 261 Sqn RAF. The two Skuas, supposed to return to the ship, were 'shanghaied' and retained for use in Malta, alongside the 12 Swordfish of 830 Sqn RN that had arrived from *Argus* on 21 June to form the nucleus of the island's striking force. *Argus* was escorted by Force H back to Gibraltar where on 4 August she joined *Valiant* for passage to Liverpool, escorted by *Faulknor* and *Forester*.

A few days after the force had returned to Gibraltar the submarines *Pandora* and *Proteus* arrived in Malta with the necessary stores.

AIRCRAFT TO MALTA

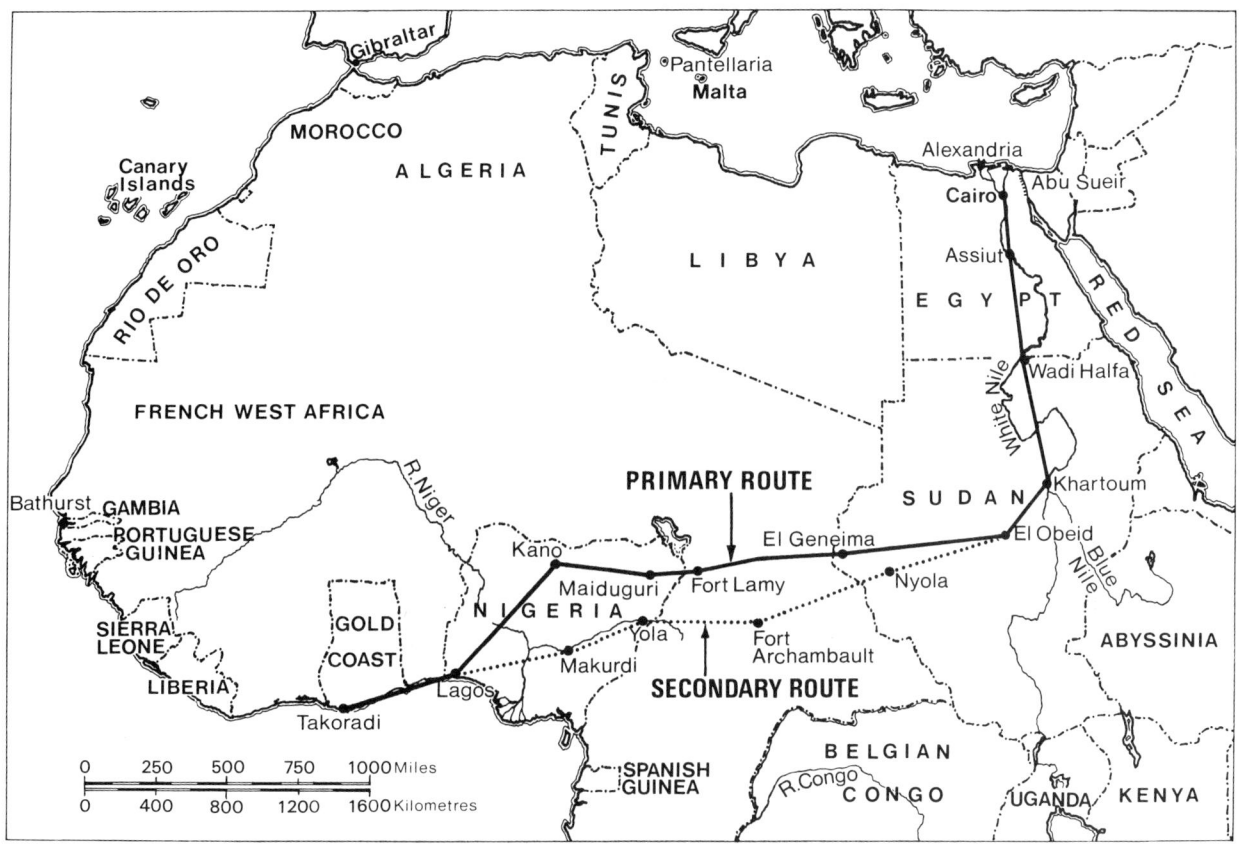

The West African Route (Takoradi 1, 5 September 1940)

The fall of France on 24 June immediately closed the overland route and the provision of an alternative became an urgent necessity to provide a means of reinforcing the Middle East without making excessive demands on shipping. Briefly, aircraft (usually in crates) would be shipped to Takoradi on the Gold Coast and, reassembled, would be flown across Africa via Lagos (378 miles) – Kano (525 miles) – Maiduguri (325 miles) – Geneima (689 miles) – Khartoum (754 miles) to Abu Sueir (1026 miles). At Abu Sueir they would be serviced before being allocated to operational units, some being sent on to Malta. Details of this route, and the alternative via Lagos – Makurdi – Yola – Fort Archambault – Nyala – El Obeid – Khartoum – Wadi Halfa and Abu Sueir are described in the HMSO publication *The Mediterranean and Middle East*, Vol 1, by Major-General I S O Playfair (London, 1954).

The first use of the route was made in September 1940. *Argus* had returned home to Britain immediately after 'Hurry' and in mid-August at Liverpool embarked 30 'tropicalised' Hurricanes plus stores for them, together with some Blenheims and Wellingtons. Without any aircraft for her own defence she sailed on the 22nd and arrived at Takoradi on 5 September. Here the Hurricanes were landed, reunited with their wings and sent on their way. *Argus* then sailed for Britain, the whole round trip taking her some six weeks.

The Cape Route

Concurrently with the first Takoradi operation, 24 Hurricanes were despatched in crates in merchant ships on the long voyage around the Cape. As this and subsequent sailings were made by merchant ships no further discussion of this route will be included in this history.

Operation 'White' (17 November 1940)

The Hurricanes flown in during August were daily being reduced in numbers by action losses, accidents, and normal wear and tear, so that by November an operation to 'top-up' the dwindling fighter force had become necessary. This second Malta ferry operation was a tragedy.

After a brief refit and short ferry trip to Iceland *Argus* returned to the Clyde on 25 October and embarked 12 Mk I Hurricanes together with 2 Skua guides. (Again, she carried no aircraft of her own.) Sailing on Armistice Day she was met by Force H on the 15th and entered the western basin of the Mediterranean. There were reports that an Italian battleship and seven cruisers were concentrating south of Naples and the flying-off position for the Hurricanes was set further west than in 'Hurry'. The fighters (which were fitted with uneconomical constant-speed propellers) took off at 06.15 and 07.15 in two flights of six each led by a Skua. A Sunderland met the first flight north of Galita Island but the Sunderland for the second flight went unserviceable, the replacement Maryland failed to rendezvous and both flights encountered a head

Furious *was a veteran of seven trips to Malta and three to the Gold Coast. This 8 August 1941 photograph shows her initial camouflage scheme.* (MoD)

wind that the pilots were not sufficiently trained to overcome, with the result that 8 of the Hurricanes (2 from the first and all from the second flight) ran out of fuel and ditched short of Malta. One Skua wandered off course and was shot down by the Italians over Sicily, and only 1 Skua and 4 Hurricanes arrived. Airmen and stores were transported from England to Malta in *Newcastle*, arriving on 19 November. *Argus* returned eventually to Britain on 14 December to prepare for another trip.

Operation 'Stripe' (Takoradi 2, 27 November 1940)

The second Takoradi operation introduced a new aircraft carrier to the route. *Furious*, fresh from delivering the final blows of the Norwegian Campaign, arrived at Gladstone Dock, Liverpool, on 7 November and loaded 34 Mk I Hurricanes of 73 Sqn RAF, plus 18 reserve aircraft and 3 Fulmars of the Fleet Air Arm. She also carried 6 Mk II Skuas of 801 Sqn RN. She sailed eight days later with the liner *New Zealand Star*, escorted by *Havelock* and *Hesperus*, and during the passage south, via Freetown, Sierra Leone (where she called on the 25th) the crated aircraft were assembled and flight tested. She arrived at Takoradi on the 27th and two days later the 34 Hurricanes were flown off to the nearby RAF airstrip: one crashed into the sea on take-off from *Furious*, but the others made it safely, together with the 18 reserve machines that were off-loaded. From Takoradi the Hurricanes flew in batches of six overland to Egypt (although six of them and one of their Blenheim guides crashed at El Fasher in Egypt) and by 12 December were in action in the Western Desert, replacing aircraft that had been sent to Greece after the Italian invasion. *Furious* returned to Liverpool on 15 December.

Operation 'Monsoon' (Takoradi 3, 10 January 1941)

At Liverpool in mid-December *Furious* loaded another 40 Mk I Hurricanes while *Argus* on the Clyde embarked 6 Swordfish of 821X Sqn and two of 825 Sqn. Two more Swordfish of 825 were in *Furious* together with 6 Mk II Skuas of 801 Sqn. *Argus* sailed on the 19th with *Bonaventure* and was followed two days later by *Furious* escorted by *Kelvin, Kipling* and *Beverley*. The two carriers joined the twenty troop and supply ships of Convoy WS5A and were in company with it when the German cruiser *Admiral Hipper* discovered the convoy on Christmas Day. The ensuing debâcle assumed the proportions of a farce – the Skuas were in *Furious* with the torpedoes while the serviceable Swordfish with bombs they were unable to carry were in *Argus*. While the Skuas took off to look for *Hipper*, space was frantically cleared in *Furious* to land on the Swordfish from *Argus*. The transfer was duly made but *Hipper* became lost in the murk and the two carriers gave up the hunt and returned to the convoy. Fortunately no damage was done to the two carriers (other than to their pride), and they arrived in Gibraltar on the 28th. Here *Argus* landed the 6 Swordfish of 821X Sqn to RAF North Front from whence they embarked in *Ark Royal* for passage to Malta. On 5 January 1941 *Argus* sailed for Britain where she arrived on the 14th.

Furious, meanwhile, sailed for Freetown and Takoradi, where she arrived on 10 January with *Delhi* and *Neptune* and flew off 39 of the 40 Hurricanes (one Hurricane went u/s) together with 9 Fulmars over the next twenty-four hours. She left the Gold Coast port with *Neptune* on the 28th and returned to Britain on 5 February to refit.

Operation 'Summer' (Takoradi 4, 22 March 1941)

Furious's last trip to the Gold Coast began on 4 March 1941 when, loaded with another batch of flyable Hurricanes besides her own air group of 825 Sqn (6 Swordfish I) and 807 Sqn (12 Fulmar I and II), she left home waters with a West African convoy and *Repulse, Alcantara, Ottawa, Assiniboine, Vansittart* and *Churchill*. She arrived at Takoradi with *Dragon* on the 22nd and quickly flew off the Hurricanes to the maintenance area; this consignment was destined for Malta to maintain, in the words of the Air Officer Commanding-in-Chief, 'a sufficient air force to sustain its defence'.

Operation 'Winch' (3 April 1941)

By January 1941 Malta had only 12 Mk I Hurricanes serviceable (plus 31 other aircraft including 10 Swordfish of 830 Sqn RN) to meet the onslaught of Fliegerkorps X, Kesselring's crack force in Sicily. Attacks on Malta were being made by formations of up to 60 bombers and 40 escorting fighters, and so many Sunderlands and Wellingtons were damaged on the ground that their squadrons had to depart in February for Egypt. On 7 March the Governor of Malta sent a personal message to the Chief of the Air Staff expressing concern that without more fighter aircraft Malta would lose much of its value as a naval and air base. On 2 March 6 Hurricanes had flown to Malta from Egypt and on the 14th 6 more flew the same route, but these were not enough pending the arrival of the latest batch from *Furious*'s Takoradi trip, and more were urgently needed.

The problems of Operation 'White' had indicated that a faster ship than *Argus* was necessary to carry the fighters nearer to Malta before flying them off and the only carrier available was *Ark Royal*, but she could not be spared from active duty to collect aircraft from Britain. Accordingly, *Argus* was again involved, loading 12 Mk II Hurricanes and 3 Skuas in Greenock over a week in mid-March, their embarkation being hindered by bad weather and mines in the Clyde. She sailed on the 21st and, with *Sheffield* and a destroyer escort, set course for Gibraltar, where she arrived eight days later. The Hurricanes and Skuas were transferred to *Ark Royal* on 2 April and this carrier sailed on the same day escorted by *Renown* and *Sheffield*. 'Ark,' being a Fleet carrier, still carried a large part of her air group: 12 Skua II of 800 Sqn, 12 Swordfish I of 818 Sqn and a similar number of 810 Sqn. At 06.00 the following morning the 12 Hurricanes, the first Mk IIs to be despatched to Malta, flew off with the 3 Skuas as guides from a position 420 miles west of the island (37° 42'N,

The highest number of trips was carried out by Ark Royal, *who made twelve between May 1941 and her loss in November.* (MoD)

Ark Royal, *seen in 1941 with her flight deck crowded with Fulmars*. (MoD)

06° 52'E). Nine Fulmars of 800X Sqn also departed for Malta, one of them shooting down an Italian Cant on the way. Having safely delivered the fighters the 3 Skuas headed back towards *Ark Royal* but encountered a scirocco, ran out of fuel and had to ditch. *Ark Royal* returned to Gibraltar and, in an exhibition of carrier versatility, was in the Atlantic the next day searching for *Gneisenau* and *Scharnhorst*. *Argus*, on 7 April, left Gibraltar for Britain accompanied by *London* and arrived in the Clyde four days later.

Operation 'Dunlop' (27 April 1941)

In the second half of April an attempt was made to reinforce Malta by means of an unescorted merchant ship, disguised and routed via territorial waters from Gibraltar. The ship, ss *Parracombe*, struck a mine and sank off Cape Bon, taking the 21 Hurricanes she carried down with her.

The weight of bombs dropped on Malta reached a new record in April and more fighters were desperately needed to defend the island. The arrival of the batch from Operation 'Winch' brought the number of serviceable Hurricanes to just over 40, a wholly inadequate total and another ferry trip was immediately set in train.

Argus had returned to the Clyde on 11 April and straight away embarked 6 replacement Swordfish for *Ark Royal*'s squadrons plus 6 Swordfish of 812 Sqn from Campbeltown for her own use. After a three-day delay while repairs were made to her boilers, the old ship sailed with *London* on the 14th. Met by *Sheffield*, *Faulknor* and *Wrestler* on the 22nd she was escorted into Gibraltar on the 24th to begin a two-week repair and maintenance period, during which the 6 replacement Swordfish were transferred to the 'Ark'. Before this, however, *Ark Royal* had been in the Atlantic hunting for the two German battlecruisers, and at the same time *Furious* (recently returned from Takoradi) had been on the Clyde loading another batch of Hurricanes, mixed Mks I and II, destined for Malta. She arrived at Gibraltar on 25 April and two days later *Ark Royal*, carrying the 24 Hurricanes, left for the flying-off position south of Sardinia. There was quite a crush on the *Ark Royal*'s flight deck and in her hangars with 24 Fulmars I and II of 807 and 808 Sqns, 21 Swordfish of 818 and 825 Sqns plus the 24 RAF machines. The ship was due to deliver the latter on the 25th but bad weather delayed the take-off until the 27th. Twenty-three of the Hurricanes (one went unserviceable with mechanical defects and was left behind) in three flights of 8, 8 and 7, arrived safely on Malta together with their 3 Skua guides.

Operation 'Splice' (21 May 1941)

The results of the aerial interceptions over Malta in early May were disappointing, possibly due to the inexperience of the pilots and the shortcomings of the Mk I Hurricanes. Accordingly, the next operation was planned to introduce more Mk II machines which were to be flown to Malta by experienced pilots of 249 Sqn and the tired ones of 261 Sqn on the island would then proceed to Egypt for a well-earned rest. At the same time a new squadron, 185, would be formed in Malta.

Furious, after a brief refit in Belfast, proceeded to Liverpool and embarked 40 Mk II Hurricanes (together with 9 Mk II Fulmars of 800X Sqn from Donibristle for her own protection – though they were 100mph slower than the Hurricanes they were protecting) and sailed on the 11th for Greenock. There she joined *London* and the two ships left the Clyde the next day for Gibraltar. On arrival on the 18th she transferred 5 of the Fulmars and 21 of the Hurricanes to *Ark Royal* by means of planks placed between the flight decks of the two carriers berthed stern to stern. The two ships (*Ark Royal* carried 41 aircraft of her own: 11 Fulmars of 808 Sqn, 12 Fulmars II of 807 and 18 Swordfish of 818 and 820 Sqns) sailed in company on the 21st, escorted by *Renown*, *Sheffield* and six destroyers, and two days later in position 37° 47'N, 06° 08'E flew off 47 Hurricanes and the 5 Fulmars before turning for Gibraltar. All the aircraft arrived without mishap and the two carriers reached Gibraltar on the 22nd.

In another demonstration of the virtue of carrier sea

power, *Ark Royal* proceeded immediately out into the Atlantic to hunt for *Bismarck*, in which operation she played a crucial part.

Operation 'Rocket' (6 June 1941)

During May much of Fliegerkorps X was withdrawn from Sicily to take part in 'Barbarossa', the German assault on Russia, and the respite from the almost incessant raids on Malta gave the Air Staff the opportunity to further reinforce the island's defences.

Concurrently with *Furious*'s first trip to Malta, *Argus* was loading another batch of Hurricanes on the Clyde. She also embarked 3 Fulmars of 800Y Sqn RN for self-protection against the FW200C Condors that patrolled the route through the Bay of Biscay. Intended for delivery to Malta the Fulmars remained in Gibraltar on completion of the operation. *Argus* sailed shortly after *Bismarck* left Germany on her one-way sortie, and arrived at Gibraltar on 31 May to unload the aircraft. *Furious* arrived the next day, carrying 48 Mk II Hurricanes, and transferred some of them to *Ark Royal* that day. *Furious* and *Ark Royal* (the latter carrying the same air group as in Operation 'Splice', plus the 3 Fulmars of 800Y Sqn) sailed in company with *Renown* and six destroyers on 4 June. South of Sardinia on the 6th, 44 of the Hurricanes were flown off from the two ships; one Hurricane returned with defects and the other 43, escorted by 8 Blenheims from Gibraltar, arrived. The two carriers returned to Gibraltar on the 8th, *Furious* sailing immediately for Britain and later joining *Argus* at sea. On arrival the two ships went to the Clyde, *Argus* for a much-needed refit and *Furious* to prepare for another trip.

Operation 'Tracer' (14 June 1941)

While Malta's immediate needs had now been met there was still a requirement for some reinforcement and the departure of the Luftwaffe presented an opportunity for Malta to be used as a 'stepping stone' to Egypt. A series of operations for the joint strengthening of Malta's and Egypt's air forces was set in motion, 'Tracer' being the first.

Neither *Argus* nor *Furious* was available for this operation: *Argus* was in refit on the Clyde and *Furious* had returned to Britain to collect another consignment. It will be recalled that *Victorious*, the new fleet carrier, on 20 May had been about to depart from Britain with 48 Hurricanes for the Western Desert when *Bismarck* broke out. By now that threat had been removed and the new carrier was able to take up where she had left off. The Hurricanes, hurriedly put ashore on 20 May, were re-embarked in the Clyde on 29 May and on the 31st *Victorious* sailed for Gibraltar in company with *Neptune*, *Norfolk* and *Wessex*. The carrier had only a token air group of her own: 12 Fulmar I of 800Z Sqn and 9 Swordfish I of 825 Sqn, but both of these had been blooded in the *Bismarck* pursuit and on the way south were put to good use searching for the enemy battleship's supply ships. One of them, *Gonzenheim*, was found by 825 Sqn and despatched by *Neptune* on 4 June, then, on the 9th, *Victorious* and her escort met *Ark Royal* with hers two days out from Gibraltar. In harbour *Victorious* transferred 24 of the Hurricanes to the 'Ark' and on the 13th they sailed in concert for the flying-off position south of the Balearic Islands. No guides were available from the carriers and the 47 Hurricanes that took off were guided to Malta by a pre-arranged flight of 4 Hudsons from Gibraltar, this part of the operation calling for accurate synchronisation of flight paths and times. The rendezvous was made and the formation set course for Malta, where the 4 Hudsons and 45 of the Hurricanes later arrived (one Hurricane ditched en route, another developed faults and was last seen heading for the coast of North Africa, and two crashed on landing). The two carriers then turned about and were back in Gibraltar on the 15th. There, *Victorious* embarked 820 Swordfish Sqn from *Ark Royal*, a fair exchange for the 825 Sqn Swordfish she had transferred to *Ark Royal* on the 11th, and on the 19th the newer ship left to return to Britain and make her delayed acquaintance with the Home Fleet in Scapa Flow.

Operation 'Railway I' (27 June 1941)

While *Victorious* was steaming south on her way to Gibraltar, *Furious* was loading her biggest batch of Hurricanes so far: 64 of them. There were so many that she had room for only 9 aircraft of her own – Swordfish of 816 Sqn – and with them she sailed from Britain on 20 June escorted by *Lance* and *Legion*. Having gained *Vanquisher*, *Faulknor*, *Fearless*, *Forester*, *Foxhound* and *Fury* on the way she arrived in Gibraltar on the 25th and there found *Ark Royal* waiting; 22 of the Hurricanes were transferred to *Ark Royal*, all that she could squeeze in besides the 24 Fulmars of 807 and 808 Sqns and the 21 Swordfish of 818 and 825 Sqns. 'Ark' sailed on the 26th for the usual flying-off position west of Sicily and the next day flew them all off to meet some Blenheims from Gibraltar. All the Blenheims and all but one of the Hurricanes subsequently arrived in Malta while *Ark Royal* returned to base.

Operation 'Railway II' (30 June 1941)

Furious had been left behind with 42 Hurricanes in Gibraltar during 'Railway I' but when *Ark Royal* arrived on the 28th, 26 of the fighters were transferred to her and the two carriers sailed together the next day for a repeat operation. The flying-off position was reached on the 30th and *Ark Royal* successfully flew off her batch. *Furious* was not so fortunate: the first 9 got away safely but the tenth crashed into the island during take-off, killing 14 men and starting a serious flight deck fire. The accident prevented the remaining 6 fighters from leaving and they had to be taken back to Gibraltar. Six Blenheims, in the now well-proven manner, escorted the fighters to Malta, all but one of the 35 Hurricanes arriving. The two carriers returned to Gibraltar where *Furious* landed the 6 Hurricanes and transferred 816 Sqn to *Ark Royal* before depart-

September, 1941 saw Ark Royal *undertake two ferry operations, 'Status I' and 'Status II', in which 59 Hurricanes were successfully flown to Malta.* (MoD)

ing for Britain with 818 Sqn (9 Swordfish) from 'Ark' for passage.

By the end of June, 224 Hurricanes had been flown to Malta since the beginning of April: 109 remained on the island and the rest flew on to Egypt to take part in the Western Desert operations against Rommel.

Operation 'Substance' (25 July 1941)

The loss of Crete and the German reoccupation of Cyrenaica increased the threat to Malta and to meet this the island needed a further reinforcement. This operation was not a ferry trip at all really, but was an important Malta convoy code-named 'Substance', and it comprised six store ships and all of Force H. The warships, including *Ark Royal*, sailed on 21 July to join the convoy and escorted it through consecutive heavy air attacks until the 23rd, when the transports left to proceed to Malta. Force H cruised off Galita Island until the 25th to counter any intervention by the Italian Fleet then *Ark Royal* flew off 6 Swordfish to join 830 Sqn on Malta, after which the force turned round for Gibraltar. All the Swordfish arrived without mishap and were soon in action against Rommel's supply convoys running between Italy and North Africa.

Operation 'Status I' (9 September 1941)

At the beginning of January 1941 the 'target' figure for fighter squadrons on Malta had been four but there was actually still only one. By the beginning of August there were 15 Mk I Hurricanes and 60 Mk II serviceable but in the month a Night Fighter Unit had to be formed to counter the increasing number of night raids, thus reducing the number of machines available for daytime use.

There were no ferry trips during August (*Argus* was going the other way with 24 Hurricanes for Russia and *Furious* was attacking the Germans in Norway) but on the 30th of that month *Furious* left Belfast carrying 49 Hurricanes for Malta, together with 3 Fulmar I of 800 Sqn and 4 Sea Hurricane IB of 880A Sqn for her own defence, and 812 Sqn of 9 Swordfish for *Ark Royal*. She arrived at Gibraltar on 6 September and transferred 40 of the Hurricanes to *Ark Royal* the next day, as well as disembarking 812 Sqn to RAF North Front. *Ark Royal* sailed on the 8th with a light escort (*Hermione* and six destroyers) and headed for the flying-off position. Only one Blenheim instead of the planned 4 from Gibraltar met the carrier at the rendezvous on the 9th so only 14 Hurricanes were flown off to Malta, the other 26 being taken back to harbour on the 11th. All the Hurricanes and their solitary Blenheim arrived.

Operation 'Status II' (13 September 1941)

An all-out effort was demanded for the next operation and two carriers were involved with a battleship for escort. On her return from 'Status I' *Ark Royal* transferred 810 Sqn (down to 6 Swordfish) to *Furious* and sailed with her the same day for the flying-off position (38°N, 04°E) escorted by *Nelson*, *Hermione*, and seven destroyers. The thirteenth was not unlucky and 46 Hurricanes took off from the two carriers to be met by 7 Blenheims from Gibraltar and shown the way to Malta. All but one (which crashed on take-off) of the Hurricanes reached Malta, and the ships returned to Gibraltar the next day.

AIRCRAFT TO MALTA

Operation 'Callboy' (18 October 1941)

In the autumn of 1941 Rommel in the North African desert was complaining to OKW in Berlin that unless attacks on the supply convoys from Italy were reduced he might be unable to assault Tobruk in November. He was, of course, referring to the work being done by the Malta-based Swordfish of 830 Sqn and the RAF Blenheims and Wellingtons. On the British side strenuous efforts were being made to further improve results against the Italian convoys and in order to increase the range of the air striking force 12 Albacores with long-range tanks were made available.

Argus, having embarked a couple of Swordfish of 818 Sqn from Machrihanish for her own protection, embarked 828 Sqn (12 Albacore I) together with their torpedoes by lighter from Abbotsinch then proceeded from the Clyde for Gibraltar with Convoy WS12. At Gibraltar on 30 September the Albacores were off-loaded and early in October were embarked in *Ark Royal* for passage to Malta. *Ark Royal* sailed on the 16th with *Rodney*, *Hermione* and seven destroyers carrying, besides 828, the Fulmars of 807 and 808 Sqns and Swordfish of 816 and 825 Sqns. The flying-off position was the same as in Operation 'White', *ie* 450 miles west of Malta, and from it on the 18th departed 11 of the Albacores and 2 Swordfish for the airfield at Hal Far. One Swordfish crashed during the flight but the other aircraft arrived safely and an Italian BR 20 was shot down by *Ark Royal*'s Fulmars the same day to even the score.

Meanwhile, back in Gibraltar, *Argus* had embarked 804 Sqn (12 Fulmars Mk I and II and Sea Hurricanes Mk IIB) from North Front and prepared to sail for Britain with *Eagle* and the destroyer *Croome*. The sailing was postponed and 804 Sqn returned to North Front on 8 October. On the 20th *Argus* loaded 7 damaged naval aircraft and 12 encased RAF engines and sailed for Britain with *Eagle* and an escort, arriving on the 26th.

Fulmars were very large fighters, as this 8 August 1941 aerial view of four (probably from 800 Sqn) on Furious's *flight deck shows. This was taken a month before the 'Status II' operation. (MoD)*

Eagle *was in the Clyde early in 1942 and sailed on 16 February for the Mediterranean and her first ferry operation. This photograph was taken on the Clyde, just before the ship departed from the UK for the last time.* (IWM)

Operation 'Perpetual' (12 November 1941)

In mid-October there were on Malta 74 aircraft of which 66 were serviceable. The forthcoming desert offensive against Rommel, code-named 'Crusader' and planned for 18 November, meant that more would be needed, both for strike and defensive roles.

On arrival in the Clyde after 'Callboy' *Argus* returned the two 818 Sqn Swordfish to Machrihanish then began embarking a load of RAF Hurricanes. The new aircraft transport *Athene* was similarly involved, as the two were to sail in company, the trip being code-named Operation 'Pantaloon'. When loading was completed on the 29th *Argus* embarked the 2 Swordfish of 818 from Machrihanish and on 1 November she also embarked 2 Sea Hurricanes IIB of 804A Sqn to provide fighter protection, before sailing with *Athene* and destroyers for Gibraltar. They arrived on the 8th and over the next two days transferred all of *Athene*'s and some of *Argus*'s Hurricanes to *Ark Royal*. Then, on 10 November, *Argus* and *Ark Royal* left Gibraltar with *Malaya, Hermione* and the 'statutory' seven destroyers. The two carriers had 37 Hurricanes on board for 242 and 605 Sqns RAF, and these were flown off on the 12th, being met by Blenheims from Gibraltar. Three of the Hurricanes vanished en route but the others arrived, together with their guides. The next day *Ark Royal* was torpedoed and, sadly, sank within sight of Gibraltar. *Argus* returned to that base and remained there as the sole carrier in the western Mediterranean.

Operation 'Spotter I' (27 February 1942)

German aircraft reappeared over Malta in December 1941 and in January 1942 the weight of bombs dropped on the island (669 tons) was greater than in the previous peak month of April 1941. Much damage was done to the dockyards and airfields and on 31 January only 28 fighters remained serviceable. The following month, February, saw 1020 tons of bombs fall on the island and by the middle of the month only 11 fighters remained airworthy. Since November no carriers had been available for ferry duties, the few fit for service being in great demand in the Atlantic and Indian Oceans.

After the loss of *Ark Royal*, *Argus* was the only aircraft carrier in the western Mediterranean but, while she was too slow for effective participation in Fleet operations, she was adequate for the occasional ferry trip, and in January 1942 she was recalled to Britain along with Force H. Before leaving Gibraltar she embarked 812 Sqn (12 Swordfish I) from North Front to provide TSR (torpedo-spotter-reconnaisance) capabilities. She loaded some 15 Spitfires on the Clyde early in February and on the 16th sailed with Force H and Convoy WS16 for Gibraltar, taking eight days on the passage. On arrival at Gibraltar *Argus* found *Eagle* (804A Flt of 1 Sea Hurricane Mk I and 813 Sqn of 9 Swordfish I and 4 Sea Hurricane Mk IB) waiting and the Spitfires were transferred to her. 807 Sqn of 9 Fulmars was embarked in *Argus* from North Front to replace the Spitfires and the two carriers sailed on the 27th, covered by Force H, *Eagle* as the ferry carrier and *Argus* with her Fulmars providing the fighter escort. During the voyage defects were discovered in the Spitfires' fuel tanks and the operation was cancelled, the ships returning to harbour the next day.

Operation 'Spotter II' (7 March 1942)

On 6 March just 32 Hurricanes on Malta were capable of taking to the air to defend the island and on that day, the fuel tank faults in the Spitfires cleared, *Eagle* and *Argus* sailed again, escorted by *Malaya, Hermione* and nine destroyers. Fifteen Spitfires, the first to serve outside Britain, were flown off on the 7th and were guided to Malta by 7 Blenheims from Gibraltar. All arrived without mishap and Force H returned to base.

AIRCRAFT TO MALTA

Operation 'Picket I' (21 March 1942)

The spirits of the hard-pressed Maltese people having been raised by the arrival from Operation 'Spotter' of the famous Spitfires, Force H redoubled its efforts and two more trips were planned for March. Neither of the two aircraft carriers took part in any operation between 'Spotter II' and the next run three weeks later. *Eagle* and *Argus* left Gibraltar together on the 20th with 9 Spitfires in the former carrier and 12 Sea Hurricanes Mk IIB of 804 Sqn in the latter. Nine Spitfires were flown off from *Eagle* on the following day and were met by 2 Blenheims from Gibraltar, the whole arriving at Malta without untoward event. The two carriers then went back to base.

Operation 'Picket II' (29 March 1942)

On her return to Gibraltar on 23 March *Eagle* embarked 7 more Spitfires and, in company with *Argus* who was acting as spare deck (with 807 Sqn – 10 Fulmars and 2 Sea Hurricanes; and 812 Sqn – 12 Swordfish I) left for the Narrows on the 27th. *Argus*, besides her escort duties, was carrying 6 Albacores who were to be flown off to reinforce 828 Sqn, the night striking force based on Malta. The flying-off position was reached on the 29th and the 7 Spitfires departed from *Eagle*, and were guided to Malta by 2 Beauforts and 3 Blenheims from Gibraltar. The planned despatch of *Argus*'s Albacores had to be abandoned because the weather over the island closed in and they were taken back to Gibraltar on the 30th.

Operation 'Calendar' (20 April 1942)

The failure of the March convoy (when all the four merchant ships, including the famous *Breconshire*, were sunk) showed that German air superiority had all but made Malta untenable, and on the 25th of the month all surface warships were cleared from the island. Between 24 March and 12 April over 2000 enemy sorties were made against Grand Harbour and 1870 tons of bombs were dropped. By mid-April most of the 31 Spitfires flown in during March had been destroyed and the number of serviceable Hurricanes from 185 and 229 Sqns fell to just 6, hopelessly outnumbered by the 250 enemy bombers and 160 fighters on Sicily. Throughout this intense period the cruiser *Penelope* was struggling to make herself seaworthy enough to escape from the dockyard, while around her numerous other ships and craft were being sunk. Another convoy was desperately needed to replenish the island's dwindling stocks of food, fuel and ammunition but it would not be possible for it to be run until the RAF had been strongly reinforced. No British carriers were available however: *Eagle* was in dock with major defects; *Argus* was training (and was too slow for a dash through enemy-dominated waters), *Victorious* and her sisters could not take Spitfires in their lifts; *Furious* was occupied elsewhere; and only a couple of destroyers were fit for service.

As it was imperative that the reinforcement of Malta be carried out speedily, Churchill asked President Roosevelt for help, his request specifically asking if USS *Wasp* could 'do one of these trips provided details are satisfactorily agreed between the Naval Staffs'. The President agreed and in early April *Wasp* arrived on the Clyde to embark 47 Spitfires. Leaving Greenock on the 14th, escorted by *Renown*, four British and two US destroyers, *Wasp* steamed non-stop to the flying-off position, being joined on the way by *Cairo* and *Charybdis*. On this occasion there were no larger aircraft to act as guides, but 46 of the fighters landed safely at Malta.

Ninety minutes after the first Spitfire had landed Fliegerkorps II on Sicily began a series of attacks on the Maltese airfields and within four days had reduced the number of Spitfires to 6.

Operation 'Bowery' (9 May 1942)

Without supplies Malta could not exist, but supplies could come only in convoys and convoys could not survive without air cover. A convoy might be run in June and until then Malta would have to survive. The onslaught unleashed by the Luftwaffe after the preceding ferry trip had reduced the defending fighters' strength to an all-time low. During April 6700 tons of bombs were dropped on Malta (the estimated weight dropped on Coventry on 14 November 1940 was 520 tons): three destroyers, three submarines, three minesweepers, five tugs, a water car-

Wasp *at the time of Operation 'Bowery' (no RAF aircraft are visible on deck).* (USN)

After the loss of Ark Royal *in November 1941,* Argus *was the sole carrier in the western Mediterranean. She is seen here returning to Gibraltar in January 1942, turning into wind to fly off a couple of Fulmars of 807 Sqn.* (IWM)

rier and a floating crane were sunk in the harbour and other ships were damaged. As a result Churchill was forced to ask President Roosevelt if *Wasp* could be spared for another trip.

This became the most famous of all the Malta ferry trips, not only because it saw the first in-concert operation of British and US aircraft carriers but also because the number of fighters delivered to the island was a record. *Wasp* had returned to Britain after 'Calendar' and at Glasgow embarked a huge batch of 64 Spitfires for Malta. She then sailed at high speed for Gibraltar where, on 7/8 May, she was met by *Eagle, Renown, Cairo, Charybdis* and eleven British and US destroyers. Seventeen of the Spitfires were transferred to *Eagle* on passage – she had left her air group at Gibraltar to make room and had no aircraft of her own on board. From a point 60 miles north of Algiers, between 06.30 and 07.30 on 9 May *Wasp* flew off her 47 Spitfires and *Eagle* her 17. One crashed on take-off, one force-landed in North Africa, one ditched and a fourth 'pranged' on landing, but 60 arrived. This time the RAF on Malta was ready for them and within hours the Spitfires were serviced, refuelled and in action.

The two carriers returned to Gibraltar on the 12th, *Eagle* entering harbour to load another batch of Spitfires while *Wasp* continued to Scapa, where she received Winston Churchill's praise in the form of the famous signal: 'WHO SAID A WASP COULDN'T STING TWICE?'

Operation 'LB' (19 May 1942)

Local air superiority had been established with the Spitfires flown in on 9 May, and to maintain this another consignment was prepared for the following week. *Argus* was available for this operation and acted as spare deck with 807 Sqn of 12 Fulmars embarked to give fighter cover to the ferry carrier, *Eagle*, who carried 17 Spitfires and the 6 Albacores that had been retained after Operation 'Picket II' as well as 813 Sqn of 9 Swordfish and 4 Sea Hurricanes. The two ships left Gibraltar on 17 May with *Charybdis* (fitted for fighter direction work) and seven destroyers, and reached the flying-off position two days later. *Eagle*'s brood of Spitfires flew safely to Malta but the clutch of Albacores developed engine trouble and struggled back to the ship, to be returned to Gibraltar for a second time. A Catalina patrolling the area was shot down by French fighters 20 miles north of Algiers and its crew were rescued by the destroyer *Ithuriel*. Two Fulmars from *Argus* covered *Ithuriel* on this task but were attacked by French Dewoitines and one was shot down. The ships arrived in harbour on the 20th and shortly afterwards *Argus* sailed for the Clyde to prepare for a major Malta convoy operation.

Operation 'Style' (3 June 1942)

Eagle stayed in Gibraltar when *Argus* departed, and at the end of May sent most of her air group ashore to North Front to make room for 31 Spitfires. This was one of those odd situations: ferrying the fast and manoeuvrable Spitfires to Malta, *Eagle* had to make do with 4 oldish Sea Hurricanes for the defence of herself and the escort force. She sailed on 2 June, in company with *Charybdis* and the only five destroyers that were fit for service, and the next day flew off the 31 Spitfires, bringing her total to date to 144. Of this latest batch four disappeared en route (shot down by Me 109s), the total number so far delivered by *Eagle* being 136. The old ship was back in harbour on the 4th to load the next lot.

Operation 'Salient' (9 June 1942)

The plan to run a convoy from each end of the Mediterranean to relieve Malta relied upon air cover being available for the ships expected to arrive and as a prelude to the joint 'Harpoon'–'Vigorous' operations another batch of Spitfires was flown in.

Sailing on 8 June, in company with *Cairo, Charybdis* and six escorting destroyers, *Eagle* carried 32 Spitfires, her largest number yet, in addition to her resident squadron (813, of 4 Sea Hurricanes and a few Swordfish). The flying-off position was 37° 18'N, 02° 30'E, south east of the Balearic Islands and was reached on 9 June. The 32 Spitfires, destined to reinforce 126, 185, 249, 601 and 605 Sqns RAF, arrived safely, as did *Eagle* who returned to Gibraltar on the 10th to prepare for the ill-fated convoy operation named 'Harpoon'. As a result of 'Salient' the number of available fighers on Malta rose to 95.

Operation 'Pinpoint' (15 July 1942)

Malta continued to serve as a base for offensive operations but their radius was restricted in order to increase the chances of success. Aviation spirit was by now in short supply and the passage of aircraft from Malta to Egypt was suspended. During July *Parthian* and *Clyde* arrived from Gibraltar with aviation spirit, while *Empire Shackleton* brought 32 crated Spitfires from Britain to Gibraltar for *Eagle* to take to Malta.

Eagle had had a month's rest after 'Harpoon' then, on 14 July, having loaded the 32 Spitfires at Gibraltar (to the exclusion of her own air group except for 6 Sea Hurricanes of 801 Sqn) she sailed on her eighth and penultimate ferry trip to Malta. Escorted by the AA cruisers *Cairo* and *Charybdis*, plus five destroyers, she reached the flying-off position on the 15th. The 32 Spitfires all took off and on their way to Malta escorted the fast minelayer *Welshman* making her third 'special stores' run to the island. The minelayer and aircraft carrier reached their destinations safely as did all but one of the fighters. This increase in Malta's defensive capability allowed the 10th Submarine Flotilla to return to the island and resume their operations against the Afrika Korps supply convoys between Italy and North Africa.

Operation 'Insect' (21 July 1942)

The enemy reacted with severity to the reinforcement of Malta's defences and during the first fortnight of July destroyed 17 aircraft on the ground and damaged many more; another 36 out of the 135 on the island were lost in combat, while the enemy lost 65. Another reinforcement therefore became necessary.

Eagle's stay in Gibraltar was just of sufficient duration for her to embark 29 Spitfires and 824 Sqn of 4 Swordfish and sail on the 20th of July for Malta. She was escorted by the usual force and later that day was attacked by the Italian submarine *Dandolo*. The four torpedoes missed. Twenty-nine Spitfires were flown off successfully and again all but one arrived, completing a total of 59 Spitfires ferried during July. *Eagle* returned to Gibraltar to prepare for the next operation, the convoy named 'Pedestal', in which she was torpedoed and sunk.

Operation 'Bellows' (11 August 1942)

At the end of July there were 80 serviceable fighters on Malta, but as the weekly wastage averaged 17 it was planned to give the strength a boost by utilising *Furious* to fly in a batch under cover of a major Malta convoy. Code-named 'Pedestal', this convoy was to become one of the most famous of all time. Five aircraft carriers were made available for this operation: *Eagle, Indomitable* and *Victorious* as the main component of the escort, *Furious*

Later in the war, during her 1942 USA refit, Furious's *colour scheme was changed. This post-refit photograph shows the old carrier in her final configuration.* (IWM)

carrying 38 Spitfires in a subsidiary operation named 'Bellows' and *Argus* with reserve aircraft. The last named left the Clyde on 2 August and on the 7th was joined by *Furious* on passage to Gibraltar. *Furious* sailed from the Clyde on 3 August in company with *Victorious, Nelson, Rodney* and escort and on the 7th joined *Argus*'s convoy in the Bay of Biscay. This force passed Gibraltar three days later, dropping off *Argus* as it did so and joining *Indomitable, Eagle* and their escort soon afterwards. On the 11th *Furious* began flying-off the 38 Spitfires from 550 miles north-west of Malta just as *Eagle* was torpedoed. One Spitfire developed engine trouble and hurriedly put down on *Indomitable*; the others arrived in Malta to join in the defence of the convoy as well as of the island. *Furious* immediately turned back for Gibraltar escorted by eight destroyers and on the way one of them, *Wolverine*, rammed and sank the Italian submarine *Dagabur*.

Operation 'Baritone' (17 August 1942)

Stocks of aviation fuel were too low at about the time of 'Pedestal' to allow the build-up of larger air striking forces on Malta and the fast minelayer *Welshman* was fitted out to carry the fuel, while submarines brought in as much as they could carry. The wastage of fighters during 'Pedestal' next had to be made good (5 RAF and 13 FAA aircraft had been lost opposing 600 German and Italian) and another batch was made ready, to be ferried by *Furious*. (The original plan had been for *Eagle* to make this trip, but after her loss *Furious* was substituted.)

This ferry trip began on 16 August, four days after *Furious* had returned to Gibraltar after 'Bellows'. *Argus* was there, having just arrived from Britain with 6 Sea Hurricanes of 804 Sqn, and so was *Empire Olive* with a load of Spitfires. The Sea Hurricanes and Spitfires were transferred to *Furious* beginning on the 13th and three days later the carrier sailed with them and 4 Albacores of 823 Sqn, escorted by *Charybdis* and twelve destroyers. The flying-off position south-east of the Balearics was reached on the 17th and the 32 Spitfires took off for Malta, all but three subsequently arriving (one crashed and the pilots of two others baled out) bringing the total numbers of aircraft ferried in since August 1940 to 670 in 27 separate operations.

Argus's last ferry trip was in March 1942 and, eight months later, she took part in the invasion of North Africa, operating Seafires. Here, one of 880 Sqn's IICs is landing on. (IWM)

Operation 'Train' (29 October 1942)

The big Malta convoy and the follow-up ferry trip had solved many of Malta's problems but one final reinforcement was necessary before the planned invasion of North Africa could take place, and this was carried out by *Furious*. After 'Baritone' this carrier, escorted by *Nelson*, had returned to Britain for two months training, and on 20 October was detached from the Home Fleet for this last ferry trip. She arrived at Gibraltar on the 27th, flew off 822 Sqn (9 Albacores and some Fulmars) and 4 Seafires Mk IB of 801 Sqn and embarked 31 Spitfires Mk VC. She left harbour the next day, accompanied by *Aurora, Charybdis* and eight destroyers, and arrived at the flying-off position on the 29th. Of the RAF fighters, two were lost en route and 29 arrived, to be in action the next day. *Furious* returned to Gibraltar on the 30th (being bombed on the way by a Ju 88) to prepare for the assault on North Africa, the success of which negated the requirement for any further reinforcement operations.

Summary

So just what did the 28 operations to Malta achieve? First and foremost, the continued survival of Malta as a base for the striking forces so essential to British command of the sea and, second, the defence of Egypt. In logistic terms, 756 aircraft ferried and 719 arrivals on the beleagured island, a success rate of just over 95 per cent (particulars are given in the table). The cost was one aircraft carrier, *Ark Royal*.

	Totals flown off	Totals arrived
Hurricanes	353	334
Spitfires	384	367
Swordfish	8	7
Albacores	17	11

Summary Of Ferry Trips Direct To Malta

Date	Operation	Carrier(s)	Aircraft flown off	Aircraft arrived
2.8.40	Hurry	*Argus*	12 Hurricanes 2 Skuas	12 Hurricanes 2 Skuas
17.11.40	White	*Argus*	12 Hurricanes 2 Skuas	4 Hurricanes 1 Skua
3.4.41	Winch	*Ark Royal*	12 Hurricanes 9 Fulmars 3 Skuas	12 Hurricanes 9 Fulmars
27.4.41	Dunlop	*Ark Royal*	24 Hurricanes 3 Skuas	23 Hurricanes 3 Skuas
21.5.41	Splice	*Ark Royal* *Furious*	48 Hurricanes 5 Fulmars	47 Hurricanes 5 Fulmars
6.6.41	Rocket	*Ark Royal* *Furious*	44 Hurricanes	43 Hurricanes
14.6.41	Tracer	*Ark Royal* *Victorious*	47 Hurricanes	45 Hurricanes
27.6.41	Railway I	*Ark Royal*	22 Hurricanes	21 Hurricanes
30.6.41	Railway II	*Ark Royal* *Furious*	35 Hurricanes	34 Hurricanes
25.7.41	Substance	*Ark Royal*	6 Swordfish	6 Swordfish
9.9.41	Status I	*Ark Royal*	14 Hurricanes	14 Hurricanes
13.9.41	Status II	*Ark Royal* *Furious*	46 Hurricanes	45 Hurricanes
18.10.41	Callboy	*Ark Royal*	11 Albacores 2 Swordfish	11 Albacores 1 Swordfish
12.11.41	Perpetual	*Ark Royal* *Argus*	37 Hurricanes	34 Hurricanes
27.2.42	Spotter I	*Eagle*	Cancelled	
7.3.42	Spotter II	*Eagle*	15 Spitfires	15 Spitfires
21.3.42	Picket I	*Eagle*	9 Spitfires	9 Spitfires
29.3.42	Picket II	*Eagle* *Argus*	7 Spitfires	7 Spitfires
20.4.42	Calendar	USS *Wasp*	47 Spitfires	46 Spitfires
9.5.42	Bowery	*Eagle* USS *Wasp*	64 Spitfires	60 Spitfires
19.5.42	LB	*Eagle*	17 Spitfires 6 Albacores	17 Spitfires
3.6.42	Style	*Eagle*	31 Spitfires	27 Spitfires
9.6.42	Salient	Eagle	32 Spitfires	32 Spitfires
15.7.42	Pinpoint	*Eagle*	32 Spitfires	31 Spitfires
21.7.42	Insect	*Eagle*	29 Spitfires	28 Spitfires
11.8.42	Bellows	*Furious*	38 Spitfires	37 Spitfires
17.8.42	Baritone	*Furious*	32 Spitfires	29 Spitfires
29.10.42	Train	*Furious*	31 Spitfires	29 Spitfires
		Total	353 Hurricanes 384 Spitfires 17 Albacores 8 Swordfish	334 Hurricanes 367 Spitfires 11 Albacores 7 Swordfish
		Grand totals	756	719

THE MIDGET SUBMARINE ATTACK ON THE TIRPITZ

The attack on the *Tirpitz* by a small band of officers and men, cooped up in tiny submarines in a struggle against both the enemy and atrocious weather, is a story of utmost gallantry. It resulted in the award of two VCs, five DSOs, a Conspicuous Gallantry Medal and five MBEs. Using official Admiralty sources, John Marriott pieces together the details of the planning and execution of this operation.

The name X Craft was applied to these very small midget submarines with a crew of three (but later they were modified to hold four men). They were 57ft long and their pressure hulls were 3.5ft in diameter. They had a maximum diving depth of 300ft and as with conventional submarines were powered by a diesel engine when on the surface and by an electric motor when submerged. The craft carried no torpedoes, but were fitted with detachable charges (or ground mines) on the sides of their hulls; each contained 2 tons of Amatol, fitted with a time fuse, which allowed up to 16 hours delay, to give the craft time to get away after laying their charges. X Craft were the brainchild of Commander Varley, a First World War submarine officer. Between the wars he ran an engineering business on the Hamble River near Southampton. After the outbreak of the Second World War he secured a contract from the Admiralty to build two more experimental X Craft and later X Craft and XE craft (for the Far East) were contracted out to other builders.

The first X Craft was called *X3*, because *X1* had been an elderly experimental British cruiser submarine and *X2* was the name given to an Italian submarine which had surrendered to the British gunboat *Moonstone* at Aden, not long after Italy had entered the war. *X3* was launched on 15 March 1942. Volunteer RN and RNVR officers were appointed to carry out trials, which took place in the Hamble River and at Fort Blockhouse, the submarine base at Portsmouth. Eventually a special base for X Craft was set up in a Hydropathic Hotel in the Isle of Bute. It was turned into a naval base, named HMS *Varbel* ('Var' for Commander Varley and 'bel' for Commander Bell, who was in charge of personnel and training at the base). The actual place chosen was Port Bannatyne, and was selected as it was very secluded yet near the main submarine base of HMS *Cyclops* in Rothesay Bay. So far as is known, the secret was well kept, for the Germans never knew of the base, let alone what went on there. *X3* was commanded by Lieutenant Donald Cameron, who was nearly killed during the trials, due to an accidental flooding. The craft had to be withdrawn and refitted, and was replaced by *X6*, with Lieutenant Geoffrey Place in command. She too had trouble, being swamped by an unusually large wave when on the surface, and was only saved by a trawler passing a wire round her and pulling her into an upright position. More X Craft were being built and eventually there were seven craft undergoing training, with a new depot ship, HMS *Bonaventure* (Captain Banks). Training continued for the remainder of 1942 and for the first eight months of 1943.

Preliminary planning

It had been hoped to mount the attack on the *Tirpitz* in the spring of 1943, but for various reasons it had to be postponed until the autumn. Spring and autumn were the only two seasons when the light was suitable in North Norway where the *Tirpitz* was based. In summer it was virtually light all night, and in winter it was virtually dark even during the day. Accordingly the attack was planned for

ATTACK ON THE TIRPITZ

The small size of the X Craft can be gauged by this postwar view of XE8. *(CPL)*

late September 1943. It was code named 'Source'. Attacks on other major units of the German fleet, also holed up in North Norway were also planned. *Tirpitz* was in Kaa Fjord, a small fjord off Alten Fjord and *Scharnhorst* was near by. *Lutzow* was in Lange Fjord not far away.

It was, of course, absolutely essential to make quite sure that the three ships would be at their berths when the time came for the attack, so use was made of aerial reconnaissance and of observers on the spot. A Norwegian, named Torsten Raaby, in the Norwegian underground movement was employed by the Meteorological Service and was passing weather information from a remote Arctic island. He later started using a secret transmitter in Tromso, but was forced to flee to Sweden and from there he went to Britain. British Intelligence decided that he was too good to be missed, and sent him back to Norway where he was secretly landed near Trondheim from the submarine *Ule*. From there he made his way to Hammerfest and thence to Alten Fjord. Working with two other Norwegians, Raaby began sending radio reports about German shipping to London. He took a house next door to a German officer, and with calculated cheek used his neighbour's receiving aerial for his HF transmitter without the German officer being any the wiser. His reports became invaluable as the day for the attack on the *Tirpitz* drew nearer. Alten Fjord was outside the range of reconnaissance aircraft from Britain, so permission was sought from the Russians to use an airfield at Vaenga inside Russia, and not too far from the Norwegian border. Mosquito aircraft were to be used for the photoreconnaissance work, but they suffered delays in getting off from Britain, due to the Russians' insistence on visas for the photographers! In the event they were not used, the job being undertaken by Spitfires instead.

It had been agreed that six X Craft should leave Loch Cairnbawn in Scotland under tow by six conventional submarines: *Truculent* (Lieutenant Alexander), *Thrasher* (Lieutenant Hezlet), *Stubborn* (Lieutenant Duff), *Syrtis* (Lieutenant Jupp), *Seanymph* (Lieutenant Oakley), and *Sceptre* (Lieutenant McIntosh). *Satyr* and *Sea Dog* were to be held in reserve at Scapa Flow. The depot ship *Titania* was to be used and she arrived in Loch Cairnbawn on 30 August. The towing submarines had to be fitted with towing tubes and slips. The towing hawsers consisted of two types – a hemp hawser, with a telephone cable embodied in it, and a nylon rope.

All was ready when, on 7 September, the first Spitfire reconnaissance flight for several days was made and reported that both the *Tirpitz* and the *Scharnhorst* were absent from their berths in Alten Fjord, and this was confirmed by the faithful Raaby by radio. In fact, as was found out later, they had gone to bombard Spitzbergen. It worried the naval staff considerably in the Admiralty, but on 10 September both ships were reported back in their berths.

The plan

The plan was that the towing submarines were to leave Loch Cairnbawn independently and make their way to a point 76 miles west of the Shetlands. They were then to proceed on parallel courses, 20 miles apart, until about

150 miles west of Alten Fjord when they were to steer for their various appointed landfalls. Each towing submarine had an area off Soroy Island just outside a declared minefield, where she was to slip her X Craft after dusk, and was then to patrol there until 27 September, waiting for the returning X Craft. The X Craft themselves were to cross the minefield on the surface and were then to make their way to Alten Fjord, bottoming during daylight hours. They were to enter Alten Fjord at dawn on the 22nd. All went well initially and quite according to plan. The X Craft had passage crews, which were to be replaced by the operational crews just before entering the Fjord. The X Craft were towed astern submerged, surfacing only every 6 hours to ventilate the craft, but they were allowed only 15 minutes on the surface.

On 14 September the photographs taken by the Spitfires reached Britain, and all possible details of the defences in the fjords were signalled to the X Craft. In addition, targets were allocated as follows: *X5*, *X6* and *X7* were to attack the *Tirpitz*; *X9* and *X10* were to attack the *Scharnhorst*; and *X5* was to attack the *Lutzow* in Lange Fjord, a long arc of Alten Fjord, some 10 miles from Kaa Fjord, where the *Tirpitz* was berthed. According to the signalled interpretation of the Spitfire photographs, there were two single nets across the entrance to Kaa Fjord, and the north-west ends of the nets joined the shore, but the south-east end of the nets had a gap of some 300ft between the nets and the shore. There was also a double anti-torpedo net stretching from the shore and running parallel to the *Tirpitz* about 170ft from her starboard side; it then continued across the battleship's bows to a gate, of which the centre was about 600ft north of her bows. Then there was also a single net to the shore which had small rafts on it. There were no gaps except at the shore end of the one net mentioned above. *Scharnhorst* was enclosed by a double anti-torpedo net on either side, but there was a movable portion of it ahead of the ship. *Lutzow* was protected by a double anti-torpedo net across her anchorage.

In point of fact, neither *Scharnhorst* nor *Lutzow* was in her berth as expected, both having gone to sea for gunnery practice. Thus, as will be seen later, the loss of *X8* and *X9*, and the fact that *X10* did not attack at all, made no

An X Craft being hoisted aboard a depot ship. (Author)

difference and did not affect the main issue.

When the towing submarines were about abreast of the Lofoten Isles, things started to go wrong. At 01.00 on the morning of the 15th, the telephone line between *X8* and *Seanymph* failed and at 04.00 the tow parted. *X8* surfaced but could not find *Seanymph* so continued in a north-westerly direction on the surface. *Seanymph* did not discover that the two had parted for a further two hours. She reversed her course but could not find *X8*. At 15.30 that afternoon the tow between *Stubborn* and *X7* also parted, but the latter surfaced immediately and another tow was passed. At this point *X8* sighted *Stubborn*. All three, with *X7* in tow of *Stubborn*, started searching for *Seanymph*, but by dawn they had had no luck. Prior to this, at about

The X Craft were towed to the target areas by larger submarines – four by 'S' class boats like the Storm *shown here, and two by larger 'T' class boats.* (CPL)

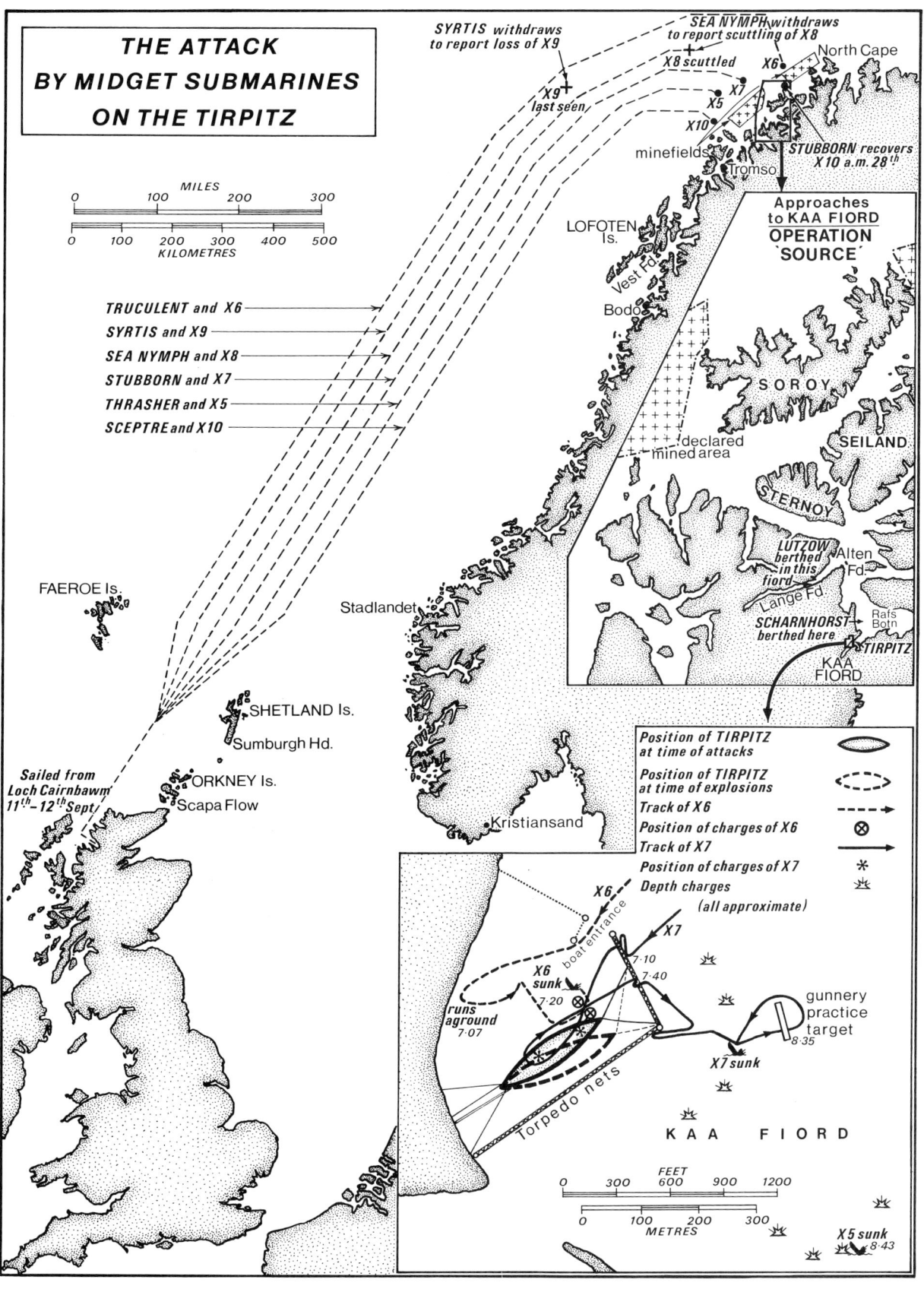

midnight, *X8* lost touch with *Stubborn* and *X7*, by steering the wrong way by mistake. At dawn *Stubborn* realised that she had lost *X7*, but at that moment she sighted *Seanymph*, who had found *X7* and taken her in tow. After transferring the operational crew to *X7*, *Stubborn* with *X7* in tow steered northwards, whilst *Seanymph* continued to search for *X8*, which she eventually found at 17.00. A new tow was prepared and at the same time the operational crew took the opportunity of taking over *X8* from the passage crew. *Seanymph* and *X8* continued their course for Alten Fjord.

First X Craft lost

Meanwhile *Syrtis*, towing *X9* submerged, found that their telephone line had failed. Shortly after, *X9* surfaced for ventilation and dived again at 01.20. The date was now the 16th. *Syrtis* increased speed gradually and set a course east-north-easterly. At dawn she dropped one hand grenade as a signal for *X9* to surface. She failed to do so and the tow was found to be parted. *Syrtis* turned back along her old course. She saw an oil slick going in an easterly direction and thought that *X9* must be making her way to Alten Fjord alone. She followed in the same direction until she reached *X9*'s furthest possible position. *X9* was never seen again. *Syrtis* eventually moved away from the Norwegian coast in order to make a signal to report what had happened, but was unable to get the signal through, and it was not until 3 October that Flag Officer Submarines knew that *X9* had been lost. The reason for her loss is of course unknown, but the possibility is that the tow parted near the towing ship's stern and the weight of the hawser attached to the *X9*'s bows dragged her under and she was unable to rise again.

Second X Craft scuttled

X8 now developed trouble in keeping her trim. Her CO (Lieutenant Macfarlane, RAN), decided to jettison the explosive charge attached to her starboard side. He set the fuse to safe, but the charge exploded when it was about half a mile distant from him. Fortunately no damage was done. With the weight of the remaining charge causing *X8* to list heavily to port, Macfarlane decided to jettison it also, but this time set the fuse to explode after two hours, thus giving him plenty of time to get away. In fact when *X8* was 3½ miles away from it, it exploded with tremendous force, severely damaging *X8*. *Seanymph*, who was dived at the time, also suffered damage, although she was even further away from the charge than was *X8*. At dawn, *Seanymph* was able to rescue the crew of *X8* and she was scuttled since she was so damaged to be of no further use. There is no clear reason why the second charge should have exploded with such force, unless *X8*'s navigation was at fault and the charge was nearer to her than she thought.

Stubborn now had trouble. She was making her final approach to the slipping position when she sighted a mine and took avoiding action, but in so doing the mine's mooring rope caught in the tow line and dragged it down onto *X7*, who was astern. *X7*'s CO, Lieutenant Place, realising that something was wrong, got onto the casing of his craft to have a look. To his horror he saw that the mine was actually in contact with the casing. He tried to submerge further and drag the mine clear, but this did not work, so very gingerly he started pushing the mine away with his feet. He managed to clear the mine from the casing and to clear the mooring wire from the towing rope. It was a truly gallant effort. From then on he had an uneventful passage to the rendezvous.

Great credit was due to the passage crews. For eight or nine days they had lived onboard the X Craft in appalling conditions, unable even to stand upright, cold and damp, often in rough seas, but somehow they had managed to keep their craft in working order for their successors. If ever there was an example of completely selfless and tiring work, this was it.

The attack

By the evening of 20 September, *X5*, *X6*, *X7* and *X10* had all slipped from their towing submarines and had begun to make their way, on the surface, over the declared minefield and towards Sorby Sound. *X6* dived at first light, and by dusk she was at Tommelholm, near the entrance to Kaa Fjord where the *Tirpitz* lay. She surfaced to recharge her batteries, but had to make an emergency dive on the approach of a patrol boat. However, by 22.30 she was able to surface in comparative safety, and shortly before midnight she was able to hide herself between two large rocks to await daylight. *X7* (Lieutenant Place) reached the rendezvous without further difficulty. Place then had a word with Lieutenant Henty-Creer of *X5* and they then went their separate ways. It was the last anyone saw of *X5*. No trace of her was ever found, but at least she had reached the rendezvous.

X10 (Lieutenant Hudspeth) had had to take over his craft with a defective periscope which the passage crew had been unable to repair. It rapidly got worse, and when the gyro compass also failed Hudspeth decided to seek shelter on the north side of the Fjord to try and repair both items. The crew worked all day on the 21st trying to repair the damage, but with little success. However, undeterred, Hudspeth pressed on to Kaa Fjord, but then the magnetic compass light failed, so he was forced to navigate by eye. On raising the periscope the lifting motor burnt out, so he was forced to go on surfaced, but at daylight, he bottomed and lay there all day, making repairs. He could see the floodlit nets at the entrance to the fjord. But now, out of the six boats that had started out, only *X6*, *X7* and *X10* had reached the attacking area.

X6 (Cameron) had decided to attack at 06.30 and he set his charges to explode at 12.30, leaving him sufficient time to escape out of the fjord to comparative safety. He had trouble with the time fuses on the charges and with his trim. Also the periscope was not working correctly. However he decided to continue with his attack. At 04.45 he approached the nets at the entrance to Kaa Fjord, intending to try and get through the gap at the south-western entrance. He could see very little, but he did see a coaster ahead of him and apparently proceeding through a

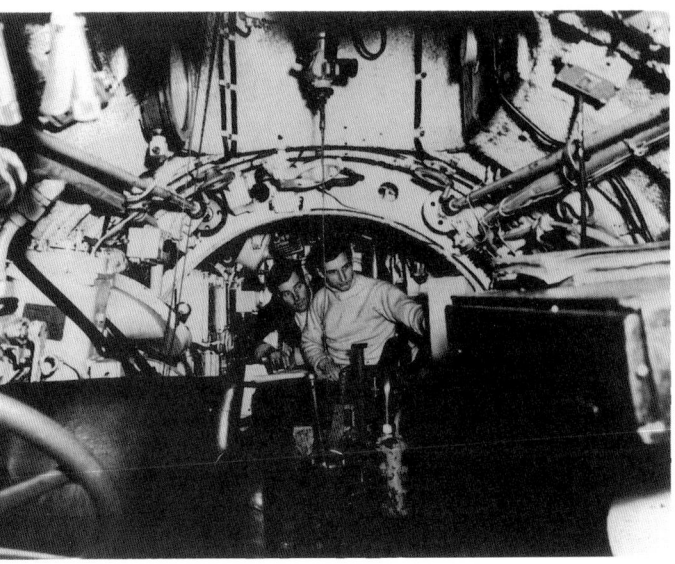

▲ *The cramped interior of an X Craft. (Author)*

Details of the casing, periscope and mast of XE8. *(CPL)* ▶

gap in the nets. He decided to surface and follow her, hoping that her wake would conceal him. His gamble paid off and he got safely through the gap, and once through, he was able to dive to 60ft and proceed towards the *Tirpitz*, while repairs to the periscope were being completed. He came to periscope depth again and was able to see the *Tirpitz* in her berth and a number of destroyers and other craft, but there was no sign of the *Scharnhorst*. He kept to the northern side of the fjord, working on dead reckoning, and at about 07.00 he was lucky to slip through a boat gap in the anti-torpedo net. His luck did not last for long as, almost immediately, he ran aground on the western shore of the fjord and broke surface. The craft was seen by those onboard the *Tirpitz* but was considered to have been a porpoise and was disregarded. He got clear and dived again, but shortly afterwards he broke surface again and was definitely seen by those onboard the battleship. He was only about 30yds away from his target. At that moment, his periscope again broke down, and to his chagrin, so did the gyro compass. However, Cameron, with no 'eyes' and no compass did his best to close the target, still submerged, relying entirely on his memory. He soon got caught in some nets, which he believed to be on the starboard side of the *Tirpitz*. He had to surface to see where he was, and was horrified to find that he was on *Tirpitz*'s port bow. He was at once met by a fusillade of small-arms fire and hand grenades, but he was too close for any of the battleship's other armament to bear. He realised that escape was not possible, but he was determined to complete his mission, and whilst burning all incriminating documents, he backed the X Craft alongside the battleship and released her side charges, right under 'B' turret. He surfaced and the crew climbed onto the casing and surrendered to a German picket boat, which promptly took the craft in tow to get her further inshore. However, *X6* had opened her Kingston valves in order to scuttle her and had put her engines astern. The German picket boat was forced to release her, to avoid being dragged under, and she sank.

Cameron and his crew were taken onboard the *Tirpitz*, which was frantically raising steam, meaning to get out of the fjord. However at 07.45 a second X Craft was sighted, which turned out to be *X7* on her way out. The *Tirpitz*'s captain had intended to go to sea, but the sighting of another X Craft made him change his mind, and in any case it would have taken too long to raise sufficient steam. *X6*'s crew were in a very difficult situation. They were of course heavily interrogated as to where they had placed their charges and when these would explode, but each man stuck rigidly to the rules regarding prisoners of war, and only gave their name, rank and number. At 08.17 there were two large explosions, causing the *Tirpitz* to leap upwards several feet. All electric power and light failed and the ship took on a list to port.

Meanwhile, *X7* (Place) had safely penetrated the boom at the entrance to Kaa Fjord, but became seriously entangled with a series of nets protecting an unoccupied berth in the middle of the fjord, of which the British had no knowledge. Place managed to break free, but his gyro compass had become defective and he had damaged a trim pump. At 06.00 *X7* tried to dive under the 50ft deep net protecting the *Tirpitz*, but found there was a second net below it, stretching right down to the sea-bed, of which he had been given no information. He got entangled again, once more broke free and surfaced, but promptly dived again, and equally promptly got entangled yet

again. The gyro compass was completely useless and Place did not know where he was, so he managed to clear the net and allowed his craft to come slowly to the surface. By a lucky chance, he found that he had somehow drifted clear of the *Tirpitz*'s anti-torpedo net and was in fact inside it, with the battleship only 30yds ahead of him. He dived to 40ft and actually collided with the *Tirpitz* abreast 'B' turret. He released one of his charges and slowly felt his way further aft under the ship's keel. He released the second charge nearly abreast 'X' turret. He then went down to 100ft and tried to find the gap where he had entered, but soon became entangled in yet another net. Once more he got free and surfaced, but like Cameron, he at once came under heavy small-arms fire, so he dived to 120ft where he hit the bottom. Getting under way again he ran into a net somewhere off *Tirpitz*'s starboard bow. At 08.17 a heavy explosion shook his craft free. Once again Place bottomed in order to inspect the damage. He realised that any hope of *X7* being able to return to Britain was out of the question, so Place brought his battered little craft to the surface, quite close to a battle practice target. He got out onto the casing, waving a white sweater, which he hoped the Germans would take as a sign of surrender. *X7* at once began to sink, so he scrambled onto the hull of the target. *X7*'s ballast tanks were ruptured and she was filling with water. The three remaining members of her crew went down with her, but one of them, Sub-Lieutenant Aitken, managed to surface using his escape apparatus. The other two, Sub-Lieutenant Whittam and ERA Whateley were drowned. Place and Aitken were taken prisoner.

It was not clear whose charges exploded or whether *X6*'s charges exploded first and probably detonated *X7*'s. In any event, *Tirpitz* certainly was seriously damaged. There were splits in the bottom of the hull and much buckling and deformation. Some of the main machinery was displaced, a propeller shaft could not be turned, and 'A' and 'X' turrets had jumped off their roller paths. The rudder was out of action, the two aircraft aboard were severely damaged, and all the radar and wireless aerials were completely useless.

The fate of the other X Craft

X8 had been scuttled, and *X9* was lost whilst in tow of *Syrtis* so this left only *X5* and *X10*. As already mentioned, nothing was heard of *X5* after she rendezvoused with *X7*, but at 08.43 on the day of the attack, *Tirpitz* had sighted a third X Craft and had opened fire on her with nearly all the weapons she had got. Several hits on her were observed. It must have been *X5* and she was thought to have been sunk with all her crew. After the war, however, the family of her CO (Lieutenant Henty-Creer) started an investigation, based on the fact that a Norwegian, living on the edge of the fjord, stated that he had seen a periscope on the morning after the attack, and had produced others who had also seen it. He has never been disproved, but, as all naval men know, it is quite possible to mistake a small object sticking out of the water for a periscope.

X10 (Lieutenant Hudspeth) had many defects and she spent all day of 22 September submerged and trying to make good some of them. By sunset, however, there were so many defects still remaining that Hudspeth decided not to attempt an attack on an enemy already alerted. He therefore made for the rendezvous, previously arranged as a meeting point after the attack for their towing submarines. He waited there for some time, and was about to give up and make for Iceland or Russia, when he sighted the towing submarine *Stubborn*. She soon took him in tow, but weather prevented the passage crew from transferring as planned. After some hours, however, the weather moderated and the crews were exchanged. *Stubborn*, towing *X10*, started for home, but the weather deteriorated again and the tow parted at least twice. Then came a signal from Flag Officer Submarines warning them of an imminent gale, and it instructed *Stubborn* to embark the crew of *X10* and to scuttle her 'at his discretion'. The weather did not seem too bad and Lieutenant Duff, *Stubborn*'s CO, was very reluctant to scuttle her,

◀ Tirpitz *lying in Kaa Fjord, as seen by a reconnaissance aircraft.* (IWM)

▼ *When surfaced the officer of the watch had no protection whatsoever.* (CPL)

but thinking that FO Submarines would know more about the forthcoming weather than he did, at 20.45 he scuttled her. The irony was that the gale did not materialise for two days, by which time *Stubborn* was safe in Lerwick Harbour in the Shetlands.

Summary

The whole operation was extremely hazardous, requiring unimaginable bravery and intense courage and endurance. Of the six X Craft that left the Shetlands, not one returned. Three men were lost on passage from *X9*. *X8* and *X10* were both scuttled without loss of life. In *X5*, *X6* and *X7*, all of whom attacked the *Tirpitz*, six men were lost and six were taken prisoner. The latter all became prisoners of war and returned home safely after the war.

The result of the attack was deemed extremely satisfactory. The *Tirpitz* was put out of action for six months. Lieutenants Cameron and Page were awarded the Victoria Cross; Sub-Lieutenant Aitken (*X7*), Lorimer and Kendall (*X6*) and Lieutenant Duff (*Stubborn*) were each awarded the DSO, and ERA Goddard the Conspicuous Gallantry Medal. Lieutenant Hudspeth (*X10*) received the DSO. The passage COs, Lieutenants Terry-Lloyd (*X5*), Wilson (*X6*), Philip (*X7*), Smart (*X8*) and Sub-Lieutenant Page (*X10*) were all awarded the MBE.

In his report to the Admiralty on the operation, the Flag Officer Submarines wrote of Lieutenants Henty-Creer, Cameron and Place, and the crews of *X5, X6,* and *X7*: 'It is clear that courage and enterprise of the very highest order was shown by these very gallant gentlemen whose daring attack will surely go down in history as one of the most dangerous acts of all time.'

No boats returned from the Tirpitz *attack but* X24 *is shown here flying a Jolly Roger as a sign of her success in the Bergen raid of April 1944. (CPL)*

One of the side charges that formed the sole armament of X Craft; they could be detached to become a powerful ground mine. (Author)

Rear-Admiral C B Barry, Flag Officer Submarines, on the deck of a training boat, during an inspection of midget submarines in February 1944 at Holy Loch. (CPL)

TWILIGHT OF THE ST LAURENTS

With the first units now out of service, Thomas G Lynch looks back at the long and complicated history of Canada's first indigenous class of major warships. Revolutionary in their day, their lives have been extended because of defence cuts and policy changes, far beyond original expectations, with an elaborate programme of refurbishment.

The announcement in November 1948, that Canada would undertake the building of two anti-submarine escort vessels of a new, unique design was the culmination of a decision-making process that had been on-going since 1944. Further, the decision to build such vessels and the definite shift into a ASW speciality role would have a dramatic effect upon naval and national defence policies for over forty years, only now being slowly altered in the last decade of the twentieth century.

Both political and military policy of the period immediately after the war was to develop a defence structure that met any need that could arise. Thus in 1947–48, the defence budget totalled C$240 million, which amounted to approximately 12 per cent of the federal budget. Of this, roughly 20 per cent or C$47 million was the Navy's share, with an establishment of nearly 7500 men. Of great aid in maintaining this level of defence spending was the ever-more hostile attitude of the Soviet Union towards its recent allies and its expansionist moves in newly 'liberated' eastern European countries. Canada, along with other like-minded countries sought to establish a collective security agreement which culminated in the Brussels Pact of 1948. Shortly thereafter, discussions began in Washington on what would ultimately become NATO.

With these developments, it now was possible to sharpen and better define Canadian defence policy, with the objectives being defined as: forces to defend against direct Soviet attack; sufficient staff, equipment and planning for rapid expansion; and the necessary infrastructure for joint defence with Canada's European and American allies in time of aggression.

Out of these objectives, a clearer definition of what was expected from the Royal Canadian Navy came about: as it had done in the Second World War, the RCN would guard the lines of communication. This political decision was all well and good, but the RCN of the day consisted of only 14 fighting ships, with a further 22 in reserve. Few of these were even marginally equipped to deal with modern diesel-electric submarines, and with a budget of a mere C$280 million in 1948–49, it was clear that a far greater effort would be necessary. The 1949 Defence White Paper stated:

> The main task of the Navy would be, as in the last war, the protection of Canadian and allied shipping and Canadian coastal waters. The Navy is constructing ships for this purpose – minesweepers, an icebreaker, fast escort vessels. A new type of escort ship designed especially for Canadian needs is under construction.[1]

Making The Decision

Deciding upon a home-grown warship design even in the mid-1940s was a daunting task. Canadian shipyards had built a few 'Tribal' class destroyers in the closing years of the war, but even then the design, drawings and specifications had been worked out by RN Naval Constructors, with subsequent modifications made to the original blueprints to make them more adaptable to RCN requirements. What was being proposed was a wholly Canadian-designed warship, using as much material and equipment as could be found or manufactured either in the US or in Canada.

The governing body in making this decision was the Canadian Naval Board. However, this article will concentrate on the technical side of the ship itself, showing how the ship systems and the bringing together of the often divergent aspirations of the operators and technical experts devolved upon two key personalities and their offices. The first was the Naval Constructor in Chief

St Laurent, *while on builder's trials in the St Lawrence, September–October 1955.* St Laurent, Assiniboine *and* Saguenay *were the only ships of class to be painted with dark grey hull and light grey superstructures and masts. This scheme, approved on 20 February 1946, was superseded by authorization to paint the ships overall light grey as of 21 June 1956. Note the open 3in/50 mounts. The 40mm 'Boffins' are covered in tarpaulins. (LYNCAN/ MARCOM Museum)*

Kootenay *during paint evaluation tests, 18 July 1965 to 16 May 1966.* Kootenay *was painted with USN Haze Grey, with USN-style 'shadow' pennant numbers, while* Nipigon *was painted with Canadian Light Grey 1-GP-61. Haze Grey was more favourably received, but in the end NDHQ in Ottawa quashed the change.* (LYNCAN/MARCOM Museum*)*

(NCC), Constructor Captain (Commodore from January 1953) Rowland Baker who was on loan from the Admiralty's Royal Corps of Naval Constructors. Baker would hold this key position from July 1948 until June 1956 and would be the driving force and creative genius that would take a general set of specifications and turn them into a workable design. The second personality was Commodore (E) (Rear-Admiral (E) from January 1949) J G Knowlton who served as Chief of Naval Technical Services (CNTS) from December 1945 until January 1956. Knowlton's department would be in charge of the overall building of the ships, with their attendant systems.

In July 1948 Constructor Captain Baker arrived in Ottawa to replace his outgoing predecessor, Captain A N Harrison. Baker arrived at a crucial moment in the decision-making process, since Commodore (E) Knowlton and his team were preparing proposals for the new escort vessels. The Naval Staff had already set some guidelines for the proposed design. These included a major emphasis on seakeeping, being able to maintain 17kts in a seaway, noise reduction, NBCW (nuclear-biological-chemical warfare) defence and damage control, a high standard of accommodation, air conditioning, possible weight-saving measures and a demand for mass-production capability in Canada.

The assessment was favourably received by the Cabinet ministers, who agreed to examine the proposed programmes in consultation with the Treasury Board, with 'it being understood . . . that the Naval Program include provision for the initial construction of three large escort vessels'.[2] With this political decision made, Baker was able to bring the matter into sharp technical focus with a lengthy paper to the Naval Staff.[3] In this memorandum, Baker referred to his own experience earlier in 1948 with the Admiralty, which had agreed to plan for a steam turbine-driven frigate, with machinery developing 30,000shp – ultimately to be built as the Type 12 *Whitby* class. However, he cautioned, the design was only in its conceptual stages and the design of the hull could not be defined until the machinery layout was available. Although the design would probably not be ready for a year or two, Baker suggested that Canadian requirements might be met by building this new Admiralty design. He further suggested that an economical alternative might be a new design, based generally on the Intermediate Class destroyer (of which Canada had three) but with a continuous forecastle which gave the extra space for an enlarged Ops Rooms, Communications Centres, etc, so desirable in modern warships.

Thus, a radically new idea in warships was proposed, alongside a much modified older concept as a cheap alternative. However, Baker was in favour of a wholly new design, for which he had some very definite ideas of his own that he wanted to incorporate. He observed that this proposed new design in many ways would be more complicated than that of the 'Tribal' class, the most ambitious naval shipbuilding project undertaken in Canada to that date. He further cautioned that the fully detailed drawings for the new proposed AS escort would have to be prepared in Canada with new ground being broken every step of the way. The latter was seen as a truly formidable problem, as there were just *six* constructor officers in Naval Headquarters, Ottawa at this time, and fully 50 per cent of this number were lieutenants.

Y-100 Drives The Design

Canada, without a native marine propulsion plant of any significant size, was forced to look offshore for suitable machinery. The choices, in practical terms, were the British 'Y-100' design being formulated for their new Type 12 design, and a 34,000shp arrangement that was being developed in the US for Brazilian destroyers.

Senior naval engineering staff were sent to the UK in the autumn of 1948 to explore the British design further, and by late October the decision was made to settle on the Y-100 design. However, since Canadian requirements were now running ahead of RN needs, it was up to the Canadian authorities to drive final machinery layout requirements. Further, Canada insisted upon full-scale shore trials to prove the design. These were conducted at the Pametrada test plant at Wallsend-on-Tyne, England, and the wisdom of such testing was soon confirmed. A serious gear-scuffing problem was identified very early in the tests of the full-scale system, something that would have seriously set the building programme back if not detected until the lead ship had been completed.[4]

Meanwhile, the Naval Board had approved the general set of particulars in mid-January 1949, allowing the real work of developing the design to proceed. The first move was for the NCC, accompanied by the director of weapons and tactics and a representative of the Engineer-in-Chief to pay a visit to the UK to review the tentative design, especially since the final layout of the Y-100 powerplant design had been completed. Baker's seemingly cautious approach was well rewarded when it was discovered that the boilers of the Y-100 would have poked through the ship's bottom of the proposed hull form! Although somewhat embarrassing, Baker solved the problem by having his colleagues in the Admiralty's Naval Construction Department redraw the hull shape so the boilers were contained.[5]

The Final Decision

On 26 March, 1949, the Minister of National Defence tabled a submission to the Governor-General in Council, noting that it was essential to provide ten additional vessels to meet, in part, the RCN's share of the plan for the defence of Canada, as spelt out in the 1949 White Paper. This proposal called for an expenditure of C$33 million and included 3 'AS frigates', 4 minesweepers and 3 gate vessels. Cabinet approved this in principle by the end of March.

Contractual arrangements were now possible on the vessels and machinery, plus preparation of hull and electrical drawings and for model hull testing in Canada and the UK. Meanwhile, the stability requirements selected by the designers called for avoidance of any capsizing moment as the result of damage. To facilitate the proving of damaged stability characteristics, a clear plastic model was prepared that allowed designers to study the effects of various flooded or damaged compartments, in any combination, and the model's behaviour in simulated sea conditions.

Thus by 28 May 1949 Baker as NCC was able to produce a final sketch design with outline plans and descriptive statement. However, Baker was wide of the mark when he suggested in his letter to CNTS that the design could be completed by December 1949, with the first of class commissioned by August 1952 or at the opening for navigation of the St Lawrence River in 1953.[6] Developments in modern submarines, weapons, tactics, plus teething problems with the transplanting of the necessary technology to build the Y-100 propulsion machinery in Canada would cause serious slippage in all of these dates.

Meanwhile, after some months of deliberation, the Naval Board decided on 15 December 1949 that the so-called Escort Vessels should be designated as Destroyer Escorts or DEs. However, in spite of these formal contracts for production, the staff requirements that would actually define what was to be created were still not complete or accepted. These 'Proposed Final Staff Requirements' were eventually presented and approved on 6 September 1949.

However, as the confrontation between the Soviet Union and the Free World worsened and the framework for

A rare photo of the Mk 2 ASW torpedo launcher, with a Mk 43 mod 1 ASW torpedo in the tray. This photo was taken aboard Restigouche, *February 1963. The St Laurent class had these throwers, housed in recesses in the aft deckhouse, but exposed to the weather. (LYNCAN/DND)*

A close-up view of the Vickers 3in/70 Mk 6 aboard Restigouche, *1960. The Mk 6 was not a favourite mount, being very prone to ammunition feed breakdowns. However, when these problems were solved in the mid-1960s, the mount was far superior to the 3in/50 Mk 33.* (LYNCAN/DND)

NATO became more concrete, Canada involved herself further and further in the business of ASW. At the first meetings of the North Atlantic Regional Planning Group in October 1949, Canada requested membership on Sub-Group B, which involved the Atlantic Ocean Lines of Communications. Further, Canada's representative, Admiral H T W Grant restricted the RCN's participation in discussions to dealing with the organization, control and protection of convoys.[7] Accordingly, in April 1950, the Canadian government increased the number of new ASW warships on order from 3 to 7, and by September, it was promising to increase the number of other vessels to be built for the RCN as well.[8]

By the time the 1951 White Paper was tabled in February 1951 by the Hon Brooke Claxton, Minister of National Defence, the new three year programme had firmed up to comprise the construction of 7 anti-submarine frigates, 14 minesweepers, 5 gate vessels and an Arctic patrol vessel (icebreaker).

Establishing The Infrastructure

No single shipyard in Canada maintained a drawing office capable of developing the systems required in modern warships. A suggestion that Canadian yards pool the design drawing staffs was quickly scuttled by traditional rivalry between the yards on the east and west coasts and the St Lawrence River; the individual yards were also afraid they would lose direct control of their design staff for commercial work. Finally, the problem was solved by the establishment of the Naval Central Drawing Office (NCDO) and its associate, the Naval Stores Central Procurement Agency (NSCPA).[9]

Setting up the NCDO under the direction of a consulting ship design firm was considered and might have worked. However, Canadian Vickers made the offer to set up an office in exchange for being designated Lead Yard. The solution was accepted in July 1949. The company's draughtsmen of the Marine Drawing Office served as the basic architects within the design team for the project. The office rapidly grew to a staff of 200 under the direction of the RCN overseeing team, and was housed in a bright new building overlooking the fitting-out basin. It was retitled the Naval Ship Design Agency in 1967 and later again, the name was changed to the Marine Design Drawing Office. It remains within the Naval organization in Ottawa in a very residual form to this day.

The NSCPA was established to assist in the task of identifying and developing Canadian sources of materiel of all sorts, including boilers, turbines, gearing, pumps, motors, winches, generators, cable, guns and everything in between, also ensuring the standardization of equipment. NSCPA became the centre for knowledge for naval procurement and served the RCN throughout three successive building programmes, plus the later modernization of these same classes. It was finally disbanded in 1967 and its task turned over to private industry.

The Final Design

Having established the groundwork for the necessary infrastructure to support Canadian construction of the warship design, Baker set out to please everyone – usually a recipe for complete disaster. There was to be a British-designed (but Canadian-built) machinery system for UK-trained naval engineers, US pattern electrical and electronic systems for Canadian electrical engineers, and a continuous, gradual effort to meet the never-ending requirements of the various other naval staff divisions. By doing so, Baker retained control of the design in order to introduce several of his own innovations.

These included a full flush upper deck that allowed plenty of extra space; well rounded deck edges, and the elimination of redundant upper deck fittings which caused maintenance problems and spray. Towards this end, the

The two Mk 10 Limbos aboard Terra Nova. *As can be seen, the power rammers and mortar projectile rails were housed port and starboard, since the mounts were opposed-sited in the well. The* St Laurent *class only retain one mount; the* IREs, *one; the* Mackenzies, *two; and the* Annapolis *class, none. (MARCOM Museum)*

anchors would be housed in pockets, covered by heated doors and the windlasses were located under the forecastle deck. A 'turtle back' forecastle for good seakeeping and smooth upper surfaces, plus the elimination of sharp corners would facilitate de-icing and decontamination of the upper deck areas in possible NBCW environments.

Other important design criteria were: special attention to stability in iced-up or damaged conditions; unitized construction as far as possible; selecting a hull form for good seakeeping ability, rather than top speed; introducing acoustic insulation and mountings; equipping the hull with efficient thermal insulation; using aluminium alloys in the superstructure, funnel casings, masts and furniture to reduce weight and top hamper and designing a central galley and messing area, the now well-known arrangement of cafeteria messing. Indeed, so much in the new design, interior-wise, was innovative that it seemed reasonable to attempt some real-time scale testing of these proposals. Accordingly, HMCS *Sioux* was reconfigured by January 1950 with bunks fitted in lieu of hammocks (a first in the RCN), plus major changes in armament, messing facilities, modern galley facilities and larger recreational spaces. Further, HMCS *Algonquin* entered a conversion refit in Esquimalt, BC, which saw her converted to a close approximation of the RN's Type 15 ASW frigate configuration by February 1953. This brought the ship's configuration and facilities very close to those of the new AS DE design and allowed valuable testing and modification of the interior layouts in the first of class.

Many detractors of the Canadian design, primarily in the UK, stated that the underwater lines of this design were directly copied from preliminary sketches of the Type 12 or *Whitby* concept. However, although both ships' criteria called for nearly-identical performance in seakeeping, handling and duties, the Canadian effort was far in advance and 'locked in' before the final Type 12 specifications were decided upon, and differed greatly in net results.

Particular care was given to the interior layout of the ship and the provision of wide passageways and access routes to allow for rapid closing-down. This design was the first within NATO to provide such close-down capability, and with NBCD filters and over-pressure within the citadel, the operations, living and working spaces within the ship were air-tight, allowing the ship to continue operations during a gas attack or entering a nuclear-hostile environment.

The electrical power generation and distribution systems were designed to the United States Navy Bureau of Ships standards, all engineered to meet American naval MILSPECS. The result was that these systems proved to be the most robust and dependable features of what would become the *St Laurent* class.

When the hull design and layout were finally sealed in 1950, the dimensions were as listed in Table 1. Mechanical, electrical and propulsion requirements were 'locked in' and the *St Laurent* class design was born.

TWILIGHT OF THE ST LAURENTS

Yukon, *the third of the* Mackenzie *class, during high speed trials off Canada's west coast in 1966. Note the first changes of Unification: the new Canadian flag being flown aft as an ensign, replacing the White Ensign. The clean lines exhibited by these, the last true descendants of the* St Laurent *line are best seen in this photo.* (LYNCAN/DND)

Propulsion

Although the Canadian application for the British Y-100 power plant would alter its layout somewhat, the design criteria remained virtually the same. By far the greatest changes came in the main gearbox and, of course the many minor changes made to translate English specifications into North American standards. However, *St Laurent* herself was somewhat the orphan even within her class, since her machinery was purchased by Canadian Vickers in its entirety from Yarrow & Co Ltd of Scotstoun. This was done to expedite her construction, but would cause logistical problems in the future and, indeed contributed greatly to her early retirement in 1974, far before her time.

The propulsion machinery comprised a two-shaft arrangement of geared turbines, each set having an underslung condenser and associated circulating water system. Lower speeds were produced by the cruising turbine. Full power applications were achieved by using the main turbine. The changeover from cruising to main turbine was automatically carried out by means of a synchromesh clutch between the cruise turbine and the main gearing. The drive from either of the turbines was then taken through double-reduction gearing. Of course the major difference that the patent MAAG hardening process allowed was the use of single-helix gears, where the Y-100 plants built by the RN used double helix gears. The MAAG process allowed for a far greater stressed and resultantly smaller or more compact gearbox. The output of the gearbox was then transferred to the twin shafts and propellers.

However, this arrangement was only applied to the *St Laurent* and *Restigouche* classes. Starting with the *Mackenzies*, the cruise turbines were eliminated from the design and the main turbines used in both speed ranges. The reasoning behind this was the numerous problems that had cropped up with the clutching arrangement in the first fourteen ships, and indeed by 1963–64, the cruise turbines in both of the first classes had been disconnected and mothballed in situ. These were gradually removed, with those in the *St Laurent*s being removed during their mid-life conversions to DDH configuration, and at various times throughout the late 1960s with the *Restigouche* class.

As in all turbine installations, the lubricating oil system was considered to be highly important. There were two forced lubricating pumps, one being motor-driven and the other turbo-driven. An automatic control was arranged in the discharge side of the pumps in order that any drop in lube oil pressure due to failure or imminent failure of the operating pump would be automatically compensated for by the cutting in of the second pump. The lube oil coolers were automatically controlled so that the oil temperature would remain constant under all exterior temperature conditions. Again, with weight reduction in mind, the drain tanks were reduced greatly in size by designing the piping system so that the maximum quantity of oil was contained in the pipe system itself, without a large reservoir being required.

Boilers

The main boilers were compact, oil-fired, water-tube 'D' boilers of the single furnace type, working at pressures of 550psi and at superheat temperatures of 675 degrees (minimum) and up to 850 degrees F. These boilers could either be operated manually, or under automatic superheat control. Both shared a common funnel and were installed athwartships in an open stokehold situated immediately forward of the engine room. Feed water requirements were handled by the latest type closed-feed system, incorporating a de-aerator feed heater and was completely automatic in its operation. Two complete evaporating plants supplied the necessary fresh water for machinery requirements and domestic services within the ship.

In general the machinery installation was arranged as an integrated single unit. By duplicating certain items of auxiliary machinery, either unit of the main machinery could be operated in a safe and economical manner in the event of damage or failure to one machinery set. As mentioned, the Canadian version of the Y-100 featured far greater automation of the machinery and boiler controls than the design used in the RN's *Whitby* class. Further, these were as centralized as far as possible in their respective compartments so that the duty watchkeeper in charge would have an excellent command of the machinery under all operating conditions.

A completely automated auxiliary boiler was installed to provide standby steam for harbour service. The capacity of this boiler was sufficient to handle all the needs of the ship while either at anchor or at a berth that did not supply the necessary steam requirements of the ship.

Electrical Generation and Distribution

The turbo-generator sets were separate units, complete with their own condenser and circulating systems. The turbo-generators consisted of two turbine-driven AC generators of 400kW capacity each, supplemented by three diesel-driven AC generators of 200kW capacity each, providing an installed generating capacity of 1750kva. Each generator set was equipped with its own means of excitation and voltage regulation. Additionally, provision was made for the 120v AC lighting system, the power being split in the Main Electrical Distribution compartment.

The turbo-generators were arranged for parallel operation and these constituted the vessels' main electrical source. One diesel-generator set was provided for harbour service but could be paralleled with either turbo if required. The remaining two diesel-generators, located one forward and one aft, operated independently of all other generators and constituted the vessel's emergency electrical source. Further, automatic relays brought these emergency generators on-line immediately if the ship's main generators failed.

Provision was made for the supply of 225v DC to equipment requiring DC power by the installation of two DC generators of 10kW capacity each, and independently, manually controlled at source through the use of field rheostats.

Steering

The steering machinery was of the electric-hydraulic type, operating twin rudders. All control was via telemotor from the main steering position, with secondary control by telemotor from an emergency conning position.

Armament

Armament included two main Mk 33, mod 2, 3in/50cal gun mountings, one forward in 'A' position, the other aft in 'Y' position. These were manufactured in Canada, under licence, by Sorel Industries gun factory which had been especially established to satisfy the needs of the new warship programme. This factory was unique in that the complete gun and mounting were manufactured from raw materials in one plant. The American GUNAR I fire control system was selected for these mounts, using the on-mount AN/SPG-48 fire control radar, with improved Mod 17 below-decks components, which featured better Target Acquisition and the Mk 7 console.[10]

As secondary or dedicated close-in AA defence, it was decided to mount two single 40mm Bofors guns just aft of the funnel and atop the deckhouse. The particular mount used was 40mm/L60 Mk 5c, sometimes referred to as the 'Boffin' gun. This was simply the powered 20mm Oerlikon Mk 5 mount, modified to accept the 40mm 60cal gun. Aiming was via local control, using the Type 6 gyro gun sight, fitted to the lefthand side of the mount. This peculiar gun mount had first seen service with the RCN in 1943–45 on late-construction 'River' class frigates.[11]

As the new design was primarily anti-submarine warfare oriented, the most modern ASW armament was specified. Therefore, the very latest in ahead-throwing mortars was sought and this proved to be the British Mk 10 NC Limbo mortar. Developed for the Royal Navy as a successor to the Squid mortar system, Limbo was first fitted aboard HMS *Rocket* for trials and tests in 1951. It superseded Squid, largely because it was more operationally flexible, had greater range and weight of projectile, plus having far greater mechanical control. Limbo was designed to be completely controlled in range, bearing and depth setting of projectiles by the sonar.

Fuzes were set remotely and, in the case of the *St Laurent* class, this, plus elevation and lateral angle was controlled by the AN/SQS-502 'Attacker' sonar, a Canadian development of the RN's Type 170 mortar control sonar. Maximum range was approximately 2200yds (2000m) and maximum depth setting was 1220ft (372m).

With the *St Laurent* design, two triple-barrelled Limbo mounts were housed in a well just aft of the after 3in gun mount, with attendant magazine/stowage rails and hoist-conveyor-rammer system. Maximum number of bombs carried was 64. The well was covered by sectional covers, that once in place, gave a reasonable amount of room for other activities. However, as the *St Laurent* design matured, so did ASW measures against rapidly-developing submarine designs. The Mk 43 lightweight ASW torpedo was the newest weapon designed to seek out submerged submarines and the new destroyers were going to have them.

To deliver the Mk 43 over the ship's sides was the next question. This was solved by taking two obsolete Mk IV depth charge throwers, removing the saddle and fabricating a suitable cradle. This was canted down at an angle of 35 degrees and when fired via a reduced impulse charge, hurled the torpedo over the side in a nose-down attitude. Upon entering the water, the torpedo was then free to initiate its search pattern. These seemingly makeshift tor-

TWILIGHT OF THE ST LAURENTS

HMCS St Laurent, Fraser *and* Ottawa *completing a scheduled refit, 1966, at Shearwater, NS. To relieve congestion in HMC Dockyard, these ships have been moved by tug to the Naval Air Station facility. The main armament has been removed for refurbishment at the Naval Armament Depot, Dartmouth, NS. Work aft appears to be centred around the VDS hoist gear of the ships.* (LYNCAN/MARCOM Museum)

pedo launchers were mounted in recesses in the aftmost deckhouse, on the main deck level and were known as Launcher Mk (NC) 2. In most photos these are covered by a canvas tarpaulin.

Plans and Contracts

Now that the design was relatively stable and the necessary infrastructure was being emplaced, the programme

Saguenay *during 'Caribops '79'. The hoist recovery hut for the SQS-504 VDS can be seen at the very stern, closest to the camera. The pole mast for TACAN is seen just forward of the twin funnels.* (LYNCAN/MARCOM Museum)

could now get into gear. The first seven ships were contracted for in 1950 and involved four yards: two on the St Lawrence River and one each on either coast. As previously stated, Canadian Vickers were designated the Lead Yard and with the NCDO becoming effective in January 1950, the drawings were soon flowing for construction of the first vessel, *St Laurent*.

The ship's hull was devised to be built in 81 prefabricated units and with a mind to wartime production, these drawings were made as simple as possible. With such a design, any fair-sized machine shop or boiler-plate shop could fabricate some of these units, which varied in weight from 5 to 26 tons. However, with peacetime construction, this fabrication was to be concentrated in seven shipyards.

These steel sections were all welded and constructed of T-bar framing members 'eggboxed' into each other, allowing both the longitudinals and athwartship frames to be continuous. Longitudinals were spaced at 2ft intervals, while athwartship frames and beams were spaced between 4ft and 5ft apart. The steel itself was especially rolled for uniformity in thickness for these vessels and strict quality control limits on carbon content were imposed to facilitate welding.

The superstructure, except for a small 'stiffener' portion in the forward end, was constructed entirely of aluminium with riveted seams. However, it was reported that those seams in *Margaree* were welded as an experiment (but it would seem this was unsuccessful, since these continued to be riveted right through the entire three follow-on classes). The foremast and outer funnel casing were also of aluminium and were suitably reinforced to accept considerable strain exerted by the heavy and eccentric loads of the radar scanners on the foremast, and the considerable side-stress imposed by 'high-line' refuelling at sea.

As the sections were moved from the fabrication areas, they were assembled on the ways in the four yards. Each unit first had to be checked for alignment, the excess material left on the joints marked, the unit removed and the excess trimmed and then the unit fitted for the final time, then welded in place. As the lower units under

machinery spaces were assembled, the larger equipment was moved into position and installed.

As can be seen from Table 2, the assembly of the hull and basic superstructure for *St Laurent* took only about one year. Most of the others in the seven-ship class were launched within eighteen months. However, the outfitting of *St Laurent* took nearly four years, reflecting the tribulations of any novel prototype. Others of the class would take about three years and the gap would steadily narrow as more and more expertise was built up in the seven yards. This is seen in the *Mackenzie* class, where the gap between launch and completion narrowed to between 1 and 2 years. The *Annapolis* class however, reflected the extra time necessary to introduce the revolutionary concepts of a hangar and deck, helicopter haul-down and variable-depth sonar.

Crisis In Construction: The Building Pace Slows

However, the optimistic launch and completion dates projected by Baker in 1949 were now proving far wide of the mark. In light of the situation in Korea and heightening of the Cold War, the Canadian government expanded the modernization of the fleet by ordering a further batch of seven DDEs to an improved design. These would eventually become the *Restigouche* class.

By 1953 the two ASW escort programmes had experienced severe slippage in their construction dates, right from the moment construction was started. Although the original completion date for the first three ships of the *St Laurent* class was projected for 30 June 1954, the work was held up initially by delays in acquiring the necessary steel, components and machine tools from foreign countries. Later, delays were caused by a never-ending series of improvements that reflected technological changes and engineering problems, especially in the area of technology transfer and establishment of necessary manufacture facilities and techniques. Lastly, the desire to spread the industrial benefits as nation-wide as possible saw contracts awarded to five separate yards: two on the St Lawrence, two on the west coast (later, three), and one on the east coast. This government fixation on preserving shipbuilding ability in Canadian yards cost the programme dearly, in time, effort and money. Hence the first ship of class, *St Laurent*, did not commission until 1955 and the last of the *Restigouche* class did not commission until 1960. It had taken slightly over twelve years, from inception to completion of these first two construction programmes.

All of these delays had had a direct financial cost as well. As projected in October 1949, each of these ships should have cost C$8 million. However, by 1955 the cost had escalated to C$15 million, and by the time *Restigouche* completed, cost per unit had reached C$23 million.[12] This figure would escalate still further over the next four years, with the last ships based on the *St Laurent* design, the *Annapolis* class, costing just over C$31 million by 1964.

Lastly, in 1954, the Navy Board once again changed the designation of these ships from DE to DDE, something that would cause great confusion in the pendant numbering of the 24 ships that would ultimately be built around this design. A prime example is the gap between *Skeena* and *Ottawa*.

Restigouche Class

On 4 June 1951, the Parliamentary Assistant to the Minister of National Defence, Ralph Campney, announced that an additional C$60 million had been added to the three-year building programme of 1949. With this money, the Canadian government was to build 12 new naval vessels. Most important to the Navy though was that this figure included 7 more destroyer escorts, bringing the total to 14. The ships were tendered in the fall and contracts awarded in mid-1952.[13]

However, these would be successors to the *St Laurent* design, incorporating several important improvements. However, the hull, machinery and other major components remained the same. Drawing upon the knowledge gleaned from the construction of the hull of *St Laurent*, the fabrication drawings were altered in such a way that the number of units delivered to the slipways was nearly cut in half. Larger units would be less trouble to align, and since these were being assembled in large, capable shipyards, the need for fabrication as envisioned under wartime conditions was felt not to be strictly necessary.

The first major improvement considered in the arma-

Nipigon, second of the Annapolis *class, RASing at sea with AOR-510* Preserver. *The fuel probe is just visible, starting down the wire from the AOR.* Nipigon *bears the 'candy stripe' around her foremast of the 5th Canadian Destroyer Squadron. Note that the 3in/50 gun is enclosed by a fibreglass housing, developed in Canada and first installed aboard the 205 class in 1962. The mount is reversed to lessen damage to the SPG-48 on the mount's face.* (LYNCAN/MARCOM Museum)

Nipigon, *April 1990. Note the additions of the lattice mast, GFCS Mk 60, deletion of the VDS and Limbo mortars and the plated-in stern. The middle fairlead (blanked off for the present) is for CANTASS, while the smaller fairleads to port are for NIXIE.* (LYNCAN/DND)

ment was the substitution of the British 3in/70 mounting for the 3in/50 Mk 33 in 'A' position. This was officially identified as the Ordnance QF 3in Mk N1 on Twin AA Mk 6 mounting. First fitted aboard the British cruisers *Tiger*, *Lion* and *Blake*, it was based upon a development of a US Bureau of Ordnance 3in/70cal design referred to as 'Broomstick' which was abandoned at the end of the war after only several installations. However, the British design, brought to a hurried completion by Vickers was impressive to say the least. The 3in/70 featured a far faster rate of fire than the US-pattern 3in/50 (60–70 versus 50 rounds per minute), higher muzzle velocity (3281fps versus 2700fps), greater range, and fully automated ammunition feed system. However, to maintain this rate of fire and muzzle velocity, the barrels were water-cooled and the bores chromium plated.[14]

Indeed, the desire to use the Mk 6 on this second class dictated the first major changes in the above-decks structures. After carefully examining the blast pattern and pressure figures supplied by the RN and Vickers, there were some very grave doubts that the aluminium bridge structure could survive the gun being fired broadside. It was the consensus of thought that in particular, the bridge face would buckle.[15] To help counter this problem, the level of the bridge was raised and strengthened. A 'breakwater' deck was incorporated on which the Mk 6 was mounted. The 'breakwater' deck also helped house the greater depth of the below-decks mount and automated feed system. Two faired bridge wing areas were built, with a radiused face contour that was designed to deflect blast. These also helped counter the loss of the pilotage position atop the enclosed bridge.[16]

Further aft, there was the addition of wing platforms to the enclosed foremast, a raised deck and installation of the Mk 69 Gun Fire Control System (GFCS) just abaft the bridge, and the main deck level superstructure aft was altered, eliminating the Mk 2 torpedo launcher recesses. Instead, these launchers were now housed inside the deckhouse, (which also served as an ASW torpedo magazine), firing through a hinged door, port and starboard, angled at 35 degrees. Today, these can still be seen aboard the three original *Restigouche* class that were not modified, and were only removed from others of the class as they were modernized to Improved *Restigouche* class ASW Escorts (IRE) in the late 1960s.

The 3in/50 Mk 33 was retained in the aft position, but the Mk 5c 40mm 'Boffin' gun mounts were deleted from the aft deckhouse, largely because the greater range of the 3in/70 rendered them obsolete. Additionally, the sonar suite was updated.

The number of yards now involved with the new destroyer programme grew to six with the ordering of the second class. These were grouped as follows: two on the west coast, three on the St Lawrence River, and one on the east coast. The cost of *Restigouche* when completed in 1958 was C$23 million.[17]

Mackenzie Class

Despite the ever-worsening situation of destroyer *vis-à-vis* submarine, the Canadian government decided to continue with the expansion of the RCN escort force through new construction. Since so many vessels of the RCN were due to be paid off in the first half of the 1960s, it was decided to build a further six Repeat *Restigouche* class. The first contract was let in 1958 and they all were on order by mid-1959.[17]

The resulting *Mackenzie* class was largely another *Restigouche* class, but with some refinements. Most were in the areas of habitability through design change and reduced complement. In the latter, crew numbers dropped to 210 from the 248 required in the *St Laurent* class. Vinyl-asbestos tile deck covering replaced the flammable linoleum; the air-conditioning was improved; the use of hot water holding tanks for domestic use was discontinued in favour of instantaneous heaters; the pre-wetting system was expanded to cover the entire upper works of the ship to combat radiation or chemical attack; and heated wipers for the bridge windows improved visibility in northern waters where icing occurred. New, delayed-cavitation propellers were first fitted on this class as well.

Diversity within the class occurred with *Qu'appelle*, who had a 3in/50 Mk 33 twin mount in both gun positions. Experience with the 3in/70 Mk 6 was showing just how hastily this mount had been brought to production. The mount was excellent when working, but the complicated magazine feed system was very prone to breakage and when a single roller pin broke, the mount was useless. The Navy itself was also contributing to the problems with the Mk 6. West coast ships so equipped were forced to wait for extended periods to have their mounts repaired, since they had to be shipped all the way from Esquimalt, BC, to the Naval Armament Depot in Dartmouth, Nova Scotia by rail. Also, the supply of parts was found sadly lacking and with the *Restigouche* class having priority in spares, *Qu'appelle* reverted to the 3in/50 Mk 33 mod 4. Later, *Yukon* gave up her 'A' mount 3in/70, to conform with *Qu'appelle*, cleanly splitting the first four ships into two armament groups. All other specifications were as per the *Restigouche* class.

Meanwhile, it was decided that the last two of what should have been a 6-ship class would be delayed while the necessary design changes were made in the blueprints to allow these two hulls to be modified to DDH configuration.[18]

Changing Tides, Shifting Technology

With the advent of nuclear power, the speed advantage of the surface ASW vessel over the submarine was virtually eliminated. This coupled with the fact that submarines could go deeper, run faster in all weather and were far more elusive seemed to forecast the demise of the surface ASW vessels. However, the Royal Canadian Navy was working on the problem, as were all other nations of the world. The US Navy was to use a nuclear submarine to negate a nuclear submarine, and the USN went on to build a fleet of specialized ASW 'hunter-killer' submarines.

For Canada, the answer was two-fold. In the first instance and to counter the far greater speed of the submerged nuclear submarine, it was the idea of coupling a relatively heavy ASW helicopter to a vessel of less than 3000 tons displacement. Secondly, to counter the tendency of submarines to be able to evade sonar by using thermal or salinity layers, the RCN developed a towed, variable-depth sonar that could be lowered through these layers, thereby locating the submarine.

Helicopters and Beartraps

Canada had been toying with the idea of using helicopters aboard RCN ships since the end of the Second World War. However, this idea had never progressed beyond the helicopter temporarily landing aboard, using some convenient, flat area, and then taking off once again.[19] The first serious experiments took place in 1956, when a steel platform was fabricated and fitted over the stern of the *Prestonian* class frigate HMCS *Buckingham*, using a HO4S-3 'Horse' helicopter. This deck was subsequently removed, modified and then installed aboard HMCS *Ottawa* in 1957, with trials being done using a H-34 (S-58) helicopter borrowed from the RCAF. As a result, it was concluded that a relatively heavy helicopter could be operated from a small ship, but that it was highly desirable to have a hanger, a method to secure the aircraft immediately after it landed, and mechanical assistance in handling the aircraft once it was on deck.[20]

The aircraft eventually chosen was the Sikorsky SH-3A Sea King, which was designated CHSS-2 in Canadian use. The system developed to handle this helicopter was known as the CHSS-2 Haul Down and Handling System.[21] Basically and very simply, this system consisted of a moveable, traversing device on the centreline of the flight deck. The helicopter, hovering over the flight deck, lowers a light steel messenger cable through a hollow probe beneath the fuselage. The messenger is received and the haul-down wire fed back up into the helicopter, lifted by the messenger, and then secured. The helicopter, maintaining hover power, is rapidly hauled down by winch until it contacts the flight deck; then the helicopter's probe is immediately seized in the jaws of the Beartrap securing device. The helicopter can promptly be shut down and the tail boom and rotor blades folded for entry into the hangar. A grid system aft of the helicopter's body aids in restraining the helicopter from lateral motion when the deck's motion is lively. When shut down and folded, the tail probe is raised and the trap traversed aft, which straightens the aircraft and trap in relation to the hangar. Then the trap is traversed forward and the helicopter guided into the hangar.[22]

The CHSS-2 Sea King was the replacement for the venerable HO4S-3 'Horse', the contract being awarded on 20 November 1962. Some 41 were eventually acquired between 1964 and 1968. Equipped with a modern 'dunking sonar" and ASW torpedoes, the Sea King was able to 'dip–sprint–dip' on any submarine, however fast and however deep, countering it with lightweight ASW torpedoes.

Annapolis class

The two ships of the *Annapolis* class were the logical, but at the same time radical, conclusion of the *St Laurent* design. Both were under construction during the time that the 205 DDH Conversion decision was being made, but in such early stages that it was possible to reconfigure the design and build the modifications in as new construction

TWILIGHT OF THE ST LAURENTS

(see below).

The *Annapolis* class when completed were very nearly the same as the Improved *St Laurents*. This class reverted to the 3in/50 Mk 33 twin mount in the 'A' position, largely as a weight-saving measure. However, they were the first class within the Canadian Navy to receive the Mk 32 triple ASW torpedo tubes, which were mounted on the quarterdeck, port and starboard, under the helicopter deck overhang.[23]

The 205 class DDH Conversions

With the preferred helicopter identified, detailed trials had to be conducted. The decision to convert the seven *St Laurents* was made on 12 September 1961 and the first ship to complete conversion was HMCS *Assiniboine* in

Fraser *and ETASS: 1987 and the 'breadboard' handling arrangement fitted to* Fraser *for evaluation of the prototype system. Fairleads to port aid in the recovery of 'tail' segments. The winch recovery control room is in the former VDS hoist control hut. The odd looking 'gun' to the hut's right is the 'bathy' launcher, which has been mounted in this area in the two converted* Annapolis *class.* (LYNCAN/DND)

June 1963. The ship was used extensively throughout 1964–66 for trials of the prototype haul-down system and in developing helicopter handling techniques.[24]

DDH conversion consisted of a 14-month long refit in which virtually everything aft of the bridge was removed to the upper deck level. Additionally, one of the two Limbo ASW mortars was removed as a weight-saving measure. The original funnel and uptakes were removed and divided in two, to make room for the forward end of the hangar. A 78ft × 40ft flight deck was installed and the space immediately below given over to accommodating the helicopter haul-down system. Meanwhile, forward accommodation spaces were re-worked as well. One of the plusses was a larger and better equipped recreation space forward, plus increased space in all messdecks.[25]

Aft, the stern of the ship had the top angle of transom and deck cut off and a variable-depth sonar well built to accommodate the AN/SQA-502 VDS handling gear, the SQS-504 towed sonar, plus the hoist control hut. In all, the modernization of *Assiniboine* consumed 2,400,000 man-hours of labour and cost C$24 million to complete. Conversion of the other six of the class cost roughly the same amount each.[26]

As well as the above, an active roll-damping system was devised and installed, albeit at a later date in *Assiniboine*. This system consisted of two non-retractable fins (one on either side of the ship), hydraulically tilted and

A close-up of the mid-ship section of Fraser *shows the latest improvements in sensors. On the foremast, bottom to top is the first of two OE-82E antennae for the WSC-3 SATCOM; the Sperry Mk 127E navigational radar; the SPS-12 and -10 radars.* Fraser *is the only ship of class to have the URN-20 TACAN mounted on a lattice mast, which resulted from her being the trials ship.* (LYNCAN/DND)

controlled by a gyro sensing unit. The fins extended out about 4½ft from the hull on a spindle and were about 9ft long. They were situated just forward of the boiler room and angled downward at 50 degrees from the horizontal. Range of movement was 15 degrees in elevation and a like amount in depression. The system was designed to limit rolling motion during extreme weather to about 10 degrees, and was successful in this role. All ships of the *St Laurent* class were retrofitted with these during or shortly after undergoing the 205 DDH Conversion Programme, while they were built into the *Annapolis* class.[27]

The DDE 257 ASW Frigate Conversions

With the decision to undertake the 205 class conversions made, the attention of Canadian naval planners turned to the *Restigouche* class. Planning began in 1961 and was accelerated after the General Purpose Frigate design was cancelled in October 1963 by the new Minister of National Defence, Paul Hellyer. However, the extensive research that had gone into the automatic digital information display system or DATAR did not go to waste.

The true success of the conversion of the four *Restigouche* class to a pure ASW role lay in the integration of sensors, displays and weapons. This was referred to as the Underwater Combat System 257 (UCS 257), and consisted of the Anti-Submarine Warfare Data System (ASWDS), one AN/SQS-505 VDS sonar set, plus the SQS-503 hull-mounted sonar and the ancillary equipment for both the hull-mounted 505 and the VDS 505. Information was fed into the ASWDS, which provides access to primary target information from the hull and VDS sonars, and secondary target information from radars. This information was processed by the SMR high-speed computer to the CCS-257. Later, the same sort of system, but utilizing two AN/SQS-505 sonar sets, would become the UCS-280, supplying the CCS-280.

The prototype of this system was evaluated in HMCS *Terra Nova* after her partial conversion in 1965–66, and, coupled with trials of the new SQS-505, took about 8 months. *Terra Nova* then entered the second phase of her modernization in 1967 and completed this in August 1968, all conversion work being handled by HMC Dockyard, Halifax, NS. Two ships, *Kootenay* and *Restigouche* were converted by Halifax Shipyards between 1970 and 1973, while *Gatineau* was converted in Esquimalt Dockyard on the west coast.[28]

The modifications to these ships were substantial. The aft 3in/50 twin mount was removed and replaced by the Mk 107 mod 2 ASROC system, with the attendant magazine built into the deckhouse immediately forward of it and to 3 deck level. This eliminated the Mk 2 ASW torpedo launchers and their magazine, forcing these ships to be without ASW torpedo tubes until after 1981. Atop this same deckhouse was mounted a 6-rail 10.3cm Bofors illumination rocket launcher. Further aft and just ahead of the Limbo mortar well, port and starboard, were mounted two, eight-barrel Corvus chaff launchers. Right aft, one of the Limbo mortars was removed and the stern was rebuilt with a reverse-slope transom, with the VDS well cut into the stern on the centreline. The VDS Hoist Control Room was built into the port inner wall of the well, something that is unique to this class. These were the first ships of the Canadian Navy to receive the new AN/SQS-505 VDS installation.

The old enclosed foremast was removed and a huge lattice mast was installed in its place, equipped with new radar and other sensors. Internally, these four ships were fitted with the AN/AQA-5 Jezebel passive sonar system. Still later, the AN/SQS-505 hull mount replaced the SQS-503, and the 502 and 10/11 sets were removed.[29]

However, by 1969 it was realized that the conversions of the *Restigouche* class were becoming very expensive – over C$12 million for the lead ship in 1970.[30] Faced with these kind of costs and the 'freeze' on defence spending that was beginning to be felt by the Department of National Defence (DND), the first ship of the class, *Chaudiere*, and the last two, *Columbia* and *St Croix* had their conversions cancelled and all three were placed in reserve in 1974.

Destroyer Life Extension Project (DELEX)

With the completion of the last of the DDH-280 'Tribal' class in late 1973, the situation looked very bleak. There were no new ships on the drawing boards for the Canadian Navy and with the unfavourable attitude of the Liberal Government towards military expenditure, it seemed that the Navy would have to soldier on with what was in service. In 1976, the DND recognized that it would be impossible to replace the Navy's nineteen destroyers at the end of their 20-year designed lifetime and that a requirement existed to maintain capability and safe operation of the fleet until they could be replaced.

Studies were conducted on project feasibility, cost implications and safety of the ships and crews as a consequence. It was found that the best option was to upgrade the sixteen operational destroyers so that their capabilities could be maintained into the 1990s, as set against a 1980–82 benchmark. Ships not included were the three remaining members of the original *Restigouche* class. Equipment that could no longer be maintained and supported would be replaced; others would be modified or updated, spares acquired, the necessary training programmes devised and instituted, and shore support provided.[31] DELEX was planned at four levels:

Level One was a basic, baseline refit that would bring the hulls and machinery back to as near-new condition as could be accomplished, without new equipment or armament being installed. Thus the elderly *St Laurent* class of six came under this level. Estimated cost per vessel was C$5 million (1980).

Level Two was the basic DELEX package as above, plus some sensor equipment that could no longer be supported would be replaced or uprated to meet original requirements. No new armament or systems were to be involved. This took in the *Mackenzie* class of four ships which ultimately had the addition of Mk 32 ASW torpedo tubes to their DELEX. Projected cost per ship was C$12 million (1980).

Level Three would only encompass the Improved *Restigouche* class, where both Levels One and Two would be achieved, plus new radar, ECM, sonar, communications, and gunfire control installed. Estimated cost per ship was C$22 million (1980).

Level Four would only take in the two newest steam-driven frigates of the *Annapolis* class. All three previous levels of refit and modernization would be undertaken, plus major modifications. Projected cost per ship was C$24 million (1980).

The original figure given as the total budget cost of this project was C$186 million (1980), and it was expected to be completed by 1986. Of the total projected, C$79 million would be allocated to the inspection and repair of the hulls and propulsion machinery in all fifteen ships, plus selective replacement of navigation and life support systems due to difficulties in maintenance. The other C$107 million would be used for the replacement of certain combat systems in ten ships (excluding the 205 class) to enable them to maintain an operational capability over the longer period of service.[32]

The first two ships, *Gatineau* and *Qu'appelle*, underwent DELEX feasibility studies as lead ships in the programme. Meanwhile, approval of the DELEX programme was announced on 8 August 1980 after it was found these two ships bore out the projected costs and requirements. In fact, the masters of the Canadian Navy had little choice: continued delays in implementing the 1978 announcement of a plan to build a new class of Patrol Frigate left no room for further postponement of DELEX.

The DELEX refits were dovetailed with a ship's regular refit cycle as far as possible. In some cases where the DELEX refits were extensive, partial programmes were implemented and completed when the ship next entered a refit, or in the case of missing equipment, whenever the equipment arrived. On the west coast, these refits were split between SRU(P) – Ship Repair Unit, Pacific – within HMC Dockyard, Esquimalt and Burrard-Yarrows Corporation. However, on the east coast, it was felt that private yards had the expertise to carry out the entire DELEX refit. Accordingly, these were put out to tender and the veteran Vickers Canada Limited yards in Montreal, Quebec were successful in the first bid. Thereafter, the ships of the *St Laurent* class were tendered as a block, and Vickers was again the successful bidder. However, it should be mentioned that SRU(A), HMC Dockyard, Halifax, NS, played an important part in both preparing the ships for refit and attending to post-refit defects.

Of course there had to be an exception to the rule, and *Margaree* was it. In 1980, she had no sooner entered refit in Montreal when the yard was hit by a serious labour strike that summer. This wore on through the year, and by December, DND were very concerned that she would be frozen in port as the St Lawrence River iced up. Accordingly, the ship was prepared for a tow and removal by naval tug from under the very noses of the strikers, arriving in Halifax on 8 December. She was drydocked at Halifax-Dartmouth Industries and between this firm and SRU(A), the DELEX was completed in time for half-power trials in June of 1981.[33]

By 1985 nine destroyers had been fully DELEXed during regularly scheduled refit periods. Two more were undergoing this update and all were expected to complete the programme by 1987. Total cost of the project had grown to C$213.8 million.³⁴

Much confusion has grown up around just what constituted part of the DELEX programme. As it progressed, 'stand-alone' projects were dovetailed into these refit cycles and the exact delineation points between the two became very blurred. The two most confusing of these were those done to the 257 class IREs and the 265 *Annapolis* class (the latter discussed more fully below).

With the 257 Improved *Restigouche* class, the modernization was extensive. *Gatineau* was first and she received the following major changes:

1. Installation of two triple Mk 32 mod 5 ASW torpedo tube mounts.
2. Removal of the 10.3cm Bofors illumination rocket launchers and the addition of the Mk 33 SRBOC chaff launcher system.
3. Removal of the top portion of the lattice mast and a pole mast installed like her sister, *Terra Nova*, which supports the SRD-501 at the top, and the CANEWS antennae.
4. Internally, the AN/SPS-10 was updated and now bears the designator SPS-501, the SPS-12 replaced by the Marconi S1820 or more commonly called SPS-503, and the navigational radar replaced by the Sperry Mk 127E. ADLIPS replaced the old navigational plot tables in the Ops Room.
5. A new and larger capacity diesel generator that supplies the ship's emergency needs was installed, and new evaporators installed.
6. The SQS-505 sonar, hull mount replaced the SQS-502 and -503 sets, the SQS-10/11 sets were deleted, and the new C3 dome eventually fixed and faired into the hull lines for better peformance.

Cost of these DELEX refits to the four of class were quoted as C$72 million in 1986, with the last, *Restigouche*, completed in late 1985.³⁵

The 265 class conversions

With the announcement in 1978 that the government was looking at a new class of frigate, it seemed the defence freeze might finally be over. However, as delay followed delay in 1978–79, it was quickly realized that the *St Laurent* class and their cousins would have to sail on operationally far beyond their projected 25-year lifetimes. This led to the Destroyer Life Extension Project (DELEX) detailed above, and out of this grew the 265 class conversions.

By 1982, it was more than apparent that the government of the day intended to delay the decision to build the new Patrol Frigates as long as possible. Meanwhile, there were systems that had to be proven long before the new ships were launched. One of these was CANTASS or Canadian Towed Array Sonar System, which was the marriage of Canadian-developed signal processors with the 'wet end' of the USN's SQR-19 TACTASS. This was tested in the experimental stage aboard HMCS *Fraser* as ETASS during 1986–87, and the decision was then made that the system was more than viable and would equip the twelve new Patrol Frigates. When operational, CANTASS will open passive detection ranges out to 100 nautical miles, with the capability of detecting, analysing, classifying and tracking dozens of targets at any given time.³⁶

Meanwhile, it was decided that the two ships of the *Annapolis* class would undergo their basic DELEX updates, but that a group of 'stand-alone' projects would be melded into what was referred to as the 265 class Conversions. Accordingly, *Nipigon* (DDH-266) entered refit on 23 June 1983 and was completed by 24 August 1984. Under this combined DELEX/265 modernization refit, *Nipigon* was altered to such a degree that one would not believe that she was a sister ship to *Annapolis*. Emerging from her refit, *Nipigon* looked like a cross between a *St Laurent* class helicopter-carrying frigate and an Improved *Restigouche* class ASW frigate, with a large lattice foremast supporting the unique antenna of the Marconi AN/SPS-503 radar. Underwater, the SQS-502, -503 and SQS-10/11 had been removed, the former two replaced by a AN/SQS-505 housed in a fixed C3 dome.³⁷

In the newly reconfigured Ops Room, two new ADLIPS stations dramatically changed and improved the ship's capabilities in processing data generated by the ship's own sensors or externally from other ship or planes. Additionally, *Nipigon* was outfitted with the Defence Research Establishment, Atlantic's newest idea in sonar processing, the Team Architecture Signal Processor or TASP. When combined with the lastest in the line of SQS-505 sonar, it is referred to as a 'smart 505' or collectively as the AN/SQS-510. The 510 will outfit the two *Annapolis* class eventually, plus the new Patrol Frigates and the Portuguese Navy's MEKO class, the latter under NATO's Mutual Aid Programme.³⁸

From here on, notes are general for both ships of the class, as some additions or alterations have been done piecemeal during regularly-scheduled refits in the past few years. The MEL-developed Canadian Naval Electronic Warfare System or CANEWS has been installed, and the Mk 69 GFCS upgraded by solid-state circuitry and the addition of the Norden SPG-515 fire control radar. Aft, the last remaining Limbo and the AN/SQA-501 VDS handling gear have been removed. The stern was plated over and the resulting space given over to accommodating the CANTASS OK-410 and NIXIE (AN/SLQ-25 acoustic torpedo countermeasures) handling gear. The former Limbo mortar magazine and handling space to port has been given over to sonobuoy and SRBOC canister stowage, plus the 'dry end' of NIXIE. The dry end compartment for CANTASS is situated on the main deck level, almost immediately under the Sonar Control Room forward, and here the signal processors are housed.

Naval engineers learned a great deal from the problems encountered by *Nipigon* during moderately rough weather in early 1985, when the whipping action of the new lattice mast threw sufficient strain against an athwartship deck joint in the Ops Room to shear off nearly 210 aluminium rivets and allowed nearly 40ft of this overlap between steel and aluminium plate to gape open.³⁹ With *Annapolis*, a large, structural cruciform was constructed that extended across the breadth of the ship at frame 21 on deck two to act as a set of 'broad shoulders' in supporting

The latest in looks for Gatineau, *and a first deployment of this class to the east coast since 1970.* Gatineau, *as part of a re-distribution of ASW assets to better balance the fleets on both coasts, was 'swapped' for one DDH-280 'Tribal' class and a helicopter detachment. She is shown on arrival in Halifax Harbour, 15 April 1987.* (LYNCAN/DND)

the weight and strain not allowed for in the original calculations in the early 1960s. It was also necessary to relocate the water-tight door at frame 21 on the same deck to starboard to accommodate this new structural member. It is hoped that *Nipigon* will have this additional support in a future refit, but her problem was found to be unusually small diameter aluminium rivets in this critical area, something that was solved by using larger bolts and nuts in lieu of rivets.

These two ships are the first in the Canadian fleet to boast the PRAIRIE/MASKER systems. MASKER was first revealed to be aboard *Annapolis* in 1987, and consists of two underwater belts, one before the boiler room and the other before the engine room. When in operation, these belts emit controlled blankets of compressed air bubbles under these noisy compartments, effectively trapping and smothering radiated noise. With PRAIRIE, especially designed propellers are fitted which bleed air through holes in the leading propeller blade edges, which effectively reduces cavitation noise. Both systems have become operational in the past two years as compressors were installed during normal refit cycles.

Nipigon's DELEX/265 Conversion took 14 months and cost C$19 million (1984); *Annapolis* entered her conversion refit in August 1985 for a scheduled 13-month period at Saint John Shipbuilding in New Brunswick. However, with additional work, the refit period was extended into January 1987 and the costs escalated to C$20 (1984).[40]

With these refits and when the production models of CANTASS are fitted in 1992–93, these ships will then be capable of soldiering on into the first decade of the next century. However, no matter how capable the systems aboard these ships, they will be 36 years old by the year 2000, and this from a class with a designed lifetime of 20–25 years.

Fading Away

The *St Laurent* design, conceived less than five years after the end of the Second World War has to have been the most successful hull design of her era to be still afloat. The hull form was used through four successive classes, spread over nearly 14 years, meeting the needs of ASW in various ways throughout the period.

Keeping ships designed for twenty years service operational for thirty-five years in some cases has been a feat of desperation on the part of the Canadian government, the Department of National Defence and the RCN's successor, Maritime Command. The disruption of building programmes began with the cancellation of the General Purpose Frigate in 1964 by a government that knew little of the needs of its navy and cared even less. The destruction of the Canadian Navy as a separate entity in 1966, when the idea of consolidation of administrative and supply branches of the three services was turned into full-blown integration by the-then Minister of National Defence, Paul Hellyer, further deranged naval planning.

The budget freezes between 1969 and 1973 totally dislocated the ship acquisition process, allowing only those ships then on the order books to be completed. By this time, the *St Laurent* class was between 12 and 14 years old, with less than 6 years remaining in their projected lifetimes. The almost leisurely pace taken by successive governments in the following years in bringing the Patrol Frigate design to the builder's yards meant that hundreds of millions of dollars had to be expended just to keep these ships marginally operational. They were without point missile defence systems, and even the electronic countermeasures suites were obsolete, with the only defence being the dubious decoying effects of chaff rockets. However, they did stay at sea when other, newer ships of the NATO fraternity cowered in harbour in foul weather. They saved lives with their Sea Kings, accounted admirably in all kinds of exercises by being utilized to their utmost capabilities by their crews.

Most of the *St Laurent* class will have disappeared by 1995, and their later sisters will fare little better, with all but the *Annapolis* class gone by the turn of the century. The *Annapolis* class will have spanned two generations of ASW helicopter, being the only ships based on this hull form that will carry the new Canadianized version of the EH-101 at the close of this decade. Meanwhile, the first few have been slipping away into history.

As mentioned, *St Laurent* (DDH-205) was paid off on 14 June 1974. She was cannibalized over the intervening years for parts for her sister ships and spent her time secured near the Bedford Magazine until June 1979 when nearly stripped bare, it was decided she would be sold as scrap. A few months later, she was sold by Crown Assets for C$76,000 to Dartmouth Salvage Limited, who stripped her of most readily salvageable scrap and then sold her gutted hull to Consolidated Andy, Brownsville, Texas. The ship then spent the next few months being readied for her tow to Texas.

On 8 January 1980, *St Laurent* left Halifax for the last time, under tow of the Norwegian tug, *Odin Salvator*. On the 12th, buffeted by the fringe of a tropical hurricane, she began to settle by the stern. After casting off her tow, the tug circled the settling hulk, as the bows rose higher and higher, before the ship gradually capsized and disappeared beneath the waves at 11.05, into nearly 2000 fathoms, some 250 miles south of Nantucket. The message flashed throughout Maritime Command finished with a brief, but heartfelt, 'Rest in Peace'.[41]

On 26 January 1988, the layup was announced of the first of the Improved *St Laurent* class frigates to make way for the new Canadian Patrol Frigates. *Assiniboine* (DDH-234), commissioned in August 1956, would be laid up as of 1 July 1988, when she would enter a 6-month long period of reduced operational readiness. Accordingly, *Assiniboine* had her last sail-past on 23 November 1988. Her last ceremonial divisions were carried out on 14 December, when the ensign, jack and commissioning pennant were lowered for the last time. The ex-*Assiniboine* was due to enter a 12-month long paying-off phase on 1 January 1989 and then enter disposal phase on 1 January 1990. However there has been a change of plans.

While under review, it was found that the steaming plant of *Assiniboine* was in excellent condition and since the ship more closely matches the configuration of the remaining 'steamers', it was decided to make this ship the alongside steam training vessel, replacing *St Croix*. No decision has been made on the disposal of *St Croix* to date. Meanwhile, the retirement of other *St Laurent* class ships are in the works. The following ships have all reached their 30th anniversary of service in the Canadian Navy: *Saguenay*, 15 December 1986; *Ottawa*, November 1986; *Skeena*, *Fraser* and *Margaree* in 1987. The next to be retired is *Saguenay* which will pay-off on 31 August 1990, and then *Ottawa* in 1991.

With their passing, the final chapters of a half-century Canadian naval history will be written. The *St Laurent*s were the first wholly Canadian warships and will have earned their place in our naval history.

1978 Pacific Fleet Review and Kootenay. *Comparing her with the photo of* Gatineau *arriving in Halifax, it can be seen that the Corvus chaff launchers, port and starboard and just ahead of the Limbo well have been replaced by two Mk 32 mod 5 ASW torpedo tube mounts, the 10.3cm Bofors illumination rocket rails atop the aft deckhouse are removed, the top of the lattice mast has been replaced with a pole mast, which also carries the CANEWS antenna at its base (just in line with the deck of the MacDonald Bridge.) The two OE-82E antennae for WSC-3 can be seen on pedestals on the bridge top of* Gatineau. *(LYNCAN/ MARCOM Museum)*

Footnotes

1. Canada, Dept of National Defence, King's Printer (Ottawa 1949), 14 (White Paper based upon DND report tabled on 19 October 1949).
2. Cabinet Defence Committee Minutes, 8 October 1948.
3. Memorandum to Staff from NCC, 'Proposed AS Escort Vessel', NSS 8200–17, 12 October 1948.
4. D K Nicholson, 'Experience With Hardened and Ground Gearing in the Royal Canadian Navy', (a Paper presented at the Institute of Marine Engineering, London, 11 April 1961).
5. Memorandum to CNTS from NCC 'Interim Report of Progress', RG24 NSS 8200–17, 18 February 1949.
6. Memorandum to CNTS from NCC, 'Sketch Design of AS Escort Vessel', RG24 NSS 8200–17, 28 May 1949.
7. Joel Sokolsky, 'The US, Canada and the Cold War in the North Atlantic: The Early Years', (A Paper presented to the 1981 Annual Meeting of the Canadian Political Science Association, May 1981).
8. Debates, House of Commons, 6 September 1950, p322, and 9 April 1951, p1726.
9. 'BDG', 'The Birthplace of a Ship', *The Crowsnest* 4 (August 1952), 1:30.
10. 'First of the Sub Killers', *Canadian Shipping & Marine Engineering News* 27, No 2 (1955), p28. Also, *GUNAR Mk NC1, mod NC1 Instruction Handbook*, Vol 1 Book No 520–10000/C, Canadian Westinghouse Co. Ltd., Hamilton, Ont, (April 1958).
11. RCN Trade Manual, *Weaponman Surface, Trade Grp One*, BRCN 3034 (63), pp169–171, and *Jane's Fighting Ships 1959–60*.
12. HOC Debates, 4 October 1949, p1065; DND Information Release, 26 October 1955, p1; and *Jane's Fighting Ships 1959–60*.
13. HOC Debates, 4 June 1951, p3690.
14. Bernard Fitzsimons (Ed) *Weapons & Warfare*, Columbia House (New York), Vol 23, p2574, and *Weaponman Surface, Trade Grp One*, pp181–183.
15. Interview with David Walker, former naval architect, German & Milne, 5 June 1990. Walker at this time was a junior architect with the naval design team working on the drawings and specifications of the *Restigouche* class.
16. *Jane's Fighting Ships*, 1962–63, p34, and correspondence with Lt (N) Stanley Stoker, BINFO, CFB Halifax, 23 March 1982.
17. HOC Debates, 8 July 1959, p5699; and 'Canada's Naval Fleet', *Canada's Navy: A Wings Magazine Commemorative Issue*, Corvus Publishing Group (Calgary, Alberta), pp53–54.
18. J H W Knox, 'An Engineer's Outline of RCN History, Part II', in *The RCN In Retrospect, 1910–1968*, James Boutilier (ed), UBC Press pp326–7.
19. T G Lynch, 'ASW Workhorse: 22 Years of Sea King', *Helicopters*, Canada's National Helicopter Magazine, Corvus Publishing Group (Fall 1986), pp45–50. Memo from Senior Officer (Fuel) Operations to DOD, 23 January 1943.
20. Ibid.
21. Lt-Cdr P Charlton, 'The CHSS-2 Haul Down and Handling System', *Canadian Aeronautics & Space Journal* (Feb 1966), pp63–68.
22. Ibid.
23. 'Canada's Naval Fleet', *Canada's Navy: A Wings Magazine Commemorative Issue*, Corvus Publishing Group (Calgary, Alberta), pp52–53.
24. 'Wedding of the Sea King', *Crowsnest*, Queen's Printer (Ottawa, March/April 1964), pp10–11.
25. Ibid.
26. Ibid.
27. 'Special Gear Aids 'Copters',' *Crowsnest*, Queen's Printer (Ottawa, February 1964), p4.
28. J H W Knox, loc cit, p331.
29. 'Canada's Naval Fleet' loc cit, pp53–54, and Unit Histories, HMC Ships, IRE DND (Ottawa 1985).
30. Captain R L Ronaldson, 'DELEX for MZ and IRE Classes – Life Extension For Old Ladies', *Canada's Navy Annual*, No 1, Corvus Pub Grp, pp69–70; and Knox, loc cit, pp330–331.
31. Lt-Cdr W R Lowe (Project Manager DELEX), 'Aide Memoire, DELEX', to the author (25 February 1985).
32. The Navy League of Canada, *Maritime Affairs Bulletin* No 3/80 and No 4/80, pp4 and 7 respectively.
33. CFBH: 1350–1 (BINFO) (5 May 1981), letter to the author concerning the *Margaree* DELEX refit.
34. Ld-Cdr W R Lowe, op cit.
35. Capt R L Donaldson, op cit, pp330–331.
36. T G Lynch, 'Canadian Towed Array Sonar System', *Canada's Navy: A Wings Magazine Commemorative Issue*, p160.
37. '*Starwars Annapolis*: From Dowdy Daughter to Cinderella Frigate', *Canada's Navy Annual* No 3, Corvus Pub Grp, pp130–132.
38. Interview with Mr Gordon Mount, Senior Vice-President, Computing Devices, Ottawa (June 1987). CDC will manufacture the UYS-501.
39. Robert Gordon, 'Captain Says: Nipigon Repair Work May Take Five Weeks', *The Mail-Star*, Halifax, NS (5 June 1985); and Gordon, 'Nipigon To Miss Show', *The Mail-Star* (13 June 1985).
40. '*Starwars Annapolis*: From Dowdy Daughter . . .', loc cit, pp130–132.
41. Message from QHM Halifax, to MARCOMHQ, 18 January 1980 based on information gathered from the marine surveyors, Evans, Yeatman and Endal. (UNCLASS) 'RIP' line preceded by comment, 'Old age'.

Table 1. SPECIFICATIONS

Dimensions	As Built	Current
St Laurent	366ft × 42ft × 13ft 2in	366ft × 42ft × 13ft 6in[1]
Restigouche	366ft × 42ft × 13ft 2in	371ft 3in × 42ft × 19ft 10in[2]
Mackenzie	366ft × 42ft × 13ft 2in	366ft × 42ft × 22ft 9in
Annapolis	366ft × 42ft × 14ft 4in	366ft × 42ft × 14ft 4in

Speed 14kts cruise; 32kts max

Range 4,750nm at 14kts

Complement 18 officers, 210 men (*Annapolis, Mackenzie* classes)
 13 officers, 201 men (Improved *Restigouche* class)
 12 officers, 236 men (*Restigouche,* Improved *St Laurent* classes)

Displacement	As built		Current	
	(light)	(full)	(light)	(full)
Improved *St Laurent*	2000t	2600t	2260t	2858t
Restigouche	2000t	2600t	2380t	2880t
Improved *Restigouche*	2000t	2600t	2714t	2899t[3]
Mackenzie	2000t	2600t	2380t	2890t
Annapolis	2400t	2858t	2600t	3000t

Machinery
2 – Babcock-Wilcox bent tube boilers
4 – English Electric design geared turbines (2 main, 2 cruise), mains = 15,000shp each or 30,000shp total.[4]
2 – shafts, twin fixed-pitch propellers; originals replaced in the mid-1970s with delayed-cavitation, curved-blade propellers.

Armament	As built	Current
St Laurent	2 – 3in/50 Mk 33 DP twin mounts	1 – 3in/50 Mk 33 DP twin mount
	2 – 40mm Mk 5c 'Boffin' single	1 – Mk 10 Limbo mortar
	2 – Mk 10 Limbo mortars	2 – Mk 32, mod 5 triple TT
	2 – Mk 2 torpedo side-launchers	1 – CH-124A Sea King helicopter
Restigouche	1 – 3in/70 Mk VI DP twin mount	1 – 3in/70 Mk VI DP twin mount
	1 – 3in/50 Mk 33 DP twin mount	1 – 3in/50 Mk 33 DP twin mount
	2 – Mk 10 Limbo mortars	2 – Mk 10 Limbo mortars
	2 – Mk 2 torpedo side-launchers	2 – Mk 2 torpedo side-launchers
Improved *Restigouche*	1 – 3in/70 Mk VI DP twin mount	1 – 3in/70 Mk VI DP twin mount
	1 – 3in/50 Mk 33 DP twin mount	1 – Mk 107, mod 2 ASROC mount
	2 – NC 10 Limbo mortars	1 – NC 10 Limbo mortar
	2 – Mk 2 torpedo side-launchers	2 – Mk 32, mod 5 triple TT
	1 – 10.3cm Bofors illumination rocket launcher	1 – Super RBOC Mk 36, mod 2 ECM
	2 – 3in 8 barrel Corvus chaff launchers	
Mackenzie	1 – 3in/70 Mk VI DP twin mount	1 – 3in/70 Mk VI DP twin mount[5]
	1 – 3in/50 Mk 33 DP twin mount	1 – 3in/50 Mk 33 DP twin mount
	2 – Mk 10 Limbo mortars	2 – Mk 10 Limbo mortars
	2 – 40mm Mk 5c 'Boffin' single	2 – Mk 32, mod 5 triple TT
	2 – Mk 2 torpedo side-launchers	
Annapolis	1 – 3in/50 Mk 33 DP twin mount	1 – 3in/50 Mk 33 DP mount
	1 – Mk 10 Limbo mortar	1 – CH-124A Sea King helicopter
	1 – CHSS-2 Sea King ASW helicopter	2 – Mk 32, mod 5 triple TT
	2 – Mk 32, mod 5 triple TT	1 – Super RBOC Mk 36, mod 2 ECM

Radar, EW, SATCOM, SATNAV

	As built	Current
St Laurent	1 – AN/SPS-12B 1 – AN/SPS-10 1 – Sperry Mk II 1 – Mk 10 IFF 1 – SRR4 AEW 2 SPG-48 w/GUNAR 1 – DAU RDF	1 – AN/SPS-12B 1 – AN/SPS-10D 1 – Sperry Mk 127E 1 – Mk 12 IFF 2 – SPG-48 w/GUNAR II 1 – URN-22A TACAN[6] 1 – SRD-501 1 – CANEWS 1 – AN/WSC-3 SATCOM 1 – SRR-1 Fleet Broadcast 1 – Omega MX 1105 LORAN 'C'
Restigouche	1 – AN/SPS-12B 1 – AN/SPS-10 1 – Sperry Mk II 1 – Mk 10 IFF 1 – SRR4 AEW 2 – SPG-48 w/Mk 69 GFCS 1 – DAU RDF	1 – AN/SPS-12B 1 – AN/SPS-10 1 – Sperry Mk II 1 – Mk 10 IFF 1 – SRR4 AEW 2 – SPG-48 w/Mk 69 GFCS 1 – DAU RDF
Improved Restigouche	1 – AN/SPS-12B 1 – AN/SPS-10 1 – Sperry Mk II 1 – Mk 10 IFF 1 – SRR4 AEW 2 – SPG-48 w/Mk 69 GFCS 1 – DAU RDF	1 – AN/SPS-503 (Marconi) 1 – AN/SPS-502 (Cardon solid-state package for SPS-10D) 1 – Sperry Mk 127E 1 – Mk 12 IFF 1 – Norden SPG-515 w/ Mk 60 GFCS 1 – WSC-3 SATCOM 1 – SRR-1 Fleet Broadcast 1 – WLR-1C (narrow band ESM) 1 – SLR-503 (comm) 1 – UPD-501 (broad band ESM) 1 – CANEWS
Mackenzie	1 – AN/SPS-12B 1 – AN/SPS-10 1 – Sperry Mk II mod 2 1 – Mk 10 IFF 2 – SPG-48 w/Mk 69 GFCS 1 – DAU RDF	1 – AN/SPS-12B 1 – AN/SPS-502 (Cardon update) 1 – Sperry Mk 127E 1 – Mk 10 IFF 2 – SPG-48 w/Mk 69 GFCS 1 – WLR-1C (narrow band ESM) 1 – UPD–501 (broad band ESM)
Annapolis	1 – AN/SPS-12B 1 – AN/SPS-10D 1 – Sperry Mk II mod 2 2 – SPG-48 w/GUNAR II 1 – WLR-1C ESM 1 – UPD-501 ESM 1 – Mk 10 IFF	1 – AN/SPS-503 (Marconi) 1 – AN/SPS-502 (Carbon solid-state update of SPS-10D) 1 – Sperry Mk 127E 1 – Norden SPG-515 w/ Mk 60 GFCS 1 – CANEWS 1 – Mk 12 IFF 1 – AN/URN-26 TACAN

Sonar, U/W Telephone, Bathy

	As built	*Current*
St Laurent	1 – AN/SQS-501 (mod Type 162) tracer	1 – AN/SQS-501
	1 – AN/SQS-502 (mod Type 170) attacker	1 – AN/SQS-502
	1 – AN/SQS-503 searcher	1 – AN/SQS-503
	1 – AN/SQS-10 scanner	1 – AN/SQS-505 VDS
	1 – AN/UQC-1B (U/W telephone)	1 – AN/UQC-1B
		1 – AN/SLQ-25 NIXIE
Restigouche	1 – AN/SQS-501 (mod Type 162) tracer	1 – AN/SQS-501
	1 – AN/SQS-502 (mod Type 170) attacker	1 – AN/SQS-502
	1 – AN/SQS-503 searcher	1 – AN/SQS-503
	1 – AN/SQS-10/11 scanner	1 – AN/SQS-505 VDS
	1 – AN/UQC-1B (U/W telephone)	1 – AN/UQC-1B
Improved *Restigouche*	1 – AN/SQS-501 (mod Type 162) bottom	1 – AN/SQS-505 (hull)
	1 – AN/SQS-502 (mod Type 170) attacker	1 – AN/SQS-505 (VDS)
	1 – AN/SQS-503 searcher	1 – AN/AQA-5 JEZEBEL passive sonar
	1 – AN/SQS-10/11 scanner	1 – AN/SSQ-56A Bathy
	1 – AN/UQC-1B (U/W telephone)	1 – AN/WQC-501 U/W telephone
		1 – AN/SLQ-25 NIXIE
Mackenzie	1 – AN/SQS-501 (mod Type 162) bottom	1 – AN/SQS-505 (hull)
	1 – AN/SQS-502 (mod Type 170) attacker	1 – AN/SQS-501
	1 – AN/SQS-503 searcher	1 – AN/AQA-5 JEZEBEL passive sonar
	1 – AN/SQS-10/11 scanner	1 – AN/SSQ-56A Bathy
	1 – AN/UQC-1B (U/W telephone)	1 – AN/WQC-501 U/W telephone
Annapolis	1 – AN/SQS-501 (mod Type 162) bottom	1 – AN/SQS-505 (hull)[7]
	1 – AN/SQS-503 searcher	1 – AN/SQS-501 (bottom)
	1 – AN/SQS-504 VDS	1 – CANTASS
	1 – AN/SQS-10/11 scanner	1 – AN/SLQ-25 NIXIE
	1 – AN/UQC-2B (U/W telephone)	1 – AN/UQC-2B

[1] With the C5 domes on these older frigates being faired into the hull in the fully extended position, deep draught is increased to approximately 19ft 10in.
[2] Improved *Restigouche* class only. Other three: 366ft length and 13ft 6in draught.
[3] *Restigouche* listed as 3007t as of 1984. All others as listed.
[4] This arrangement for the first 14 ships of the *St Laurent* and *Restigouche* classes only. Discontinued, beginning with the *Mackenzie* class. Original 14 suites largely had cruise turbines disconnected by 1964.
[5] The twin 3in/70 Mk VI in 'A' position on *Yukon* has been replaced by a 3in/50 Mk 33 twin mount. *Qu'appelle* was built in this configuration. *Mackenzie* and *Saskatchewan* retain their 3in/70 mounts.
[6] Except *Fraser* (DDH-233) which has a URN-20A on distinctive lattice mast.
[7] *Nipigon* served as trials ship for the DRE(A)-developed AN/SQS-510 TASP system. The system marries eight Computing Devices of Canada UYS-501 computers with the latest 505 variant sonar. The resultant '*Smart* 505' resulted in the SQS-510 TASP, which will be fitted in the *Halifax*, *Montreal* and *Annapolis* classes, the latter after the requirements of the new frigates are met. These are also being supplied to the Portuguese Navy for use in their new MEKO class frigates.

Table 2. BUILDING DATA

Name	Pennant No	Builder	Laid down	Launched	Commissioned
St Laurent Class					
St Laurent	DDE-205	Canadian Vickers, Montreal, Que	24.11.50	30.11.51	29.10.55
Saguenay	DDE-206	Halifax Shipyard, Halifax, NS	04.04.51	30.07.53	15.12.56
Skeena	DDE-207	Burrard DD & SB, N Vancouver, BC	01.06.51	19.08.52	30.03.57
Ottawa	DDE-229	Canadian Vickers, Montreal, Que	08.06.51	29.04.53	10.11.56
Margaree	DDE-230	Halifax Shipyard, Halifax, NS	12.09.51	29.03.56	05.10.57
Fraser	DDE-223	Burrard/Yarrows, Esquimalt, BC	11.12.51	19.02.53	28.06.57
Assiniboine	DDE-234	Marine Industries, Sorel, Que	19.05.52	12.02.54	16.08.56
Restigouche Class					
Restigouche	DDE-257	Canadian Vickers, Montreal, Que	15.07.53	22.11.54	07.06.58
Gatineau	DDE-236	Davie SBm Lauzon, Que	30.04.53	03.06.57	17.02.59
Kootenay	DDE-258	Burrard, Vancouver, BC	21.08.52	15.06.54	07.03.59
Terra Nova	DDE-259	Victoria Machinery, Victoria, BC	14.11.52	21.06.55	06.06.59
Chaudiere	DDE-235	Halifax Shipyard, Halifax, NS	30.07.53	13.11.57	14.11.59
Columbia	DDE-260	Burrard, Vancouver, BC	11.06.53	01.11.56	07.11.59
St Croix	DDE-256	Marine Industries, Sorel, Que	15.10.54	17.11.57	04.10.58
Mackenzie Class					
Mackenzie	DDE-261	Canadian Vickers, Montreal, Que	15.12.58	25.05.61	06.10.62
Saskatchewan	DDE-262	Victoria Machinery, Victoria, BC	29.10.59	01.02.61	16.02.63
Yukon	DDE-263	Burrard, Vancouver, BC	25.10.59	27.07.61	25.05.63
Qu'appelle	DDE-264	Davie SB., Lauzon, Que	14.01.60	02.05.62	14.09.63
Annapolis Class					
Annapolis	DDH-265	Halifax Shipyard, Halifax, NS	02.09.61	27.04.63	19.12.64
Nipigon	DDH-266	Marine Industries, Sorel, Que	05.08.60	10.12.61	30.05.64

Farewell to St Laurent – *a very tired warrior slowly slips beneath the waves while being towed to Brownsville, Texas for breaking up, 12 January 1980.* (LYNCAN/C Squires)

WARSHIP NOTES

This section comprises a number of short articles and notes, generally highlighting little-known aspects of warship history.

DANISH TUMLEREN TORPEDO BOATS

Tom Wismann describes some of the Danish Navy's first sea-going torpedo craft.

Initially, the Orlogsværftet (the Royal Naval Dockyard in Copenhagen) did not have the skills or the technology necessary for building these very complicated vessels; the first 22 torpedo-boats for the RDN were built abroad (1874–89). In 1908 it was decided to construct nine large torpedo-boats, beginning with two comparative classes each of three vessels.

Two of the world's leading torpedo-boat construction companies, Schichau in Elbing and Yarrow in Glasgow, were chosen to build the leading boat of the two classes; the follow-on vessels would then be built in Denmark. The two classes were of the same size, had the same horsepower, and the same armament, to see which company could produce the better vessel.

The *Tumleren* boats were one of these classes.

When the boats had been built a comparison between the German and the British designed boats showed that the German boats were better in technical and tactical respects, whereas the sea-keeping ability of the British designed boats was superior. During the First World War the Imperial German Navy's *A26* class torpedo-boats were built to a design that closely resembled the *Tumleren* class.

1. Building.
The *Tumleren* (Porpoise), as the lead boat, was built at the German F Schichau shipyard in Elbing (hull number 852) at a price of 500,000 Marks, the two following sisters, *Vindhunden* (Greyhound) and *Spækhuggeren* (Killer Whale), being built to German drawings, at the Orlogsværftet with hull numbers 104 and 105 respectively.

2. Technical description.
The ships were built of steel, and it was mentioned in the contract with the German yard that both workmanship and materials should be 'first class standard'. The delivery of the first unit was to take place 14 months after the signing of the contract. If the building was delayed the Yard would pay a fine of 10 pounds sterling a day.

	laid down	launched	trial	commissioned
Tumleren	. . . .	1.3.1911	8.8.1911	28.8.1911
Vindhunden	21.10.1910	16.12.1911	1912	. . . . . .
Spækhuggeren	29.10.1910	7.10.1911	1912	. . . . . .

2.1 Pennant numbers.
The boats had through their lifetimes the following pennant numbers.

Period	Tum	Vind	Sfaek
1920–23	T 19	T 18	T 17
1923–29	C 1	C 2	C 3
1929–35	N 1	N 2	N 3

3. Main Particulars

Length, overall	56.00m
Length, pp	54.00m
Breadth, moulded	6.00m
Depth, keel to deck beam line	3.00m
Depth, keel to gunwale	2.55m
Draught, forwards and midship	1.60m
Draught, rear at rudder	2.00m
Draught, full load	max 2.30m
Displacement, loaded	282t

3.1 Hull Construction.
The hull was constructed of steel, with deck and shell plating of 'Torpedobootstahl III' (torpedo-boat steel III); all other plates, stiffeners and frames were of 'Torpedobootstahl II' (torpedo-boat steel II). The hull was transversed framed, with a frame spacing of 500mm, there was one centre girder and two side girders on each side. The 11 water-tight bulkheads made up the vessel's water-tight subdivision. There was no water-tight double bottom. The engine room bulkheads were placed at frames 29 and 46, the later being the after boiler room bulkhead, with the other boiler-room bulkheads at frame 61 and frame 76. The bow was of forged steel, and the stern frame of steel casting. The steel deck was covered with a double layer of anti-slip canvas.

3.2 Weight distribution (Vindhunden-Spækhuggeren).

Hull	88t
Machinery	112t
Electrical machinery	4t
Artillery	5t
Torpedo Equipment	12t
Equipment	11t
Coal	50t
Loaded Displacement	282t

4. Accommodation. The quarters for ordinary seamen were in the bow and stern. A separate room for the wireless set was incorporated into the forward living spaces. Just aft of the ordinary seamen's quarters there was a mess for the ships' 7 petty officers. The cabins, wardroom, ship's office, bathroom, and pantry for the commanding officer and officers were placed aft of the turbine room. The galley was above deck in a deckhouse on top of which was the bridge.

All living quarters, wireless room included, were steam heated. The heating was designed to obtain a temperature of 20 degrees C above the ambient temperature, as long as the ambient temperature was higher than -10 degrees C. All compartments were supplied with electric light, but there was emergency light by means of oil lamps in the living quarters and boiler rooms.

All rooms were ventilated by natural ventilation, except the wardroom and the officers' living quarters which had electrical ventilators. The 'heads' for the officers and crew were placed in the superstructure under the bridge, and as stressed in the contract, properly ventilated.

The complement was 4 officers, 7 petty officers, and 24 seamen.

5. Colour Scheme. The bottom of the hull was given three coats of 'Holzapfel' anti-fouling composition. Topside, deck, coaming and funnel were finished in matt black.

6. Boats. Two whaleboats (5.5m and 4m long) were carried on chocks on the weatherdeck.

7. Armament. The ships were equipped with two 75mm L/30 guns without shields, one on the fore deck and one on the quarterdeck. Each gun had a peacetime/wartime allocation of 30/99 rounds. A 8mm machine gun completed the gun armament. A 1m rangefinder was also shipped. The arc of fire for the forward gun was 0 to 150 degrees on each bow; for the after gun arc was dead astern to 155 degrees forward on each bow. The magazine was placed under the forward living quarters and was able to hold 300 rounds of 75mm ammunition. It was possible to flood the magazine in less than 10 minutes.

The ships mounted five 450mm torpedo tubes. One tube was built into the bow (forward living quarters), and two on each side on the weatherdeck fore and aft. No reserve torpedoes were carried. The torpedo tubes on deck were heated by steam pipes. The arc of fire for the forward torpedo tubes were from 6 to 100 degrees, and for the after tubes the arcs were from 10 degrees forward to 172 aft. A magazine for the five torpedo warheads was placed under the forward living quarters, forward of the 75mm magazine.

8. Machinery. The *Tumleren* boats were the first in the Royal Danish Navy with turbine machinery. All three ships were equipped with two boilers in separate boiler rooms. The boilers supplied steam to two turbines placed in one engine room, each turbine directly driving one shaft.

Vindhunden, *notice the very low freeboard of the boats. They must have been quite wet during a winter gale.* (Royal Danish Navy.)

Side view of Tumleren. *All plans redrawn from Schichau originals by Tom Wismann 1989.*

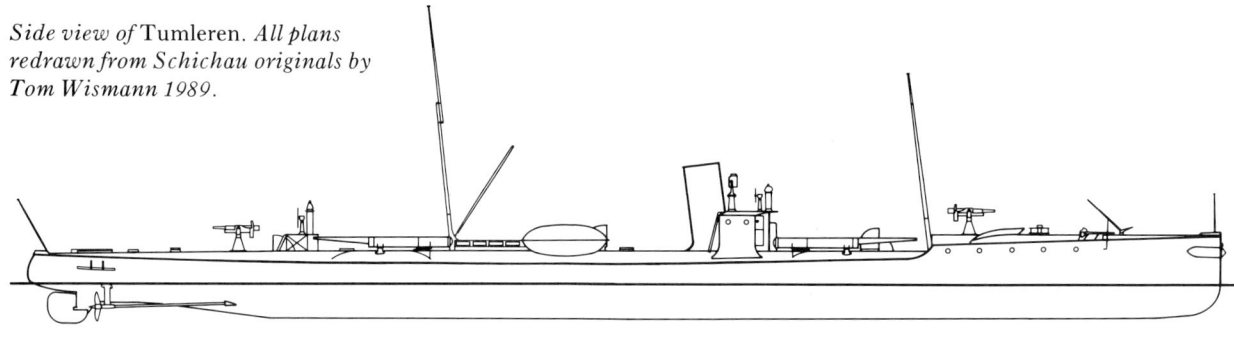

Internal arrangement.

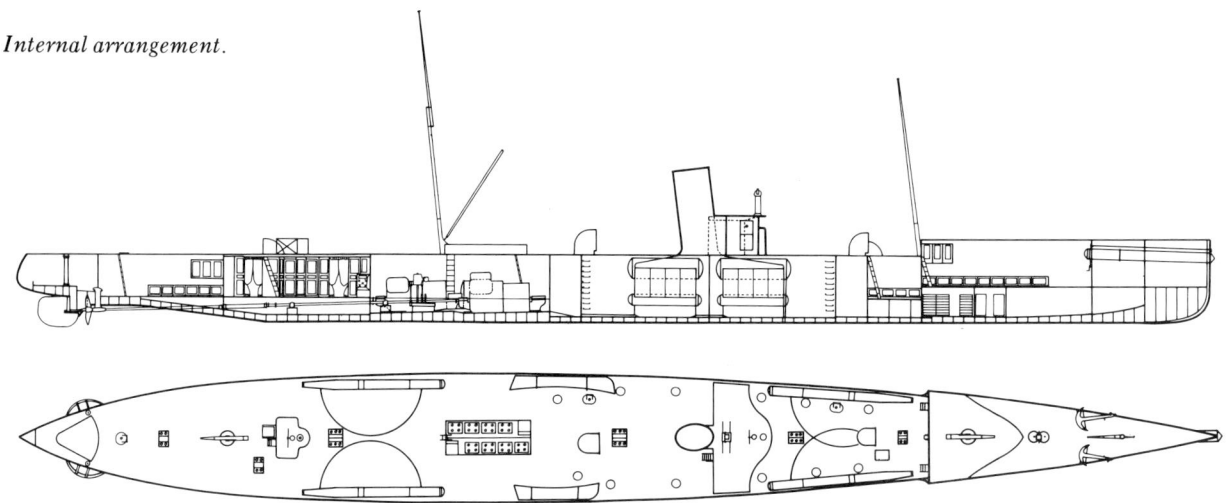

Deck plan. Notice the rails for the torpedo tubes which gave the boats very wide torpedo arcs.

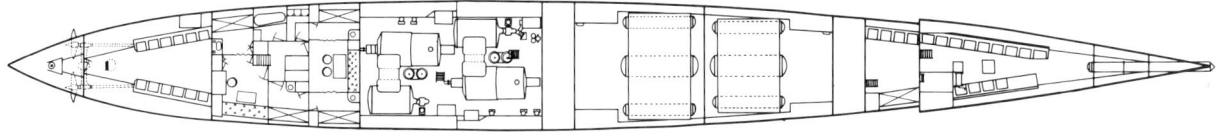

Internal arrangement. As can be seen there was a bath but no toilet facilities in the officers' quarters. The heads were placed in the superstructure under the bridge, side by side with the galley.

Boilers	Tum	Vind and Spæk
Type	Schichau	OV*
Boiler pressure	16.5 bar	17.0 bar
Stokeholds	2	2
Furnaces	2	1
Draught	Forced	Forced
Grate size	12.0m2	12.8m2
Heating surface	705m2	598m2

*OV = Orlogsværftet

The turbines in all ships were identical and built by Schichau. Each turbine (single stage) delivered 2500shp giving the ships a maximum speed of 27.5kts. The astern turbine was able to stop the ship in 45 seconds and able to drive the ship astern at 14kts. The propellers had three blades and a diameter of 1.25m. During the trials the following data were obtained:

Continuous	Tum	Vind	Spæk
Propeller (rpm)	716	664	664
Power (shp)	3426	2940	2940
Coal consumption (kg/shp/hr)	1.05	1.20	1.20
Speed (kts)	24.8	22.5	22.5
Average draught (m)	1.82	1.91	1.91
Full power trials			
Propeller (rpm)	825	829	829
Power (shp)	4970	5005	4930
Coal consumption (kg/shp/hr)	1.06	1.36	1.29
Speed (kts)	27.5	27.8	27.8
Radius at 14kts (nm)	–	750	750

WARSHIP NOTES

A quarter view of a model of Tumleren. (Photo by Thorsten Lindhe, courtesy of Orlogsmuseet, Royal Danish Naval Museum).

The coal bunkers together held 50 tonnes: 12 tonnes in the hold forward of the foremost boiler room; 6 tonnes in the holds on each side of the forward boiler room; 8 tonnes in the holds on each side of the after boiler room, and 10 tonnes in the hold aft of the after boiler room.

8.1 Internal communications.
There were speaking tubes from:
1. the after steering position to the forward turbine control position;
2. from the bridge to the after steering position;
3. from the bridge to the turbine room;
4. from the turbine room to both boiler rooms;
5. from engineering officer's cabin to the turbine room;
6. from the bridge to the wireless room.

There were engine telegraphs from the bridge to boiler and turbine rooms.

9. Steering. The boats were fitted with one rudder of 2.74m². Steering from the open bridge was assisted by a steam driven steering engine. A hand-operated auxiliary steering pedestal was provided on the quarterdeck. For emergency steering it was possible to operate the rudder by blocks and tackles direct on the rudder tiller. Maximum rudder angle was 38 degrees.

10. Electrical plant. From the beginning the ships were supplied with a reciprocating steam engine driving a DC dynamo which delivered 110-volt, 80-amp electricity at 9kW. A 400mm searchlight was placed on the bridge.

11. Windlass, anchor and cables. There was one steam windlass on the forecastle, with its engine placed below deck. It was possible to operate the windlass by hand. There were two anchors of each 240kg and each had 80m and 60m respectively of anchor chain.

12. Careers. All were commissioned in 1911–12, and after duty with the training squadron, joined the 1st Torpedo-Boat Flotilla of the First Squadron protecting Danish neutrality during the First World War. *Tumleren* remained a frontline unit until 1929 when she and *Spækhuggeren* were transferred to the reserve, to be joined by *Vindhunden* in 1930. All were stricken from the navy list in 1935 and sold to the breakers Petersen & Albeck in Copenhagen.

Tumleren *in 1911. The white ring around the funnel together with the circle a little more than half way up the mainmast are the identification marks for* Tumleren. *The other boats had different markings.* (Royal Danish Navy).

YANGTSZE RIVER GUNBOATS

The following photos of China gunboats come from a remarkable album compiled by George Henry Smith, then serving on the *Kinsha*, and employed surveying the Yangtsze in 1903. He later saw action in the Mediterranean during the First World War, and was awarded the DSM for conspicuous bravery during the Dardanelles evacuation. Having gone to sea aged 15 in one of the Navy's last training brigs, when he retired from the Navy as a Chief Petty Officer, it was natural for him to return to sail. He joined the *Cap Pilar* on her famous voyage around the world, as described in her skipper Adrian Seligman's classic book *Voyage of the Cap Pilar*. This later led Smith to serve as Mate on the replica *Santa Maria* during the filming of *Christopher Columbus* in the West Indies.

His photo album is now the property of his descendents, and we are grateful to Mr and Mrs Ronald F Berry for permission to publish the selection that follows. The ships depicted are the British side-wheel steamer *Pioneer* (later converted to a gunboat at Shanghai and renamed *Kinsha* – 616 tons, sold 1921) and the purpose-built gunboats *Woodcock* and *Woodlark* (built 1897, 150 tons, sold 1928). There is also a single depiction of the French gunboat *Olry* (purchased in China in 1901, tonnage unknown, served until 1910). We have followed the original short captions in the album.

The Pioneer *in her original form.*

▲ Kinsha *at Su Chow Fu, July 1903.*

▶ *A bow view of* Kinsha *at Chungking, October 1903.*

◀ Kinsha *(ex-*Pioneer*) at Chungking on the upper Yangtsze, October 1903.*

▲ *The squadron lying off Chungking, 1600 miles from the sea.*

▶ *The French gunboat* Olry *at Loo Chou, 1904.*

▶ *The squadron dressed overall, Chungking.*

◀ Woodlark *at Su Chow Fu, July 1903.*

Woodcock *beached for repairs at Chungking.*

WARSHIP NOTES

THE MYSTERIOUS FATE OF THE POLTAVA

Throughout the 1920s and 1930s the naval annuals repeatedly listed a Soviet battleship, the Poltava *(and later* Mihail Frunze*), generally speculating on its exact status. However, none could explain why the ship continued to lie alongside in Leningrad rather than being sent to the breaker's yard. In this article, René Greger offers some explanations.*

The first four dreadnoughts for the Czarist navy were all laid down on 16 June 1900. More were projected, but in the event only four of the class were built. *Poltava*, the second of what became the *Sevastopol* class (Russian warship classes being named after the first ship in service, not the first built), was launched on 10 July 1911, ran trials in November 1914, and joined the fleet on 14 December 1914. However, she was not combat-ready since her main armament directors were not fitted and the fire-control station was not operational. Problems with the latter were not resolved before the 1917 armistice, so the ship was never committed to battle.

After the October Revolution the *Poltava* remained with the rest of the battlefleet at Helsingfors until returned to Kronstadt in March 1918 with the first squadron to break through the ice. Her crew was dispersed to fight in the Civil War, and since there was no fuel *Poltava* and her sister *Gangut* were towed to Leningrad, where they were to be refitted. Given the conditions prevailing at the time, it is unlikely that anything was done; according to Soviet literature in May 1919 it was planned to use her 12in (305mm) guns against the White Russian forces of General Judenich, but they never came within range. From that date onwards the *Poltava* became a taboo subject for Soviet naval historians, not being mentioned again for over 60 years – until 1980 in fact, when brief details of her renaming (*Frunze* or *Mihail Frunze*) and fate appear in a few articles. However, they do not address themselves to the claim made in the 1919 edition of *Jane's* that the ship was aground in the River Neva (at Leningrad). No explanation is given, so what had happened?

Early Soviet sources mention a severe fire in 1921 or 1923, but an article in the magazine *Sudostroenie (Shipbuilding)* said that the fire occurred on 24 November 1919, and spread from the forward boiler room to the fire-control station, severely damaging much of the ship's interior. However, the date seems unlikely, because apart from the statement in

Poltava *on trials in November–December 1914 reached 24.1kts, and was faster than her sisters. (Author).*

Jane's, an order of 18 December 1920 from the Bolshevik naval command mentions *Poltava* among the battleships in best condition for refitting with a view to service in 1921. Since the naval command was also in Leningrad, it seems unlikely that they would have been unaware of the state of the ship, from which we must conclude that the fire occurred later, or possibly that there were two fires between 1919 and 1923. Whatever the date, the fire-control station was almost certainly destroyed, and for many years there were no plans for the reconstruction of the vessel as a battleship. However, other projects did arise.

In 1924 the Soviet government launched one of many schemes to strengthen its navy. Plans included refitting the three remaining *Sevastopol*s, completing the four cruisers of the *Svetlana* class, and the construction of two aircraft carriers. This was far beyond the capacity of Soviet industry, but the naval command believed it could obtain the carriers by utilizing the hulls of the uncompleted battlecruiser *Izmail* and the damaged *Poltava* – now useless as a big-gun ship since her fire-control station had been destroyed. The 1925–31 programme scheduled con-

This photo has been captioned on Gangut *during the transfer through the ice from Helsinfors to Kronstadt in March 1918. In fact it is* Poltava *on the same occasion.* (Author).

version of both ships for 1925. The *Izmail* would have carried 90 aircraft and the smaller *Poltava* 50; sketches show the latter as completely flush decked with no island, in the manner of the first Japanese carriers.

Even this limited programme was beyond Soviet shipbuilding capabilities, so the conversions were cancelled. Nevertheless, *Poltava*'s reconstruction was close enough to warrant renaming her *Mihail Frunze* in 1926 (nobody would rename a ship that was about to be discarded). At this time other conversion schemes were proposed, ranging from a floating battery to a fast battlecruiser. The latter type was prohibited under the 1921 Washington Treaty, but since the Soviet Union was not a signatory, this had no influence. A battlecruiser feasibility study was ordered as late as 1928, two variants being produced by early 1933. Each version envisaged retaining three of the original triple 305mm (12in) turrets, with the new secondary armament of sixteen 130mm (5in) in single casements concentrated amidships. Where the variants differed was in the AA armament (eight single 100mm in the first version, six twin 100mm in the second, which also had two funnels instead of one). The guns were of Italian manufacture, and having been ordered, were later used to modernise the cruisers of the Black Sea Fleet.

The turbines would also have been built in Italy (the 110,000shp sets were originally ordered for the cruiser *Kirov*) and should have given the *Frunze* a maximum speed of 27kts.

The first version of a proposed battlecruiser conversion of Frunze, *1932. The second variant, prepared several months later, showed two funnels and six twin AA guns; main armament was the same.* (Author).

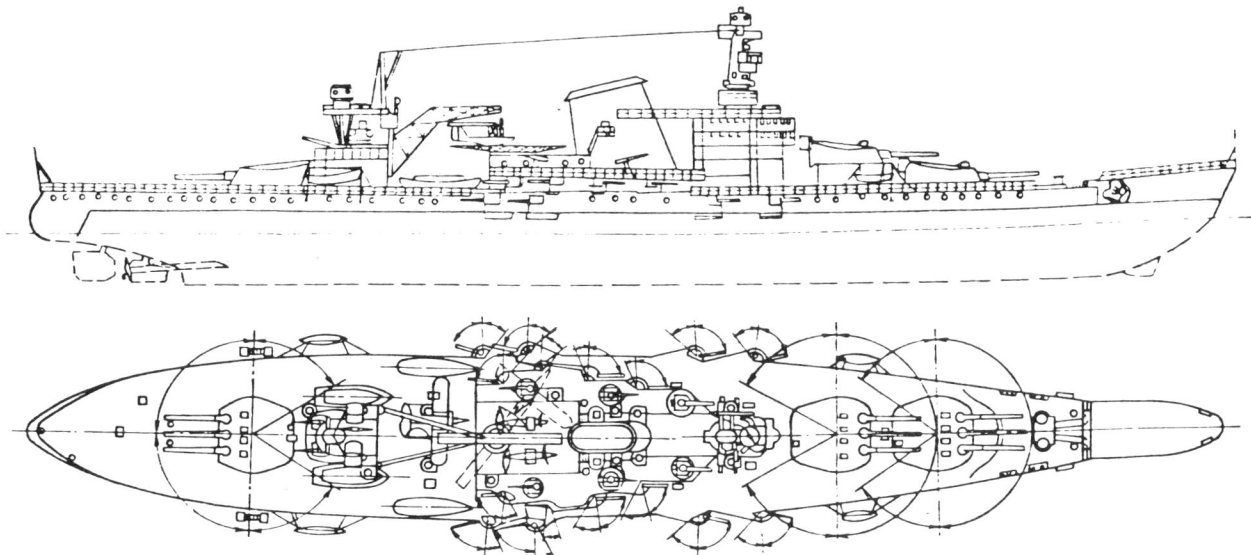

To achieve this speed the hull had to be lengthened by about 10m (33ft), but the longer forecastle would have given the battlecruiser an advantage in seaworthiness over her modernised sister ships.

Frunze's conversion was postponed until 1935, but although the plans were finalised, it was never carried out. In the meantime Stalin had decided to build new and very large capital ships, armed with nine 406mm (16in) guns, and when the Italian design became available in the summer of 1936, the *Frunze* conversion compared very badly. All preparations for the reconstruction ceased and her conversion to a training ship was suggested; later it was decided to remove all equipment and use the hull as a target. This work started in the late summer of 1939, but was interrupted by the outbreak of war in the west two weeks later. The bow had already been removed and the ship then lay minus superstructure in Leningrad's coal harbour until the German invasion. German reconnaissance aircraft noticed the hull and wrongly identified it as an unfinished aircraft carrier, an illusion which wartime propaganda perpetuated.

The reality was less glamorous. Fearing a German assault on Leningrad, the Soviets planned to close the only deep channel by scuttling *Frunze* as a blockship. In 1941 when the threatened attack took place, the ship was towed out towards its planned position, but German artillery spotted the movement and sank the hulk with a few well-aimed salvoes. The hull did not seal the entrance but was so restrictive to shipping movements that the Soviets decided to raise the ship as soon as the front line retreated far enough to permit it (carried out January–May 1944). There was talk of cannabalising the *Poltava* to help repair her sister *Marat* (lying at Kronstadt without her forward turret, bridge or fore funnel), but the day of the battleship was over; *Marat* survived where she was for a few more years, but the remains of the *Poltava* were broken up in 1946.

This ended the long and somewhat mysterious career of a battleship that had never left its own coastal waters and had never been in action.

BRITISH DESTROYER REQUIREMENTS AND THE SECOND WORLD WAR

John English looks at the immediately pre-war 'L' class and the 1944–45 Gallant *class as indicators of the effects of wartime experience on destroyer design.*

The eight *Gallants* were originally projected as part of the 1944 War Emergency Programme, as a development of the 'Weapons', whilst the 'L' class were to form the 2nd Flotilla of destroyers projected under the 1937/38 Estimates. The Staff Requirement of the *Gallants* issued during July 1944, listed the functions of the proposed vessels as:

1. to attack enemy ships with torpedoes; 2. to attack enemy light craft with gunfire; 3. to screen against attack from enemy ships, submarines, E-boats and aircraft.

These requirements had hardly changed since pre-war days and could have been used to describe the functions of the 'L' class some seven years before and did not reflect the changes in the operational environment the vessels were likely to encounter or the technical developments that had occurred during the war.

1937/38 'L' class. These vessels – a development of the 'J/K' classes had a prolonged gestation period, following the request by the then Controller (Vice-Admiral R C Henderson) to have destroyer-type vessels that were comparable to the large foreign destroyers – the Japanese *Asashio*s, the German *Von Roeder*s and especially the French *Mogador*s that were considered superior to current British designs (the 'Tribals' and the 'J's and 'K's, then under construction). Initially five designs were developed with the following arrangements:

The vessels differed from the 'J's and 'K's in the following ways.

1. The vessels were to be fitted with weatherproof gun mountings, which would be 40 tons per twin mounting, compared with the 29-ton gun mountings of the 'J's. To this 33 tons of extra weight for the three twin mountings were added an increase of 14 tons in the weight of cordite charges and shell carried, as well as a penalty of 5 tons for heavier lubricant pumps.
2. The proposed destroyers would mount weapons with 50° elevation to provide better high-angle fire.
3. There was a desire to increase the maximum speed in deep loaded condition from 32kts to 33kts. Thus machinery to provide the power would have to be enlarged. This was to ensure that the speed advantage of fleet destroyers would be maintained at 10kts over the *King George V* class battleships then under construction.

The C-in-Cs of the Home and Mediterranean Fleets were cabled on 27 September 1937 for their views on the proposed super destroyer – a design titled L72 (see earlier) and a modified 'J' class with a speed of 32kts in deep condition. Admiral Pound, the C-in-C Mediterranean Fleet made the following comments:

1. that the 1650-ton type ('J' class modified) be adopted;
2. that 14 more 'Tribals' be built to make up our deficiency in cruisers;
3. that destroyers of future programmes should be of the 1650-ton type.

Admiral Pound commented further:

> If we adopted the 2750-ton super destroyer type, the shortage [of destroyers] is bound to be accentuated, not only because we may not be able to afford a large number whatever nations built, but because

Design	Engine Rooms	Gearing rooms	Boiler rooms
L44 – 44,000 shp	1	1	2
L56 – 56,000 shp	1	1	3
L60 – 60,000 shp	2	–	3
L63 – 63,000 shp	2	–	3
L72 – 72,000 shp	2	–	3

Lively, *one of the class completed with 4in guns.* (IWM)

other nations may follow our lead and it may become the standard type.

He continued, by doubting whether 'the 1650-type [the 'J's] was outclassed by other destroyers', and he referred to a conversation with his French Liaison officer, who stated that the *Mogodor*s were not being repeated, as they had been found to be too unwieldy in flotilla attacks.

On 14 October 1937, Vice-Admiral Henderson, reported the C-in-C's comments to the Board meeting. The ACNS supported the C-in-C's views on the destroyer. The L44 design was criticised for the lack of short-range anti-aircraft armament. The meeting concluded, that the torpedo type (the 'J's) should be developed for the new destroyer instead of the gun type ('Tribals').

The legend of particulars of 20 October 1937, differed from the 'J's in the following ways:
1. Displacement increased by 140 tons to 1835 tons for the leader and by 125 tons to 1815 tons for the destroyer.
2. Draught increased by 3in.
3. Shaft Horse Power increased by 8000.
4. Speed increased by 1½ kts in the standard condition and 1kt deep loaded.
5. 50 degree twin 4.7in weatherproof mounts, instead of the 40 degree twin mounts of the 'J's.
6. To compensate for increased weights, one bank of torpedo tubes was dropped.

The vessels were estimated to cost £715,000, compared with the £590,000 for the 'J' class and only £367,000 for the 'I' class. By the next month, the weights of the twin mounting had increased by a further 10 tons per mounting and further alterations to the design were now made. Two additional designs were proposed:

Design L48C: a 'J' class form pulled out to 37ft beam, with a waterline length of 354ft, displacement of 1920 tons (light) and 2542 tons (deep).

Design L48D: as L48C with 37½ft beam, 354ft waterline length, a light displacement of 1940 tons and deep loaded 2552 tons.

The decision was made to develop design L48C. Later a modified form of scantlings was agreed, which reduced displacement by 15 tons.

The modification of four vessels during March–April 1940. On 28 February 1940, the Director of Naval Construction, Sir Stanley Goodall, on being informed of the serious delays then occurring in the supply of twin 4.7in mountings, requested his destroyer section to investigate the possibility of equipping four of the 'L' class with 4in twin HA/LA mountings, then being fitted to the 'Hunt' class. The first design proposed the fitting of three twin 4in, but later investigation showed that a four twin-mounting vessel was feasible. On 29 March 1940, the proposed armament of the vessels was given as follows:

Four 4in twin HA/LA Mk XIX mounting with Mk XVI guns;
One quadruple 2pdr pompom;
two 0.5in machine-guns;
two quadruple 21in torpedo tubes;

Final Legend of particulars for L class destroyers 30.3.38

Detail	Destroyer	Leader
Length pp (ft)	345½	345½
Length wl (ft)	354	354
Length oa (ft)	362½	362½
Beam (ft)	37	37
Displacement (tons)	1920	1935
Mean draught std (ft–in)	9–11	10–0
Mean draught deep (ft–in)	12–1	12–2
Shaft horse power	48,000	48,000
Shafts	2	2
Speed std (kts)	37	37
Speed deep (kts)	22	33
Endurance (nm)	5450	5450
Weights (tons): equipment	85	90
machinery	650	650
armament	260	260
hull	925	935
Standard displacement (tons)	1920	1935

Preliminary Legend of Particulars (October 1944) – 1944 'Weapon' Class Design ('G' Class)

Detail	1943 'Weapon' (App Board Minute 3888)	Proposed 1944 'Weapon'	1944 'Weapon' (App Board Minute 3984)
Dimensions (ft)			
Length pp	341½	341½	341½
Length oa	365	365	365
Breadth (extreme)	38	39½	39½
Standard condition			
Displacement (tons)	1965	1985	1995
Draught forward (ft–in)	9–2	8–11	9–1
Draught (aft) (ft–in)	10–2	9–11	10–1
Deep condition			
Displacement (tons)	2700	2720	2730 (est)
Draught (mean) (ft–in)	12–2	11–10	12–1
Shaft horse power	40,000	40,000	40,000
Shafts	2	2	2
Speed (kts)	34	33¾	33¾
Speed (deep) (kts)	30	29¾	29¾
Endurance at 20 kts (nm)	5000	4900	5000
Complement	230	230	251
(as leader)	260	N/A	279
Armament (rounds)			
4in (twin Mk XIX mountings)	6	–	–
4.5in (twin Mk VI mountings)		4 (350)	4 (350)
40mm (twin STAAG mountings)	4 (1440)	4 (1440)	4 (1440)
20mm (twin powered mountings)	4 (2400)	4 (2400)	4 (2400)
21in torpedo tubes	8	8	10
Depth charges	50	50	50
Weights (tons)			
General equipment	103	103	103
Machinery	570	570	570
Electrical generation	30	30	30
Armament	241	286	290
Hull	1008	996	1002
Margin	13	–	–
Total	1965	1985	1995

110 depth charges on eight throwers and three chutes.

Deep displacement was now estimated at 2631 tons. The design was sanctioned by the Controller on 10 April 1940. The four vessels were completed during 1940–41. Subsequently during construction, 20mm Oerlikons replaced the 0.5in machine-guns, *Lance* was fitted with new radio equipment for test purposes and in *Lively* the depth charge arrangements were altered to meet new practice. All four vessels were to have short careers with *Gurkha* (ex-*Larne*) being torpedoed by *U33* off Sollum on 17 January 1942, *Legion* and *Lance* lost to air attack at Malta on 26 March and 5 April 1942 and *Lively* sunk, again by air attack, on 11 May 1942 off Sollum.

The 1944 Gallants The eight *Gallant*s were projected during July 1944 as part of the 1944 War Emergency Programme and were derivatives of the 'Weapons' and for a period they were referred to as the 1944 Weapon class. The principal difference between these vessels and the earlier 'Weapons' was the requirement to mount two twin 4.5in 80 degree mountings, on the same basic hull. The vessels were to be built at the same yards as those building the 'Weapons' and standard displacement was restricted to 2000 tons. This restriction was to cause problems all the way through their development and was one of the causes of their cancellation. It is a good example of how an artificial ceiling on displacement was to result in a vessel that did not fully meet requirements.

The adoption of the twin 4.5in mounting resulted in a considerable weight penalty compared with the Weapons. Much discussion took place over the armament to be fitted to the vessels, before the design was finally approved during 10 October 1944. The main arguments concerned

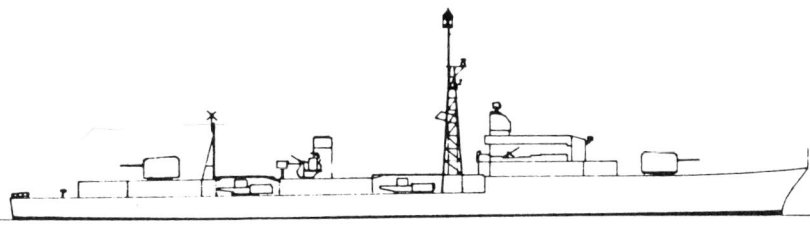

Outline of the 'G' class design, 1946.

1. The numbers of depth charge patterns carried against the number of torpedoes. These alterations were discussed:
a) 4 throwers, 2 rails, 100 depth charges and 1 bank of torpedo tubes;
b) 4 throwers, 2 rails, 150 depth charges and no torpedo tubes;
c) As (a) but 75 depth charges and 1 bank of torpedo tubes.
2. What weapons were to constitute the close-range anti-aircraft armament – whether 20mm or 40mm.
The vessels were estimated to cost £750,000.

Problems of Weight and Stability October 1944–November 1945. The legend of particulars had not included a Board Margin and this made the proposed vessels weight-critical from the start, and the weight increases that were occurring at this time on the Mk VI 4.5in mounting and the STAAG mounting accentuated the problem. It had been hoped to fit a Squid ASW mortar, even though this had not been mentioned on the legend of particulars, but on 4 December 1944, it was decided not to fit the weapon, because of its weight and the fact that the space saved could be used for additional accommodation and storage.

However, weight saved by reducing frame weight, upper deck beams and hold flats – a total of 17.20 tons, was more than compensated by weight additions:

1. The substitution of two single Bofors in lieu of twin Oerlikons:
 7.25 tons
2. Addition of a barrage direction:
 2.50 tons
3. Increase in the weight of the STAAG mountings:
 8.00 tons
 Total: 17.75 tons

However, there was a growing realisation that no flotilla vessel could undertake all the duties of a fleet escort, defined as being:
(i) capable of a full scale torpedo attack;
(ii) able to destroy enemy light forces by gunfire;
(iii) able to defend itself and to assist in defending the fleet against all forms of air attack;
(iv) able to screen and defend the fleet against submarine attack and to destroy every submarine in the vicinity of the fleet.

The modern ASW weapons necessary to hunt and destroy submarines cannot be combined in one ship with effective HA/LA armament and full scale torpedo armament, without greatly increasing the displacement of the ship to take her 'out of her class'. Such large vessels lacked manoeuvrability, had increased manpower, greater cost with a reduction in the numbers available. 'It is suggested that the *Gallant* type is not strictly speaking a fleet destroyer but a hybrid type, which falls short of modern requirements.' The DNC was stating by 24 September 1945, 'It is becoming a question of serious consideration, whether these vessels should be redesigned on a larger basis.'

In light of the above and the financial stringency of the time, it was not surprising, that the decision to cancel the *Gallant*s was made on 12 December 1945.

Conclusions on the design, construction, armament, and sensors of the two classes. The fact that the *Gallant*s were never completed only highlights the changes in the role and the technology of the destroyer that had taken place during the war years. The pace of change is emphasised by the fact that a group of vessels, that incorporated 80 degree 4.5in twin mounts, Bofors, a full complement of radar, advanced sonars and torpedoes as the *Gallant*s were to be equipped, would be regarded as obsolescent in 1945. It also highlights the relative paucity of the equipment of the 'L's as designed in 1938. The *Gallant*s in 1938 would have been regarded as first rate fleet escorts. The changes can be listed as follows:

Construction. The 'L' class were of conventional riveted construction, whilst the *Gallant*s in line with the decision of the DNC (Lillicrap) of 3 March 1944, were to be of all welded construction, as were all subsequent destroyers. On 7 July 1944, it was decided that the *Gallant*s were to use aluminium in the construction of their main bulkheads, galley, funnel casings and bridge deck. In weight-critical vessels such as these the 23 tons saved through the use of aluminium was of great benefit to the Constructors.

Sensors. In 1938, the primary sensor on the 'L's was its Asdic set and the Mark I eyeball! The greatest change was the development of radar and by the war's end the sole survivor of the 'L's, *Lookout*, was fitted with surveillance and gunnery sets. The *Gallant*s, however, were to be fitted with a comprehensive suite, which consisted of the air warning and gunnery sets – Types 291, Type 293 and Type 275. The originally proposed STAAG mountings were to be controlled by Type 242 sets. This equipment was completed by the fitting of an Action Information Organisation to analyse the threats and provide a quick response.

Armament. The 'L' class were plagued with the weight problems of their twin 4.7in powered mountings. These problems combined with problems of manufacture, meant that four vessels were completed with 4in guns. The *Gallant*s, although the weight problems of the Mk 6 twin 4.5in had yet to be resolved, would have been armed with one of the most successful mounts ever operated by the Royal Navy. The superiority of this weapon, together with its radar control and Action Information Organisation was total. The short-range armament had also been transformed, with the 0.5in machine-guns of the 'L's having been superseded by the 20mm Oerlikon and finally by the 40mm Bofors. The *Gallant*s were to have been armed with power-operated STAAG mounts with self-contained prediction and control.

If they had been completed, the 'G' class would have resembled the 'Weapons' (Crossbow, seen here in April 1948 is an example) but with the 4.5in turret that was fitted to the Darings. (CPL)

This was to consist of the American Mk 37 Stabilised Director, with Type 275 Radar and a 15ft rangefinder. The 'L's had limited director control only.

One bank of torpedo tubes was retained in the *Gallant*s but was primarily required to fire anti-submarine homing torpedoes then under development and was not for surface actions.

Power generation. The growth in the power demanded by the different groups of sensors to be operated by the *Gallant*s was quite marked over the 'L's. The power was to be supplied by two 300kW turbo-generators and two 150kW diesel generators.

Machinery/Speed/Endurance. Power for the 'L's was supplied by two Admiralty 3-drum boilers at 300psi at 660 degrees F on two shafts with Parsons geared turbines which produced 36kts at standard displacement and 32.5kts deep loaded. The *Gallant*s were to be powered by two Foster Wheeler boilers, with pressure increased to 400psi at a temperature of 750 degrees F, indicating the technical improvements that had taken place. The speed in the standard and deep conditions was 3kts less than the 'L's. This reduction reflected the fact that the nominal speed of vessels was no longer regarded as important as it had been pre-war; sustained sea speed was now the important criterion. The reduction in the power of the machinery required and hence weight, could be utilised for other more desirable characteristics. Endurance for the *Gallant*s was estimated as 5000 miles, some 450 miles less than the 'L's; however, this endurance could be achieved at 20kts instead of the 15kts of the 'L's.

However, although the *Gallant*s were a considerable advance on the 'L's, they would have been incredibly cramped compared with the 'L's as their complement was 280 instead of the 190 of the 'L's. Thus, the *Gallant*s although weight-critical and never completed, would have been far superior in every respect to the 'L's and even then they were regarded as being obsolescent. The 'L' class, although some of the most handsome destroyers ever built for the Royal Navy, had several shortcomings – their main armament only elevated to 50 degrees, their anti-aircraft armament as designed was obsolete and their sensors almost non-existent. These drawbacks were to be highlighted by their losses in the Mediterranean in 1942.

Sources:
Ships Cover 630 'L' class with 4in guns
Ships Cover 576 'L' class
Ships Cover 711 Destroyer 1944 'Weapon' class (all at National Maritime Museum)

NAVAL BOOKS OF THE YEAR

The reviews are divided into three main sections: firstly, full reviews; then short notices and finally, a straightforward listing of books announced but not received. In all sections the order is alphabetical by author.

D K Brown, Before the Ironclad: Development of Ship Design, Propulsion and Armament in the Royal Navy 1815–60, *published by Conway Maritime Press, 1990. 295 x 248mm, 224 pages, 100 photographs, 25 drawings. ISBN 0-85177-532-2. £30.00*

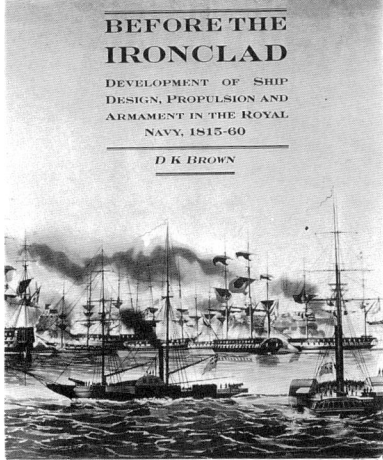

This book should be the final instalment in the prolonged effort required to overturn the absurd idea that the Royal Navy opposed advances in naval and maritime technology during the nineteenth century. D K Brown RCNC, until recently Head of Ship Design Policy at the MoD, is well known to all readers of *Warship*. In this book he has produced a comprehensive technical study of a hitherto largely neglected area. Britain was the world leader in nineteenth century maritime development, giving the book universal relevance. It should be recalled that even in the 1850s France and Russia were forced to buy British engines for their battleships, while pioneering efforts in the United States were heavily influenced by British technology.

The individual chapters cover: the lessons of war, 1793 to 1815; the development of marine and hydrodynamic science; the policy framework of the postwar navy; the last sailing warships; the paddle steam warship; early iron ships; the development of the screw propeller; the Russian War; postwar wooden ships; and a concluding chapter on HMS *Warrior*.

In view of the unparalleled engineering development that separates the *Victory* from the *Warrior* it is a mark of the author's mastery of the subject that the technical coverage is never less than excellent. The naval architect's view of that well worn subject, the speed of sailing warships, is worthy of note. Hull form, he says, made no worthwhile contribution to performance, given the compromise nature of the wooden warship hull and the limitations on design. As a result the innumerable squadrons of evolution of the period could not provide reliable evidence. Any that resulted in clear cut results merely encouraged political attacks and ill-tempered recriminations. Their only real merit – and even that should be qualified – was the emphasis they gave to seamanship. As the period progressed this became exaggerated into an obsession of the sort common to all navies at peace.

As part of the process of rebutting charges of negligence aimed at the Admiralty the book emphasises the degree to which the weaknesses of paddle-wheel warships made them entirely unsuitable for the close collision of a first class naval battle. They remained auxiliaries, particularly suited to amphibious warfare, for which Admiral Napier's *Sidon* was designed. The same approach to steam carried over into the screw fleet. At the outbreak of the Russian War the Admiralty issued orders that screw steamships were to go into action with only atmospheric pressure in their boilers, and the propeller housed to avoid becoming fouled. These were ignored by officers afloat. *Warrior* was the first front line warship with priority given to speed under steam. The final chapter, concerning the *Warrior*, understates the close connection between the last wooden frigates, the *Mersey* class, and the ironclads, which adopted their hull form and engines.

The author adopts technology and the men who handled it as the central theme. Attacking the concept of a reactionary Admiralty from the standpoint of the in-house technologists undervalues the role of politics and political decision-making. The discussion of the screw propeller misses the economic and political aspects of the process. The Ship Propeller Company was formed to make money from the patent; in consequence the whig Admiralty of Lord Minto appointed Brunel, a liberal with no financial interest to supervise the *Rattler*. This was overtaken by the return of a tory administration more in tune with the Ship Propeller Company. The resulting misunderstandings were more complex than is suggested here. Nevertheless, the technical discussion is the best yet published.

In addition the book has the secondary aim of demonstrating how far the subject under discussion was influenced by the pupils of the First School of Naval Architecture, 1810–1832. In terms of sailing ship design it is clear that the pupils of the School tended to follow the models of Chapman, rather than producing more original work. The *Orion* class sailing battleships of 1848 were not Symondites as suggested on page 165; they were designed months after Symonds had left office, by Watts and Large, and Augustin Creuze admitted they were an enlarged Chapman design.

Equally, the First Chief Naval Engineer, Peter Ewart (1767–1842), deserves more credit for the successful steam programme of the late 1830s. Ewart had been trained by James Watt, and considered for a partnership. His cautious policy of selecting the best machinery contrasted strongly with that of Thomas Lloyd, for whom the highest praise is reserved. The engines ordered by Lloyd in the 1840s were in many cases less satisfactory than those of the preceding decade.

While the book adopts an apolitical stance, it is essential to observe the extent to which the policy framework was dominated by politics. The post-war tory government prepared for another twenty-year war against the European navies. The greatest efforts were expended on building up the reserve fleet, at the expense of the force in commission. Political instability and international tension forced succeeding ministries to spend more money on the active fleet. The whig Reform Ministry abolished the Navy Board in 1832, and with it the long-term policy framework. Admiralty control of materiel programmes saved money, and reduced defence estimates were the financial bribe that persuaded a House of Commons that remained tory to vote for political reform. In place of the Controller, a major naval figure with an independent power base, they selected an over-age Captain with powerful political patrons. It was particularly misleading that he should have the title Surveyor of the Navy – in truth he was a construction policy programmer without the influence of his predecessor. The real replacement for the innovative Seppings was the Deputy Surveyor, the properly praised John Edye, although it should be observed that Edye retired in 1857, not 1848.

The Controller from 1815 to 1831, Admiral Sir Thomas Byam Martin, was among the most influential policy-makers of the period. Like Symonds he was a political creature, his dismissal and the abolition of the Navy Board being largely conditioned by party politics. Having been selected by a tory administration the Master Shipwrights and pupils of the abolished School of Naval Architecture were driven by the whig ministers' appointment of Symonds to support the tory party. In 1841 Oliver Lang carried Cockburn, the tory First Sea Lord, to his election, his reward coming with orders to build the *Terrible* and the *Royal Albert*. Similarly Symonds falling out with the tory Admiralty of 1841–6 had nothing to do with his views on technical questions. He was an unpaid advisor to the opposition, providing them with sensitive naval information, much of which was then used in the House of Commons. That the Admiralty chose to counter-attack is hardly surprising. The returning whigs finally forced Symonds to retire in 1847, to enable them to reform naval policy-making. After 1848 the new Surveyor, Captain Baldwin Walker, assumed control of the Steam Department and re-established the influence of the materiel department on naval policy.

Overall this is an important work, required reading for all those interested in nineteenth century navies. It is well produced; although it should be noted that there are several errors in the captions. As an example the ship described on page 131 as the *Edgar* is in fact the *Sans Pareil*: given the fundamental differences between the two vessels (the former an all new steamship, the latter a poor experimental conversion from a half-built vessel), this is particularly unfortunate.

Dr Andrew Lambert

J G Coad, The Royal Dockyards 1690–1850, *published by Scolar Press, 1989.*
295 x 200mm, 399 pages, 298 plates, 21 plans.
ISBN 0-89567-803-2. £45.00.

This is an important and beautiful book which will be of interest to all who serve the Navy. The author was Assistant Inspector of Ancient Monuments and is a leading member of many Societies dealing with naval history.

His book tells the story of the building and engineering works in Dockyards from the end of the seventeenth century to the middle of the nineteenth. The account is selective; yards discussed are Chatham, Portsmouth, Devonport, Gibraltar, Minorca, Malta, Antigua and Bermuda; hence there is no mention of Woolwich and the first Steam Factory.

There is a short introduction on the organisation and management of the yards. Wars with France led to increasing emphasis on the south coast yards at the expense of those on the Thames. Though much steady development went on in the eighteenth century, there was an acceleration in 1795 when the Board, headed by Lord Spencer and Admiral Middleton (later Lord Barham) brought in Samuel Bentham as Inspector General. He created posts for the Architect and Engineer, the Mechanist and the Chemist. Many of the buildings were still designed locally, with success, by the Master Shipwright. It is interesting that the early office buildings lacked internal communication and to speak to another department it was necessary to go outside – still a feature of life in Bath.

Great attention was paid to the risk of fire and wooden buildings were replaced by brick and stone, whilst Admiralty architects were pioneers in metal framed buildings.

The most technically interesting chapter is that on docks and slips. Most yards had dry docks by 1700 but they were built of wood and needed frequent repair. In 1746 the Board decided that ships should no longer be built in dock but only on slipways. At the end of the seventeenth century, Edward Dummer revolutionised dock construction, using stone. There were early problems with foundations but these were overcome. Nos 5 & 6 Docks at Portsmouth are not dissimilar, despite alterations, from Dummer's concept with access stairs, altars and chutes to get timber down. He designed the entrance as an inverted arch giving strength to the gate supports. In 1802, Bentham designed a caisson which was simpler to operate than gates and which could carry a roadway across the entrance. The final step came in 1799 when Portsmouth gained a steam pump.

During the 1830s, building slips were roofed, the last wooden roof being at Chatham in 1838. From 1845 roofs with iron columns, arched roof trusses and corrugated iron cladding were introduced. These pre-date the better known railway station roofs. Greene's boathouse at Sheerness was, in 1859, the first multi-storey metal-framed building and owed much to his earlier work on roofing the slips.

The most conspicuous buildings were the immensely long ropewalks. A 74-gun ship needed some 14,000ft of rope and it required frequent replacement. It is indeed fortunate that the Chatham ropewalk remains in use with its early nineteenth century machinery. It is a pity that Devonport's execution cell, one of only two in working order, does not get a mention.

Steam power entered the yards in 1799 but was not very economic for intermittent work such as pumping docks. Marc Brunel's block mills were working under steam by 1803 and in 1808 they turned out 130,000 blocks. Ten unskilled men replaced 100 blockmakers and the capital cost was recovered in three years. This was a major milestone in the Industrial Revolution.

The Navy needed facilities other than dockyards such as ordnance yards and victualling yards. There is a nice story of the first 'instant' soup, credited to Mrs Dubois, in 1756. The Navy cared for its men much better than most contemporary organisations as shown by the great naval hospitals of which Haslar is the best known.

The illustrations are very well selected, using a blend of early and modern photographs, reproductions of building plans and thoughtful use of details from the elaborate models of the yards dating from the end of the eighteenth century. There are plans of the yards at various dates with surviving buildings marked.

There are few complaints: the author does confuse displacement (weight) with tonnage (builder's measurement), a crude representation of volume; Marc Brunel did not sever all connection with the Admiralty in 1812 but after the war initiated and carried out trials of steamships for the Admiralty.

Navies, then and now, require considerable support. The Admiralty of the eighteenth and nineteenth centuries used advanced technology to design a remarkable range of buildings, fit for purpose, generally fairly inexpensive and attractive in appearance. Mr Coad has done them credit.

D K Brown RCNC

T Gibbons, Warships and Naval Battles of the US Civil War, *published by Dragon's World, 1989.*
310 x 260mm, 176 pages, 180 colour illustrations.
ISBN 1-85028-094-0. £16.95

The author is an illustrator who has made a long study of the ships of the US Civil War. The numerous coloured illustrations of the ships are both beautiful and accurate and there are also five paintings of key battles. This work is, however, far from being just a picture book.

In the main sections of the book, all important ships of both sides are not only illustrated but described in considerable detail and there is a brief operational history of each ship. They are grouped under the headings of Ironclads, Gunboats, Raiders, Cruisers, Blockade runners and Submarines. There are also annexes listing particulars of some 1500 ships of the Federal and Confederate States Navies.

This war saw the first extensive use

The wooden sidewheel steamer Peosta, *one of the illustrations from* Warships and Naval Battles of the US Civil War.

of ironclads, some of advanced technology and others, crude improvisations. The river war on the Mississippi posed unique operational and technical problems. There were a number of heroic attempts to build and operate submarines culminating in the first success when the Confederate *Hunley* sank the USS *Housatonic* on 17 February 1864. The author has done great service in describing these fascinating vessels in such attractive style.

D K Brown RCNC

N Polmar and P B Mersky, Amphibious Warfare, The Illustrated History, *published by Blandford Press, 1988.*
270 x 200mm, 192 pages, 197 illustrations.
ISBN 0-7137-1827-7. £19.95

The book opens with brief accounts of early combined operations such as Alexandria (1802), the Dardanelles, Zeebrugge and early feats of the US Marines at Tripoli and elsewhere. The story proper opens with the Japanese assault on China and their early successes in the Pacific.

The great invasions of the Second World War, North Africa, the Mediterranean, Normandy etc, are fully described and there are good descriptions of the ships and craft used. Though the authors are Americans, full credit is given to the work of other countries, even the British concept for the LST(2) getting a mention. The United States reconquest of the Pacific forms the major part of the book, a topic not as well known as it should be to British readers.

Postwar operations in Korea, Suez, Vietnam and the Falklands follow, with a final section describing the capabilities of the US Marine Corps and of other countries. Submarine launched attacks during and after the war are given prominence; even that of 41 Commando, Royal Marines from USS *Perch* against North Vietnam. The only criticism which can be levelled against this fascinating book is that it is too short and some sections seem a bit hurried in consequence. The numerous illustrations are clear and well chosen. At a time when Britain is still debating the future of its amphibious force, this book is well worth reading.

D K Brown RCNC

Ray Sturtivant, British Naval Aviation: The Fleet Air Arm 1917–1990, *published by Arms and Armour, 1990.*
270 x 200mm, 254 pages, 170 illustrations.
ISBN 0-85368-938-5. £19.95.

The limitations of potted history are shown by Ray Sturtivant's *British Naval Aviation* which covers the Fleet Air Arm in its various guises from 1917 until now. Some 220 pages allow space for the wood or the trees but not both; Sturtivant inclines towards the latter, and the result is a mine of information but not history à la Roskill. Much of the earlier coverage comes from verbatim reminiscences of participants, who are well chosen from among the author's many Fleet Air Arm contacts. A very wide variety of postwar events and developments are each briefly described. Overall, the focus is on air operations but with anecdotal coverage of some supporting elements. The author's mastery of aviation facts matches that shown in his *Squadrons of the Fleet Air Arm*, an earlier invaluable source book, but aircraft carrier matters are less well served, as shown by some dubious claims in the annex listing 'British Naval Aviation Firsts'. The many photographs naturally include some classics but most are new to this reviewer.

One minor curiosity. HMS *Indomitable* was badly mauled by an air launched torpedo on the night 15/16 July 1943 after covering the invasion of Sicily. Although Ray Sturtivant like some other writers attributes the deed to a German Junkers 88, I and others believe that the culprit was an Italian SM 79 from one of the Aerosilurante (Air Torpedo) Gruppos. Surprising that such a detail is in doubt so long after the event.

Among its topics the book jogs memories about the number and extent of Fleet Air Arm operational activities since the war. One thinks of Korea, Suez, the 'junglies' in Borneo and lastly the Falklands; but there were other warlike sideshows and any amount of on the spot deterrence. Hence the distinctive 'sharp end' flavour of a specialty in which, in piping days of peace, it has been more usual for people to have campaign experience than not. Ray Sturtivant offers a worthy addition to its chronicles.

David Stanley

SHORT NOTICES

'Anatomy of the Ship Series':
Peter Goodwin, The Bomb Vessel Granado 1742
Al Ross, The Destroyer Campbeltown
Portia Takakjian, The 32-Gun Frigate Essex
all published by Conway Maritime Press Ltd, 1989–90.
Each: 240 x 254mm, 128 pages, approx 20 photographs and 300 line drawings.
Granado *ISBN 0-85177-522-5 £18.00.*
Campbeltown *ISBN 0-85177-543-8 £18.00.*
Essex *ISBN 0-85177-541-1 £18.00.*

The latest additions to this well established series range from the highly specialised bomb vessel (the shore bombardment ship of the age of sail) through the American frigate *Essex* of 1799 to the famous ex-'four stacker' expended in the St Nazaire raid of March 1942. This latter 'Anatomy' depicts the ship as built (USS *Buchanon*), as an RN Lend-Lease escort, and as converted for the raid.

As with all previous volumes in the series, the books are based on numerous detailed drawings, although they also contain a photo section and brief introduction.

Anon, Fuehrer Conferences on Naval Affairs 1939–1946, *with a Foreword by Jak P Mallmann Showell, published by Greenhill Books, 1990.*
232 x 145mm, 480 pages.
ISBN 1-85367-060-X. £19.95.

This is a facsimile reprint of the limited-circulation Admiralty translation of notes kept by Raeder and Dönitz (as C-in-C) of the regular meetings with Hitler to review naval matters. They are mostly in note form and are effectively minutes, but they do allow considerable insight into naval thinking at the highest level. The material has been published before (in *Brassey's* for 1948), but this new edition will make it far more easily available. The addition of an index would have been valuable, but it does contain a useful glossary.

Ronald Atkin, Pillar of Fire: Dunkirk 1940, *published by Sidgwick & Jackson in association with the Imperial War Museum, 1990.*
232 x 156mm, 264 pages, 19 illustrations.
ISBN 0-283-99697-8. £12.95.

For the next five years we will be afflicted with 50th anniversary offerings celebrating various landmarks of the Second World War. This year it is the turn of the Fall of France and the Battle of Britain, and of course the victory-in-defeat that constituted the Dunkirk evacuation. Of a number of titles relating to this epic of improvisation, *Pillar of Fire* is probably the most readable. It is essentially a collection of personal reminiscences, skilfully stitched together by an *Observer* journalist. It claims to 'expose the myth of Dunkirk' – and it is true that it was not all unalloyed heroism and brilliant organisation – but the overwhelming impression is still one of daring and ingenuity justly rewarded.

William M Arkin and Joshua Handler, Naval Accidents 1945–1988, *published by Greenpeace and the Institute for Policy Studies, 1989.*
280 x 210mm, 88 pages, paperback. No price quoted.

A compilation by date of around 1300 accidents to naval vessels since the end of the war, designed to support Greenpeace's Nuclear Free Seas campaign by showing how frequently potentially dangerous incidents occur. As a pure chronicle it is useful, with a number of previously unpublished events, but to the informed observer it suggests quite the opposite of its intention – it actually highlights how rarely there is any real danger, considering the hostile environment of the oceans, although where nuclear radiation and pollution is concerned, no risk must be preferable to even the most infinitesimal.

Bernard Blake, Jane's Underwater Warfare Systems 1989–90, *published by Jane's Information Group, 1989.*
316 x 216mm, 208 pages, 300 illustrations.
ISBN 0-7106-0884-5. £80.00.

With *Jane's Fighting Ships* now costing £100, there seems little point in reviewing it in a journal whose readership is primarily non-professional. As a marketing strategy, it might make sense to concentrate on the military and the defence industry, but the interested layman is entitled to feel aggrieved at his exclusion from up-to-date information on the grounds of price. A particularly blatant example of this approach is the division of *Jane's Weapon Systems* into eight parts, each costing much the same as the original combination. Judging from the *Underwater Warfare* volume, for your money, you get a lot of press-release photos, some very general description (possibly from the same source) and little idea of the whole thrust of development or how various bits of kit fit into the overall picture.

Just as *Combat Fleets* is eroding the *Fighting Ships* market, so the launch by Naval Institute Press of a *Naval Weapons* volume (by Norman Friedman) should give the technically minded enthusiast a preferable alternative to Jane's multi-part product.

David Brown, Warship Losses of World War Two, *published by Arms and Armour, 1990.*
232 x 156mm, 256 pages.
ISBN 0-85368-802-8. £16.95.

A very useful reference book, including not only details of each sinking (time, position and circumstances, where known) but also statistical analyses of losses by type, country, area, year and major navy. There are also sketch maps, and tabular statistics of weapons and warship classes, although the latter are inevitably sketchy.

Fotofax series: The US Navy 1942–1943 by Robert C Stern; British Submarines of World War One by Paul J Kemp. Both *published by Arms and Armour, 1990.*
Each: 246 x 189mm, 48 pages c90 illustrations. £4.95.

The latest in this pictorial series share the major drawback of all the others, namely the poor standard of halftone printing. Both are well (and interestingly) captioned, but the photos in the submarine volume are rarer, whereas the US Navy collection is rather commonplace.

Erich Groener, German Warships 1815–1945, Vol 1: Major Surface Vessels, *published by Conway Maritime Press, 1990.*
295 x 248mm, 256 pages, 430 line drawings.
ISBN 0-85177-533-0. £30.00

Groener's work should need no introduction to readers of this journal, and this translation is based on the much revised and expanded edition by Dieter Jung and Martin Maass currently being published in Germany (6 volumes to date). When finished it will be monumentally comprehensive, including besides naval vessels proper, Army and Luftwaffe craft, and every commandeered merchantman, not excluding even the small craft taken up for the intended invasion of Britain in 1940.

The translated edition makes two significant changes: firstly, to employ a larger format, and consequently a more manageable number of volumes; and secondly, to replace the German's formidable battery of symbols with more 'user-friendly' data tables, so that the book can be consulted on an occasional basis without recourse to twenty pages of explications. This can only be an improvement.

Eric J Grove, Nato Major Warships – Europe, *published by Tri-Service Press, 1990.*
127 x 190mm landscape, 208 pages, c100 photographs.
ISBN 1-85400-006-3. £7.95.

The latest in a long line of pocket books, this series demonstrates the increasing sophistication of the market. A bare list of data is no longer enough, and each entry now has a short but enlightening analysis of the design. Perhaps not something for the reader of *Warship*, but a better 'beginners' reference than was available 20 years ago.

Bernard Ireland, Sea Power 2000, *published by Arms and Armour, 1990.*
241 x 184mm, 160 pages, c150 illustrations.
ISBN 0-85368-979-2. £14.95.

With the year 2000 so close, this is less an exercise in crystalball-gazing, than an attempt to describe the most important current trends in technology and tactics. It is a very short (and heavily illustrated) book, so expect no depth of analysis, but it does tackle all the major concerns. Although one would not agree with all the author's opinions and judge-

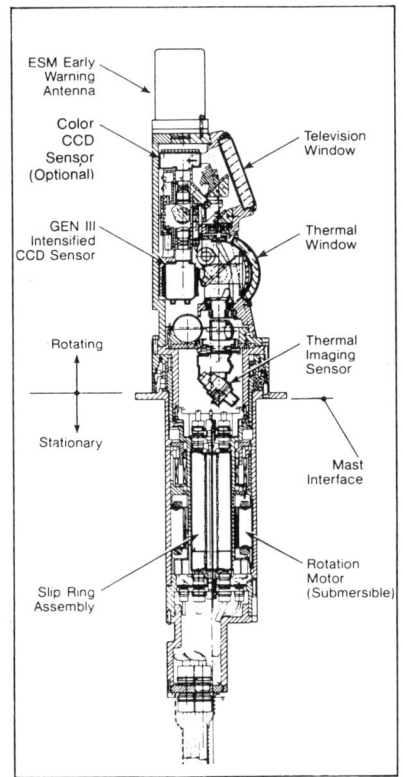

No longer a simple periscope, the Optronic Mast provides several means of imaging and does not penetrate the pressure hull. An illustration from Sea Power 2000.

ments, the book is a unique summary pitched at the level of the intelligent layman, and very useful for that.

Peter Kirsch, The Galleon: The Great Ships of the Armada Era, *published by Conway Maritime Press, 1990.*
260 x 200mm, 224 pages, 150 illustrations.
ISBN 0-85177-546-2. £25.00.

Primarily intended for modelmakers, this book sifts all the available evidence in order to reconstruct a typical large warship of about 1610. The author's handling of the sources makes the book worthy of the general ship historian's attention.

John Lambert and Al Ross, Allied Coastal Forces of World War II, Volume I: Fairmile Designs and US Submarine Chasers, *published by Conway Maritime Press, 1990.*
295 x 248mm, 256 pages, 211 photographs, 500 line drawings.
ISBN 0-85177-519-5. £35.

The first of a three-volume series, essentially much enlarged versions of the 'Anatomy of the Ship' approach, with large numbers of detailed drawings of each type, its variations, equipment, machinery and armament. Both the authors are well known authorities on coastal forces and skilled draughtsmen, and the volume packs in a wealth of information in an under-researched subject area.

John Lippiett, Modern Combat Ships 5: Type 21, *published by Ian Allan, 1990.*
233 x 170mm, 112 pages, c150 illustrations.
ISBN 0-7110-1903-7. £13.95.

The latest in this series of monographs is written by the CO of *Amazon*, who also served in *Ambuscade* during the Falklands, so the 'user angle' is well covered. Given that the type has come in for a fair degree of criticism, it is interesting to see them given sympathetic and knowledgeable treatment. The book also deals with the various proposed improvements and commercial frigate derivations.

Leo Marriott, Royal Navy Frigates since 1945, *published by Ian Allan, 1990.*
233 x 170mm, 160 pages, c160 illustrations.
ISBN 0-7110-1915-0. £12.95.

A revised edition of a book first published in 1983, this is a useful general survey, although being based on secondary sources has nothing entirely new to say. The line draw-

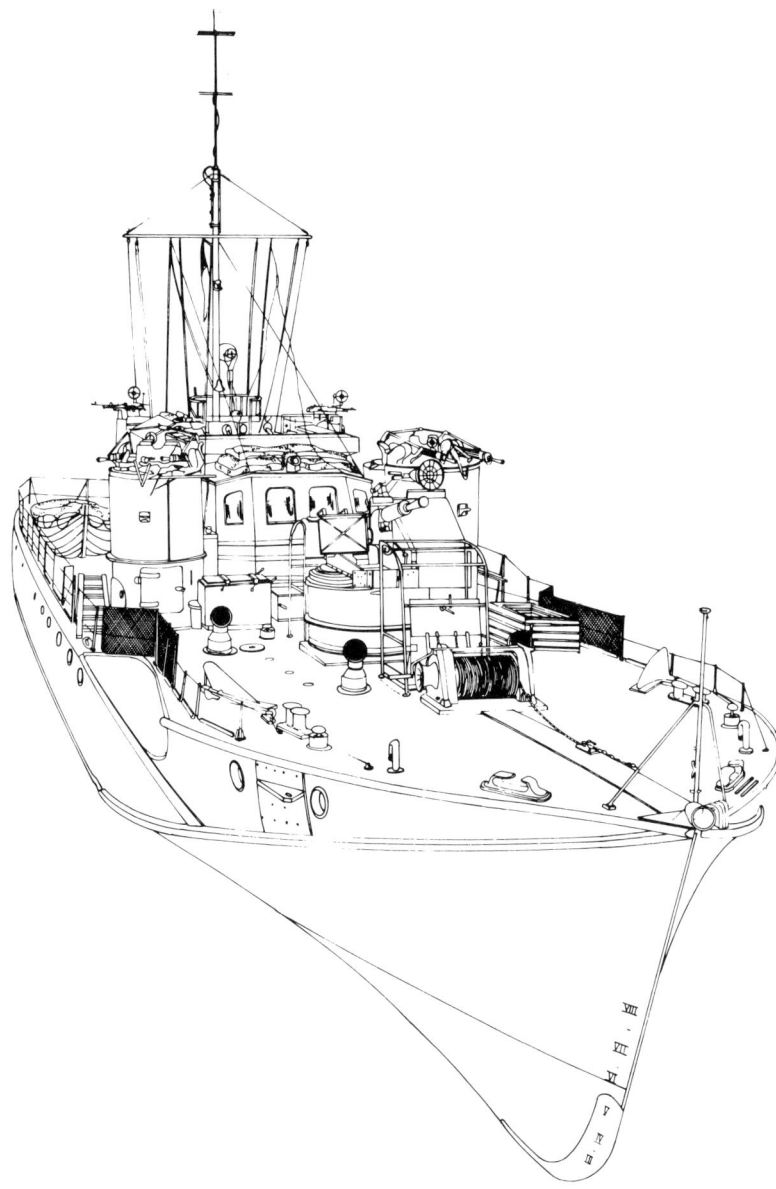

One of John Lambert's drawings (a Fairmile 'D') from Allied Coastal Forces.

ings are a bit crude, but there is a good selection of photographs covering ships from the war-standard escorts of 1945 to the Type 23s, plus a selection of commercial proposals (hardly likely to be adopted by the Royal Navy) and the already defunct NFR-90.

Ian H Marshall, Armored Ships, *published by Conway Maritime Press, 1990.*
254 x 254mm, 176 pages, 58 colour plates, 15 pencil sketches.
ISBN 0-85177-558-6. £25.00.

A portfolio of watercolour paintings devoted to some of the greatest warships (predominantly capital ships) of the last century and a half. The paintings are, technically speaking, highly accurate, but they also have a real feeling for the character of the individual ships depicted, and each is shown in a specific location at a particular time, adding to the authenticity of the rendering.

Samuel Eliot Morison, The Two-Ocean War: A Short History of the United States Navy in the Second World War, *published by Little, Brown & Co, 1989.*
234 x 156mm, 640 pages, 35 photographs and 54 maps.
ISBN 0-316-58352-9. £9.95 paperback.

A reprint of this classic distillation from Morison's definitive 15-volume history of US naval operations. Now a little dated in places, it is still the most readable single book on the subject.

Russell Plummer, The Ships that saved an Army, *published by Patrick Stephens Ltd, 1990.*
245 x 190mm, 240 pages, c200 illustrations.
ISBN 0-85260-210-4. £17.99.

Although this book essays a chapter on 'The Seafarers' Stories', it could hardly be more of a contrast to *Pillar of Fire* (mentioned earlier), being essentially a listing of as many vessels involved in the Dunkirk evacuation as the author could track down. Well represented are the famous 'Little Ships' (none smaller than the 15ft dinghy *Tamzine*, now in the Imperial War Museum), but it was the larger vessels – cross-Channel ferries, paddle steamers and coasters – that actually brought home the majority of the troops. These are fully documented with contemporary photographs wherever possible, and the warships involved are also listed (their particulars are widely available elsewhere). There may have been as many as 1300 craft of all types at Dunkirk, and the author has done a marvellous job of assembling information on the ships and their role in the evacuation – with so much never committed to paper at the time, and the power of memory fading with the passing years, this book may well be unsurpassed.

Kenneth Poolman, Allied Submarines of World War Two, *published by Arms and Armour, 1990.*
276 x 216mm, 160 pages, c150 illustrations.
ISBN 0-85368-942-3. £19.95.

This is a slightly surprising book in that the title, large format, and high proportion of illustrations leads one to expect a technical reference book. Instead, it turns out to be a somewhat over-written operational narrative. It is mainly concerned with retelling the well-known story of US and British submarines, although a short appendix does summarise Greek, Dutch, Norwegian, Polish, Soviet and Yugoslav efforts. The photographs are mostly well-known, and are not well reproduced, some being clearly copied from earlier publications.

Peter Schenk, The Invasion of England 1940: The Planning of Operation Sealion, *published by Conway Maritime Press, 1990.*
220 x 148mm, 384 pages, c150 illustrations.
ISBN 0-85177-548-9. £20.00.

One of this year's 50th anniversaries concerns a non-event: the proposed German invasion of Britain. This book was originally published in German and is the most detailed reconstruction of the planning so far attempted. It contains a store of fascinating information on the special craft developed, the barge conversions and a host of ingenious and makeshift arrangements. The author sees the preparations as an important, but ignored, step in the development of amphibious warfare and compares the German solutions to the later Allied achievements in the Normandy landings.

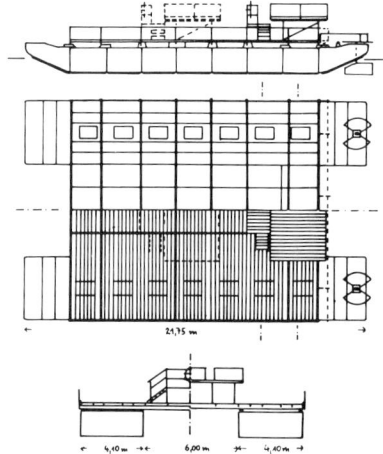

One of the many ingenious craft devised for the planned German invasion of England, this ferry was contrived from a pair of army assault bridge pontoons. An illustration from The Invasion of England 1940.

Charles S Thomas, The German Navy in the Nazi Era, *published by Unwin Hyman, 1990.*
230 x 156mm, 304 pages.
ISBN 0-04-445493-7. £35.00.

An academic history of the Kriegsmarine's relationship with its political masters. There is not much of specific technical interest, but the book provides important background.

David A Thomas, The Atlantic Star 1939–45, *published by W H Allen, 1990.*
232 x 156mm, 320 pages, 40 photographs, 12 maps and tables.
ISBN 1-85227-147-7. £14.95.

It is not easy to write a history of so diverse and lengthy an event as the Battle of the Atlantic, and although this book has a chronological framework, its strength is the working in of personal accounts by those involved. Most of the photographs were taken by survivors and are previously unpublished.

Brian Tunstall, Naval Warfare in the Age of Sail: The Evolution of Fighting Tactics 1680–1815, *edited by Dr Nicholas Tracy, published by Conway Maritime Press Ltd, 1990.*
295 x 248mm, 288 pages, 150 photographs, 150 line drawings.
ISBN 0-85177-544-6. £35.00.

This was Brian Tunstall's master work, a comprehensive and highly original study of sailing ship tactics, left as an unedited typescript on his death. Carefully edited to half its original length (it is still about 300,000 words), with battle charts and paintings of the famous engagements, it is now presented in a form more readily appreciated by the layman.

A Van Dijk, Voor Pampus, *published by De Bataafsche Leeuw, 1987.*
280 x 215mm, 176 pages, c100 illustrations.
ISBN 90-6707-148-X. No price quoted.

Although published several years back, a review copy of this title has only recently arrived, and is too significant to be ignored, since very

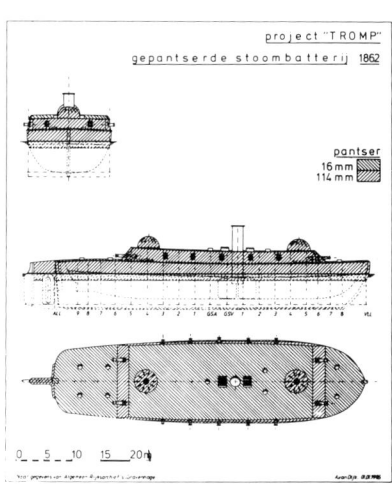

A plan of the projected conversion of the Tromp *into an armoured steam battery – one of numerous drawings in* Voor Pampus.

little of technical merit on the mid-nineteenth century Dutch navy has ever been published. The book looks at the naval technical revolution of steam, steel and shellfire from the Netherlands point of view, and although it is principally in Dutch, there is an English summary and numerous illustrations.

John Winton, The Naval Heritage of Portsmouth, *published by Ensign Publications, 1990. 244 x 187mm, 234 pages, c100 illustrations. ISBN 1-85455-002-0. £12.95.*

A study of the relationship between the Royal Navy and its premier base. An interesting social history, by this well-known writer.

PUBLICATIONS ANNOUNCED

John D Alden, The American Steel Navy, *new edition, published by Naval Institute Press, £32.95.*

John D Alden, Flush Deck and Four Pipes, *new edition, published by Naval Institute Press, £19.95.*

Michael Evans, Amphibious Operations, *published by Brassey's (No 4 in the 'Sea Power' series), £19.95.*

N L R Franks, Search, Find and Kill: Coastal Command's U-Boat Successes in World War 2, *published by Aston Publications, £16.95.*

Norman Friedman, World Naval Weapons Systems, *published by Naval Institute Press, £59.95.*

Eric Grove, Maritime Strategy and European Security, *published by Brassey's, £16.95.*

Michael Glover, Invasion Scare 1940, *published by Leo Cooper, £14.95.*

Stephen Howarth, The Shining Sea: A History of the US Navy 1775–1989, *published by Weidenfeld, £25.00.*

R D Layman, The Hybrid Warship, *published by Conway Maritime Press, £25.00.*

Ken Macksey, Invasion: The German Invasion of England, July 1940, *published by Greenhill Books, £14.95.*

Gordon Swanborough and Peter Bowers, United States Navy Aircraft since 1911, *published by Putnam Aeronautical, £35.00.*

Anthony Watts, The Imperial Russian Navy, *published by Arms and Armour, £19.95.*

Two of the specially commissioned battle charts from Naval Warfare in the Age of Sail, *depicting the attack on the Danish fleet in 1801.*

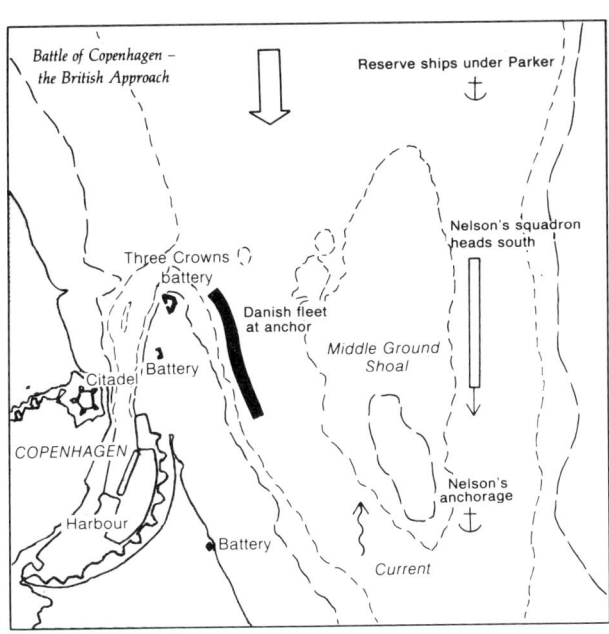
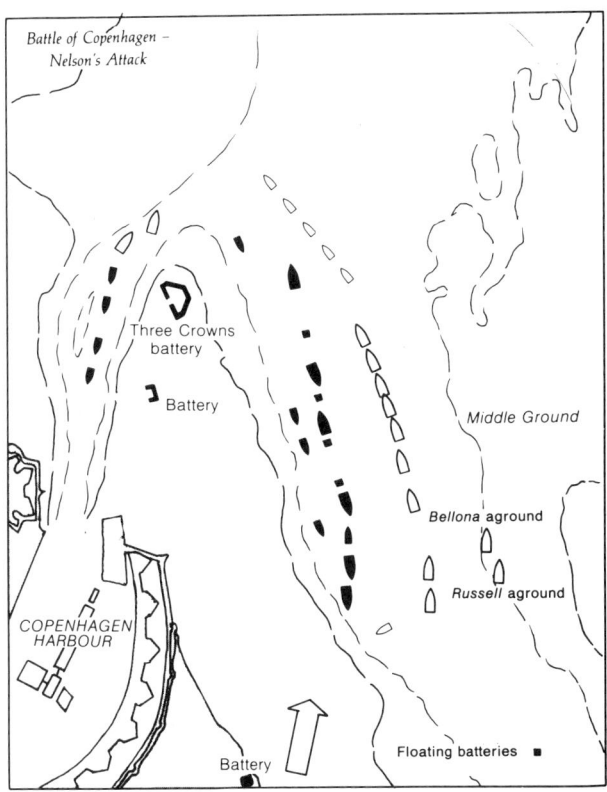

THE NAVAL YEAR IN REVIEW

The events covered by this review stretch from approximately May 1989 to May 1990, with some reference before and after. Compiled by Ian Sturton.

A. INTRODUCTION

The year in review began with continuing improvements in East–West relations, both blocs negotiating towards arms treaties, while Moscow's decision not to support unpopular satellite regimes precipitated the collapse of the old order in Eastern Europe. The first months of 1990 saw non-communist governments elected, the Warsaw Pact in shreds and German reunification imminent. Downward pressures on defence spending will affect East and West alike; the smaller navies of the year 2000 will spend much time on protecting EEZ resources, enforcing environmental and anti-drug controls, and preventing illegal immigration.

Further east, defence spending is up in the Pacrim area, where, as the US shield shrinks, prospering countries cast wary eyes on stronger neighbours – China, India, Japan and the Soviet Union. In the Middle East, mutual hatred and fear have increased investments in military equipment, but Latin America and Africa have little to spare on arms.

B(i). THE STRATEGIC BALANCE

The likelihood of an East–West crisis culminating in hostilities receded; NATO sources reckoned that the West would be able to rely on 33–44 days' warning of an attack from a 'standing start', in place of the 14 days previously used in planning. Much else is in a state of flux, even the future political geography of Europe being uncertain. The number of US carriers, needed to implement the US/NATO forward maritime strategy, is as yet uncut, but the totals of planes and escorts per group have already been reduced, so that non-US NATO countries may be asked to provide more ASW-heavy task forces for the Norwegian Sea.

The USSR seems to be turning to 'defensive sufficiency', the concept of minimum defence; in the Norwegian area, naval exercises are increasingly defensive, and against attack from the north.

B(ii). DISARMAMENT

The proposed arms treaties are to reduce conventional forces in Europe (CFE, between NATO and the Warsaw Pact) and to limit long-range strategic weapons (START, between USA and USSR). The year saw a renewed Soviet campaign to include naval forces in CFE talks, a move opposed by NATO, which claims that its navies are 'non-negotiable'. Soviet unilateral naval cuts to date, although very numerous, comprise outdated units only; the incentive for scrapping effective ships remains low because the West is so much stronger at sea. NATO states that its superiority in surface ships is less impressive than suggested by numbers, because Atlantic sea lanes, essential for the transport of troops and supplies, have to be protected. All Soviet needs in war would be obtainable within the country or would be importable over land frontiers. In reply, the USSR states that the USN strike carriers, each with about 40 strike planes able to attack land targets with nuclear or conventional weapons, are not defensive weapons, projecting far more power than is needed to protect communications, transports or convoys in wartime. In contrast, the argument continues, Soviet carriers are essentially defensive; they carry fighters rather than strike aircraft and can only launch lightly loaded planes.

Similarly, the USSR has tried to include land attack SLCM (Sea Launched Cruise Missiles) with nuclear warheads in the START talks. According to the US, which has invested immensely in cruise missile

THE NAVAL YEAR IN REVIEW

Table 1. *MAJOR WARSHIP TYPES OF PRINCIPAL NAVIES, 1 APRIL 1990*

Type	USA	USSR	UK	France	China	India	Japan	Italy
CV (large)	15	–	–	–	–	–	–	–
CV (medium)	–	4	–	2	–	1	–	–
CV (small)	–	–	3	–	–	1	–	1
Battleship	4	–	–	–	–	–	–	–
Cruiser (helicopter)	–	2	–	1	–	–	–	1
Cruiser (missile)	42	31	–	1	–	–	–	2
Destroyer	59	39	13	17	19	5	42	4
Frigate (fleet)	100	38	33	6	37	12	16	14
(escort)	–	142	–	17	–	9	–	4
SSBN	36	63	4	6	1	–	–	–
SSGN	96	52	–	–	–	–	–	–
SSN		85	16	4	4	1	–	–
SS (all types)	–	149	10	10	c55	18	14	10
MCMV (ocean and coastal)	24	311	39	19	c130	12	32	23

Note: The 15 US carriers include one in SLEP. Many of the older Soviet escort frigates, patrol submarines and MCMV in the above totals are unserviceable.

variants, the SLCM is a tactical, not a strategic missile, and in any case the number present with nuclear, not conventional, warheads is not readily verifyable (the USN's Tomahawks can have either type).

C. BUDGET PROPOSALS AND NEW PROGRAMMES

C(i). USA, NATO and Allies

In June 1989, NATO Ministers reiterated the annual goal of a 3 per cent real increase in defence spending for each country. In practice, in the previous twelve months, only Greece, Portugal, Denmark and Canada increased spending in real terms.

MAJOR NATO NAVIES

(a) United States
The defence budget for FY90, beginning 1 October 1989, was agreed eventually (14 April 1989) at $295.6b, about 1 per cent less in real terms than the final FY89 figure of $290.2b. The Administration's FY91 request (January 1990) was for $295.1, some 2.6 per cent below FY90 in real terms. Both FY90 and FY91 figures were scaled down from earlier Bush proposals (zero real increase in FY90, +1 per cent in FY91, FY92 and +3 per cent in FY93), reflecting demands for tighter spending in a less menacing world. Cuts of $180b were ordered for FY92 through FY94, and the armed forces are preparing options, including the reduction of deployable carriers from 14 to 12. FY89, FY90 and FY91 (request) figures for the US Navy were $97.4b, $97.8b and $99.5b.

The USN will reduce ship numbers by retiring elderly fleet submarines and missile destroyers faster than replacements are commissioned. Ten *Knox* class frigates will be put in reserve (4 in FY90, 6 in FY91) to join the 24 modern frigates already there. FY90 cuts include retiring *Coral Sea* when *Abraham Lincoln* is completed, keeping for the moment the total of deployable carriers at 14, with 15 air wings, but reducing the number of surface combatants per battle group. The Administration's axe fell on the F-14D new production programme, although the F-14E upgrading con-

USS *Florida (SSBN-729), the third Ohio class SSBN. The ninth (Tennessee) and later boats will have longer-range Trident II D5 missiles.* (General Dynamics, Electric Boat Division)

tinued; only development funds were left for the Marine Corps' V-22 tilt-rotor aircraft. Proposals for FY91 included retirement of the battleships *New Jersey* and *Iowa* in 1991; the CGNs *Truxtun* and *Bainbridge*, first proposed for withdrawal in FY94 and FY92 respectively, will almost certainly also go in 1991. The fleet will comprise 546 deployable ships by FY91.

(b) United Kingdom.
The 1989–90 Defence Estimates were for £20.3b ($34.1b), a reduction in real terms of 0.7 per cent; planned real increases of 1.7 per cent for 1990–91 and 1.3 per cent for 1991–92 depend on unrealistic low predicted rates of inflation. The 1989–90 provision for maritime defence was £2.56b ($4.30b), an actual reduction of £40m ($67m). The existing pattern of ship construction continued, with new orders for Type 23 frigates and Single Role Minehunters (SRMH) placed or imminent. The RN's total of destroyers and frigates was 49, of which 44 could be ready in a very short time. Orders for the Aviation Support

'Delta IV' SSBN. A sixth 'Delta IV' was launched in 1988; a more accurate version of the SS-N-23 ICBM was tested at sea in the same year. (From Soviet Military Power 1989)

Ship and the third Trident SSBN are expected later in 1990, while *Fearless* and *Intrepid* will probably be replaced by new construction. For the fourth consecutive year, total estimated costs for the Trident II programme fell in real terms (the January

Table 2. *USN SHIPBUILDING PROGRAMMES, 1988–1993*

New Construction	Approved (authorised and funded)			Proposed (subject to amendment)		
	FY88	FY89	FY90	FY91	FY92	FY93
SSBN *Ohio*	1	1	1	1	1	1
SSBN-688 *Los Angeles*	3	2	2	–	–	–
SSN-21 *Seawolf*	–	1	–	2	3	3
CVN	2	–	–	–	–	–
CG-47 *Ticonderoga*	5	–	–	–	–	–
DDG-51 *Arleigh Burke*	–	5	5	5	5	5
MCM *Avenger*	–	–	3	–	–	–
MHC *Osprey*	–	–	2	3	4	4
LHD *Wasp*	1	1	–	1	1	1
LSD (cargo variant)	1	1	1	1	1	1

Note: Projections beyond FY91 unlikely to be authorised or fully funded.

An 'Oscar' class cruise missile submarine (SSGN). These quiet, very large boats carry 24 SS-N-19 450km-range cruise missiles, with HE or nuclear warheads. (From Soviet Military Power *1988)*

1990 figure was £9.38b ($15.85b), a fall of £432m ($730m) in 1989 and a reduction in real terms of £2.63b on 1982 estimates). February's decision to allow members of the WRNS to serve at sea followed trends in the army and air force.

(c) Canada

The defence budget for 1989–90 was fixed at $9.4b, an increase of only 1.2 per cent on 1988–89, inflation being forecast at 4.5 per cent. Defence took the brunt of the April 1989 cuts, the extra spending planned for 1989–1994 being reduced by $2.27b. For the next two years, defence spending is to increase by 5 per cent annually before inflation, the proposed figure for 1990–91 being $9.89b and for 1991–92 $10.38b. The SSN cancellation effectively ended plans for Arctic control; the patrol submarine programme may be revived, with air-independent propulsion (AIP) for limited under-ice operations possible. More maritime patrol aircraft would provide extra coastal and Arctic surveillance, but the projected nuclear-powered Polar icebreaker was cancelled in 1990. Two companies are competing in the project definition phase of the 12-MCMV programme.

(d) West Germany

The 1990 defence budget was increased by a real 3.3 per cent, but long-term plans include major cuts in the Baltic and a reduction in naval personnel to 31,000. By the year 2000, there will be 16 frigates, 18 or fewer submarines and 20 modern MCMVs, a reduction in active units of nearly a half. The new Type 212 submarines will be ocean-going, and the present coastal submarines and FAC will be hard hit. Fuller details of future force composition and major arms programmes are to be determined later.

(e) Italy

The 1989 Italian defence budget of approximately $17b, was reduced by around 9.5 per cent in 1990. The major review 'Project 2000' begun in July 1988 assumed an annual 2.5 per cent of GNP on defence, but balance of payments deficits reduced this figure to 2 per cent, and, if CFE talks are successful, there will be pressure to go much lower. The present Navy is considered the minimum for adequate peacetime defence, and some

USS Yorktown (CG-48). Later units of this class are fitted with vertical launch systems (VLS) for Standard MR-2 missiles; the DD-963/DDG-993/CG-47 hull is too small to take the much longer ER-2. (Ingalls)

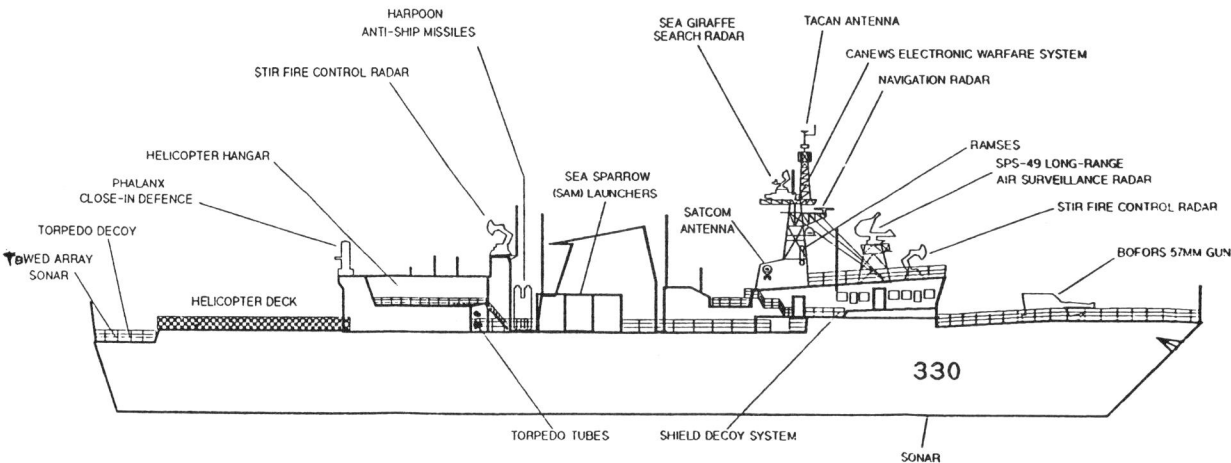

money for new construction is already coming from outside the defence budget. The naval procurement budget for 1989–91 was $2.65b, and existing ship construction programmes continue.

(f) Netherlands

After much debate, the Dutch defence budget for 1990 was frozen, followed by a 1 per cent reduction in 1991; further cuts planned will depend on progress of the CFE talks and events in Eastern Europe. No major new orders are planned until after 2000, apart from the joint MCMV force, the Marines' Amphibious Assault Ship and the Fast Combat Support Ship. Orders for two *Moray* class submarines are unlikely, and the viability of an eventual four-unit submarine force has been called into question.

(g) The South–Eastern Flank

Greece's order of three Meko 200 frigates from Skaramanga on 16 May was followed (January 1990) by the

▲ *Schematic elevation of Canadian patrol frigate* Halifax *('City' class) with modified masting etc, showing weapons and sensors (Official).*

▶ HMS *Sandown, the first SRMH, commissioned 9 June 1989. (Vosper Thornycroft)*

▼ *The Italian light carrier* Giuseppe Garibaldi. *Preliminary approval has been given for 18 AV-8B plus rotary-wing aircraft for this ship; the SH-3D ASW helicopters will be replaced by EH 101. (Fincantieri)*

THE NAVAL YEAR IN REVIEW

public prosecutor's investigation of contract irregularities. **Turkey's** defence budget fell by a real 10 per cent; the first of two new Type 1400 submarines was begun, following the contract signed in February 1988. The fifth and sixth Meko frigates were ordered, and a further two are possible.

LESSER NATO NAVIES

Norway's 1990 defence budget showed real growth of over 2 per cent, and Kvaerner has the MCMV programme in hand. **Denmark's** navy is to have four more Standard Flex 300 craft, and will modernise two additional submarines. **Belgian** austerity measures include keeping ships at sea 50 days annually on average instead of 83, cutting the budget by $42m to $2.6b.

FRANCE AND SPAIN

Cooperate with NATO but are not full military members.
France. The 1990 French Defence Budget, for $29.6b, was up by 3.9 per cent from 1989. Cuts during 1989

▲ *First of a pair of economical, medium-sized assault ships, the Italian LPD* San Giorgio *has a bow ramp, floodable dock aft and upper deck spotted for large helicopters, but no aircraft hangar. Sister ship* San Marco *was funded by the Ministry of Civil Protection, for a peacetime role in disaster relief.* (Fincantieri)

THE NAVAL YEAR IN REVIEW

included a reducton in the growth rate from 6 to 4 per cent, slowing many programmes. The carrier *Charles de Gaulle* will be completed in 1998, not 1996, the light frigates will be delayed by about one year each, but the surveillance frigates will be unaffected; 3 instead of 5 Atlantique 2s will be acquired annually, while the *Amethyste* class SSNs may also be delayed.

◀ *The Turkish frigate* Yavuz, *the first of four ordered in 1982. Two more ordered in 1989 will have CODOG instead of CODAD propulsion, and VLS Sea Sparrow; a further pair may be ordered in place of the cancelled transfer of four US frigates.* (Blohm & Voss)

▶ *The Dutch Tripartite-type minehunter* Alkmaar. *Ten of this class were built for France, ten for Belgium, fifteen for the Netherlands and two of modified type for Indonesia. A Kuwait order for two was not taken up, although an export licence was granted; six were ordered for Pakistan in August 1989, two to be built in France and four at Karachi.* (Directie Voorlichting, KM)

▼ *HNlMS* Jan van Brakel, *one of ten* Kortenaer *class frigates; two more were completed for Greece. Six of the class will be modernised in the 1990s, four reduced to reserve.* (Directie Voorlichting, KM)

Spain. The modernisation of the Navy continues unabated. The 10-year Alta Mar plan specifies 15 modern escorts in service in 2002; four F-100 ASW-specialised frigates will be built from 1994–2001 as *Gearing* replacements, and the *Baleares* class will be replaced by the new F-110 from 2003. The *Agosta* class submarines will be modernised, the *Daphne* class replaced by a new S-80 type, the first to be laid down in 1999. Eight SRMHs will be delivered between 1993 and 1998.

US ALLIES

Japan. Japan continues to spend almost exactly 1 per cent of GNP on

▲ *Elevations of the Meko 200 PN and HN frigates, under construction for Portugal and Greece respectively.* Vasco da Gama, *launched 26 June 1989, is due to commission in January 1991.* (Blohm & Voss)

▼ HNIMS Tromp *is due for replacement near the end of the century, without the planned mid-life modernisation.* (Directie Voorlichting, KM)

the Self Defence Forces; the proposed FY90 budget was $30b, an increase of 6.35 per cent and representing around 6.5 per cent of government expenditure. In addition to the conventional submarines, AEGIS type destroyers and frigates in hand, the MSDF will build three *Sparviero* type missile/gun hydrofoils in FY90, to assist frigates in the control of vital sea straits around Japan. Equipment plans include TASS on warships and special new surveillance ships, the SH-60J ASW helicopter and development of the new GRX-4 ASW torpedo has started.

Australia. The Australian Defence budget for 1989–90 was $6.5b, totalling 9.6 per cent of Federal spending and 2.3 per cent of GNP, and showing no growth in real terms from 1988–89. The AMECO consortium's Meko 200 ANZ won the Australia–New Zealand frigate competition (announced 29 August). Initial orders were 8 for Australia and 2, with options on 2 more, for New Zealand; the first should be ready in 1996. Full details of weapon and sensor fits have not been finalised. The option on the seventh and eight submarines will not be taken up, and the Navy may

THE NAVAL YEAR IN REVIEW

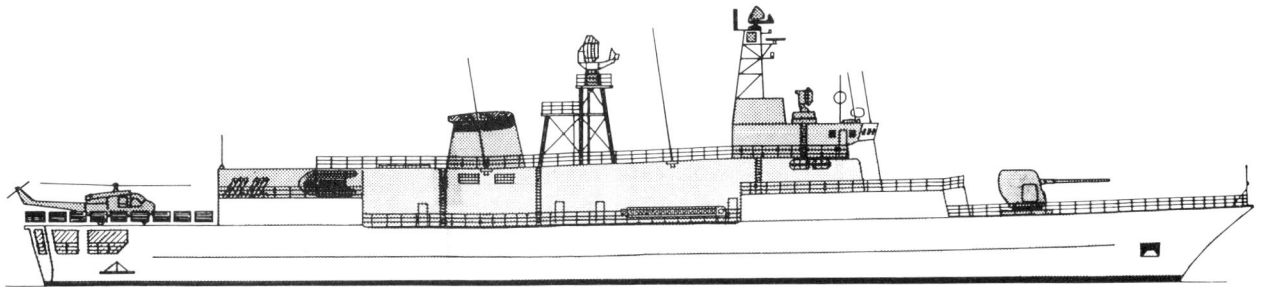

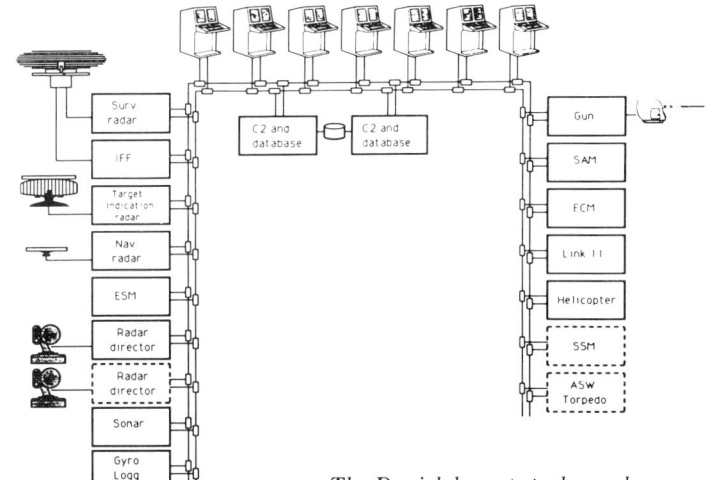

A provisional layout of the ANZAC frigate and its Bofors Electronics command and control system. (Bofors)

request a dedicated helicopter carrier/support ship instead; the training and logistics support ship *Jervis Bay* is undergoing an interim conversion. No more *Rushcutter* class MCMVs will be ordered until difficulties with the present ships' engines and sensors are overcome.

C (ii). Neutral European Nations

Sweden. Diminished defence spending continues to reduce Sweden's

The Danish large patrol vessel Flyvefisken, *first of the very versatile Standard Flex 300 class. Plug-in weapon and sensor modules can be changed in 48 hours, allowing class to operate as fast attack craft (torpedo), seaward defence craft, or MCMV. (Danyard A/S)*

military credibility, but, subject to final approval, the new A 19 submarine class will be built for the mid-1990s.

C (iii). Warsaw Pact and Associated Nations

USSR. Western and Soviet figures for the USSR's military spending are converging. In June, Moscow's defence budget for 1989, excluding civil programmes with military applications, was announced as $118b, 15.6 per cent of the national budget, 9 per cent of GNP and about four times more than the $31b previously stated, which apparently only covered military pay and allowances. For 1990, the proposed figure was $108b, a reduction of 8.3 per cent, with a

Three views of Principe de Asturias, *commissioned 30 May 1988. Spain's carrier, regarded as vulnerable in high threat areas such as the Straits of Gibraltar and approaches, and the West Mediterranean, will be the centrepiece of a North Atlantic ASW task force.* (Bazan)

further cut of some $5.3b for 1991. By 1995, it was hoped to reduce military spending to between 7.8 and 10.4 per cent of the national budget.

Western sources put total defence spending closer to $230b–$260b at current prices (curiously, a TASS report early in 1990 listed 1989 expenditure as $264b), and estimate a real annual growth rate of around 3 per cent from 1982 to 1988. Total spending declined slightly in 1989, although for much of the year there was no evidence for near-term reductions, and spending on new ships, particularly submarines, rose sharply, because of their long lead and building times.

The Soviet Navy is becoming 'leaner and meaner'; numerous obsolete ships are being deleted, new advanced platforms – missile cruisers, ships with phased array radars, the naval variant of the Su-27 'Flanker' – are entering service. New types in hand include the enlarged *Tbilisi* class carrier (reportedly the first of four), but construction of a new cruiser, perhaps with nuclear propulsion but smaller than *Kirov*, was stopped to make way for merchant ships. The 'Typhoon' class SSBN has been terminated, apparently prematurely. Western sources estimate that Soviet fleet strength will bottom out at 8 carriers of various types, around 20 cruisers and battlecruisers, 120 destroyers and frigates and 120 nuclear submarines of all types (75–80 SSN).

The operational tempo has flattened out, after a 10–15 per cent decline in recent years, and distant patrols have been reduced. In the north, naval activities are being concentrated in the Barents Sea, with less intelligence gathering along the Norwegian Coast. Most warships at the Cam Ranh base have returned to Vladivostock.

▲ Novorossiysk, *the third* Kiev *class carrier. Although* Novorossiysk *entered service in 1982, the Cross Sword fire control radars for the SA-N-9 systems were not on board as late as 1989.* Baku *had all four Cross Swords in 1988*, Tbilisi *was shown to the press in autumn 1989 with three out of four. (From* Soviet Military Power *1988)*

Ivan Rogov, *the first large Soviet landing ship, completed in 1978. The third of the class was completed in 1990. (From* Soviet Military Power *1988)*

◀ *The Su-27 'Flanker' has 150 per cent more speed, a 50 per cent greater ceiling and more than ten times the range of the Yak-38 'Forger', the first embarked fixed-wing aircraft. (From* Soviet Military Power *1989)*

C (iv). Middle East

Israel's defence spending of $4.3b includes $1.8b from the USA. The order for two HDW-designed submarines, largely funded by US Foreign Military Sales, was finally approved. **Saudi Arabia** and France agreed in outline on the construction of two or three AAW frigates, while France will probably win the Saudi

◀ *The 'Yankee-Notch' conversion of former 'Yankee' ballistic missile submarines has a new 'notch-waisted' central section containing cruise missiles, which may also be fitted in modified torpedo tubes. (From* Soviet Military Power *1989)*

▼ *The sixth and subsequent Sovremenniy class destroyers are fitted with Top Plate air search radar. (From* Soviet Military Power *1989)*

patrol submarine competition. **Oman** is to order at least three 1200t patrol vessels, possibly in Britain. **Egypt** is negotiating to replace her ex-Soviet 'Romeo' fleet with ex-RN *Oberon*s.

The Saudi SRMH Al Jawf, *seen after launch, was begun as* HMS *Inverness. The Saudi minehunters have a twin Emmerson Electric 30mm forward, the British a single Oerlikon/DES 30mm.* (Vosper Thornycroft)

▼ *Soviet 'Krivak I' class frigate* Druzhny; *32 'Krivak I' and 'II' were completed between 1970 and 1981; the helicopter variant, 'Krivak III', continues to be built for the KGB at one a year.* (USN).

The South Korean corvette Chon An, *fourteenth of eighteen 1180-ton ships, is fitted with Western weapons and sensors; these corvettes are generally similar to the larger* Ulsan *class frigates.* (Marconi Radar Systems)

C (v). Pacific Rim ('PACRIM') and Indian Ocean

(a) China

The Chinese Navy's antiquated, ill-equipped ships continue to illustrate the stultifying effect of the Cultural Revolution on all aspects of technology. Defence cooperation with the West began in the early 1980s, but contracts were suspended in June 1989 after the Tiananmen Square shootings; the only up-to-date ships building, two frigates for Thailand, will have Western sensors and equipment.

(b) India
continues to stride ahead as regional great power; the 1989–90 defence estimates were for $8.5b, a 10 per cent reduction from 1988–89 in real terms, of which the Navy will receive 13.5 per cent. Old submarines are being replaced by indigenous new construction or transfers from the USSR, while new destroyers and frigates advance slowly. The carrier replacement for *Vikrant* is to be built between 1991 and 1997. India may develop a naval version of its light combat aircraft (LCA) for this carrier, or may buy Soviet or French planes.

LESSER NAVIES

South Korea ordered (September) three more Type 209 submarines, to be built locally; the 1988 trio will probably now all be built in West Germany. **Taiwan** wants to follow its eight FFG-7 (Taiwan PFG-2) frigates with six lighter vessels but France's offer of the *Lafayette* class had to be withdrawn when Peking objected. The **Philippines** will begin its much-needed modernisation with a fast patrol craft programme. **Thailand** is reported to be adding a 7800-ton helicopter support ship from West Germany to its programme of Chinese-built frigates. Contrary to earlier reports, the competition for **Malaysia's** submarine squadron, approved in principle in April 1988, is open, with France overtaking Britain as the front-runner. **Brunei's** order for three 1000-ton 'blue water' patrol corvettes may go to Vosper Thornycroft, while **Bangladesh** is buying frigates from China. Britain has tried reviving **Pakistan's** interest in Type 23 frigates, but the limited procurement funds are earmarked for tripartite minecraft and for outfitting the eight ex-US frigates.

C (vi). Latin America

Argentine's much reduced defence spending has greatly delayed the local submarines and frigates. **Brazil** is slightly better off, and the indigenous submarine and missile programmes continue; the light helicopter for the *Inhauma* class frigates has not been decided. **Chile's** defence budget for 1989 was $720m, allowing limited modernisations only.

C (vii). Africa

The **South African** defence budget for 1989–90 was $2.35b, a real increase of 2.3 per cent. However, the military withdrawal from Namibia and Angola will produce major force cuts, particularly in the Navy and Marine Corps, which may be disbanded. Plans for new submarines

▲ *Offshore patrol vessels (OPV)* Thompson *and* Prefecte Fique *of the Prefectura Naval, the Argentine Coast Guard. Such lightly armed patrol boats, displacing around 1000 tons, are increasingly taking over security and safety duties in territorial waters and EEZs.* (Bazan)

▶ *The Brazilian submarine* Tupy, *first of four Type 1400 boats, was completed by HDW in 1988; three more are building at Rio de Janeiro. Brazil intends to follow these with two of an enlarged S-NAC1 type, also locally built, and, in the distant future, by a nuclear-powered derivative, S-NAC2* (HDW).

were shelved in July 1988, but construction may be taking place covertly; HDW papers regarding the alleged transfer of submarine plans were seized by the West German Public Prosecutor. There is no news of the proposed **Nigerian** submarine procurement, the navy being generally in poor condition, while in 1988–89 **Ghana** scrapped most of its navy, leaving just four fast attack craft.

D. WARSHIP BUILDING

D (i). New Designs and Principal Orders

Nato Frigate The eight-nation NATO frigate project (NFR 90) collapsed, six nations pulling out between September and December. The UK, the first to go, could not agree a timetable or design with the other partners and objected to the main weapon system not being developed to the same timetable as the ship. NFR 90 would be ready too early for West Germany, and the NAAWS, if chosen, too capable.

(*Note:* Tables 3, 4 and 5, listing data on recent carriers, destroyers and frigates, include ships on order or building).

(a) United States. The carrier construction programme, fully funded in FY88, is unaffected by cuts. The *Arleigh Burke* (DDG-51) AEGIS destroyer programme is running behind schedule and above cost; thirteen are building, on order or authorised. Bath Iron Works, the lead yard, has encountered numerous design and construction problems, and the delivery date of the lead ship has slipped still further, from September 1990 to March 1991. At year's end, both DDG-51 and SSN-21 *(Seawolf)* programmes were coming under critical review, following analysis by GAO. The DDG-82 destroyer design, intended to follow the DDG-51, will be 12.2m longer and have an electric drive.

(b) United Kingdom. The UK Trident programme continues, within budget and on schedule for the in-service date of the mid-1990s, although much of the 'slack' in the timetable has been used. The third boat will be ordered in mid-1990, six months late; the fourth should follow in 1991, to be in service in time for *Vanguard*'s first refit. If the fourth boat were cancelled – changes in Eastern Europe will give much longer warning of a Soviet attack – then about £500m ($850m) would be saved, although there would be cancellation charges. Factors causing de-

The Type 23 frigate Norfolk *on contractor's trials. Accepted by the RN one week late because of port shaft bearing problems,* Norfolk *commissioned in June 1990.* (Yarrow)

THE NAVAL YEAR IN REVIEW

Table 3. AIRCRAFT CARRIER TYPES

Country	USA	USSR	France
Ship	*Abraham Lincoln*	*Tbilisi*	*Charles de Gaulle*
No in class	5 + 3	1 + 1	1 + ?1
Builder	Newport News SB	Nikolayev South	Brest NYd
Building Dates	1984–1989	1983–1990	1989–1998
Displacement, max	102,000t	65,000t–67,000t	36,600t
L×b×d (max), metres	332.9 × 40.8 × 11.9	302 × 38.5 × 11	261.5 × 31.8 × 8.5
Missiles	3 NATO Sea Sparrow SAM	SS–N–19 SA–N–9 VLS	Aster 15 VLS SAM 2 Sadral PDMS
Guns	4–20mm Phalanx CIWS	8–30mm Gatling-type	8–20mm CIWS
Aircraft (normal)	81 fixed wing 6 helicopters	Prob 24 fixed wing 15–18 helicopters	20–25
(max)	90+	60	35–40
Machinery	Nuclear, steam turbines	Conventional, steam turbines	Nuclear, steam turbines
SHP	260,000	c200,000	83,000
Speed (kts)	30+	30+	27

Note: Abraham Lincoln is the first warship to exceed 100,000t.

lays include the command system and sonar, the warhead production facility at Aldermaston and part of the works programme at Faslane, including certain safety aspects of the submarine lift.

A new procurement procedure is being enforced for the SSN 20 (or 'W') class; to increase competition and reduce costs, contracts will not be awarded automatically to approved companies. For these reasons and to avoid overstretching VSEL, a joint venture company was formed for the project definition phase. Three current SSN will be decommissioned by the end of the decade; as the first SSN 20 class will not be ordered until 1993 or 1994 and will not enter service until 2000, SSN totals will fall. The SSN 20 will be the first British class with an optronic periscope/mast.

Three more Type 23 frigates, *Northumberland*, *Westminster* and *Richmond*, were ordered from Swan Hunter on 19 December for service in the mid-1990s; the hulls will not be lengthened and there will be no CIWS. The order increased the Type 23 total to 10; tenders for the next batch will be invited later in 1990, and an eventual total of at least 17 is likely. The contract for their command system, replacing the Ferranti CACS-4, was awarded to Dowty-Sema (SSCS). Tenders for 7 SRMHs were invited in early 1990 bringing the class total to 12.

(c) Canada. Realistic delivery dates for the patrol frigates are now: *Halifax* late in 1990, 4 in 1991 and the sixth in 1992. A possible lengthening of the last four ships by 10m, for separate accommodation of women crew members and more VLS missiles, is still being considered.

The USS Missouri and Kitty Hawk represent respectively the centrepieces of the US Navy's surface action groups and carrier battle groups. Economic realities will number the days of the former; two battleships are due to decommission in 1991. (From Soviet Military Power 1989*)*

WARSHIP 1990

Table 4. *Destroyer Types*

Country	USA	Japan	Italy
Class	*Arleigh Burke*	AEGIS type	*Animoso*
No in class	13 + 19	2 + ?6	2
Builder(s)	Bath IW	Mitsubishi	Fincantieri
	Ingalls	? Others	
Building Dates	1988–c2000	1990–?	1988–1992
Displacement (max)	8315t	8900t	5400t
L×b×d (max), metres	153.8 × 20.4 × 9.3	161 × 21 × 6.1	147.7 × 16.1 × 5
Missiles	Tomahawk SLCM/SSM	8 Harpoon	8 OTOMAT 2
	8 Harpoon	SM–2MR SAM	SM–1MR SAM
	SM–2MR SAM	VLS ASROC	Albatros PDMS
	VLS ASROC		
Guns	1–5in/54	1–5in/54	1–5in/54
	2–20mm CIWS	2–20mm CIWS	3–3in/62
ASW	6–12.75in TT	6–12.75in TT	6–12.75in TT
Helicopters	Platform for LAMPS III	Platform for LAMPS III	2 AB 212
Machinery	Gas turbine	Gas turbine	CODOG
Max SHP	100,000	80,000	55,000
Speed (kts)	30+	31	31.5

Table 5. FRIGATE TYPES

Country	Australia	Canada	Greece	Thailand
Class	Meko 200 ANZ	City	Meko 200 HN	025T
No in class	8	12	4	2
Builder(s)	Newcastle Williamstown DYd	St Johns SB Marine, Sorel	1 Blohm & Voss 3 Skaramanga	China
Building Dates	c1991–?	1990–1996	1990–1997	1990–1993
Displacement (max)	3495t	4750t	3350t	2900t
L×b×d (max), metres	118 × 14.8 × —	134.1 × 16.4 × 4.9	117 × 14.8 × 4.1	119 × 13 × 3.8
Missiles	? Harpoon Sea Sparrow VLS	8 Harpoon Sea Sparrow VLS	8 Harpoon 1 × 8 Sea Sparrow	8 Harpoon
Guns	1–5in/54 ?2–20mm CIWS	1–57mm 1–20mm CIWS	1–5in/54 2–20mm CIWS	1–5in/54 4–37mm (2×2)
ASW	?6–12.75in TT	4–12.75in TT	6–12.75in TT	6–12.75in TT
Helicopters	1 Seahawk size	2 Sea King	1 SH-2	1 SH-2
Machinery	CODOG	CODOG	CODOG	CODOG
Max SHP	c30,000	41,000	50,000	50,000
Speed (kts)	27	28	31	32

Note: Meko 200 ANZ frigates for New Zealand may have lighter armament.

▶ *The new AOR* RFA *Fort Victoria nearing completion at Harland & Wolff, 12 June 1990.* (Harland & Wolff)

◀ *The British submarine* Upholder *on trials.* Upholder *was delivered at the end of 1989, for commissioning in July 1990. The torpedo tubes were sealed at delivery because of a hydraulic fault, but sensational press reports of a near-catastrophic power failure on trials were grossly exaggerated.* (VSEL)

▶ HNIMS Witte de With, *one of the two AAW/command ship variants of the* Kortenaer. *Note the Goalkeeper CIWS aft, currently being installed in the* Kortenaers. (Directie Voorlichting, KM)

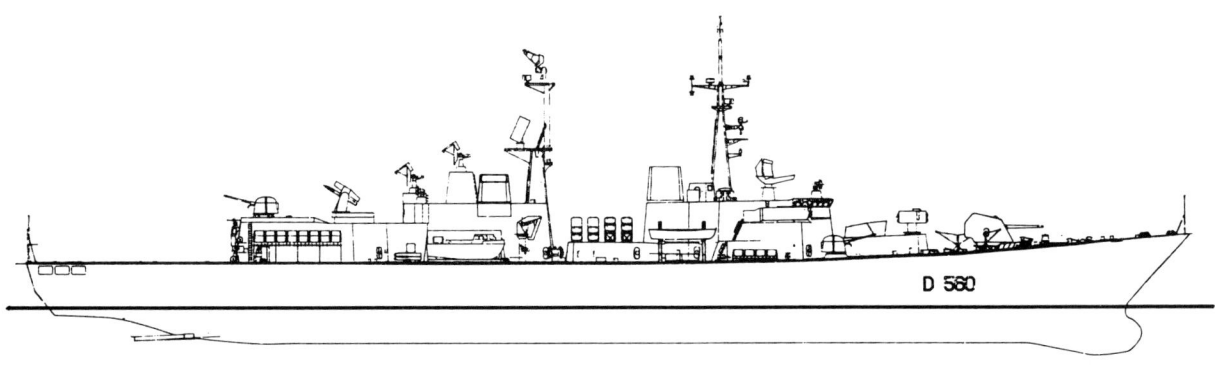

▲ *The Italian destroyers* Animoso *and* Ardentimoso *are being built to replace the two* Impavidos. *Two more are planned to replace the* Audace *class.*

◀ *Soviet 'Akula' class SSN. This class has replaced the 'Victor III' as the mainline Soviet fleet submarine; a second production line has been opened in the Far East. (From* Soviet Military Power *1989)*

(d) West Germany. The first Type 212 submarine is to be ordered in 1991; *Deutschland*, the first Type 123 frigate, will be built 1992–94.

(e) Italy. The Type S 90 submarine is at the project definition stage; it will not include Maritalia's GST technology.

(f) Netherlands. The first M class frigate, *Karel Doorman*, is due to go to sea in November 1990, six months late because of delays in the command and control automatisation process.

(g) France. The second pair of surveillance frigates, *Nivose* and *Ventose*, were ordered in January 1990 for delivery early in 1992. The construction of the first ocean-going MCMV has been put back to 1992–94.

(h) Spain. Frigates five and six of the

▲ *The* Tramontana, *Spain's newest submarine, is the last of four French* Agosta *class, built at Cartagena under licence.* (Bazan)

FFG-7 type, authorised in 1989, will be ordered in 1990.

(j) USSR. The 75,000t Soviet carrier *Ul'yanovsk*, laid down in 1988, will have a catapult launch system (necessary for operation of the Su-24 'Fencer'), but apparently not nuclear propulsion. Soviet statements that

THE NAVAL YEAR IN REVIEW

The Soviet carrier Baku. *(From* Soviet Military Power *1989)*

The nuclear-powered missile cruiser Frunze. *The fourth in the class*, Yuriy Andropov, *was launched in 1989. (From* Soviet Military Power *1989)*

this third carrier will mainly operate air defence fighters, not strike aircraft with land attack capability, must be recorded with reserve, because of the variety of aircraft being tried in *Tbilisi*. The new frigate 'Balcom 8', the 'Krivak' successor, was not sighted during the year.

The frigate Numancia, *latest of Spain's FFG-7 variants to enter service. The Spanish ships are 0.6m wider than their US counterparts, and mount the Meroka CIWS instead of the Vulcan Phalanx.* (Bazan)

The new Soviet carrier Tbilisi, *May 1990.* (TASS)

(k) Thailand. Two frigates ordered from China in September will be of enlarged 'Jianghu' type, with Western weapons and sensors.

(l) Iraq. The frigates and corvettes of the 1981 order, held up because of the Gulf War, have been 'freed for delivery', but were still in Italian ports early in 1990.

D (ii). Ships entering service during the year

These are listed in Table 6 (the figures for the Soviet Union and China are approximate).

The Soviet carrier *Tbilisi*, undoubted ship of the year, was formally unveiled in the autumn; her trials were delayed from late 1989 to 1990, possibly putting back the in-service date to 1991. Photos and generalised data from Soviet sources were another example of *glasnost* in operation and incidentally corrected much of the information in open Western sources. Moscow's initial classification of the ship as an 'aircraft carrier' was hurriedly altered to 'heavy aircraft-carrying cruiser', to comply with the provisions of the 1936 Montreux Convention limiting exit from the Black Sea.

Tbilisi has a *Baku*-type island and full-length flight deck, with an angled extension amidships. The usual Soviet battery of anti-ship missiles is flush-mounted under the flight deck, allowing aircraft operations when the missiles are not in use. Other features include steam turbine machinery, two deck-edge and one centreline elevators, four arrestor wires, but no catapults; jet-blast deflectors are fitted to assist take-off over the 10–12-degree ski jump.

Contrary to Western expectations, *Tbilisi* is not to be a V/STOL carrier; the Yak-38 'Forger' and the forthcoming Yak-41 appear to be reserved for the *Kiev* class. Three types of aircraft that had undergone land-based trials, the Su-27 'Flanker', Mig-29 'Fulcrum' and Su-25UT 'Frogfoot', all landed aboard and took off on 21 November.

D (iii). Reconstructions

(a) United States. USCGC *Hamilton* was the first high-endurance cutter to complete FRAM modernisation; new weaponry includes Harpoon, Phalanx CIWS, uprated helicopter facilities for LAMPS I, and an OTO Melara 3in gun.

(b) United Kingdom. *Illustrious* paid off into reserve at Portsmouth for 'Preservation by Operation'. Her 1991–93 refit, to bring her up to improved *Invincible* standard, will include four Sea Wolf GWS 26 Mod 2 lightweight launchers. The repairs to *Southampton* at Swan Hunter will cost £45m ($74m). The Type 22s' CACS1 and Type 42s' ADAWS command and control systems are being upgraded by Ferranti.

THE NAVAL YEAR IN REVIEW

Table 6. NEW SHIPS ENTERING SERVICE, 1 APRIL 1989 TO 31 MARCH 1990 (USSR, CHINA IN 1989)

Type	USA	USSR	UK	France	China	India	Japan	Italy
CV (large)	CVN-72	–	–	–	–	–	–	–
CV (medium)	–	–	–	–	–	–	–	–
CV (small)	–	–	–	–	–	–	–	–
BB	–	–	–	–	–	–	–	–
CAH	–	–	–	–	–	–	–	–
CG	CG-60 CG-62	–	–	–	–	–	–	–
DD	–	2 *Sovremenniy* 1 *Udaloy*	–	1 F-70	1	–	3	–
FF (Fleet)	FFG–31	1 'Krivak III'	2 Type 22	–	4	–	2	–
(escort)	–	2 'Grisha V' 5 'Parchim II'	–	–	–	2	–	–
SSBN	SSBN–735	1 'Typoon' 1 'Delta IV'	–	–	–	–	–	–
SSGN	SSN–750 SSN-753	1 'Oscar II'	–	–	–	–	–	–
SSN	SSN-754	1–2 'Akula' 1 'Victor III'	–	–	–	–	–	–
SS (all)	–	3 'Kilo'	–	–	c1	2	–	1

Note: One or more of above 'Kilos' may be for export.

A detail of the after end of Tbilisi's *flight deck, with a Su-27 'Flanker' on the elevator.* (TASS)

Table 7. *USN DELETIONS, 1989–91*

Type	FY89	FY90	FY91
SSBN	1	2	?
SSN	1 *Permit*	3 *Permit*	6 *Permit*
		3 *Skipjack*	
		SSN–685	
SS	3	–	–
CV	–	*Coral Sea*	–
BB	–	–	*New Jersey*
			Iowa
DDG	–	2 *Coontz*	2 *Coontz*
	–	8 *Charles F Adams*	8 *Charles F Adams*

Note: FY92 deletions to include two more *Coontz* class.

(c) Other reconstructions may be summarised more briefly. **Canada's** very complex TRUMP AAW modernisation programme is about one year behind schedule; *Algonquin*, due to complete in November 1989, should now be ready late in 1990. Three of the thirteen USSR 'Yankee' SSBN have completed 'Yankee Notch' conversions; the new, longer, missile section contains 3000km-range SS-N-21 cruise missiles. The **Argentine** carrier *25 de Mayo's* rebuilding has been suspended, for financial and labour reasons. **Brazil** plans to refit the *Niteroi* class frigates with a PDMS, possibly Sea Wolf or Crotale.

D (iv). Fleet depletions (decommissionings, transfers etc)

Noteworthy items in this category are summarised below.

(a) United States. Table 7 shows USN disposals for FY89, FY90 and FY91 (proposed). The planned transfer of four US frigates to Turkey was cancelled, for cost reasons.

(b) United Kingdom. The ex-RN *Oberon* and *Walrus*, the sale of which to Malaysia fell through, have been purchased from Seaforth by Egypt and will enter service after a two-year refit. *Olympus* was sold to Canada in August as alongside basic training submarine at Halifax. *Falmouth* departed for scrapping in Spain on 4 May; *Londonderry* was sunk as a target on 25 June, and *Leander* in September in the NATO exercise 'Sharp Spear'. *Hul Vul* (ex-*Naiad*) was used as a target for mining trials in September and should have been expended in March 1990; *Achilles* decommissioned March 1990. RFA *Sir Lancelot* was sold to commercial interests, while *Appleleaf* went to Australia for five years as *Westralia*, replacing *Stalwart*.

(c) West Germany. *Braunschweig* was transferred to Turkey for spares on 6 June.

(d) Netherlands. The last two *Van Speijks* were sold to Indonesia on 13 May. The decommissioned submarine *Zeehond* will be used for sea trials of an air-independent propulsion system.

(e) Spain. The former carrier *Dedalo* docked at New Orleans, to be a museum ship.

(f) USSR. According to the Soviet press, 12 diesel submarines, including three 'Golf II' SSBs will be deleted by the end of 1989, while a total of 26 submarines (7 with nuclear missiles) and 45 surface ships will go by the end of 1990. All four of the Baltic Fleet's 'Golf II' will go, although NATO claims that their targets have been re-allocated to 'Yankee' SSBNs in the Norwegian Sea. The UK MoD estimated that the Soviets withdrew two SSKs in 1988, at least 35 in 1989, and another 35, plus 70 surface ships, in 1990. In May 1989, a soft-drinks company took a cruiser, a destroyer, a frigate and 17 submarines as scrap in part payments for its products sold in the USSR. US estimates suggest that by the mid-1990s, the USSR will have scrapped more than 100 older SSK hulls, some 24 nuclear, including 'November' and 'Echo I' boats. Lists and totals aside, it is clear that all 'Whiskey' and 'Foxtrot' SSKs, all non-missile cruisers, all pre-'Kashin' destroyers (and some 'Kashins'), all 'Riga' and many 'Petya' and 'Mirka' frigates are going or have gone. At least three old submarines were lost in tow in 1989, and one in January 1990. A second nuclear submarine was scheduled for transfer to India and renaming *Chitra*. It was not clear whether the first transfer, *Chakra*, reported to have had radiation problems, was being returned to the USSR.

E. NAVAL WEAPON SYSTEMS

Salient developments in naval weapon systems are listed below.

E (i). Missiles, including Ballistic Missiles

(a) United States. The first two submerged test firings of the Trident II D5 missile from *Tennessee* failed, 21 March and 15 August 1989. The failure was remedied by strengthening the connection between the first stage rocket motor and its nozzle, slightly reducing missile range. The third missile's successful launch, on 4 December, was followed by seven more before the end of March 1990.

E (ii). Maritime Aircraft

(a) United States. The USN plans to spend $10.2b between 1990 and FY94 on 106 of its proposed 450 A-12 Advanced Tactical Aircraft, successor to the venerable A-6E Intruder and a joint project with the USAF.

(b) United Kingdom. An order placed for 10 new Sea Harriers FRS2 will go in parallel with the conversion of 29 existing FRS1 to FRS2 standard (Blue Vixen radar, AMRAAM missiles). No production order was placed for the EH-101 Merlin helicopter, as no agreement was reached on maximum cost; the initial order may be scaled down from 50 to 25.

(c) France. Plans to buy the F/A-18 for *Clemenceau* and *Foch* were dropped in January 1990; the existing Crusaders are to be upgraded at half the cost and the naval Rafale accelerated to be ready in 1998 for *Charles de Gaulle*. It is hoped to recover some Rafale development costs by promoting the plane for the new Indian carrier.

(d) USSR. Aircraft tested aboard *Tbilisi* in November included the STOL variant of the Su-27 'Flanker', fitted with canards, and a folded-wing version of the Mig-29 'Fulcrum'. Problems with the single-purpose Pegasus-type engine of the Yak-41, the supersonic, radar-equipped successor to the Yak-38 'Forger', have delayed the plane's development, but its flight test programme has started. A possible helicopter AEW provision for *Tbilisi* was suggested, but in March 1990, US sources suggest that the An-74 'Madcap' could be adapted to provide an AEW capability.

E (iii). Anti-Aircraft and Anti-Missile Warfare (AAW)

Major future threats to surface ships are multiple attacks by supersonic sea-skimming anti-ship missiles and fast, agile strike aircraft. To counter these threats, two Western consortia are developing rival short-medium range missile systems for future destroyers and frigates. The US-led NAAWS (NATO Anti-Air Warfare System), intended for the now-defunct NFR 90 and for retrofitting in existing US warships, is the more comprehensive, including command and control aspects. The European-based FAMS (Family of Anti-Air Missile Systems), designed around the Franco–Italian Aster 15/30, depends on a common missile, with different boosters for different ranges and national requirements. In December Britain decided to join FAMS, possibly adding BAe's VLS Sea Wolf technology to the Franco–Italian Aster.

(a) UK. Lightweight Sea Wolf and Marconi 805SW tracker radar are to be fitted in Type 42 Batch 3 destroyers and the three ASW carriers, starting with *Illustrious* (Swan Hunter was awarded a contract for technical support for the modernisation of these classes in February 1989). BAe and Marconi are to study a possible upgrade of the Sea Wolf missile systems and guidance radar.

(b) Spain. Bazan's Weapon Division has started preliminary studies of a combined gun/missile CIWS to replace the Meroka 20mm CIWS. The proposed system, designated SARDON, is intended for the advanced frigate F-110, to meet saturation attacks by supersonic anti-ship missiles.

(c) USSR The new PDMS/CIWS (Western CADS-N-1) in *Kalinin* combines a 30mm Gatling-type gun (2km range), two quadruple SA-18 missile systems (8km) and a fire-control radar on a single pedestal.

(d) Chile is to re-equip its surface fleet with the Israeli Barak 1 PDMS, starting with the four ex-RN 'County' class destroyers.

E (iv). Anti-Submarine Warfare (ASW)

New, very quiet Soviet submarines entering service will increasingly expose the limitations of current ASW systems; for example, NATO finds the 'Oscar' SSGN hard to detect, as it is very silent and seldom comes into areas patrolled by NATO aircraft. Although it will be many years before quiet Soviet submarines are in the majority (and submarines become noisier after 2–3 years at sea), the US and NATO continue to improve acoustic and develop non-acoustic methods of detecting submarines. Further tests of synthetic aperture radar for submarine tracking (by detecting 'wake scarring', the disturbance on the surface caused by submerged motion) were continued on Loch Linnhe in 1989. A third consortium may enter the Anglo-US bilateral Surface Ship Torpedo Defence System (SSTDS) contest; the UK MoD has agreed that this programme, unlike the Advanced Sea Mine, will not be summarily terminated. As regards weapons, the US Mk 50 advanced lightweight ASW torpedo is completing full scale development and the submarine-launched heavyweight Mk 48 entering front-line service. The US trials submarine *Memphis* is to test the 762mm (30in) TT intended for SSN-21, allowing a much larger warhead, and also permitting the more silent launch of 533mm (21in) weapons which can 'swim out' instead of being ejected.

The Soviet Navy is faced with similar problems, and, according to US testimony, is following parallel lines of research.

E (v). Guns

United States. The Block 2 development of the Phalanx CIWS is likely to have a larger calibre gun than the Block 1's 20mm, but will use the present mount. Anglo–US live trials of the 25mm Goalkeeper are unlikely to lead to a choice of this system.

Others. At least two groups, HSA and a BAe/Melara consortium, are developing correctable ammunition systems (CORAS), involving steerable shells with retractable fins, for use in existing 3in (76.2mm) weapons.

E (vi). Other Weapon Systems

The RN's pilot-dazzling shipborne laser 'gun' achieved brief (and ill-informed) notoriety in the national press.

F. NAVAL EVENTS

F (i). Areas of Conflict and Naval Actions

(a) The Gulf. The last three US MCMVs left the gulf in March 1990, but some 20 US ships, including the USS *Enterprise* task force, remain in the area; the British Armilla patrol was reduced from three destroyers/frigates to two. With the Iran/Iraq dispute unresolved, the area remains in a state of tension and minor incidents abound. On 9 May a Kuwaiti coastguard patrol vessel pursuing illegal immigrants was seized by Iranian Revolutionary Guards near the maritime border. The vessel was returned in July, after the release of the crew.

(b) Lebanon. The continued crisis in Lebanon and detention of foreign hostages resulted in US and French naval forces on alert off Beirut. The US 6th Fleet was concentrated in the Eastern Mediterranean between 1 and 8 August, while in mid-August France sent the carrier *Foch* to reinforce the destroyer *Duquesne* and the frigate *D'Estienne D'Orves*. At 04.51 GMT on 24 February, the 3987-ton Marlines ferry *Baroness M*, on regular night passage from Cyprus to Lebanon, was attacked by a Syrian gunboat about 30 miles off Jounieh. One passenger was killed and at least 18 wounded.

(c) Indian Ocean. Indian naval forces, with carrier support, were present off Sri Lanka between August 1989 and March 1990 as the Indian expeditionary force was withdrawn. In the Comoro Islands, foreign mercenaries took control on 26 November, after the President's murder. Intense French pressure, including units of the Indian Ocean squadron on patrol off Moroni, forced the mercenaries to surrender and leave the country on 15 December.

(d) The Far East. The UN Armistice Commission complained that there had been 24 naval intrusions by North Korea into South Korean waters between January and May 1989, compared with 25 in all of 1988.

(e) The Americas. US forces are to increase flight hours against drug trafficking by 220 per cent in FY90 over FY89 and ship days by about 80 per cent. The RN gave support; for example, in September the frigate *Alacrity*, which, with RFA *Brambleleaf*, had been providing relief after Hurricane 'Hugo', turned to anti-narcotics patrols. Operation 'Just Cause', the US airborne invasion of Panama, resulted in AC-130 gunships destroying 9 Panamanian patrol craft, while 7 were captured. Following the Panama invasion, and at the height of the drugs scare, US naval forces briefly blockaded Colombia. The restoration of diplomatic relations between Britain and Argentina in February coincided with the reduction of the 240km protection zone round the Falkland Islands to 80km for warships and 110km for military aircraft.

(f) Caucasus. As nationalist unrest and ethnic strife escalated in the Caucasus, Moscow sent in the Army, Navy and KGB (decree signed 15 January). Troops went in to Baku on 20 January by land and sea, thousands landing from motorboats and assault vessels. The harbour blockade which had prevented oil tankers leaving was lifted, and Armenian refugees enabled to flee across the Caspian.

(g) Baltic. Swedish naval forces including a helicopter chased a suspected foreign submarine off Stockholm. Controlled mines were detonated, and anti-submarine grenades dropped from the helicopter, but the submarine was not hit. Sweden detected fewer unidentified submarines in 1989 than in earlier years.

F (ii). Major Casualties At Sea, 1 April 1989 to 31 March 1990

The spate of accidents to Soviet and American warships recorded below caused much comment and concern. A Soviet Admiral blamed his country's repeated submarine mishaps on design and building errors, and lax practices within the Navy; the USN for a time even suspended non-essential operations at sea, while safety practices were reviewed.

(a) The wreck of the Soviet submarine *Komsomolets* (NATO 'Mike'), which caught fire and sank off Norway on 7 April 1989, was located and photographed by the Soviets, apparently still in one piece. Details of the disaster were released in the Soviet press, an example of *glasnost* rare in submarine operations. A short-circuit aft sparked a fire which, fed by a ruptured compressed-air

The ill-fated submarine Komsomolets. *According to Soviet statements, this solitary 'Mike' (NATO designation) class SSN had a titanium-strengthened hull and a maximum diving depth of 1000m; when lost, it was carrying two weapons with nuclear warheads. (From* Soviet Military Power *1989)*

USS America. *The Reagan Administration planned to increase the total of deployable carriers to 15 (plus 1 in SLEP). However, the total has remained at 14, and may drop to 12. (From* Soviet Military Power 1989*)*

pipe, spread rapidly, forcing the submarine to surface. Five hours later, the burning, exploding and evacuated submarine lost hull integrity and sank.

(b) USS *Iowa* (BB-61) redeployed in May 1989 with 'B' turret, damaged by an explosion on 19 April 1989, inactive. The 16in guns in 'A' and 'Y' turrets were not fired again until August. The report on the explosion was unable to find any accidental cause, and attributed it to a disgruntled member of the turret crew; although residual traces of foreign material were found in the gun barrel, the precise nature of an explosive device believed to have been placed there between two powder bags was uncertain. As the ship is being decommissioned in 1991, the turret will not be repaired, saving an estimated $14.7m. The matter is not closed: the inquiry will be re-opened, and Congressional hearings are impending.

(c) The USS *Blueback* (SS-581), forced to surface by a machinery fire off the coast of south California, was towed to San Diego; this was the second accident to the USN's very few non-nuclear submarines in just over a year.

(d) An engine-room fire in USS *White Plains* (AFS-4) killed 6 and injured 5 on 9 May.

(e) A Soviet 'Echo II' class SSBN limped home after a fire on board, 26 June; a burst pipe put the reactor out of action and leaked radioactivity into the surrounding water. This class has a particularly poor safety record.

(f) An 'Alfa' class submarine was observed to surface and emit smoke, 27 July; an onboard fire was denied, the smoke coming from starting diesels after part of the battery short-circuited.

(g) A Soviet 'Yurka' class ocean minesweeper sank in the Black Sea after an explosion, 19 August.

(h) A T-2 Buckeye trainer crashed on to the flight deck of the training carrier USS *Lexington* (AVT-16) and burst into flames, killing 5 and injuring 2 on 29 October.

(j) The next day, an F/A-18 from USS *Midway* (CV-41) accidentally bombed the cruiser *Reeves* (CG-24). The 500lb (226kg) bomb exploded and blew a hole in the main deck, injuring 5.

(k) On 1 November a freak wave hit USS *Dwight D Eisenhower* (CVN-69), killing 3 and washing 38 Sidewinder missiles overboard.

(l) A hairline crack in the primary reactor cooling system in HMS *Warspite*, under refit at Plymouth, was announced 30 January, leading to checks in other British nuclear submarines.

F (iii). Footnotes

(a) The wreck of the German battleship *Bismarck* was located on 8 June at a depth of 15,617ft (4760m), and photographed. The *Bismarck* capsized as it sank, 27 May 1941, losing the four 15in turrets, but settled upright on the ocean floor. The precise location of the wreck, some 600 miles

USS Iowa (BB-61) firing 'A' turret. All 16in gun firings by US battleships were halted, 24 May 1990, pending further investigation of the disastrous 1989 explosion in Iowa's 'B' turret. (Ingalls)

west of Brest, was concealed to deter unauthorised visitors, a problem elsewhere in the world; in mid-March 1990, the RN discovered that propellers and other items had been removed by divers from the wrecks of the battleship *Prince of Wales* and battlecruiser *Repulse*, sunk off Kuantan, Malaya, 10 December 1941. Resting at depths of less than 200ft (60m), the British ships were readily plundered by experienced divers without regard for their war graves status.

(b) Further details were published of the December 1965 incident in which a nuclear weapon from the flight deck of USS *Ticonderoga* (CVA-14) fell to a depth of 15,750ft (4800m), 133km off the south coast of Japan. 1989 tests found only background levels of plutonium in the area, and it was declared safe.

(c) The first Soviet account of the short-lived mutiny in the Soviet destroyer *Storozhevoi*, 8–9 November 1975, was published in *Izvestia* in February 1990, adding to the outline known in the West. The deputy commander took over the ship in port and headed for Sweden. Soviet aircraft dropped bombs ahead of the ship, forcing it to stop, without causing damage or casualties. The deputy commander, wounded in the leg by the ship's commander, was later tried and shot.

H. STOP PRESS

As *Warship* closed for press (mid-August), the West's response to the Iraqi invasion of Kuwait at the beginning of the month was involving the deployment of substantial naval forces to the region. To defend Saudi Arabia and support UN sanctions, the USN battle groups based on the carriers *Independence* and *Eisenhower* were in position with two other groups led by *Saratoga* and the battleship *Wisconsin* reported to be following. A French carrier group (*Clemenceau*, *Colbert* and two frigates) were to act independently, and Britain was adding three 'Hunt' class MCMVs to the Armilla patrol (*York*, *Battleaxe* and *Jupiter*). Australia had dispatched two FFGs and the Netherlands was sending the AAW frigate *Witte de With* and one other frigate.

INDEX

Italicised page numbers refer to illustrations and diagrams. An illustrated page may also carry relevant text.

Abo, Kiyotane 119
Abraham Lincoln 223, *239*
Achilles 25, 29, 246
Aconite 33
Admiral Hipper 154
AEGIS type destroyers *240*
Affondatore 19, 31
AG class submarines 81, 90
Agano 128–30
aircraft carriers 105, 133, 137, 139, *239*
  see also *Yorktown* class
airships 93, 99
Aitken, Sub-Lt 173–4
Akamatsu, Noroyoshi 42
Akashi 118–31, *119*
  construction 119–23, *120, 129, 130, 131*
  facilities 123–5
  career 124–30
Akula 81
Alacrity 248
Al Jawf 235
Albatross 83
Albemarle 31
Alcantara 155
Alexander-Sinclair, Rear-Admiral E S 110, 114
Akula class *242*
Algonquin 180, 246
Alkmaar 229
Alligator 76, 78, 82, 84, 88–9
Amazonas 31
America 249
Amethyste class 229
Ancona 19, 31
Anderson 132
Animoso destroyers *240, 242*
Aoba 129
Annapolis 190–1, 197
Annapolis class 186–90, 192
ANZAC frigates *231*
Antelope 33
Appleleaf 246
Arcadion 32
Ardentimoso 242
Arethusa 115

Arethusa class 110, 112
Argentina 236, 246, 250
Argus 133, 151–62, 164–5, *152, 162, 164*
Ariel 32
Arkansas 31
Ark Royal 151–2, 154–60, 165, *156, 158*
Arleigh Burke 240
Artois class 10, 16, *11*
Asahi 118
Assiniboine 29, 33, 155, 176, 187, 191
Athene 160
Atlantic, Battle of 28–9
Aube, Admiral 28
Augsburg 83
Aurora 164
Australia 230–1, 246

B 109 (German destroyer) 95
B 110 (German destroyer) 45
Bainbridge 224
Baker, Commodore R (RCNC) 177–9
Baku 233, *243*
Bangladesh 236
Barham 97
Barnaby, K C 27
Baroness M (ferry) 248
Barry, Rear-Admiral C B *174*
Bars class submarines 80–1, 83, 90
Bars 83–4
Battleaxe 250
'battle scouts' 105, 109
Bauer, William 77
Bayern class 115
Bayou City 31
Beatty, Vice-Admiral Sir David 93–6, 99–100, 106, 109–10
Beauregard 31
Behrings, Rear-Admiral Ehler 82
Bellerophon 29
Bellona 11–12, 16
Bellona class 9–17, *10–17*
Berry, W J 104
Bertin, Louis Emile 35, 37, 40, 42
Beverley 154
Bianca 89–90

Birkenhead 94
Birmingham 32, 108
Bismarck 249–50
Blake 185
Blanco Encalada 32
Blueback 249
Bodisco, Admiral 16
Bonaventure 154, 166
Boston 14
Bouvet 32
Boyle, Captain 114
Brambleleaf 248
Braunschweig 246
Brazil 236, 246
Breconshire 161
Bredow, Sub-Lt H von 110, 112
Bremen 84
British Transport 32
Brooklyn 31
Brunei 236
Brussels 28
Buckingham 186

Cadillac, Project 145
Cadmus 33
Cairo 161–3
Caledon 110, 112–15, *114, 116*
Calvi 33
Calypso 110, 113–15, *111*
Cameron, Lt Donald 166, 170–1, 174
Campbell 33
Camilla 11–16
Camperdown 22–6, 30, *25*
Canada 175–93, 225, 246
Canada 110
Caradoc 113
Cardiff 111, 113, *116*
Cardiff class 110
Carless, O/S J H 114
Carondelet 31
Cederström, Admiral R 13–15
Cerbere class 27
Ceres 113
Cervera, Admiral 73
Ch 28 130
Chambly 33
Champion 96, 110

Chapman frigates 9–17, *15*
Charles de Gaulle 229, 239
Charles F Adams class *246*
Charybdis 161–4
Chen Yuen 52–3, *36, 37, 38, 41*
Chester class 108
Chile 236, 247
China 35–6, 51–3, 102, 118, *202–5*
  current developments in 236, *223, 245*
Churchill, Winston 102–3, 106, 109, 161–2
Churchill 155
City class *241*
Colbert 250
Colorado 141
Courageous 104–5
Cincinatti 31
Clemenceau 247, 250
Clowes, Sir William Laird 20, 30
Clyde 163
Cobalto 33
Cochrane 32
Colossus class 56
Commodore Perry 31
Congress 18
Constitution class 9
Coontz class *246*
Coral Sea 246
Corallo 33
Cordelia 95
Courageous 106, 109–10, 112, *107*
Courageous class 103–17
Covadonga 32
Cowan, Commodore 110, 112
Crocus 33
Croome 159
Cumberland 18, 31
Cunningham, Admiral 152
CVA-01 109
Cyclops 166

Dagabur 33, 164
Dale, Captain 13–14
Decatur, Commodore 15
Dedalo 246
de Lôme, Depuy 27
Delhi 154
Denmark 9, 13–14, 16, 227
Desterro 90
D'Estienne d'Orves 248
Deutschland 242
Devastation 30
D'Eyncourt, Tennyson 103–4, 106
Diable Marin 77
Diana 11–12, 16
Dianthus 33
Dogger Bank, battle of 106
Donald, Flt Lt Graham 94–5, 98–9
Dorita, ss 90
Dragon 155
Drakon 76, 78, 82–4, 88–9
Dreadnought 25, 32, 102
Druzhny 235
Duff, Lt 173–4

Duquesne 248
Dwight D Eisenhower 249–50

E-1 (submarine) 85
E-9 (submarine) 86
E-18 (submarine) 90
Eagle 133, 159, 160–5, *160*
Edwards, Captain 114
Egypt 151, 154–5, 235
Elbing 97
Ella and Anne 31
Empire Olive 164
Empire Shackleton 163
Empress 94
Enchantress 33
Encounter 152
Engadine 93–101, *94, 95, 98, 100*
Enterprise (CV-6) 132, 135, 140–6, 148–50, *136, 140, 141, 144, 145, 146, 147, 148, 149, 150*
Erebus 108
Esmeralda 32
Erzherzog Ferdinand Max 18–19, 31
Essen, Admiral Nikolai von 76, 82–3
Essex (c1802) 14
Essex (c1862) 31
Essex (CV-9) 132
Essex class 148–50
Euredice 11–12, 16
European Gateway (ferry) 25

Fairy 32
Falklands 104, 248
Falmouth (WW II) 94–5
Falmouth 246
Fame 33
Farragut class 141, 143
Faulknor 152, 156
Fearless 224
Finland 78–9
  Gulf of 81, 83, 85–6, 88–9
Fisher, Admiral Sir John 102–4, 106, 108–9
'Flanker' (SU-27) *234*
Fleet, General von der 82
Fletcher, Admiral Frank 105
Flyvefisken 231
Florida 31
Forester 152
Flower class 29
Forelle 77–8
Foch 247–8
France 9–10, 35, 40, 42–3, 50, 108, 151–2, 153
  current developments in 227, 229, 234, 242, 247, *223, 245*
Frankfurt 97, 110
Fraser 192, *183, 187, 188*
Friedrich Carl 83
Friedrich der Grosse 19
Fröja 11–16, *17*
Frunze see *Poltava*
Frunze (missile cruiser) *243*
Fryatt, Captain 28
Furious 108–9, 115, 117, 151, 154–8,

161–5, *107, 154, 159, 163*
Fuso 36

G-35 (destroyer) 83
Galatea 95, 97, 112–15
Galathea 10–11, 16
Gallant 152
Gallant class 208, 210–12, *210, 211, 212*
Gatineau 189–190
Gazelle 83
Gearing class 229
Gedania 88
General Bragg 31
General Price 31
General Steuben 90
General van Dorn 31
Gepard 83, 88
Gerda Vith 89
Germany 77–8, 80, 108–10, 225, 242, 246
Ghana 237
Giuseppe Garibaldi 226
Gloire 18, 29
Glorious 106, 109, 110, 112, 115, *103, 104, 108*
Gloucester 94
Gneisenau 156
Goddard, ERA 174
Golf II class SSBs 246
Goodall, Stanley 104
Gorgon 30
Governor Moore 31
Greyhound 152
Grosser Kurfurst 22, 25
Gurkha 210

H-2 catapult 139–40
H-2 mine 110
Halifax 226
Hamaguchi, Yuko 119
Handcock, Lt 94, 99
Harriet Lane 31
Hartford 31
Harvester 33
'Harveyizing' 63–5
Hashidate 35, 41–3, 50–1, 53–4, *46, 47, 48–9, 52, 53, 54*
Hector 29
Heinrich of Prussia, Grand-Admiral 83
Heligoland 103, 110
  3rd Battle of 110–15, *114*
Henty-Creer, Lt 170, 174
Hera 89–90
Hermes 133
Hermione 33, 158, 160
Hesperus 29, 33
Hiei 36
Hindenburg 110
Hipper, Vice-Admiral Franz 84, 93, 96–7
Hood, Admiral Samuel 16
Hood 108
Hornet (CV-8) 132, 135–6, 140–5,

INDEX

148, *133, 134–5, 137, 138, 139, 142, 143, 150*
Hosho 133
Hotspur 27, 33, *26–7*
Hotspur (WW II) 152
Huascar 32
Hudspeth, Lt 170, 173–4
Hul Vul 246
Husar 13

I-158 (submarine) *132*
Iljinskij, Lt N N 83–4
Illustrious 244
Inconstant 95, 112, 115
Indefatigable 96–7
Independence class 148
Independence 250
Independencia 32
India 236, *223*
Indiana 56, 63, *69*
Indiana class 56, *60, 68, 69*
Indianola 31
Indomitable 163–4
Intrepid 224
Invincible 104
Iowa 224, 249, *246*
Iran/Iraq dispute *248*
Iraq *244*
Iron Duke 22, *20*
Iron Duke class 110
Israel 234
Italy 18, 77, 102, 225–6, 242, *223, 240, 245*
Ithuriel 29, 33, 162
Itsukishima 40–2, 50–4, *44, 50, 51, 52*
Ivan Rogov 233
Izzedin 32

Jan van Brakel 229
Japan 35–55, 118–27, 132, 146
  current developments in 229–30, *223, 245*
Jarramas 15–16
Jeguy 31
Jellicoe, Vice-Admiral Sir John 93–5 97, 99, 106
Jerome, Midshipman 112
Jervis Bay 229
Jupiter 134, 250
Jussuf Bay 13–15
Jutland, Battle of 93–101, 109, 112

K-1 (submarine) 110
Kaiman (submarine) 76, 78, 82, 84, 86–90, *77*
Kaiman class submarines 76–92
Kaiser 19, 31, 110
Kaiserin 110, 115
Kambala 78
Kanto 118
Karas 78
Karel Doorman 242
Karp 78
Karp class 78

Katahdin 28
Kearney, N J 150
Kehdingen 110–12
Keller, Count 86
Kelvin 154
Kendall, Lt 174
Keystone State 31
Khabarovsk 81
Kilduin 12
King George V class 102
Kinsha 202
Kipling 154
Kitty Hawk 239
Knowlton, Rear-Admiral J G (RCN) 177
Kolberg 84
Kolga 89–90
Komsomolets 249, *248*
König Wilhelm 22
Kongo 36
Königsberg 110, 114
Kootenay 177, 188
Korea 248
Krokodil 76, 78, 84, 88, 90
Kuma class 120

L class destroyers 208–210
L20e Alpha 117
Lackawanna 31
Lafole 33
Lake, Simon S 78
Lance 210
Langley 134
Leander 246
Lebanon 248
Legion 210
Levitkij, Rear-Admiral 80
Lexington 134, 140, 148, 249
Liberty 32
Lion 97, 99, 106, 185
Lion class 110
Lissa, Battle of 18–20, 41
Lively 210, *209*
London 156
Londonderry 246
London Treaty (1930) 119, 141
Lookout 211
Lord Clyde 29
Lorimer, Lt 174
Lovell 31
Lübeck 82
Lulworth 33
Lutzow 167–8

MacFarlane, Lt, (RAN) 170
Mackenzie 194–7
Mackenzie class 181, 185–6
McNeil, Captain D 14
Madison, President 15
Magellanes 32
Maine 56
Makaroff 84
Makrel (submarine) 81, 89
Malaya 103, 160
Malaysia 236

Malta 151–65
Mamiya 118
Manassass 31
Manchuria 118
Manchurian incident 119
Marat 208
Margaree 189, 192
Marinesko, Captain Alexandr 90
Mario Pia 31
Marquez de Olinda 31
Marten, Captain 112
Massachusetts 56, *66*
Matabesett 31
Matsushima 40–2, 45, 50–4, *39, 41, 42, 43, 44*
Matsushima class 35–49
Medusa 119–21, 123–4
Medway 114, 119
Meko 200 frigates *241*
Merkushov, V A 78
Messer, Lt Ivan V 76, 86, 88–90, *79, 80, 90*
Meteor 32
Miami 31
Midway 249
Mikasa 54
Miller, Captain 109
Milne 32
Minerva 11–12, 16
Minoga 81
Missouri 239
Miyabara, Vice-Admiral Jiro 51
Mississippi 31
Mogami 128
Molteno, Captain V B 98
Moltke 84–5, 110, *85*
Monarch 22, 31
Monitor 18, 31
Monongahela 31
Moose Jaw 33
Moresby 96–7
Mound City 31
Mustin 132

Naniwa 40
Napier, Rear-Admiral Trevylyan 94, 96, 110, 112, 114–15
NATO 222–7, 238, 246
Nelson 158, 164
Neptune (19th century) 31
Neptune (World War II) 154
Nerissa 114
Netherlands 13–14, 226–7, 242, 246
Newcastle 154
New Jersey 224, *246*
New Zealand 110
NFR 90 (NATO frigate) 238
Nigeria 237
Niphon 31
Nipigon 190, 191, *184, 185*
Niteroi class 246
Nivose 242
Niwada, Vice-Admiral Shozo 120
No 43 (submarine) 118
No 70 (submarine) 118

253

Noel, Cdr G H 28
Norfolk 238
Northampton 132, *133*
Northumberland 239
Norway 227
Novorossiysk 233
Numancia 243

Oakville 33
Oberon 246
Ocean 29
Oikaze 130
Okun 81
Olry 202, *205*
Olympic 32
Olympus 246
Oman 234–5
Onslow 96–7
Operation Baritone 164, 165
    Bellows 163–4, 165
    Bowery 161–2, 165
    Calendar 161, 165
    Callboy 159, 165
    Dunlop 156, 165
    Hurry 152, 165
    Insect 163, 165
    LB 162, 165
    Monsoon 154
    Perpetual 160, 165
    Picket 161, 165
    Pinpoint 162, 165
    Railway 157–8, 165
    Rocket 157, 165
    Salient 162–3, 165
    Splice 156, 165
    Spotter 160, 165
    Status 158, 165
    Stripe 154
    Style 162, 165
    Substance 158, 165
    Summer 155
    Tracer 157, 165
    Train 164
    White 153–4, 165
    Winch 155–6, 165
Oracle 32
Oregon 56–75, *57, 58–9, 60–1, 62, 63, 64, 67, 68, 72, 73, 74, 75*
Oribi 33, *29*
Orion 102
Oscar class SSGN 247, *225*
Osetr 78
Ossipee 31
Ottawa 155, 186, 192, *183*

P-56 32
P-57 32
P-61 32
P-62 32
Pakenham, Vice-Admiral 110, 112
Page, Lt 174
Page, Sub-Lt 174
Pakistan 236
Palau 124
Palestro 18, 31

Pallada 85
Pallas 29
Palmetta State 31
Panama 248
Pandora 152
Parracombe 156
Parthian 163
Pathfinder 33
P-boats 28
Pearl Harbor 140, 142, *145*
Pedestal convoy 163–4
Penelope 161
Pensacola 31
Permit class *246*
Peters, L/S V 112
Petsjora 89
Philadelphia 14–15
Philip, Sub-Lt 174
Philippines 236
Phillimore, Rear-Admiral R F 114–15
Pietà 89
Pillau 84, 97, 110, 112
Pioneer 202
Place, Lt Geoffrey 166, 170, 171, 173–4
Plaskett, CEA 112
Playfair, Major-General I S O 153
Pollen, Arthur Hungerford 102
Poltava (Frunze) 206–8, *206, 207*
Polyphemus 26–7
Prefecte Fique 237
President 14
Prince Adalbert 83
Prince of Wales 250
Principe de Asturias 232
Price 31
Princess Royal 99
Project Cadillac 145
Protector 78
Proteus 152

Qu'Appelle 186, 189
Queen Alexandra 32
Queen Elizabeth class 103–4
Queen Mary 97, 99, 102
Queen of the West 31

Ramillies 109
ramming 18–34, *22, 26*
  accidental 21–4
  design for 25–8, *26–7*
  efficacy of 20–1, 29–30, 34
  protection against 25
  and submarines 28
  in war 18–21, 41
Ranger 134–5, 140–1
Re d'Italia 18–19, 31
Re di Portogallo 31
Reed, Sir Edward 28, 36
Renown 103, 155–6, 162
Repulse (WW I) 103–6, 109, 110, 114–15, *112*
Repulse 155, 250
Resource 119
Restigouche 188, *178, 179, 194–7*

Restigouche class 181, 184–5, 188–9
Reuter, Rear-Admiral Ludwig von 110–11, 115
Riachuelo 56
Richmond (1860s) *31*
Richmond (1990s) 239
Riviera 94
Robinson, Lt Charles G 94, 97–9
Rodney 159, 164
Roxborough 32
Royalist 112
Royal Oak 18
Royal Sovereign 25, 109 *26*
Rupert 27
Russia 9, 12, 76–92, 102
  Caucasus crisis 248
  current developments 222, 232–3, 242–3, 246–50, *223, 239, 245*
Russo–Japanese War 54, 76, 118
Rutland, Flt Lt F J 97, 99–100, *96*

S-13 90
S-142 84
Saguenay 176, 192 *183*
St Croix 192
St Laurent 176, 192, 194–7, *183, 197*
St Laurent class 175–97
  design 178–80
  propulsion 181–2
  armament 182, 186, *178, 179, 180*
  construction 183–4
  DDH conversions 187–9
  and DELEX 189–91
  specifications and data 194–7
Saudi Arabia 234
Salem class 105
Salto 31
Sampson, Admiral 73
San Giorgio 27
San Jacinto 150
'Sankeikan' 35–49
Sans Pareil 43
Santiago Bay, battle of 73–4
Saratoga 134, 140, 148, 250, *150*
Sartorious, Admiral Sir George 18, 28
Sassacus 31
Satyr 167
Scamp (submarine) 128
Sceptre 167
Scharnhorst 156, 167–8, 170
Scheer, Vice-Admiral Rheinhardt 93
Schwaben 90
Schwarzenberg 31
Sea Bird 31
Sea Dog 167
Seanymph 167–8, 170
Serbino 86
Seydlitz 84, 93, *85*
Seymour, Lt-Cdr Ralph 97
Shah 32
Shanghai incident 119
Shannon 26
Sharpshooter 29, 33
Sheffield 155–6
Shepheard, Victor 109

Sheldon, Gilbert 9
Sicily 152, 155
Sig (submarine) 81
Simpson, Rear-Admiral G W G 151
Sino-Japanese War 51–3
Sioux 180
Sir Lancelot 246
Skeena 192
Skipjack class *246*
Slava 84
Smart, Sub-Lt 174
Smith, George Henry 202–5
Söderström, Admiral *see* Cederström
Som (submarine) 89
Somerville, Admiral 152
South Africa 236–7
Southfield 31
Southampton 244
South Korea 236
Sovremenniy class *234*
Spain 141, 229, 242, 246–7
Spiess, Johann 86
Spaekhuggeren 198
Sprengsporten 13–14
SSBN-685 *246*
Stahleck 89
Stalwart 246
Stonewall Jackson 31
Stork 33
Storm 168
Storozhevoi 250
Stubborn 167–8, 170, 173–4
Sweden 9–17, 82, 88, 231, 248
Syria, SS 90
Syrtis 167, 170

Takachiho 40
Takoradi (Gold Coast) 153–6, *156*
Tarleton, Vice-Admiral Sir W 22
Taureau 27
Tbilisi 243–4, *239, 244, 245*
Tei Yuen 52
Tembien 33
Tennessee 31
Tennessee (BB-43) 141
Terra Nova 188, *180*
Terry-Lloyd, Lt 174
Tersmeden, Admiral 9
Texas 56
TF-16 132
TF-17 132
Thailand 236, 244
Thetis (frigate) 11–16
Thetis (light cruiser) 83–4, *84*
Thompson 237
Thrasher 167
Ticonderoga 250
Tiger 99, 105, 185
Tiger class 103
Tirpitz 117, 166–74, *172*
Titania 167
Titanic 25

'torpedo battleships' 105–6, 109
torpedoes 25, 27–8, 78–9, 83–4
torpedo nets 35
Tovey, Cdr JC 114
Tramontana 242
Trident programme 238
Trolle, Admiral Henrik af 9
Trewin, Asst Paymaster G S 96–7, 100, *101*
Truculent 167
Truxton 224
Tryon, Admiral 22–3
Tsukushi 121
Tudor, Rear-Admiral F C T 104, 109
Tumleren 198–201, *200, 201*
Tupy 237
Turkey 246
Turku Islands 79, 81–2, 91
U-boats 28–9, 32–3
　Type IIA 91
　Type VIIA 91
Ule 167
UK, current developments in 224–5, 238, 244, 246–7, *223, 245*
Ul'yanovsk 242–3
Umpire 114
Undine 83
Upholder 241
Urchin 114
Ursa 114
USA, current developments 223–4, 238, 244, 246–9, *240, 245*
Utö Island 82–4, 86–8, *81, 86, 87*

V-100 (destroyer) 90
V and W class 29
Valentine 114
Valrond, Lt R 84, 89
Vanessa 33
Vanguard (1860s) 22, 25
Vanguard (1990s) 238
Vanoc 33
Vanquisher 114
Vansittart 155
Van Speijk class 246
Varbel 166
Varley, Cdr 166
Varuna 31
Vassilis Giorgious 108
Vendetta 110–11, 114
Ventose 242
Venus 10–12, 16, *10*
Vetehinen class submarines 91
Victoria 22–3, 43, *23–4*
Victorious 157, 161, 163–5
Viper (submarine) 83, 90
Ville de Quebec 33
Vindhunden 198, *199*
Virginia 18–19, 31
Viscount 33
Volk (submarine) 76, 89–90, *90*
Von der Tann 84, *85*

Wachusett 31
Walker 33
Warden, Admiral 28
Warrior (1860) 18, 27, 29
Warrior (1905) 98–9
Warspite 249
Washington Treaty (1922) 105, 117, 119, 134–5, 140
Wasp 135–6, 161–2, 165, *161*
Watts, Sir Philip 105
Webb 31
Weddigen, Otto 86
Welshman 163–4
Westcott 33
Westminster 239
Westralia 246
Whateley, ERA 173
White Plains 249
Whittam, Sub-Lt 173
Wiesbaden 97
Wilhelm Gustloff 90
Wilson, Lt 174
Wilson, Ahmet 15
Wilson, Sir A K 103
Winthers, Admiral de 14
Wisconsin 250
Witte de With 241, 250
Wolverine 33, 164
Woodcock 202, *204*
Woodlark 202, *204*
Wrestler 156

X class submarines 166–74, *168, 171, 173, 174*

Yalu, battle of 40, 51–3
Yamato 121, 124
Yamato class 40
Yankee class submarines *234*
Yarmouth 94
Yavuz 228
Yevropa 81
York 250
Yorktown 132, 135, 140–3, 145, 148, 225, *133, 134*
Yorktown class 132–150
　armament 140–2
　armour 135, 146–7
　aviation features 136, 137–40
　design 133–7
　fire control systems 142–5
Yoshimatsu, Rear-Admiral Sigetaro 54
Ysevoloch 16
Yukon 181
Yuri Andropov 243

Zeehond 246
Zemire 11–12, 16

025T frigates 241
25 de Mayo 246
96 (trawler) 32